THE CODE
OF CANON LAW

In English translation

THE CODE
OF CANON LAW

in English translation

Prepared by
The Canon Law Society of Great Britain and Ireland
in association with
The Canon Law Society of Australia and New Zealand
and The Canadian Canon Law Society

COLLINS
WILLIAM B. EERDMANS PUBLISHING COMPANY

Collins Liturgical Publications
187 Piccadilly, London W1V 9DA

Distributed in the United States of America by
William B. Eerdmans Publishing Company
255 Jefferson Avenue, S.E.
Grand Rapids, Michigan 49503

Distributed in Canada by
Publications Service, Canadian Conference of Catholic Bishops
90 Parent Avenue
Ottawa, Ont. K1N 7B1

ISBN 0 88997 090 4 (Canada)
0-8028-1978-8 (U.S.A.)
Reprinted, January 1984

First published this edition 1983

Imprimatur: George Basil Hume OSB
Cardinal Archbishop of Westminster
Westminster, 13 July 1983

Typographical design by Colin Reed
Data capture and manipulation by
Morton Word Processing Ltd, Scarborough, England
Typeset by Computape (Pickering) Ltd, Pickering, England
Printed and bound in the United States of America

CONTENTS

INTRODUCTION

'A journey, literally a generation long, has just drawn to a conclusion, as exactly twenty-four years have passed since the unforgettable Pope John XXIII announced the reform of the Code, together with the proclamation of the Council.' Thus said Pope John Paul II on 3 February 1983, in the Hall of Benedictions over the portico of the Vatican Basilica, on the occasion of the solemn presentation of the new Code of Canon Law. On that occasion the Holy Father also repeated the phrase from St. Augustine, 'Tolle, lege': he wished the Code to be read by as wide an audience as possible. To this end, for the first time permission has been given for the Code to be translated into the vernacular, subject to the approval of the appropriate Episcopal Conferences, and subject in particular to the clear understanding that the only official and binding version of the Code is the Latin text.

It was not long after the Second World War that there was a very strong feeling both in scholarly circles and especially amongst pastors of souls, that there was a need to bring the 1917 Code up to date and to adapt it to the changed circumstances of the world. Pope John XXIII, when announcing the Second Vatican Council, clearly appreciated that after the conclusion of the Council a revision of the Code would be essential; and in 1977 Pope Paul VI said that 'the new Code must prove to be an instrument most finely adapted to the life of the Church'. Part of that adaptation means that translations must be made available, as widely as possible.

This translation has been prepared by the Canon Law Society of Great Britain and Ireland, which is privileged to acknowledge with a particular gratitude the singular and invaluable contribution made to the work, especially in its latter stages, by the Canon Law Society of Australia and New Zealand. With pleasure the Society acknowledges also the generous help which it has received from the Canadian Canon Law Society.

The work of translation itself has had, and indeed will continue to have in the future, its own special problems. It is always difficult to provide a translation which is not to some extent an interpretation. In the context of a legal document, this has its own peculiar difficulties and dangers.

These are perhaps heightened when it comes to the matter of translating Latin into English. A strictly literal translation is simply not possible, even if it were desirable. At the very fundamental level of words, English labours under difficulties which are not found in the classical language. To take but one contemporary example, English requires more complex constructions than does Latin to provide accurately and adequately for the expression of gender which our cultural climate now demands. At the level of phrases, the problem intensifies. Latin has its own peculiar succinctness, its capacity for linking a chain of subordinate or even disparate ideas together in one complicated sentence, its ability to introduce nuances of meaning by moving through a variety of declensions, moods and tenses. In English, these matters have to be catered for otherwise.

To confront these and related problems in this translation, a basic principle was adopted. It was decided that the aim must be to establish a text which, while always striving to achieve an acceptable style in English, would in the first place express accurately the sense of the Latin legal terminology, thereby as far as possible avoiding the danger of interpretation.

This principle, which highlights the point that only the Latin text is the official and authoritative one, has had a number of consequences, some of which for the information of the readers may be briefly mentioned.

Not infrequently, but always deliberately, the translation has, in face of a complex Latin sentence, resorted to a number of shorter sentences, and sometimes to an inversion of the original sentence, in order to reproduce a pattern of thought more intelligible in the English language. When this device has been adopted, every effort has been made to reproduce accurately the sense of the Latin text.

It has sometimes been found advisable to render a singular form in the plural, or vice versa. In so far, for example, as the Latin rarely distinguishes a male or a female subject, adaptations have in most cases been made to indicate 'he or she'; where, however, this formulation was felt to introduce an unnecessary inelegance of style, a singular form has been turned into the plural, provided the essential meaning was not altered.

In the same sense, it has on occasion been found helpful to change from the passive to the active voice, and vice versa.

In the matter of words and terms, the aim has been to translate all and every one of those which could find a reasonable measure of acceptance in the English language. There were some few, however, which it was decided to leave in the original Latin, either because they were virtually untranslatable or because they were already widely accepted in their Latin form. These have been italicised in the text, and remitted to a Glossary (p.319) where their meaning is briefly explained.

A special word must be said here about the term *christifideles*. It is a completely new term in the Code. It clearly emanates from the thinking and the documents of the Second Vatican Council. It has manifest theological implications. There are varying views as to how best it ought to be translated. There is the further problem that the Code itself is not consistent in this regard: sometimes, and without apparent explanation, it reverts to the term *fideles* ('the faithful'), which in earlier terminology was often meant to indicate only the laity; it is quite certain that it no longer has this connotation. Against this background, the present translation has rendered *christifideles* as 'Christ's faithful'. It has departed from this usage, substituting 'the faithful[†]', only when it has been felt that felicity of style required it. A dagger sign ([†]) is employed to differentiate this use from the Latin text's use of the simple word *fideles*.

A final observation concerns the use of capital letters. The principle adopted was to follow the form used in the Latin text, except where otherwise demanded by accepted usage in English.

It is hoped that this English version of the Code will be a fitting resource for an attentive and fruitful study of the law of the Church. It is hoped, above all, that this translation will contribute to making the Code 'an effective instrument by the help of which the Church will be able to perfect itself in the spirit of the Second Vatican Council and show itself ever more equal to carry out its salvific role in the world' (Apos. Const., John Paul II: *Sacrae Disciplinae Leges*, 25 January 1983).

APOSTOLIC CONSTITUTION

To Our Venerable Brothers
the Cardinals, Archbishops, Bishops,
Priests, Deacons
and to the other members of the People of God

JOHN PAUL BISHOP

Servant of the Servants of God

For an Everlasting Memorial

Over the course of time, the Catholic Church has been wont to revise and renew the laws of its sacred discipline so that, maintaining always fidelity to the Divine Founder, these laws may be truly in accord with the salvific mission entrusted to the Church. With this sole aim in view, we today, 25 January 1983, bring to fulfilment the anticipation of the whole Catholic world, and decree the publication of the revised Code of Canon Law. In doing so, our thoughts turn back to this same date in 1959, when our predecessor, John XXIII of happy memory, first publicly announced his personal decision to reform the current body of canonical laws which had been promulgated on the feast of Pentecost 1917.

This decision to renew the Code was taken with two others, of which that Pontiff spoke on the same day: they concerned his desire to hold a synod of the diocese of Rome and to convoke an Ecumenical Council. Even if the former does not have much bearing on the reform of the Code, the latter on the other hand, namely the Council, is of the greatest importance for our theme and is closely linked with its substance.

If one asks why John XXIII had clearly perceived the need to reform the current Code, perhaps the answer is found in the 1917 Code itself. There is however another reason, the principal one, namely that the reform of the Code of Canon Law was seen to be directly sought and requested by the Council itself, which had particularly concentrated its attention upon the Church.

As is quite clear, when the first announcement of the revision of the Code was made, the Council was something totally in the future. Moreover, the acts of its teaching authority, and particularly its teaching on the Church, were to be developed over the years 1962–65. Nevertheless, one cannot fail to see that John XXIII's insight was most accurate, and his proposal must rightly be acknowledged as one which looked well ahead to the good of the Church.

Therefore, the new Code which appears today necessarily required the prior work of the Council and, although it was announced together with that ecumenical gathering, it follows it in order of time, since the tasks needed for its preparation could not begin until the Council had ended.

Turning our thoughts today to the beginning of that long journey, that is to 25 January 1959 and to John XXIII himself, the originator of the review of the Code, we must acknowledge that this Code drew its origin from one and the same intention, namely the renewal of christian life. All the work of the Council drew its norms and its shape principally from that same intention.

If we now turn our attention to the nature of the labours which preceded the promulgation of the Code and to the manner in which they were performed, especially during the Pontificates of Paul VI, John Paul I and then up to this present day, it is vital to make quite clear that these labours were brought to their conclusion in an eminently collegial spirit. This not only relates to the external composition of the work, but it affects also the very substance of the laws which have been drawn up.

This mark of collegiality by which the process of this Code's origin was prominently characterised, is entirely in harmony with the teaching authority and the nature of the Second Vatican Council. The Code therefore, not only because of its content but because also of its origin, demonstrates the spirit of this Council in whose documents the Church, the universal sacrament of salvation (cf Const. *Lumen Gentium*, n. 9, 48), is presented as the People of God, and its hierarchical constitution is shown as founded on the College of Bishops together with its Head.

For this reason therefore, the Bishops and Episcopal Conferences were invited to associate themselves with the work of preparing the new Code, so that through a task of such length, in as collegial a manner as possible, little by little the juridical formulae would come to maturity and would then serve the whole Church. During the whole period of this task, experts also took part, people endowed with particular academic standing in the areas of theology, history and especially canon law, drawn from all parts of the world.

To each and every one of them we express our deepest gratitude today.

We recall, first of all, those Cardinals, now deceased, who headed the preparatory Commission, Cardinal Pietro Ciriaci who began the work, and Cardinal Pericles Felici who over a period of several years guided the labours almost to their goal. We think then of the Secretaries of this Commission, Monsignor, later Cardinal, Giacomo Violardo and Father Raimondo Bidagor SJ, both of whom lavished their talents of learning and wisdom on their role. Together with them, we recall the Cardinals, Archbishops and Bishops, and all who were members of this Commission, as well as the Consultors of the individual study groups engaged over these years in that strenuous task. God has called these to their eternal reward in the meantime. For all of them our suppliant prayer is raised to God.

With pleasure we also refer to the living: in the first place, to the present Pro-President of the Commission, our venerable brother Rosalio Castillo Lara, who has worked so outstandingly for so long in a role of such responsibility. Next, we refer to our beloved son, Monsignor William Onclin, who has contributed to the successful outcome of the task with assiduous and diligent care. Then there are others who played an inestimable part in this Commission, in developing and completing a task of such volume and complexity, whether as Cardinal members, or as officials, consultors and collaborators in the various study groups or in other roles.

In promulgating this Code today, therefore, we are fully conscious that this act stems from our pontifical authority itself, and so assumes a primatial nature. Yet we are no less aware that in its content this Code reflects the collegial solicitude for the Church of all our brothers in the episcopate. Indeed, by a certain analogy with the Council itself, the Code must be viewed as the fruit of collegial cooperation, which derives from the combined energies of experienced people and institutions throughout the whole Church.

A second question arises: what is the Code? For an accurate answer to this question, it is necessary to remind ourselves of that distant heritage of law contained in the books of the Old and New Testaments. It is from this, as from its first source, that the whole juridical and legislative tradition of the Church derives.

For Christ the Lord in no way abolished the bountiful heritage of the law and the prophets which grew little by little from the history and experience of the People of God in the Old Testament. Rather he fulfilled it (cf Matt.5,17), so that it could, in a new and more sublime way, lead to the heritage of the New Testament. Accordingly, although St Paul in expounding the mystery of salvation teaches that justification is not obtained through the works of the law but through faith (cf Rom.3,28; Gal.2,16), nonetheless he does not exclude the binding force of the Decalogue (cf Rom.13,8–10; Gal.5,13–25; 6, 2), nor does he deny the importance of discipline in the Church (cf 1 Cor.5 and 6). Thus the writings of the New Testament allow us to perceive more clearly the great importance of this discipline and to understand better the bonds which link it ever more closely with the salvific character of the Gospel message.

Granted this, it is sufficiently clear that the purpose of the Code is not in any way to replace faith, grace, charisms and above all charity in the life of the Church or of Christ's faithful. On the contrary, the Code rather looks towards the achievement of order in the ecclesial society, such that while attributing a primacy to love, grace and the charisms, it facilitates at the same time an orderly development in the life both of the ecclesial society and of the individual persons who belong to it.

As the Church's fundamental legislative document, and because it is based on the juridical and legislative heritage of revelation and tradition, the Code must be regarded as the essential instrument for the preservation of right order, both in individual and social life and in the Church's zeal. Therefore, over and above the fundamental elements of the hierarchical and organic structure of the Church established by the Divine Founder, based on apostolic or other no less ancient tradition, and besides the principal norms which concern the exercise of the threefold office entrusted to the Church, it is necessary for the Code to define also certain rules and norms of action.

The instrument, such as the Code is, fully accords with the nature of the Church, particularly as presented in the authentic teaching of the Second Vatican Council seen as a whole, and especially in its ecclesiological doctrine. In fact, in a certain sense, this new Code can be viewed as a great effort to translate the conciliar ecclesiological teaching into canonical terms. If it is impossible perfectly to transpose the image of the Church described by conciliar doctrine into canonical language, nevertheless the Code must always be related to that image as to its primary pattern, whose outlines, given its nature, the Code must express as far as is possible.

Hence flow certain fundamental principles by which the whole of the new Code is governed, within the limits of its proper subject and of its expression, which must reflect that subject. Indeed it is possible to assert that from this derives that characteristic whereby the Code is regarded as a complement to the authentic teaching proposed by the Second Vatican Council and particularly to its Dogmatic and Pastoral Constitutions.

From this it follows that the fundamental basis of the 'newness' which, while never straying from the Church's legislative tradition, is found in the Second Vatican Council and especially in its ecclesiological teaching, generates also the mark of 'newness' in the new Code.

Foremost among the elements which express the true and authentic image of the Church are: the teaching whereby the Church is presented as the People of God (cf Const. *Lumen Gentium*, n. 2) and its hierarchical authority as service (ibid n. 3); the further teaching which portrays the Church as a communion and then spells out the mutual relationships which must intervene between the particular and the universal Church, and between collegiality and primacy; likewise, the teaching by which all members of the People of God share, each in their own measure, in the threefold priestly, prophetic and kingly office of Christ, with which teaching is associated also that which looks to the duties and rights of Christ's faithful and specifically the laity; and lastly the assiduity which the Church must devote to ecumenism.

If, therefore, the Second Vatican Council drew old and new from the treasury of tradition, and if its newness is contained in these and other elements, it is abundantly clear that the Code receives into itself the same mark of fidelity in newness and newness in fidelity, and that its specific content and corresponding form of expression is in conformity with this aim.

The new Code of Canon Law is published precisely at a time when the Bishops of the whole Church are not only asking for its promulgation but indeed are insistently and vehemently demanding it.

And in fact a Code of Canon Law is absolutely necessary for the Church. Since the Church is established in the form of a social and visible unit, it needs rules, so that its hierarchical and organic structure may be visible; that its exercise of the functions divinely entrusted to it, particularly of sacred power and of the administration of the sacraments, is properly ordered; that the mutual relationships of Christ's faithful are reconciled in justice based on charity, with the rights of each safeguarded and defined; and lastly, that the common initiatives which are undertaken so that christian life may be ever more perfectly carried out, are supported, strengthened and promoted by canonical laws.

Finally, canonical laws by their very nature demand observance. For this reason, the greatest care has been taken that during the long preparation of the Code there should be an accurate expression of the norms and that they should depend upon a sound juridical, canonical and theological foundation.

In view of all this, it is very much to be hoped that the new canonical legislation will be an effective instrument by the help of which the Church will be able to perfect itself in the spirit of the Second Vatican Council, and show itself ever more equal to carry out its salvific role in the world.

It is pleasing to set out these reflections of ours in a trusting spirit as we promulgate this principal body of ecclesiastical laws for the latin Church.

May God grant that joy and peace, with justice and obedience, may commend this Code, and that what is bidden by the head will be obeyed in the body.

Relying, therefore, on the help of divine grace, supported by the authority of the Blessed Apostles Peter and Paul, with certain knowledge and assenting to the pleas of the Bishops of the whole world who have laboured with us in collegial good will, by the supreme authority which is ours, and by means of this Constitution of ours which is to have effect for the future, we promulgate this present Code as it has been compiled and reviewed. We order that henceforth it is to have the force of law for the whole latin Church, and we commit its observance to the care and vigilance of all who are responsible. In order, however, that all may properly investigate these prescriptions and intelligently come to know them before they take effect, we decree and command that they shall come into force from the first day of Advent of the year 1983, all ordinances, constitutions and privileges, even those meriting special and individual mention, as well as contrary customs, notwithstanding.

We, therefore, exhort all our beloved children to observe, with sincere mind and ready will, the precepts laid down, buoyed up by the hope that a zealous Church discipline will flourish anew, and that from it the salvation of souls also will be ever more fervently promoted, with the assistance of the Blessed Virgin Mary, Mother of the Church.

Given at Rome, in the Vatican, on the 25th day of January 1983, in the fifth year of our Pontificate.

JOHN PAUL II

Book I
GENERAL NORMS

Can. 1   The canons of this Code concern only the latin Church.

Can. 2   For the most part the Code does not determine the rites to be observed in the celebration of liturgical actions. Accordingly, liturgical laws which have been in effect hitherto retain their force, except those which may be contrary to the canons of the Code.

Can. 3   The canons of the Code do not abrogate, nor do they derogate from, agreements entered into by the Apostolic See with nations or other civil entities. For this reason, these agreements continue in force as hitherto, notwithstanding any contrary provisions of this Code.

Can. 4   Acquired rights, and likewise privileges hitherto granted by the Apostolic See to either physical or juridical persons, which are still in use and have not been revoked, remain intact, unless they are expressly revoked by the canons of this Code.

Can. 5   §1 Universal or particular customs which have been in effect up to now but are contrary to the provisions of these canons and are reprobated in the canons of this Code, are completely suppressed, and they may not be allowed to revive in the future. Other contrary customs are also to be considered suppressed, unless the Code expressly provides otherwise, or unless they are centennial or immemorial: these latter may be tolerated if the Ordinary judges that, in the circumstances of place and person, they cannot be removed.
   §2 Customs apart from the law, whether universal or particular, which have been in effect hitherto, are retained.

Can. 6   §1 When this Code comes into force, the following are abrogated:
   1° the Code of Canon Law promulgated in 1917;
   2° other laws, whether universal or particular, which are contrary to the provisions of this Code, unless it is otherwise expressly provided in respect of particular laws;
   3° all penal laws enacted by the Apostolic See, whether universal or particular, unless they are resumed in this Code itself;
   4° any other universal disciplinary laws concerning matters which are integrally reordered by this Code.
   §2 To the extent that the canons of this Code reproduce the former law, they are to be assessed in the light also of canonical tradition.

TITLE I: ECCLESIASTICAL LAWS

Can. 7   A law comes into being when it is promulgated.

Can. 8   §1 Universal ecclesiastical laws are promulgated by publication in the 'Acta Apostolicae Sedis', unless in particular cases another manner of promulgation has been prescribed. They come into force only on the expiry of three months from the date appearing on the particular issue of the 'Acta', unless because of the nature of the case they bind at once, or unless a shorter or a longer interval has been specifically and expressly prescribed in the law itself.

§2 Particular laws are promulgated in the manner determined by the legislator; they begin to oblige one month from the date of promulgation, unless a different period is prescribed in the law itself.

Can. 9 Laws concern matters of the future, not those of the past, unless provision is made in them for the latter by name.

Can. 10 Only those laws are to be considered invalidating or incapacitating which expressly prescribe that an act is null or that a person is incapable.

Can. 11 Merely ecclesiastical laws bind those who were baptised in the catholic Church or received into it, and who have a sufficient use of reason and, unless the law expressly provides otherwise, who have completed their seventh year of age.

Can. 12 §1 Universal laws are binding everywhere on all those for whom they were enacted.

§2 All those actually present in a particular territory in which certain universal laws are not in force, are exempt from those laws.

§3 Without prejudice to the provisions of can. 13, laws enacted for a particular territory bind those for whom they were enacted and who have a domicile or quasi-domicile in that territory and are actually residing in it.

Can. 13 §1 Particular laws are not presumed to be personal, but rather territorial, unless the contrary is clear.

§2 *Peregrini* are not bound:

    1° by the particular laws of their own territory while they are absent from it, unless the transgression of those laws causes harm in their own territory, or unless the laws are personal;

    2° by the laws of the territory in which they are present, except for those laws which take care of public order, or determine the formalities of legal acts, or concern immovable property located in the territory.

§3 *Vagi* are bound by both the universal and the particular laws which are in force in the place in which they are present.

Can. 14 Laws, even invalidating and incapacitating ones, do not oblige when there is a doubt of law. When there is a doubt of fact, however, Ordinaries can dispense from them provided, if there is question of a reserved dispensation, it is one which the authority to whom it is reserved is accustomed to grant.

Can. 15   §1 Ignorance or error concerning invalidating or incapacitating laws does not prevent the effect of those laws, unless it is expressly provided otherwise.

§2 Ignorance or error is not presumed about a law, a penalty, a fact concerning oneself, or a notorious fact concerning another. It is presumed about a fact concerning another which is not notorious, until the contrary is proved.

Can. 16   §1 Laws are authentically interpreted by the legislator and by that person to whom the legislator entrusts the power of authentic interpretation.

§2 An authentic interpretation which is presented by way of a law has the same force as the law itself, and must be promulgated. If it simply declares the sense of words which are certain in themselves, it has retroactive force. If it restricts or extends the law or resolves a doubt, it is not retroactive.

§3 On the other hand, an interpretation by way of a court judgement or of an administrative act in a particular case, does not have the force of law. It binds only those persons and affects only those matters for which it was given.

Can. 17   Ecclesiastical laws are to be understood according to the proper meaning of the words considered in their text and context. If the meaning remains doubtful or obscure, there must be recourse to parallel places, if there be any, to the purpose and circumstances of the law, and to the mind of the legislator.

Can. 18   Laws which prescribe a penalty, or restrict the free exercise of rights, or contain an exception to the law, are to be intepreted strictly.

Can. 19   If on a particular matter there is not an express provision of either universal or particular law, nor a custom, then, provided it is not a penal matter, the question is to be decided by taking into account laws enacted in similar matters, the general principles of law observed with canonical equity, the jurisprudence and practice of the Roman Curia, and the common and constant opinion of learned authors.

Can. 20   A later law abrogates or derogates from an earlier law, if it expressly so states, or if it is directly contrary to that law, or if it integrally reorders the whole subject matter of the earlier law. A universal law, however, does not derogate from a particular or from a special law, unless the law expressly provides otherwise.

Can. 21   In doubt, the revocation of a previous law is not presumed; rather, later laws are to be related to earlier ones and, as far as possible, harmonised with them.

Can. 22   When the law of the Church remits some issue to the civil law, the latter is to be observed with the same effects in canon law, insofar as it is not contrary to divine law, and provided it is not otherwise stipulated in canon law.

TITLE II: CUSTOM

Can. 23   A custom introduced by a community of the faithful has the force of law only if it has been approved by the legislator, in accordance with the following canons.

Can. 24   §1 No custom which is contrary to divine law can acquire the force of law.
§2 A custom which is contrary to or apart from canon law, cannot acquire the force of law unless it is reasonable; a custom which is expressly reprobated in the law is not reasonable.

Can. 25   No custom acquires the force of law unless it has been observed, with the intention of introducing a law, by a community capable at least of receiving a law.

Can. 26   Unless it has been specifically approved by the competent legislator, a custom which is contrary to the canon law currently in force, or is apart from the canon law, acquires the force of law only when it has been lawfully observed for a period of thirty continuous and complete years. Only a centennial or immemorial custom can prevail over a canonical law which carries a clause forbidding future customs.

Can. 27   Custom is the best interpreter of laws.

Can. 28   Without prejudice to the provisions of can. 5, a custom, whether contrary to or apart from the law, is revoked by a contrary custom or law. But unless the law makes express mention of them, it does not revoke centennial or immemorial customs, nor does a universal law revoke particular customs.

TITLE III: GENERAL DECREES AND INSTRUCTIONS

Can. 29   General decrees, by which a competent legislator makes common provisions for a community capable of receiving a law, are true laws and are regulated by the provisions of the canons on laws.

Can. 30   A general decree, as in can. 29, cannot be made by one who has only executive power, unless in particular cases this has been expressly authorised by the competent legislator in accordance with the law, and provided the conditions prescribed in the act of authorisation are observed.

Can. 31 §1 Within the limits of their competence, those who have executive power can issue general executory decrees, that is, decrees which define more precisely the manner of applying a law, or which urge the observance of laws.

§2 The provisions of can. 8 are to be observed in regard to the promulgation, and to the interval before the coming into effect, of the decrees mentioned in §1.

Can. 32 General executory decrees which define the manner of application or urge the observance of laws, bind those who are bound by the laws.

Can. 33 §1 General executory decrees, even if published in directories or other such documents, do not derogate from the law, and any of their provisions which are contrary to the law have no force.

§2 These decrees cease to have force by explicit or implicit revocation by the competent authority, and by the cessation of the law for whose execution they were issued. They do not cease on the expiry of the authority of the person who issued them, unless the contrary is expressly provided.

Can. 34 §1 Instructions, namely, which set out the provisions of a law and develop the manner in which it is to be put into effect, are given for the benefit of those whose duty it is to execute the law, and they bind them in executing the law. Those who have executive power may, within the limits of their competence, lawfully publish such instructions.

§2 The regulations of an instruction do not derogate from the law, and if there are any which cannot be reconciled with the provisions of the law, they have no force.

§3 Instructions cease to have force not only by explicit or implicit revocation by the competent authority who published them or by that authority's superior, but also by the cessation of the law which they were designed to set out and execute.

TITLE IV: SINGULAR ADMINISTRATIVE ACTS

Chapter I

COMMON NORMS

Can. 35 Within the limits of his or her competence, one who has executive power can issue a singular administrative act, either by decree or precept, or by rescript, without prejudice to can. 76 §1.

Can. 36 §1 An administrative act is to be understood according to the proper meaning of the words and the common manner of speaking. In doubt, a strict interpretation is to be given to those administrative acts which concern litigation or threaten or inflict penalties, or restrict the rights of persons, or harm the acquired rights of others, or run counter to a law in favour of private persons; all other administrative acts are to be widely interpreted.

§2 Administrative acts must not be extended to cases other than those expressly stated.

Can. 37 An administrative act which concerns the external forum is to be effected in writing; likewise, if it requires an executor, the act of execution is to be in writing.

Can. 38 An administrative act, even if there is question of a rescript given *Motu proprio*, has no effect in so far as it harms the acquired right of another, or is contrary to a law or approved custom, unless the competent authority has expressly added a derogatory clause.

Can. 39 Conditions attached to an administrative act are considered to concern validity only when they are expressed by the particles 'if', 'unless', 'provided that'.

Can. 40 The executor of any administrative act cannot validly carry out this office before receiving the relevant document and establishing its authenticity and integrity, unless prior notice of this document has been conveyed to the executor on the authority of the person who issued the administrative act.

Can. 41 The executor of an administrative act to whom the task of execution only is entrusted, cannot refuse to execute it, unless it is quite clear that the act itself is null, or that it cannot for some other grave reason be sustained, or that the conditions attached to the administrative act itself have not been fulfilled. If, however, the execution of the administrative act would appear to be inopportune, by reason of the circumstances of person or place, the executor is to desist from the execution, and immediately inform the person who issued the act.

Can. 42 The executor of an administrative act must proceed in accordance with the mandate. If, however, the executor has not fulfilled essential conditions attached to the document, or has not observed the substantial form of procedure, the execution is invalid.

Can. 43 The executor of an administrative act may in his prudent judgement substitute another for himself, unless substitution has been forbidden, or he has been deliberately chosen as the only person to be executor, or a specific person has been designated as substitute; however, in these cases the executor may commit the preparatory acts to another.

Can. 44 An administrative act can also be executed by the executor's successor in office, unless the first had been chosen deliberately as the only person to be executor.

Can. 45 If there has been any error in the execution of an administrative act, the executor may execute it again.

Can. 46 An administrative act does not cease on the expiry of the authority of the person issuing it, unless the law expressly provides otherwise.

Can. 47 The revocation of an administrative act by another administrative act of the competent authority takes effect only from the moment at which the person to whom it was issued is lawfully notified.

Chapter II

SINGULAR DECREES AND PRECEPTS

Can. 48 A singular decree is an administrative act issued by a competent executive authority, whereby in accordance with the norms of law a decision is given or a provision made for a particular case; of its nature this decision or provision does not presuppose that a petition has been made by anyone.

Can. 49 A singular precept is a decree by which an obligation is directly and lawfully imposed on a specific person or persons to do or to omit something, especially in order to urge the observance of a law.

Can. 50 Before issuing a singular decree, the person in authority is to seek the necessary information and proof and, as far as possible, is to consult those whose rights could be harmed.

Can. 51 A decree is to be issued in writing. When it is a decision, it should express, at least in summary form, the reasons for the decision.

Can. 52 A singular decree has effect in respect only of those matters it determines and of those persons to whom it was issued; it obliges such persons everywhere, unless it is otherwise clear.

Can. 53 If decrees are contrary one to another, where specific matters are expressed, the specific prevails over the general; if both are equally specific or equally general, the one later in time abrogates the earlier insofar as it is contrary to it.

Can. 54 §1 A singular decree whose application is entrusted to an executor, has effect from the moment of execution; otherwise, from the moment when it is made known to the person on the authority of the one who issued it.

§2 For a singular decree to be enforceable, it must be made known by a lawful document in accordance with the law.

Can. 55 Without prejudice to cann. 37 and 51, whenever a very grave reason prevents the handing over of the written text of a decree, the decree is deemed to have been made known if it is read to the person to whom it is directed, in the presence of a notary or two witnesses; a record of the occasion is to be drawn up and signed by all present.

Can. 56 A decree is deemed to have been made known if the person to whom it is directed has been duly summoned to receive or to hear the decree, and without a just reason has not appeared or has refused to sign.

Can. 57 §1 Whenever the law orders a decree to be issued, or when a person who is concerned lawfully requests a decree or has recourse to obtain one, the competent authority is to provide for the situation within three months of having received the petition or recourse, unless a different period of time is prescribed by law.

§2 If this period of time has expired and the decree has not yet been given, then as far as proposing a further recourse is concerned, the reply is presumed to be negative.

§3 A presumed negative reply does not relieve the competent authority of the obligation of issuing the decree, and, in accordance with can. 128, of repairing any harm done.

Can. 58 §1 A singular decree ceases to have force when it is lawfully revoked by the competent authority, or when the law ceases for whose execution it was issued.

§2 A singular precept, which was not imposed by a lawful document, ceases on the expiry of the authority of the person who issued it.

Chapter III

RESCRIPTS

Can. 59 §1 A rescript is an administrative act issued in writing by a competent authority, by which of its very nature a privilege, dispensation or other favour is granted at someone's request.

§2 Unless it is otherwise established, provisions laid down concerning rescripts apply also to the granting of permission and to the granting of favours by word of mouth.

Can. 60 Any rescript can be obtained by all who are not expressly prohibited.

Can. 61 Unless it is otherwise established, a rescript can be obtained for another, even without that person's consent, and it is valid before its acceptance, without prejudice to contrary clauses.

Can. 62   A rescript in which there is no executor, has effect from the moment the document was issued; the others have effect from the moment of execution.

Can. 63   §1 Except where there is question of a rescript which grants a favour *Motu proprio*, subreption, that is, the withholding of the truth, renders a rescript invalid if the request does not express that which, according to canonical law, style and practice, must for validity be expressed.

§2 Obreption, that is, the making of a false statement, renders a rescript invalid if not even one of the motivating reasons submitted is true.

§3 In rescripts of which there is no executor, the motivating reason must be true at the time the rescript is issued; in the others, at the time of execution.

Can. 64   Without prejudice to the right of the Penitentiary for the internal forum, a favour refused by any department of the Roman Curia cannot validly be granted by another department of the same Curia, or by any other competent authority below the Roman Pontiff, without the approval of the department which was first approached.

Can. 65   §1 Without prejudice to the provisions of §§2 and 3, no one is to seek from another Ordinary a favour which was refused by that person's proper Ordinary, unless mention is made of the refusal. When the refusal is mentioned, the Ordinary is not to grant the favour unless he has learned from the former Ordinary the reasons for the refusal.

§2 A favour refused by a Vicar general or an episcopal Vicar cannot be validly granted by another Vicar of the same Bishop, even when he has learned from the Vicar who refused the reasons for the refusal.

§3 A favour refused by a Vicar general or an episcopal Vicar and later, without any mention being made of this refusal, obtained from the diocesan Bishop, is invalid. A favour refused by the diocesan Bishop cannot, without the Bishop's consent, validly be obtained from his Vicar general or episcopal Vicar, even though mention is made of the refusal.

Can. 66   A rescript is not rendered invalid because of an error in the name of the person to whom it is given or by whom it is issued, or of the place in which such person resides, or of the matter concerned, provided that in the judgement of the Ordinary there is no doubt about the person or the matter in question.

Can. 67   §1 If it should happen that two contrary rescripts are obtained for one and the same thing, where specific matters are expressed, the specific prevails over the general.

§2 If both are equally specific or equally general, the one earlier in time prevails over the later, unless in the later one there is an express mention of the earlier, or unless the person who first obtained the rescript has not used it by reason of deceit or of notable personal negligence.

§3   In doubt as to whether a rescript is invalid or not, recourse is to be made to the issuing authority.

Can. 68   A rescript of the Apostolic See in which there is no executor must be presented to the Ordinary of the person who obtains it only when this is prescribed in the rescript, or when there is question of public affairs, or when it is necessary to have the conditions verified.

Can. 69   A rescript for whose presentation no time is determined, may be submitted to the executor at any time, provided there is no fraud or deceit.

Can. 70   If in a rescript the very granting of the favour is entrusted to the executor, it is a matter for the executor's prudent judgement and conscience to grant or to refuse the favour.

Can. 71   No one is obliged to use a rescript granted in his or her favour only, unless bound by a canonical obligation from another source to do so.

Can. 72   Rescripts granted by the Apostolic See which have expired, can for a just reason be extended by the diocesan Bishop, but once only and not beyond three months.

Can. 73   No rescripts are revoked by a contrary law, unless it is otherwise provided in the law itself.

Can. 74   Although one who has been granted a favour orally may use it in the internal forum, that person is obliged to prove the favour for the external forum whenever this is lawfully requested.

Can. 75   If a rescript contains a privilege or a dispensation, the provision of the following canons are also to be observed.

Chapter IV

PRIVILEGES

Can. 76   §1   A privilege is a favour given by a special act for the benefit of certain persons, physical or juridical; it can be granted by the legislator, and by an executive authority to whom the legislator has given this power.

§2   Centennial or immemorial possession of a privilege gives rise to the presumption that it has been granted.

Can. 77   A privilege is to be interpreted in accordance with can. 36 §1. The interpretation must, however, always be such that the beneficiaries of the privilege do in fact receive some favour.

Can. 78   §1   A privilege is presumed to be perpetual, unless the contrary is proved.

§2 A personal privilege, namely one which attaches to a person, is extinguished with the person.

§3 A real privilege ceases on the total destruction of the thing or place; a local privilege, however, revives if the place is restored within fifty years.

Can. 79   Without prejudice to can. 46, a privilege ceases by revocation on the part of the competent authority in accordance with can. 47.

Can. 80   §1 No privilege ceases by renunciation unless this has been accepted by the competent authority.

§2 Any physical person may renounce a privilege granted in his or her favour only.

§3 Individual persons cannot renounce a privilege granted to a juridical person, or granted by reason of the dignity of a place or thing. Nor can a juridical person renounce a privilege granted to it, if the renunciation would be prejudicial to the Church or to others.

Can. 81   A privilege is not extinguished on the expiry of the authority of the person who granted it, unless it was given with the clause 'at our pleasure' or another equivalent expression.

Can. 82   A privilege which does not burden others does not lapse through non-use or contrary use; if it does cause an inconvenience for others, it is lost if lawful prescription intervenes.

Can. 83   §1 Without prejudice to can. 142 §2, a privilege ceases on the expiry of the time or the completion of the number of cases for which it was granted.

§2 It ceases also if in the judgement of the competent authority circumstances are so changed with the passage of time that it has become harmful, or that its use becomes unlawful.

Can. 84   A person who abuses a power given by a privilege deserves to be deprived of the privilege itself. Accordingly, after a warning which has been in vain, the Ordinary, if it was he who granted it, is to deprive the person of the privilege which he or she is gravely abusing; if the privilege has been granted by the Apostolic See, the Ordinary is obliged to make the matter known to it.

Chapter V

DISPENSATIONS

Can. 85   A dispensation, that is, the relaxation of a merely ecclesiastical law in a particular case, can be granted, within the limits of their competence, by those who have executive power, and by those who either explicitly or implicitly have the power of dispensing, whether by virtue of the law itself or by lawful delegation.

Can. 86 In so far as laws define those elements which are essentially constitutive of institutes or of juridical acts, they are not subject to dispensation.

Can. 87 §1 Whenever he judges that it contributes to their spiritual welfare, the diocesan Bishop can dispense the faithful from disciplinary laws, both universal laws and those particular laws made by the supreme ecclesiastical authority for his territory or his subjects. He cannot dispense from procedural laws or from penal laws, nor from those whose dispensation is specially reserved to the Apostolic See or to some other authority.

§2 If recourse to the Holy See is difficult, and at the same time there is danger of grave harm in delay, any Ordinary can dispense from these laws, even if the dispensation is reserved to the Holy See, provided the dispensation is one which the Holy See customarily grants in the same circumstances, and without prejudice to can. 291.

Can. 88 The local Ordinary can dispense from diocesan laws and, whenever he judges that it contributes to the spiritual welfare of the faithful, from laws made by a plenary or a provincial Council or by the Episcopal Conference.

Can. 89 Parish priests and other priests or deacons cannot dispense from universal or particular law unless this power is expressly granted to them.

Can. 90 §1 A dispensation from an ecclesiastical law is not to be given without a just and reasonable cause, taking into account the circumstances of the case and the importance of the law from which the dispensation is given; otherwise the dispensation is unlawful and, unless given by the legislator or his superior, it is also invalid.

§2 A dispensation given in doubt about the sufficiency of its reason is valid and lawful.

Can. 91 In respect of their subjects, even if these are outside the territory, those who have the power of dispensing can exercise it even if they themselves are outside their territory; unless the contrary is expressly provided, they can exercise it also in respect of *peregrini* actually present in the territory; they can exercise it too in respect of themselves.

Can. 92 A strict interpretation is to be given not only to a dispensation in accordance with can. 36 §1, but also to the very power of dispensing granted for a specific case.

Can. 93 A dispensation capable of successive applications ceases in the same way as a privilege. It also ceases by the certain and complete cessation of the motivating reason.

TITLE V: STATUTES AND ORDINANCES

Can. 94 §1 Statutes properly so called are regulations which are established in accordance with the law in aggregates of persons or of things, whereby the purpose, constitution, governance and manner of acting of these bodies are defined.

§2 The statutes of an aggregate of persons bind only those persons who are lawfully members of it; the statutes of an aggregate of things bind those who direct it.

§3 The provisions of statutes which are established and promulgated by virtue of legislative power, are regulated by the provisions of the canons concerning laws.

Can. 95 §1 Ordinances are rules or norms to be observed both in assemblies of persons, whether these assemblies are convened by ecclesiastical authority or are freely convoked by the faithful[†], and in other celebrations: they define those matters which concern their constitution, direction and agenda.

§2 In assemblies or celebrations, those who take part are bound by these rules of ordinance.

TITLE VI: PHYSICAL AND JURIDICAL PERSONS

Chapter I
THE CANONICAL STATUS OF PHYSICAL PERSONS

Can. 96 By baptism one is incorporated into the Church of Christ and constituted a person in it, with the duties and the rights which, in accordance with each one's status, are proper to christians, in so far as they are in ecclesiastical communion and unless a lawfully issued sanction intervenes.

Can. 97 §1 A person who has completed the eighteenth year of age, has attained majority; below this age, a person is a minor.

§2 A minor who has not completed the seventh year of age is called an infant and is considered incapable of personal responsibility; on completion of the seventh year, however, the minor is presumed to have the use of reason.

Can. 98 §1 A person who has attained majority has the full exercise of his or her rights.

§2 In the exercise of rights a minor remains subject to parents or guardians, except for those matters in which by divine or by canon law minors are exempt from such authority. In regard to the appointment of

14

guardians and the determination of their powers, the provisions of civil law are to be observed, unless it is otherwise provided in canon law or unless, in specific cases and for a just reason, the diocesan Bishop has decided that the matter is to be catered for by the appointment of another guardian.

Can. 99   Whoever habitually lacks the use of reason is considered as incapable of personal responsibility and is regarded as an infant.

Can. 100   A person is said to be: an *incola*, in the place where he or she has a domicile; an *advena*, in the place of quasi-domicile; a *peregrinus*, if away from the domicile or quasi-domicile which is still retained; a *vagus*, if the person has nowhere a domicile or quasi-domicile.

Can. 101   §1 The place of origin of a child, and even of a neophyte, is that in which the parents had a domicile or, lacking that, a quasi-domicile when the child was born; if the parents did not have the same domicile or quasi-domicile, it is that of the mother.

§2 In the case of a child of *vagi*, the place of origin is the actual place of birth; in the case of a foundling, it is the place where it was found.

Can. 102   §1 Domicile is acquired by residence in the territory of a parish, or at least of a diocese, which is either linked to the intention of remaining there permanently if nothing should occasion its withdrawal, or in fact protracted for a full five years.

§2 Quasi-domicile is acquired by residence in the territory of a parish, or at least of a diocese, which is either linked to the intention of remaining there for three months if nothing should occasion its withdrawal, or in fact protracted for three months.

§3 Domicile or quasi-domicile in the territory of a parish is called parochial; in the territory of a diocese, even if not in a parish, it is called diocesan.

Can. 103   Members of religious institutes and of societies of apostolic life acquire a domicile in the place where the house to which they belong is situated. They acquire a quasi-domicile in the house in which, in accordance with can. 102 §2, they reside.

Can. 104   Spouses are to have a common domicile or quasi-domicile. By reason of lawful separation or for some other just reason, each may have his or her own domicile or quasi-domicile.

Can. 105   §1 A minor necessarily retains the domicile or quasi-domicile of the person to whose authority the minor is subject. A minor who is no longer an infant can acquire a quasi-domicile of his or her own and, if lawfully emancipated in accordance with the civil law, a domicile also.

§2 One who for a reason other than minority is lawfully entrusted to the guardianship or tutelage of another, has the domicile and quasi-domicile of the guardian or curator.

15

Can. 106 Domicile or quasi-domicile is lost by departure from the place with the intention of not returning, without prejudice to the provisions of can. 105.

Can. 107 §1 Both through domicile and through quasi-domicile everyone acquires his or her own parish priest and Ordinary.

§2 The proper parish priest or Ordinary of a *vagus* is the parish priest or Ordinary of the place where the *vagus* is actually residing.

§3 The proper parish priest of one who has only a diocesan domicile or quasi-domicile is the parish priest of the place where that person is actually residing.

Can. 108 §1 Consanguinity is reckoned by lines and degrees.

§2 In the direct line there are as many degrees as there are generations, that is, as there are persons, not counting the common ancestor.

§3 In the collateral line there are as many degrees as there are persons in both lines together, not counting the common ancestor.

Can. 109 §1 Affinity arises from a valid marriage, even if not consummated, and it exists between the man and the blood relations of the woman, and likewise between the woman and the blood relations of the man.

§2 It is reckoned in such a way that the blood relations of the man are related by affinity to the woman in the same line and the same degree, and vice versa.

Can. 110 Children who have been adopted in accordance with the civil law are considered the children of that person or those persons who have adopted them.

Can. 111 §1 Through the reception of baptism a child becomes a member of the latin Church if the parents belong to that Church or, should one of them not belong to it, if they have both by common consent chosen that the child be baptised in the latin Church: if that common consent is lacking, the child becomes a member of the ritual Church to which the father belongs.

§2 Any candidate for baptism who has completed the fourteenth year of age may freely choose to be baptised either in the latin Church or in another autonomous ritual Church; in which case the person belongs to the Church which he or she has chosen.

Can. 112 §1 After the reception of baptism, the following become members of another autonomous ritual Church:

    1° those who have obtained permission from the Apostolic See;

    2° a spouse who, on entering marriage or during its course, has declared that he or she is transferring to the autonomous ritual

Church of the other spouse; on the dissolution of the marriage, however, that person may freely return to the latin Church;

3° the children of those mentioned in nn. 1 and 2 who have not completed their fourteenth year, and likewise in a mixed marriage the children of a catholic party who has lawfully transferred to another ritual Church; on completion of their fourteenth year, however, they may return to the latin Church.

§2 The practice, however long standing, of receiving the sacraments according to the rite of an autonomous ritual Church, does not bring with it membership of that Church.

Chapter II

JURIDICAL PERSONS

Can. 113   §1 The catholic Church and the Apostolic See have the status of a moral person by divine disposition.

§2 In the Church, besides physical persons, there are also juridical persons, that is, in canon law subjects of obligations and rights which accord with their nature.

Can. 114   §1 Aggregates of persons or of things which are directed to a purpose befitting the Church's mission, which transcends the purpose of the individuals, are constituted juridical persons either by a provision of the law itself or by a special concession given in the form of a decree by the competent authority.

§2 The purposes indicated in §1 are understood to be those which concern works of piety, of the apostolate or of charity, whether spiritual or temporal.

§3 The competent ecclesiastical authority is not to confer juridical personality except on those aggregates of persons or of things which aim at a genuinely useful purpose and which, all things considered, have the means which are foreseen to be sufficient to achieve the purpose in view.

Can. 115   §1 Juridical persons in the Church are either aggregates of persons or aggregates of things.

§2 An aggregate of persons, which must be made up of at least three persons, is collegial if the members decide its conduct by participating together in making its decisions, whether by equal right or not, in accordance with the law and the statutes; otherwise, it is non-collegial.

§3 An aggregate of things, or an autonomous foundation, consists of goods or things, whether spiritual or material, and is directed, in accordance with the law and the statutes, by one or more physical persons or by a college.

Can. 116   §1 Public juridical persons are aggregates of persons or of things which are established by the competent ecclesiastical authority so that, within the limits allotted to them in the name of the Church, and in accordance with the provisions of law, they might fulfil the specific task entrusted to them for the public good. Other juridical persons are private.

§2 Public juridical persons are given this personality either by the law itself or by a special decree of the competent authority expressly granting it. Private juridical persons are given this personality only by a special decree of the competent authority expressly granting it.

Can. 117 No aggregate of persons or of things seeking juridical personality can acquire it unless its statutes are approved by the competent authority.

Can. 118 Those persons represent, and act in the name of, a public juridical person whose competence to do so is acknowledged by universal or particular law, or by their own statutes; those persons represent a private juridical person who are given this competence by their statutes.

Can. 119 In regard to collegial acts, unless the law or the statutes provide otherwise:

1° in regard to elections, provided a majority of those who must be summoned are present, what is decided by an absolute majority of those present has the force of law. If there have been two inconclusive scrutinies, a vote is to be taken between the two candidates with the greatest number of votes or, if there are more than two, between the two senior by age. After a third inconclusive scrutiny, that person is deemed elected who is senior by age;

2° in regard to other matters, provided a majority of those who must be summoned are present, what is decided by an absolute majority of those present has the force of law. If the votes are equal after two scrutinies, the person presiding can break the tie with a casting vote;

3° that which affects all as individuals must be approved by all.

Can. 120 §1 A juridical person is by its nature perpetual. It ceases to exist, however, if it is lawfully suppressed by the competent authority, or if it has been inactive for a hundred years. A private juridical person also ceases to exist if the association itself is dissolved in accordance with the statutes, or if, in the judgement of the competent authority, the foundation itself has, in accordance with the statutes, ceased to exist.

§2 If even a single member of a collegial juridical person survives, and the aggregate of persons has not, according to the statutes, ceased to exist, the exercise of all the rights of the aggregate devolves upon that member.

Can. 121 When aggregates of persons or of things which are public juridical persons are so amalgamated that one aggregate, itself with a juridical personality, is formed, this new juridical person obtains the patrimonial goods and rights which belonged to the previous aggregates; it also accepts the liabilities of the previous aggregates. In what concerns particularly the arrangements for the goods and the discharge of obligations, the wishes of the founders and benefactors, and any acquired rights, must be safeguarded.

Can. 122   When an aggregate which is a public juridical person is divided in such a way that part of it is joined to another juridical person, or a distinct public juridical person is established from one part of it, the first obligation is to observe the wishes of the founders and benefactors, the demands of acquired rights and the requirements of the approved statutes. Then the competent ecclesiastical authority, either personally or through an executor, is to ensure:

    1° that the divisible common patrimonial goods and rights, the monies owed and the other liabilities, are divided between the juridical persons in question in due proportion, in a fashion which is equitable and right, taking account of all the circumstances and needs of both;

    2° that the use and enjoyment of the common goods which cannot be divided, be given to each juridical person, and also that the liabilities which are proper to each are the responsibility of each, in due proportion, in a fashion which is equitable and right.

Can. 123   On the extinction of a public juridical person, the arrangements for its patrimonial goods and rights, and for its liabilities, are determined by law and the statutes. If these do not deal with the matter, the arrangements devolve upon the next higher juridical person, always with due regard for the wishes of the founders or benefactors and for acquired rights. On the extinction of a private juridical person, the arrangements for its goods and liabilities are governed by its own statutes.

TITLE VII: JURIDICAL ACTS

Can. 124   §1 For the validity of a juridical act, it is required that it be performed by a person who is legally capable, and it must contain those elements which constitute the essence of the act, as well as the formalities and requirements which the law prescribes for the validity of the act.

§2 A juridical act which, as far as its external elements are concerned, is properly performed, is presumed to be valid.

Can. 125   §1 An act is invalid if performed as a result of force imposed from outside on a person who was quite unable to resist it.

§2 An act performed as a result of fear which is grave and unjustly inflicted, or as a result of deceit, is valid, unless the law provides otherwise. However, it can be rescinded by a court judgement, either at the instance of the injured party or that party's successors in law, or ex officio.

Can. 126   An act is invalid when performed as a result of ignorance or of error which concerns the substance of the act, or which amounts to a condition sine qua non; otherwise it is valid, unless the law provides differently. But an act done as a result of ignorance or error can give rise to a rescinding action in accordance with the law.

Can. 127 §1 When the law prescribes that, in order to perform a juridical act, a Superior requires the consent or the advice of some college or group of persons, the college or group must be convened in accordance with can. 166, unless, if there is question of seeking advice only, particular or proper law provides otherwise. For the validity of the act, it is required that the consent be obtained of an absolute majority of those present, or that the advice of all be sought.

§2 When the law prescribes that, in order to perform a juridical act, a Superior requires the consent or advice of certain persons as individuals:

1° if consent is required, the Superior's act is invalid if the Superior does not seek the consent of those persons, or acts against the vote of all or of any of them;

2° if advice is required, the Superior's act is invalid if the Superior does not hear those persons. The Superior is not in any way bound to accept their vote, even if it is unanimous; nevertheless, without what is, in his or her judgement, an overriding reason, the Superior is not to act against their vote, especially if it is a unanimous one.

§3 All whose consent or advice is required are obliged to give their opinions sincerely. If the seriousness of the matter requires it, they are obliged carefully to maintain secrecy, and the Superior can insist on this obligation.

Can. 128 Whoever unlawfully causes harm to another by a juridical act, or indeed by any other act which is deceitful or culpable, is obliged to repair the damage done.

TITLE VIII: POWER OF GOVERNANCE

Can. 129 §1 Those who are in sacred orders are, in accordance with the provisions of law, capable of the power of governance, which belongs to the Church by divine institution. This power is also called the power of jurisdiction.

§2 Lay members of Christ's faithful can cooperate in the exercise of this same power in accordance with the law.

Can. 130 Of itself the power of governance is exercised for the external forum; sometimes however it is exercised for the internal forum only, but in such a way that the effects which its exercise is designed to have in the external forum are not acknowledged in that forum, except in so far as the law prescribes this for determinate cases.

Can. 131 §1 Ordinary power of governance is that which by virtue of the law itself is attached to a given office; delegated power is that which is granted to a person other than through an office.

§2 Ordinary power of governance may be proper or vicarious.

§3 One who claims to have been delegated has the onus of proving the delegation.

Can. 132 §1 Habitual faculties are governed by the provisions concerning delegated power.

§2 However, unless the grant has expressly provided otherwise, or the Ordinary was deliberately chosen as the only one to exercise the faculty, an habitual faculty granted to an Ordinary does not lapse on the expiry of the authority of the Ordinary to whom it was given, even if he has already begun to exercise the faculty, but it passes to the Ordinary who succeeds him in governance.

Can. 133 §1 A delegate who exceeds the limits of the mandate, with regard either to things or to persons, performs no act at all.

§2 A delegate is not considered to have exceeded the mandate when what was delegated is carried out, but in a manner different to that determined in the mandate, unless the manner was prescribed for validity by the delegating authority.

Can. 134 §1 In law the term Ordinary means, apart from the Roman Pontiff, diocesan Bishops and all who, even for a time only, are set over a particular Church or a community equivalent to it in accordance with can. 368, and those who in these have general ordinary executive power, that is, Vicars general and episcopal Vicars; likewise, for their own members, it means the major Superiors of clerical religious institutes of pontifical right and of clerical societies of apostolic life of pontifical right, who have at least ordinary executive power.

§2 The term local Ordinary means all those enumerated in §1, except Superiors of religious institutes and of societies of apostolic life.

§3 Whatever in the canons, in the context of executive power, is attributed to the diocesan Bishop, is understood to belong only to the diocesan Bishop and to those others in can. 381 §2 who are equivalent to him, to the exclusion of the Vicar general and the episcopal Vicar except by special mandate.

Can. 135 §1 The power of governance is divided into legislative, executive and judicial power.

§2 Legislative power is to be exercised in the manner prescribed by law; that which in the Church a legislator lower than the supreme authority has, cannot be delegated, unless the law explicitly provides otherwise. A lower legislator cannot validly make a law which is contrary to that of a higher legislator.

§3 Judicial power, which is possessed by judges and judicial colleges, is to be exercised in the manner prescribed by law, and it cannot be delegated except for the performance of acts preparatory to some decree or judgement.

21

§4 As far as the exercise of executive power is concerned, the provisions of the following canons are to be observed.

Can. 136 Persons may exercise executive power over their subjects, even when either they themselves or their subjects are outside the territory, unless it is otherwise clear from the nature of things or from the provisions of law. They can exercise this power over *peregrini* who are actually living in the territory, if it is a question of granting favours, or of executing universal or particular laws by which the *peregrini* are bound in accordance with can. 13 §2, n. 2.

Can. 137 §1 Ordinary executive power can be delegated either for an individual case or for all cases, unless the law expressly provides otherwise.

§2 Executive power delegated by the Apostolic See can be subdelegated, either for an individual case or for all cases, unless the delegation was deliberately given to the individual alone, or unless subdelegation was expressly prohibited.

§3 Executive power delegated by another authority having ordinary power, if delegated for all cases, can be subdelegated only for individual cases; if delegated for a determinate act or acts, it cannot be subdelegated, except by the express grant of the person delegating.

§4 No subdelegated power can again be subdelegated, unless this was expressly granted by the person delegating.

Can. 138 Ordinary executive power, and power delegated for all cases, are to be interpreted widely; any other power is to be interpreted strictly. Delegation of power to a person is understood to include everything necessary for the exercise of that power.

Can. 139 §1 Unless the law prescribes otherwise, the fact that a person approaches some competent authority, even a higher one, does not mean that the executive power of another competent authority is suspended, whether that be ordinary or delegated.

§2 A lower authority, however, is not to interfere in cases referred to higher authority, except for a grave and urgent reason; in which case the higher authority is to be notified immediately.

Can. 140 §1 When several people are together delegated to act in the same matter, the person who has begun to deal with it excludes the others from acting, unless that person is subsequently impeded, or does not wish to proceed further with the matter.

§2 When several people are delegated to act as a college in a certain matter, all must proceed in accordance with can. 119, unless the mandate provides otherwise.

§3 Executive power delegated to several people is presumed to be delegated to them together.

Can. 141 If several people are successively delegated, that person is to deal with the matter whose mandate was the earlier and was not subsequently revoked.

Can. 142 §1 Delegated power lapses: on the completion of the mandate; on the expiry of the time or the completion of the number of cases for which it was granted; on the cessation of the motivating reason for the delegation; on its revocation by the person delegating, when communicated directly to the person delegated; and on the retirement of the person delegated, when communicated to and accepted by the person delegating. It does not lapse on the expiry of the authority of the person delegating, unless this appears from clauses attached to it.

§2 An act of delegated power exercised for the internal forum only, which is inadvertently performed after the time limit of the delegation, is valid.

Can. 143 §1 Ordinary power ceases on the loss of the office to which it is attached.

§2 Unless the law provides otherwise, ordinary power is suspended if an appeal or a recourse is lawfully made against a deprivation of, or removal from, office.

Can. 144 §1 In common error, whether of fact or of law, and in positive and probable doubt, whether of law or of fact, the Church supplies executive power of governance for both the external and the internal forum.

§2 The same norm applies to the faculties mentioned in cann. 883, 966, and 1111 §1.

TITLE IX: ECCLESIASTICAL OFFICES

Can. 145 §1 An ecclesiastical office is any post which by divine or ecclesiastical disposition is established in a stable manner to further a spiritual purpose.

§2 The duties and rights proper to each ecclesiastical office are defined either by the law whereby the office is established, or by a decree of the competent authority whereby it is at one and at the same time established and conferred.

Chapter I

THE PROVISION OF ECCLESIASTICAL OFFICE

Can. 146 An ecclesiastical office cannot be validly obtained without canonical provision.

Can. 147   The provision of an ecclesiastical office is effected: by its being freely conferred by the competent ecclesiastical authority; by appointment made by the same authority, where there has been a prior presentation; by confirmation or admission by the same authority, where there has been a prior election or postulation; finally, by a simple election and acceptance of the election, if the election does not require confirmation.

Can. 148   Unless the law provides otherwise, the provision of an office is the prerogative of the authority which is competent to establish, change or suppress the office.

Can. 149   §1 In order to be promoted to an ecclesiastical office, one must be in communion with the Church, and be suitable, that is, possessed of those qualities which are required for that office by universal or particular law or by the law of the foundation.

§2 The provision of an ecclesiastical office to a person who lacks the requisite qualities is invalid only if the qualities are expressly required for validity by universal or particular law or by the law of the foundation; otherwise it is valid, but it can be rescinded by a decree of the competent authority or by a judgement of an administrative tribunal.

§3 The provision of an office made as a result of simony, is invalid by virtue of the law itself.

Can. 150   An office which carries with it the full care of souls, for which the exercise of the order of priesthood is required, cannot validly be conferred upon a person who is not yet a priest.

Can. 151   The provision of an office which carries with it the care of souls is not to be deferred without grave reason.

Can. 152   Two or more offices which are incompatible, that is, which cannot be exercised at the same time by the same person, are not to be conferred upon anyone.

Can. 153   §1 The provision of an office which in law is not vacant is by that very fact invalid, nor does it become valid by subsequent vacancy.

§2 If, however, there is question of an office which by law is conferred for a determinate time, provision can be made within six months before the expiry of this time, and it takes effect from the day the office falls vacant.

§3 The promise of any office, by whomsoever it is made, has no juridical effect.

Can. 154   An office which in law is vacant, but which someone unlawfully still holds, may be conferred, provided that it has been properly declared that such possession is not lawful, and that mention is made of this declaration in the letter of conferral.

Can. 155   One who confers an office in the place of another who is negligent or impeded, does not thereby acquire any power over the person on whom the office is conferred; the juridical condition of the latter is the same as if the provision of the office had been carried out in accordance with the ordinary norm of law.

Can. 156   The provision of any office is to be made in writing.

Article 1: Free Conferral

Can. 157   Unless the law expressly states otherwise, it is the prerogative of the diocesan Bishop to make appointments to ecclesiastical offices in his own particular Church by free conferral.

Article 2: Presentation

Can. 158   §1 Presentation to an ecclesiastical office by a person having the right of presentation must be made to the authority who is competent to make an appointment to the office in question; unless it is otherwise lawfully provided, presentation is to be made within three months of receiving notification of the vacancy of the office.

§2 If the right of presentation belongs to a college or group of persons, the person to be presented is to be designated according to the provisions of cann. 165–179.

Can. 159   No one is to be presented who is unwilling. Accordingly, one who is proposed for presentation must be consulted, and may be presented if within eight canonical days a refusal is not entered.

Can. 160   §1 One who has the right of presentation may present one or more persons, either simultaneously or successively.

§2 No persons may present themselves. However a college or a group of persons may present one of its members.

Can. 161   §1 Unless the law prescribes otherwise, one who has presented a person who is judged unsuitable, may within a month present another candidate, but once only.

§2 If before the appointment is made the person presented has withdrawn or has died, the one with the right of presentation may exercise this right again, within a month of receiving notice of the withdrawal or of the death.

Can. 162   A person who has not presented anyone within the canonical time prescribed by can. 158 §1 and can. 161, or who has twice presented a candidate judged to be unsuitable, loses the right of presentation for that case. The authority who is competent to appoint may then freely provide for the vacant office, but with the consent of the proper Ordinary of the person appointed.

Can. 163   The authority to whom, in accordance with the law, it belongs to appoint one who is presented, is to appoint the person lawfully presented whom he has judged suitable, and who has accepted. If a number lawfully presented are judged suitable, he is to appoint one of them.

Article 3: Election

Can. 164   Unless it has been otherwise provided in the law, the provisions of the following canons are to be observed in canonical elections.

Can. 165   Unless it is otherwise provided in the law or in the statutes of the college or group, if a college or a group of persons enjoys the right to elect to an office, the election is not to be deferred beyond three canonical months, to be reckoned from the receipt of notification of the vacancy of the office. If the election does not take place within that time, the ecclesiastical authority who has the right of confirming the election or the right to make provision otherwise, is freely to provide for the vacant office.

Can. 166   §1 The one who presides over the college or group is to summon all those who belong to the college or group. When it has to be personal, the summons is valid if it is made in the place of domicile or quasi-domicile or in the place of residence.

§2 If someone who should have been summoned was overlooked and was therefore absent, the election is valid. However, if that person insists and gives proof of being overlooked and of absence, the election, even if confirmed, must be rescinded by the competent authority, provided it is juridically established that the recourse was submitted within no more than three days of having received notification of the election.

§3 If more than one third of the voters were overlooked, the election is invalid by virtue of the law itself, unless all those overlooked were in fact present.

Can. 167   §1 When the summons has been lawfully made, those who are present on the day and in the place specified in the summons have the right to vote. Unless it is otherwise lawfully provided in the statutes, votes cast by letter or by proxy cannot be admitted.

§2 If an elector is present in the building in which the election is being held, but because of infirmity is unable to be present at the election, a written vote is to be sought from that person by the scrutineers.

Can. 168   Even if someone has a right to vote in his or her own name by reason of a number of titles, that person may cast only one vote.

Can. 169   In order that an election be valid, no one may be allowed to vote who does not belong to the college or group.

Can. 170   If the freedom of an election has in any way been in fact impeded, the election is invalid by virtue of the law itself.

Can. 171   §1 The following are legally incapable of casting a vote:
    1° one incapable of a human act;
    2° one lacking active voice;
    3° one who is excommunicated, whether by judgement of a court or
      by a decree whereby this penalty is imposed or declared;
    4° one who notoriously defected from communion with the Church.
  §2 If any of the above persons is admitted, the vote cast is invalid. The election, however, is valid, unless it is established that, without this vote, the person elected would not have gained the requisite number of votes.

Can. 172   §1 For a vote to be valid, it must be:
    1° free; a vote is therefore invalid if, through grave fear or deceit,
      someone was directly or indirectly made to choose a certain
      person or several persons separately;
    2° secret, certain, absolute and determinate.
  §2 Conditions attached to a vote before an election are to be considered non-existent.

Can. 173   §1 Before an election begins, at least two scrutineers are to be appointed from among the college or group.
  §2 The scrutineers are to collect the votes and, in the presence of the one who presides at the election, to check whether the number of votes corresponds to the number of electors; they are then to examine the votes and to announce how many each person has received.
  §3 If the number of votes exceeds the number of electors, the act is null.
  §4 All the proceedings of an election are to be accurately recorded by the one who acts as notary. They are to be signed at least by that notary, by the person who presides and by the scrutineers, and they are to be carefully preserved in the archive of the college.

Can. 174   §1 Unless the law or the statutes provide otherwise, an election can be made by compromise, that is the electors by unanimous and written consent transfer the right of election for this occasion to one or more suitable persons, whether they belong to the college or are outside it, who in virtue of this authority are to elect in the name of all.
  §2 If the college or group consists solely of clerics, the persons to whom the power of election is transferred must be in sacred orders; otherwise the election is invalid.
  §3 Those to whom the power of election is transferred must observe the provisions of law concerning an election and, for the validity of the election, they must observe the conditions attached to the compromise, unless these conditions are contrary to the law. Conditions which are contrary to the law are to be regarded as non-existent.

Can. 175   A compromise ceases, and the right to vote reverts to those who transferred it, when:
    1° it is revoked by the college or group before it has been put into
      effect;

2° a condition attached to the compromise has not been fulfilled;
3° the election has been held, but invalidly.

Can. 176 Unless it is otherwise provided in the law or the statutes, the person who has received the requisite number of votes in accordance with can. 119, n. 1, is deemed elected and is to be proclaimed by the person who presides over the college or group.

Can. 177 §1 The election is to be notified immediately to the person elected who must, within eight canonical days from the receipt of notification of the election, intimate to the person who presides over the college or group whether or not he or she accepts the election; otherwise, the election has no effect.

§2 The person elected who has not accepted loses every right deriving from the election, nor is any right revived by subsequent acceptance; the person may, however, be elected again. The college or group must proceed to a new election within a month of being notified of non-acceptance.

Can. 178 If the election does not require confirmation, by accepting the election the person elected immediately obtains the office with all its rights; otherwise, he or she acquires only a right to the office.

Can. 179 §1 If the election requires confirmation, the person elected must, either personally or through another, ask for confirmation by the competent authority within eight canonical days of acceptance of the office; otherwise that person is deprived of every right, unless he or she has established that there was just reason which prevented confirmation being sought.

§2 The competent authority cannot refuse confirmation if he has found the person elected suitable in accordance with can. 149 §1, and the election has been carried out in accordance with the law.

§3 Confirmation must be given in writing.

§4 Before receiving notice of the confirmation, the person elected may not become involved in the administration of the office, neither in spiritual nor in material affairs; any acts possibly performed by that person are invalid.

§5 When confirmation has been notified, the person elected obtains full right to the office, unless the law provides otherwise.

Article 4: Postulation

Can. 180 §1 If a canonical impediment, from which a dispensation is possible and customary, stands in the way of the election of a person whom the electors judge more suitable and prefer, they can, unless the law provides otherwise, postulate that person from the competent authority.

§2 Those to whom the power of electing has been transferred by compromise may not make a postulation, unless this is expressly stated in the terms of the compromise.

Can. 181 §1 For a postulation to have effect, at least two thirds of the votes are required.

§2 A vote for postulation must be expressed by the term 'I postulate', or an equivalent. The formula 'I elect or postulate', or its equivalent, is valid for election if there is no impediment; otherwise, it is valid for postulation.

Can. 182 §1 The postulation must be sent, within eight canonical days, by the person who presides to the authority which is competent to confirm the election, to whom it belongs to grant the dispensation from the impediment or, if he has not this authority, to seek the dispensation from a superior authority. If confirmation is not required, the postulation must be sent to the authority which is competent to grant the dispensation.

§2 If the postulation is not forwarded within the prescribed time, it is by that very fact invalid, and the college or group is for that occasion deprived of the right of election or of postulation, unless it is proved that the person presiding was prevented by a just impediment from forwarding the postulation, or did not do so in due time because of deceit or negligence.

§3 The person postulated does not acquire any right from the postulation; the competent authority is not obliged to admit the postulation.

§4 The electors may not revoke a postulation made to the competent authority, except with the consent of that authority.

Can. 183 §1 If a postulation is not admitted by the competent authority, the right of election reverts to the college or group.

§2 If the postulation has been admitted, this is to be notified to the person postulated, who must reply in accordance with can. 177 §1.

§3 The person who accepts a postulation which has been admitted, immediately obtains full right to the office.

Chapter II

LOSS OF ECCLESIASTICAL OFFICE

Can. 184 §1 An ecclesiastical office is lost on the expiry of a predetermined time; on reaching the age limit defined by law; by resignation; by transfer; by removal; by deprivation.

§2 An ecclesiastical office is not lost on the expiry, in whatever way, of the authority of the one by whom it was conferred, unless the law provides otherwise.

§3 The loss of an office, once it has taken effect, is to be notified as soon as possible to those who have any right in regard to the provision of the office.

Can. 185 The title 'emeritus' may be conferred on one who loses office by reason of age, or of resignation which has been accepted.

Can. 186 Loss of office by reason of the expiry of a predetermined time or of reaching the age limit, has effect only from the moment that this is communicated in writing by the competent authority.

Article 1: Resignation

Can. 187   Anyone who is capable of personal responsibility can resign from an ecclesiastical office for a just reason.

Can. 188   A resignation which is made as a result of grave fear unjustly inflicted, or of deceit, or of substantial error, or of simony, is invalid by virtue of the law itself.

Can. 189   §1 For a resignation to be valid, whether it requires acceptance or not, it must be made to the authority which is competent to provide for the office in question, and it must be made either in writing, or orally before two witnesses.

§2 The authority is not to accept a resignation which is not based on a just and proportionate reason.

§3 A resignation which requires acceptance has no force unless it is accepted within three months. One which does not require acceptance takes effect when the person resigning communicates it in accordance with the law.

§4 Until a resignation takes effect, it can be revoked by the person resigning. Once it has taken effect, it cannot be revoked, but the person who resigned can obtain the office on the basis of another title.

Article 2: Transfer

Can. 190   §1 A transfer can be made only by the person who has the right to provide both for the office which is lost and at the same time for the office which is being conferred.

§2 A grave reason is required if a transfer is made against the will of the holder of an office and, always without prejudice to the right to present reasons against the transfer, the procedure prescribed by law is to be observed.

§3 For a transfer to have effect, it must be notified in writing.

Can. 191   §1 In the process of transfer, the first office is vacated by the taking of canonical possession of the other office, unless the law or the competent authority has prescribed otherwise.

§2 The person transferred receives the remuneration attached to the previous office until the moment of obtaining canonical possession of the other office.

Article 3: Removal

Can. 192   One is removed from office either by a decree of the competent authority lawfully issued, observing of course the rights possibly acquired from a contract, or by virtue of the law in accordance with can. 194.

Can. 193   §1 No one may be removed from an office which is conferred on a person for an indeterminate time, except for grave reasons and in accordance with the procedure defined by law.

§2 This also applies to the removal from office before time of a person on whom an office is conferred for a determinate time, without prejudice to can. 624 §3.

§3 When in accordance with the provisions of law an office is conferred upon someone at the prudent discretion of the competent authority, that person may, upon the judgement of the same authority, be removed from the office for a just reason.

§4 For a decree of removal to be effective, it must be notified in writing.

Can. 194   §1 The following are removed from ecclesiastical office by virtue of the law itself:
> 1° one who has lost the clerical state;
> 2° one who has publicly defected from the catholic faith or from communion with the Church;
> 3° a cleric who has attempted marriage, even a civil one.

§2 The removal mentioned in nn. 2 and 3 can be insisted upon only if it is established by a declaration of the competent authority.

Can. 195   If by a decree of the competent authority, and not by the law itself, someone is removed from an office on which that person's livelihood depends, the same authority is to ensure that the person's livelihood is secure for an appropriate time, unless this has been provided for in some other way.

Article 4: Deprivation

Can. 196   §1 Deprivation of office, that is, as a punishment for an offence, may be effected only in accordance with the law.

§2 Deprivation takes effect in accordance with the provisions of the canons concerning penal law.

TITLE X: PRESCRIPTION

Can. 197   Prescription, as a means of acquiring or of losing a subjective right, or as a means of freeing oneself from obligations, is, apart from the exceptions prescribed in the canons of this Code, accepted by the Church in the manner in which it is adopted in the civil legislation of each country.

Can. 198   No prescription is valid unless it is based on good faith, not only in its beginning, but throughout the whole time required for the prescription, without prejudice to can. 1362.

Can. 199   The following are not affected by prescription:
> 1° rights and obligations which are of divine law, whether natural or positive;

2° rights which can be obtained only by apostolic privilege;

3° rights and obligations which bear directly on the spiritual life of Christ's faithful;

4° the certain and undisputed boundaries of ecclesiastical territories;

5° Mass offerings and obligations;

6° the provision of an ecclesiastical office which, in accordance with the law, requires the exercise of a sacred order;

7° the right of visitation and the obligation of obedience, so that Christ's faithful could not be visited by an ecclesiastical authority and would no longer be subject to any authority.

TITLE XI: THE RECKONING OF TIME

Can. 200 Unless the law provides otherwise, time is to be reckoned in accordance with the following canons.

Can. 201 §1 Continuous time means unbroken time.

§2 Canonical time is time which a person can so use to exercise or to pursue a right that it does not run when one is unaware, or when one is unable to act.

Can. 202 §1 In law, a day is understood to be a space of twenty-four hours, to be reckoned continuously and, unless expressly provided otherwise, it begins at midnight; a week is a space of seven days; a month is a space of thirty days, and a year a space of three hundred and sixty-five days, unless it is stated that the month and the year are to be taken as in the calendar.

§2 If time is continuous, the month and the year are always to be taken as in the calendar.

Can. 203 §1 The first day is not to be counted in the total, unless its beginning coincides with the beginning of the day, or unless the law expressly provides otherwise.

§2 Unless the contrary is prescribed, the final day is to be reckoned within the total; if the total time is one or more months, one or more years, one or more weeks, it finishes on completion of the last day bearing the same number or, if the month does not have the same number, on the completion of the last day of that month.

Book II
THE PEOPLE OF GOD

Part I
CHRIST'S FAITHFUL

Can. 204   §1 Christ's faithful are those who, since they are incorporated into Christ through baptism, are constituted the people of God. For this reason they participate in their own way in the priestly, prophetic and kingly office of Christ. They are called, each according to his or her particular condition, to exercise the mission which God entrusted to the Church to fulfil in the world.

§2 This Church, established and ordered in this world as a society, subsists in the catholic Church, governed by the successor of Peter and the Bishops in communion with him.

Can. 205   Those baptised are in full communion with the catholic Church here on earth who are joined with Christ in his visible body, through the bonds of profession of faith, the sacraments and ecclesiastical governance.

Can. 206   §1 Catechumens are linked with the Church in a special way since, moved by the Holy Spirit, they are expressing an explicit desire to be incorporated in the Church. By this very desire, as well as by the life of faith, hope and charity which they lead, they are joined to the Church which already cherishes them as its own.

§2 The Church has a special care for catechumens. While it invites them to lead an evangelical life, and introduces them to the celebration of the sacred rites, it already accords them various prerogatives which are proper to christians.

Can. 207   §1 By divine institution, among Christ's faithful there are in the Church sacred ministers, who in law are also called clerics; the others are called lay people.

§2 Drawn from both groups are those of Christ's faithful who, professing the evangelical counsels through vows or other sacred bonds recognised and approved by the Church, are consecrated to God in their own special way and promote the salvific mission of the Church. Their state, although it does not belong to the hierarchical structure of the Church, does pertain to its life and holiness.

TITLE I
THE OBLIGATIONS AND RIGHTS OF ALL CHRIST'S FAITHFUL

Can. 208 Flowing from their rebirth in Christ, there is a genuine equality of dignity and action among all of Christ's faithful. Because of this equality they all contribute, each according to his or her own condition and office, to the building up of the Body of Christ.

Can. 209 §1 Christ's faithful are bound to preserve their communion with the Church at all times, even in their external actions.

§2 They are to carry out with great diligence their responsibilities towards both the universal Church and the particular Church to which by law they belong.

Can. 210 All Christ's faithful, each according to his or her own condition, must make a wholehearted effort to lead a holy life, and to promote the growth of the Church and its continual sanctification.

Can. 211 All Christ's faithful have the obligation and the right to strive so that the divine message of salvation may more and more reach all people of all times and all places.

Can. 212 §1 Christ's faithful, conscious of their own responsibility, are bound to show christian obedience to what the sacred Pastors, who represent Christ, declare as teachers of the faith and prescribe as rulers of the Church.

§2 Christ's faithful are at liberty to make known their needs, especially their spiritual needs, and their wishes to the Pastors of the Church.

§3 They have the right, indeed at times the duty, in keeping with their knowledge, competence and position, to manifest to the sacred Pastors their views on matters which concern the good of the Church. They have the right also to make their views known to others of Christ's faithful, but in doing so they must always respect the integrity of faith and morals, show due reverence to the Pastors and take into account both the common good and the dignity of individuals.

Can. 213 Christ's faithful have the right to be assisted by their Pastors from the spiritual riches of the Church, especially by the word of God and the sacraments.

Can. 214 Christ's faithful have the right to worship God according to the provisions of their own rite approved by the lawful Pastors of the Church; they also have the right to follow their own form of spiritual life, provided it is in accord with Church teaching.

Can. 215 Christ's faithful may freely establish and direct associations which serve charitable or pious purposes or which foster the christian vocation in the world, and they may hold meetings to pursue these purposes by common effort.

Can. 216   Since they share the Church's mission, all Christ's faithful have the right to promote and support apostolic action, by their own initiative, undertaken according to their state and condition. No initiative, however, can lay claim to the title 'catholic' without the consent of the competent ecclesiastical authority.

Can. 217   Since Christ's faithful are called by baptism to lead a life in harmony with the gospel teaching, they have the right to a christian education, which genuinely teaches them to strive for the maturity of the human person and at the same time to know and live the mystery of salvation.

Can. 218   Those who are engaged in fields of sacred study have a just freedom to research matters in which they are expert and to express themselves prudently concerning them, with due allegiance to the *magisterium* of the Church.

Can. 219   All Christ's faithful have the right to immunity from any kind of coercion in choosing a state in life.

Can. 220   No one may unlawfully harm the good reputation which a person enjoys, or violate the right of every person to protect his or her privacy.

Can. 221   §1 Christ's faithful may lawfully vindicate and defend the rights they enjoy in the Church, before the competent ecclesiastical forum in accordance with the law.
§2 If any members of Christ's faithful are summoned to trial by the competent authority, they have the right to be judged according to the provisions of the law, to be applied with equity.
§3 Christ's faithful have the right that no canonical penalties be inflicted upon them except in accordance with the law.

Can. 222   §1 Christ's faithful have the obligation to provide for the needs of the Church, so that the Church has available to it those things which are necessary for divine worship, for apostolic and charitable work and for the worthy support of its ministers.
§2 They are also obliged to promote social justice and, mindful of the Lord's precept, to help the poor from their own resources.

Can. 223   §1 In exercising their rights, Christ's faithful, both individually and in associations, must take account of the common good of the Church, as well as the rights of others and their own duties to others.
§2 Ecclesiastical authority is entitled to regulate, in view of the common good, the exercise of rights which are proper to Christ's faithful.

TITLE II: THE OBLIGATIONS AND RIGHTS OF THE LAY MEMBERS OF CHRIST'S FAITHFUL

Can. 224 Lay members of Christ's faithful have the duties and rights enumerated in the canons of this title, in addition to those duties and rights which are common to all Christ's faithful and those stated in other canons.

Can. 225 §1 Since lay people, like all Christ's faithful, are deputed to the apostolate by baptism and confirmation, they are bound by the general obligation and they have the right, whether as individuals or in associations, to strive so that the divine message of salvation may be known and accepted by all people throughout the world. This obligation is all the more insistent in circumstances in which only through them are people able to hear the Gospel and to know Christ.

§2 They have also, according to the condition of each, the special obligation to permeate and perfect the temporal order of things with the spirit of the Gospel. In this way, particularly in conducting secular business and exercising secular functions, they are to give witness to Christ.

Can. 226 §1 Those who are married are bound by the special obligation, in accordance with their own vocation, to strive for the building up of the people of God through their marriage and family.

§2 Because they gave life to their children, parents have the most serious obligation and the right to educate them. It is therefore primarily the responsibility of christian parents to ensure the christian education of their children in accordance with the teaching of the Church.

Can. 227 To lay members of Christ's faithful belongs the right to have acknowledged as theirs that freedom in secular affairs which is common to all citizens. In using this freedom, however, they are to ensure that their actions are permeated with the spirit of the Gospel, and they are to heed the teaching of the Church proposed by the *magisterium*, but they must be on guard, in questions of opinion, against proposing their own view as the teaching of the Church.

Can. 228 §1 Lay people who are found to be suitable are capable of being admitted by the sacred Pastors to those ecclesiastical offices and functions which, in accordance with the provisions of law, they can discharge.

§2 Lay people who are outstanding in the requisite knowledge, prudence and integrity, are capable of being experts or advisors, even in councils in accordance with the law, in order to provide assistance to the Pastors of the Church.

Can. 229 §1 Lay people have the duty and the right to acquire the knowledge of christian teaching which is appropriate to each one's capacity and condition, so that they may be able to live according to this teaching, to proclaim it and if necessary to defend it, and may be capable of playing their part in the exercise of the apostolate.

§2 They also have the right to acquire that fuller knowledge of the sacred sciences which is taught in ecclesiastical universities or faculties or in institutes of religious sciences, attending lectures there and acquiring academic degrees.

§3 Likewise, assuming that the provisions concerning the requisite suitability have been observed, they are capable of receiving from the lawful ecclesiastical authority a mandate to teach the sacred sciences.

Can. 230   §1 Lay men whose age and talents meet the requirements prescribed by decree of the Episcopal Conference, can be given the stable ministry of lector and of acolyte, through the prescribed liturgical rite. This conferral of ministry does not, however, give them a right to sustenance or remuneration from the Church.

§2 Lay people can receive a temporary assignment to the role of lector in liturgical actions. Likewise, all lay people can exercise the roles of commentator, cantor or other such, in accordance with the law.

§3 Where the needs of the Church require and ministers are not available, lay people, even though they are not lectors or acolytes, can supply certain of their functions, that is, exercise the ministry of the word, preside over liturgical prayers, confer baptism and distribute Holy Communion, in accordance with the provisions of the law.

Can. 231   §1 Lay people who are pledged to the special service of the Church, whether permanently or for a time, have a duty to acquire the appropriate formation which their role demands, so that they may conscientiously, earnestly and diligently fulfil this role.

§2 Without prejudice to the provisions of can. 230 §1, they have the right to a worthy remuneration befitting their condition, whereby, with due regard also to the provisions of the civil law, they can becomingly provide for their own needs and the needs of their families. Likewise, they have the right to have their insurance, social security and medical benefits duly safeguarded.

TITLE III: SACRED MINISTERS OR CLERICS

Chapter I

THE FORMATION OF CLERICS

Can. 232   It is the duty and the proper and exclusive right of the Church to train those who are deputed to sacred ministries.

Can. 233   §1 It is the duty of the whole christian community to foster vocations so that the needs of the sacred ministry are sufficiently met in the entire Church. In particular, this duty binds christian families, educators and, in a special way, priests, especially parish priests. Diocesan Bishops, who must show the greatest concern to promote vocations, are to instruct the people entrusted to them on the importance of the sacred ministry and the need for ministers in the Church. They are to encourage and support initiatives to promote vocations, especially movements established for this purpose.

§2 Moreover, priests and especially diocesan Bishops are to be solicitous that men of more mature years who believe they are called to the sacred ministries are prudently assisted by word and deed and are duly prepared.

Can. 234 §1 Minor seminaries and other institutions of a similar nature promote vocations by providing a special religious formation, allied to human and scientific education; where they exist, they are to be retained and fostered. Indeed, where the diocesan Bishop considers it expedient, he is to provide for the establishment of a minor seminary or similar institution.

§2 Unless the circumstances of certain situations suggest otherwise, young men who aspire to the priesthood are to receive that same human and scientific formation which prepares their peers in their region for higher studies.

Can. 235 §1 Young men who intend to become priests are to receive the appropriate religious formation and instruction in the duties proper to the priesthood in a major seminary, for the whole of the time of formation or, if in the judgement of the diocesan Bishop circumstances require it, for at least four years.

§2 Those who lawfully reside outside the seminary are to be entrusted by the diocesan Bishop to a devout and suitable priest, who will ensure that they are carefully formed in the spiritual life and in discipline.

Can. 236 Those who aspire to the permanent diaconate are to be formed in the spiritual life and appropriately instructed in the fulfilment of the duties proper to that order, in accordance with the provisions made by the Episcopal Conference:

    1° young men are to reside for at least three years in a special house, unless the diocesan Bishop for grave reasons decides otherwise;

    2° men of more mature years, whether celibate or married, are to prepare for three years in a manner determined by the same Episcopal Conference.

Can. 237 §1 Where it is possible and advisable, each diocese is to have a major seminary; otherwise, students preparing for the sacred ministries are to be sent to the seminary of another diocese, or an inter-diocesan seminary is to be established.

§2 An inter-diocesan seminary may not be established unless the prior approval of the Apostolic See has been obtained, both for the establishment of the seminary and for its statutes. Approval is also required from the Episcopal Conference if the seminary is for the whole of its territory; otherwise, from the Bishops concerned.

Can. 238   §1 Seminaries which are lawfully established have juridical personality in the Church by virtue of the law itself.

§2 In the conduct of all its affairs, the rector acts in the person of the seminary, unless for certain matters the competent authority has prescribed otherwise.

Can. 239   §1 In all seminaries there is to be a rector who presides over it, a vice-rector, if circumstances warrant this, and a financial administrator. Moreover, if the students follow their studies in the seminary, there are to be professors who teach the various subjects in a manner suitably coordinated between them.

§2 In every seminary there is to be at least one spiritual director, though the students are also free to approach other priests who have been deputed to this work by the Bishop.

§3 The seminary statutes are to determine the manner in which the other moderators, the professors and indeed the students themselves, are to participate in the rector's responsibility, especially in regard to the maintenance of discipline.

Can. 240   §1 Besides ordinary confessors, other confessors are to come regularly to the seminary; while maintaining seminary discipline, the students are always to be free to approach any confessor, whether inside or outside the seminary.

§2 In deciding about the admission of students to orders, or their dismissal from the seminary, the vote of the spiritual director and the confessors may never be sought.

Can. 241   §1 The diocesan Bishop is to admit to the major seminary only those whose human, moral, spiritual and intellectual gifts, as well as physical and psychological health and right intention, show that they are capable of dedicating themselves permanently to the sacred ministries.

§2 Before they are accepted, they must submit documentation of their baptism and confirmation, and whatever else is required by the provisions of the Charter of Priestly Formation.

§3 If there is question of admitting those who have been dismissed from another seminary or religious institute, there is also required the testimony of the respective superior, especially concerning the reason for their dismissal or departure.

Can. 242   §1 In each country there is to be a Charter of Priestly Formation. It is to be drawn up by the Episcopal Conference, taking account of the norms issued by the supreme ecclesiastical authority, and it is to be approved by the Holy See; moreover, it is to be adapted to new circumstances, likewise with the approval of the Holy See. This Charter is to define the overall principles governing formation in the seminary and the general norms which take account of the pastoral needs of each region or province.

§2 The norms of the Charter mentioned in §1 are to be observed in all seminaries, whether diocesan or inter-diocesan.

Can. 243 In addition, each seminary is to have its own rule, approved by the diocesan Bishop or, in the case of an inter-diocesan seminary, by the Bishops concerned. In this, the norms of the Charter of Priestly Formation are to be adapted to the particular circumstances and developed in greater detail, especially on points of discipline affecting the daily life of the students and the good order of the entire seminary.

Can. 244 The spiritual formation and the doctrinal instruction of the students in a seminary are to be harmoniously blended. They are to be so planned that the students, each according to his talents, simultaneously develop the requisite human maturity and acquire the spirit of the Gospel and a close relationship with Christ.

Can. 245 §1 Through their spiritual formation students are to be fitted for the fruitful exercise of the pastoral ministry, and are to be inculcated with a sense of mission. They are to learn that a ministry which is always exercised with lively faith and charity contributes effectively to their personal sanctification. They are to learn to cultivate those virtues which are highly valued in human relationships, in such a way that they can arrive at an appropriate harmony between human and supernatural values.

§2 Students are to be so trained that, filled with love for Christ's Church, they are linked to the Roman Pontiff, the successor of Peter, in humble and filial charity, to their own Bishop as his faithful co-workers, and to their brethren in friendly cooperation. Through the common life in the seminary, and by developing relationships of friendship and of association with others, they are to be prepared for the fraternal unity of the diocesan *presbyterium*, in whose service of the Church they will share.

Can. 246 §1 The celebration of the Eucharist is to be the centre of the whole life of the seminary, so that the students, participating in the very charity of Christ, may daily draw strength of soul for their apostolic labour and for their spiritual life particularly from this richest of sources.

§2 They are to be formed in the celebration of the liturgy of the hours, by which the ministers of God, in the name of the Church, intercede with Him for all the people entrusted to them, and indeed for the whole world.

§3 Devotion to the Blessed Virgin Mary, including the rosary, mental prayer and other exercises of piety are to be fostered, so that the students may acquire the spirit of prayer and be strengthened in their vocation.

§4 The students are to become accustomed to approach the sacrament of penance frequently. It is recommended that each should have a director of his spiritual life, freely chosen, to whom he can trustfully reveal his conscience.

§5 Each year the students are to make a spiritual retreat.

Can. 247   §1 By appropriate instruction they are to be prepared to observe celibacy and to learn to hold it in honour as a special gift of God.

§2 The students are to be given all the requisite knowledge concerning the duties and burdens which are proper to the sacred ministers of the Church, concealing none of the difficulties of the priestly life.

Can. 248   The doctrinal formation given is to be so directed that the students may acquire a wide and solid teaching in the sacred sciences, together with a general culture which is appropriate to the needs of place and time. As a result, with their own faith founded on and nourished by this teaching, they ought to be able properly to proclaim the Gospel to the people of their own time, in a fashion suited to the manner of the people's thinking.

Can. 249   The Charter of Priestly Formation is to provide that the students are not only taught their native language accurately, but are also well versed in latin, and have a suitable knowledge of other languages which would appear to be necessary or useful for their formation or for the exercise of their pastoral ministry.

Can. 250   The philosophical and theological studies which are organised in the seminary itself may be conducted either in succession or conjointly, in accordance with the Charter of Priestly Formation. These studies are to take at least six full years, in such a way that the time given to philosophical studies amounts to two full years and that allotted to theological studies to four full years.

Can. 251   Philosophical formation must be based on the philosophical heritage that is perennially valid, and it is also to take account of philosophical investigations over the course of time. It is to be so given that it furthers the human formation of the students, sharpens their mental edge and makes them more fitted to engage in theological studies.

Can. 252   §1 Theological formation, given in the light of faith and under the guidance of the *magisterium*, is to be imparted in such a way that the students learn the whole of catholic teaching, based on divine Revelation, that they make it a nourishment of their own spiritual lives, and that in the exercise of the ministry they may be able properly to proclaim and defend it.

§2 Students are to be instructed with special care in sacred Scripture, so that they may acquire an insight into the whole of sacred Scripture.

§3 Lectures are to be given in dogmatic theology, based always on the written word of God and on sacred Tradition; through them the students are to learn to penetrate more deeply into the mysteries of salvation, with St. Thomas in particular as their teacher. Lectures are also to be given in moral and pastoral theology, canon law, liturgy, ecclesiastical history, and other auxiliary and special disciplines, in accordance with the provisions of the Charter on Priestly Formation.

Can. 253   §1 The Bishop or the Bishops concerned are to appoint as teachers in philosophical, theological and juridical subjects only those who are of outstanding virtue and have a doctorate or a licentiate from a university or faculty recognised by the Holy See.

§2   Care is to be taken that different professors are appointed for sacred Scripture, dogmatic theology, moral theology, liturgy, philosophy, canon law and church history, and for other disciplines which are to be taught by their own distinctive methods.

§3   A professor who seriously fails in his or her duty is to be removed by the authority mentioned in §1.

Can. 254   §1 In their lectures, the professors are to be continuously attentive to the intimate unity and harmony of the entire doctrine of faith, so that the students are aware that they are learning one science. To ensure this, there is to be someone in the seminary who is in charge of the overall organisation of studies.

§2   The students are to be taught in such a way that they themselves are enabled to research various questions in the scientific way appropriate to each question. There are, therefore, to be assignments in which, under the guidance of the professors, the students learn to work out certain subjects by their own efforts.

Can. 255   Although the whole formation of students in the seminary has a pastoral purpose, a specifically pastoral formation is also to be provided there; in this the students are to learn the principles and the techniques which, according to the needs of place and time, are relevant to the ministry of teaching, sanctifying and ruling the people of God.

Can. 256   §1 Students are to be carefully instructed in whatever especially pertains to the sacred ministry, particularly in catechetics and homiletics, in divine worship and in a special way in the celebration of the sacraments, in dealing with people, including non-catholics and unbelievers, in parish administration and in the fulfilment of other tasks.

§2   The students are to be instructed about the needs of the universal Church, so that they may have a solicitude for encouraging vocations, for missionary and ecumenical questions, and for other pressing matters, including social problems.

Can. 257   §1 The formation of students is to ensure that they are concerned not only for the particular Church in which they are incardinated, but also for the universal Church, and that they are ready to devote themselves to particular Churches which are beset by grave need.

§2   The diocesan Bishop is to ensure that clerics who intend to move from their own particular Church to a particular Church in another region, are suitably prepared to exercise the sacred ministry there, that is, that they learn the language of the region, and have an understanding of its institutions, social conditions, usages and customs.

Can. 258   In order that the students may also by practice learn the art of exercising the apostolate, they are in the course of their studies, and especially during holiday time, to be initiated into pastoral practice by suitable assignments, always under the supervision of an experienced priest. These assignments, appropriate to the age of the student and the conditions of the place, are to be determined by the Ordinary.

Can. 259   §1 It belongs to the diocesan Bishop or, in the case of an inter-diocesan seminary, to the Bishops concerned to determine those matters which concern the overall control and administration of the seminary.

§2 The diocesan Bishop or, in the case of an inter-diocesan seminary, the Bishops concerned, are frequently to visit the seminary in person. They are to oversee the formation of their students, and the philosophical and theological instruction given in the seminary. They are to inform themselves about the vocation, character, piety and progress of the students, in view particularly to the conferring of sacred orders.

Can. 260   In the fulfilment of their duties, all must obey the rector, who is responsible for the day to day direction of the seminary, in accordance with the norms of the Charter of Priestly Formation and the rule of the seminary.

Can. 261   §1 The rector of the seminary is to ensure that the students faithfully observe the norms of the Charter of Priestly Formation and the rule of the seminary; under his authority, and according to their different positions, the moderators and professors have the same responsibility

Can. 262   The seminary is to be exempt from parochial governance. For all those in the seminary, the function of the parish priest is to be discharged by the rector of the seminary or his delegate, with the exception of matters concerning marriage and without prejudice to the provisions of can. 985.

Can. 263   The diocesan Bishop must ensure that the building and maintenance of the seminary, the support of the students, the remuneration of the teachers and the other needs of the seminary are provided for. In an inter-diocesan seminary this responsibility devolves upon the Bishops concerned, each to the extent allotted by their common agreement.

Can. 264   §1 To provide for the needs of the seminary, the Bishop can, apart from the collection mentioned in can. 1266, impose a levy in the diocese.

§2 Every ecclesiastical juridical person is subject to the levy for the seminary, including even private juridical persons, which have a centre in the diocese. Exception is made for those whose sole support comes from alms, or in which there is actually present a college of students or of teachers for furthering the common good of the Church. This levy should be general, proportionate to the revenue of those who are subject to it, and calculated according to the needs of the seminary.

Chapter II

THE ENROLMENT OR INCARDINATION OF CLERICS

Can. 265 Every cleric must be incardinated in a particular church, or in a personal Prelature, or in an institute of consecrated life or a society which has this faculty: accordingly, acephalous or 'wandering' clergy are in no way to be allowed.

Can. 266 §1 By the reception of the diaconate a person becomes a cleric, and is incardinated in the particular Church or personal Prelature for whose service he is ordained.

§2 A member who is perpetually professed in a religious institute, or who is definitively incorporated into a clerical society of apostolic life, is by the reception of the diaconate incardinated as a cleric in that institute or society unless, in the case of a society, the constitutions determine otherwise.

§3 A member of a secular institute is by the reception of the diaconate incardinated into the particular Church for whose service he was ordained, unless by virtue of a concession of the Apostolic See he is incardinated into the institute itself.

Can. 267 §1 To be validly incardinated in another particular Church, a cleric who is already incardinated must obtain a letter of excardination signed by the diocesan Bishop, and in the same way a letter of incardination signed by the diocesan Bishop of the particular Church in which he wishes to be incardinated.

§2 Excardination granted in this way does not take effect until incardination is obtained in the other particular Church.

Can. 268 §1 A cleric who has lawfully moved from his own particular Church to another is, by virtue of the law itself, incardinated in that latter Church after five years, if he has declared this intention in writing to both the diocesan Bishop of the host diocese and his own diocesan Bishop, and neither of the two Bishops has indicated opposition in writing within four months of receiving the cleric's written request.

§2 By perpetual or definitive admission into an institute of consecrated life or a society of apostolic life, a cleric who in accordance with can. 266 is incardinated in that institute or society, is excardinated from his own particular Church.

Can. 269 A diocesan Bishop is not to incardinate a cleric unless:

    1° the need or the advantage of his particular Church requires it, and the provisions of law concerning the worthy support of the cleric are observed;

    2° he knows by a lawful document that excardination has been granted, and has also obtained from the excardinating Bishop, under secrecy if need be, appropriate testimonials concerning the cleric's life, behaviour and studies;

3° the cleric declares in writing to the same Bishop that he wishes to enter the service of the new particular Church in accordance with the norms of law.

Can. 270   Excardination can be lawfully granted only for a just reason, such as the advantage of the Church or the good of the cleric. It may not, however, be refused unless grave reasons exist; it is lawful for a cleric who considers himself to be unfairly treated and who has a Bishop to receive him, to have recourse against the decision.

Can. 271   §1 Except for a grave need of his own particular Church, a Bishop is not to refuse clerics seeking permission to move whom he knows to be prepared and considers suitable to exercise the ministry in regions which suffer from a grave shortage of clergy. He is to ensure, however, that the rights and duties of these clerics are determined by written agreement with the diocesan Bishop of the place to which they wish to move.

§2 A Bishop can give permission to his clerics to move to another particular Church for a specified time. Such permission can be renewed several times, but in such a way that the clerics remain incardinated in their own particular Church, and on returning there enjoy all the rights which they would have had if they had ministered there.

§3 A cleric who lawfully moves to another particular Church while remaining incardinated in his own, may for a just reason be recalled by his own Bishop, provided the agreements entered into with the other Bishop are honoured and natural equity is observed. Under the same conditions, the Bishop of the other particular Church can for a just reason refuse the cleric permission to reside further in his territory.

Can. 272   The diocesan Administrator cannot grant excardination nor incardination, nor permission to move to another particular Church, unless the episcopal see has been vacant for a year, and he has the consent of the college of consultors.

Chapter III

THE OBLIGATIONS AND RIGHTS OF CLERICS

Can. 273   Clerics have a special obligation to show reverence and obedience to the Supreme Pontiff and to their own Ordinary.

Can. 274   §1 Only clerics can obtain offices the exercise of which requires the power of order or the power of ecclesiastical governance.

§2 Unless excused by a lawful impediment, clerics are obliged to accept and faithfully fulfil the office committed to them by their Ordinary.

Can. 275 §1 Since all clerics are working for the same purpose, namely the building up of the body of Christ, they are to be united with one another in the bond of brotherhood and prayer. They are to seek to cooperate with one another, in accordance with the provisions of particular law.

§2 Clerics are to acknowledge and promote the mission which the laity, each for his or her part, exercises in the Church and in the world.

Can. 276 §1 Clerics have a special obligation to seek holiness in their lives, because they are consecrated to God by a new title through the reception of orders, and are stewards of the mysteries of God in the service of His people.

§2 In order that they can pursue this perfection:

    1° they are in the first place faithfully and untiringly to fulfil the obligations of their pastoral ministry;

    2° they are to nourish their spiritual life at the twofold table of the sacred Scripture and the Eucharist; priests are therefore earnestly invited to offer the eucharistic Sacrifice daily, and deacons to participate daily in the offering;

    3° priests, and deacons aspiring to the priesthood, are obliged to carry out the liturgy of the hours daily, in accordance with their own approved liturgical books; permanent deacons are to recite that part of it determined by the Episcopal Conference;

    4° they are also obliged to make spiritual retreats, in accordance with the provision of particular law;

    5° they are exhorted to engage regularly in mental prayer, to approach the sacrament of penance frequently, to honour the Virgin Mother of God with particular veneration, and to use other general and special means to holiness.

Can. 277 §1 Clerics are obliged to observe perfect and perpetual continence for the sake of the Kingdom of heaven, and are therefore bound to celibacy. Celibacy is a special gift of God by which sacred ministers can more easily remain close to Christ with an undivided heart, and can dedicate themselves more freely to the service of God and their neighbour.

§2 Clerics are to behave with due prudence in relation to persons whose company can be a danger to their obligation of preserving continence or can lead to scandal of the faithful.

§3 The diocesan Bishop has authority to establish more detailed rules concerning this matter, and to pass judgement on the observance of the obligation in particular cases.

Can. 278 §1 The secular clergy have the right of association with others for the achievement of purposes befitting the clerical state.

§2 The secular clergy are to hold in high esteem those associations especially whose statutes are recognised by the competent authority and which, by a suitable and well tried rule of life and by fraternal support, promote holiness in the exercise of their ministry and foster the unity of the clergy with one another and with their Bishop.

§3 Clerics are to refrain from establishing or joining associations whose purpose or activity cannot be reconciled with the obligations proper to the clerical state, or which can hinder the diligent fulfilment of the office entrusted to them by the competent ecclesiastical authority.

Can. 279   §1 Clerics are to continue their sacred studies even after ordination to the priesthood. They are to hold to that solid doctrine based on sacred Scripture which has been handed down by our forebears and which is generally received in the Church, as set out especially in the documents of the Councils and of the Roman Pontiffs. They are to avoid profane novelties and pseudo-science.

§2 Priests are to attend pastoral courses to be arranged for them after their ordination, in accordance with the provisions of particular law. At times determined by the same law, they are to attend other courses, theological meetings or conferences, which offer them an occasion to acquire further knowledge of the sacred sciences and of pastoral methods.

§3 They are also to seek a knowledge of other sciences, especially those linked to the sacred sciences, particularly insofar as they benefit the exercise of the pastoral ministry.

Can. 280   Some manner of common life is highly recommended to clerics; where it exists, it is as far as possible to be maintained.

Can. 281   §1 Since clerics dedicate themselves to the ecclesiastical ministry, they deserve the remuneration that befits their condition, taking into account both the nature of their office and the conditions of time and place. It is to be such that it provides for the necessities of their life and for the just remuneration of those whose services they need.

§2 Suitable provision is likewise to be made for such social welfare as they may need in infirmity, sickness or old age.

§3 Married deacons who dedicate themselves full-time to the ecclesiastical ministry deserve remuneration sufficient to provide for themselves and their families. Those, however, who receive a remuneration by reason of a secular profession which they exercise or exercised, are to see to their own and to their families' needs from that income.

Can. 282   §1 Clerics are to follow a simple way of life and avoid anything which smacks of worldliness.

§2 Goods which they receive on the occasion of the exercise of an ecclesiastical office, and which are over and above what is necessary for their worthy upkeep and the fulfilment of all the duties of their state, they may well wish to use for the good of the Church and for charitable works.

Can. 283   §1 Clerics, even if they do not have a residential office, are not to be absent from their diocese for a considerable time, to be determined by particular law, without the at least presumed permission of their proper Ordinary.

§2 They may, however, take a rightful and sufficient holiday every year, for the length of time determined by general or by particular law.

Can. 284 Clerics are to wear suitable ecclesiastical dress, in accordance with the norms established by the Episcopal Conference and legitimate local custom.

Can. 285 §1 Clerics are to shun completely everything that is unbecoming to their state, in accordance with the provisions of particular law.

§2 Clerics are to avoid whatever is foreign to their state, even when it is not unseemly.

§3 Clerics are forbidden to assume public office whenever it means sharing in the exercise of civil power.

§4 Without the permission of their Ordinary, they may not undertake the administration of goods belonging to lay people, or secular offices which involve the obligation to render an account. They are forbidden to act as surety, even concerning their own goods, without consulting their proper Ordinary. They are not to sign promissory notes which involve the payment of money but do not state the reasons for the payment.

Can. 286 Clerics are forbidden to practise commerce or trade, either personally or through another, for their own or another's benefit, except with the permission of the lawful ecclesiastical authority.

Can. 287 §1 Clerics are always to do their utmost to foster among people peace and harmony based on justice.

§2 They are not to play an active role in political parties or in directing trade unions unless, in the judgement of the competent ecclesiastical authority, this is required for the defence of the rights of the Church or to promote the common good.

Can. 288 Permanent deacons are not bound by the provisions of cann. 284, 285 §§3 and 4, 286, 287 §2, unless particular law states otherwise.

Can. 289 §1 As military service ill befits the clerical state, clerics and candidates for sacred orders are not to volunteer for the armed services without the permission of their Ordinary.

§2 Clerics are to take advantage of exemptions from exercising functions and public civil offices foreign to the clerical state, which are granted in their favour by law, agreements or customs, unless their proper Ordinary has in particular cases decreed otherwise.

Chapter IV

LOSS OF THE CLERICAL STATE

Can. 290 Sacred ordination once validly received never becomes invalid. A cleric, however, loses the clerical state:

1° by a judgement of a court or an administrative decree, declaring the ordination invalid;

2° by the penalty of dismissal lawfully imposed;

3° by a rescript of the Apostolic See; this rescript, however, is granted to deacons only for grave reasons and to priests only for the gravest of reasons.

Can. 291   Apart from the cases mentioned in can. 290, n. 1, the loss of the clerical state does not carry with it a dispensation from the obligation of celibacy, which is granted solely by the Roman Pontiff.

Can. 292   A cleric who loses the clerical state in accordance with the law, loses thereby the rights that are proper to the clerical state and is no longer bound by any obligations of the clerical state, without prejudice to can. 291. He is prohibited from exercising the power of order, without prejudice to can. 976. He is automatically deprived of all offices and roles and of any delegated power.

Can. 293   A cleric who has lost the clerical state cannot be enrolled as a cleric again save by rescript of the Apostolic See.

TITLE IV: PERSONAL PRELATURES

Can. 294   Personal prelatures may be established by the Apostolic See after consultation with the Episcopal Conferences concerned. They are composed of deacons and priests of the secular clergy. Their purpose is to promote an appropriate distribution of priests, or to carry out special pastoral or missionary enterprises in different regions or for different social groups.

Can. 295   §1 A personal prelature is governed by statutes laid down by the Apostolic See. It is presided over by a Prelate as its proper Ordinary. He has the right to establish a national or an international seminary, and to incardinate students and promote them to orders with the title of service of the prelature.

§2 The Prelate must provide both for the spiritual formation of those who are ordained with this title, and for their becoming support.

Can. 296   Lay people can dedicate themselves to the apostolic work of a personal prelature by way of agreements made with the prelature. The manner of this organic cooperation and the principal obligations and rights associated with it, are to be duly defined in the statutes.

Can. 297   The statutes are likewise to define the relationships of the prelature with the local Ordinaries in whose particular Churches the prelature, with the prior consent of the diocesan Bishop, exercises or wishes to exercise its pastoral or missionary activity.

TITLE V: ASSOCIATIONS OF CHRIST'S FAITHFUL

Chapter I
COMMON NORMS

Can. 298 §1 In the Church there are associations which are distinct from institutes of consecrated life and societies of apostolic life. In these associations, Christ's faithful, whether clerics or laity, or clerics and laity together, strive with a common effort to foster a more perfect life, or to promote public worship or christian teaching. They may also devote themselves to other works of the apostolate, such as initiatives for evangelisation, works of piety or charity, and those which animate the temporal order with the christian spirit.

§2 Christ's faithful are to join especially those associations which have been established, praised or recommended by the competent ecclesiastical authority.

Can. 299 §1 By private agreement among themselves, Christ's faithful have the right to constitute associations for the purposes mentioned in can. 298 §1, without prejudice to the provisions of can. 301 §1.

§2 Associations of this kind, even though they may be praised or commended by ecclesiastical authority, are called private associations.

§3 No private association of Christ's faithful is recognised in the Church unless its statutes have been reviewed by the competent authority.

Can. 300 No association may call itself 'catholic' except with the consent of the competent ecclesiastical authority, in accordance with can. 312.

Can. 301 §1 It is for the competent ecclesiastical authority alone to establish associations of Christ's faithful which intend to impart Christian teaching in the name of the Church, or to promote public worship, or which are directed to other ends whose pursuit is of its nature reserved to the same ecclesiastical authority.

§2 The competent ecclesiastical authority, if it judges it expedient, can also establish associations of Christ's faithful to pursue, directly or indirectly, other spiritual ends whose attainment is not adequately provided for by private initiatives.

§3 Associations of Christ's faithful which are established by the competent ecclesiastical authority are called public associations.

Can. 302 Associations of Christ's faithful are called clerical when they are under the direction of clerics, presuppose the exercise of sacred orders, and are acknowledged as such by the competent authority.

Can. 303 Associations whose members live in the world but share in the spirit of some religious institute, under the overall direction of the same institute, and who lead an apostolic life and strive for Christian perfection, are known as third orders, or are called by some other suitable title.

Can. 304   §1 All associations of Christ's faithful, whether public or private, by whatever title or name they are called, are to have their own statutes. These are to define the purpose or social objective of the association, its centre, its governance and the conditions of membership. They are also to specify the manner of action of the association, paying due regard to what is necessary or useful in the circumstances of the time and place.

§2 Associations are to select for themselves a title or name which is in keeping with the practices of the time and place, especially one derived from the purpose they intend.

Can. 305   §1 All associations of Christ's faithful are subject to the supervision of the competent ecclesiastical authority. This authority is to ensure that integrity of faith and morals is maintained in them and that abuses in ecclesiastical discipline do not creep in. The competent authority has therefore the duty and the right to visit these associations, in accordance with the law and the statutes. Associations are also subject to the governance of the same authority in accordance with the provisions of the canons which follow.

§2 Associations of every kind are subject to the supervision of the Holy See. Diocesan associations are subject to the supervision of the local Ordinary, as are other associations to the extent that they work in the diocese.

Can. 306   To enjoy the rights and privileges, indulgences and other spiritual favours granted to an association, it is necessary and sufficient that a person be validly received into the association in accordance with the provisions of the law and with the association's own statutes, and be not lawfully dismissed from it.

Can. 307   §1 The admission of members is to take place in accordance with the law and with the statutes of each association.

§2 The same person can be enrolled in several associations.

§3 In accordance with their own law, members of religious institutes may, with the consent of their Superior, join associations.

Can. 308   No one who was lawfully admitted is to be dismissed from an association except for a just reason, in accordance with the law and the statutes.

Can. 309   Associations that are lawfully established have the right, in accordance with the law and the statutes, to make particular norms concerning the association, for the holding of meetings, and for the appointment of moderators, officials, ministers and administrators of goods.

Can. 310 A private association which has not been constituted a juridical person cannot, as such, be the subject of duties and rights. However, the faithful[†] who are joined together in it can jointly contract obligations. As joint owners and joint possessors they can acquire and possess rights and goods. They can exercise these rights and obligations through a delegate or a proxy.

Can. 311 Members of institutes of consecrated life who preside over or assist associations which are joined in some way to their institute, are to ensure that these associations help the apostolic works existing in the diocese. They are especially to cooperate, under the direction of the local Ordinary, with associations which are directed to the exercise of the apostolate in the diocese.

Chapter II
PUBLIC ASSOCIATIONS OF CHRIST'S FAITHFUL

Can. 312 §1 The authority which is competent to establish public associations is:
  1° the Holy See, for universal and international associations;
  2° the Episcopal Conference in its own territory, for national associations which by their very establishment are intended for work throughout the whole nation;
  3° the diocesan Bishop, each in his own territory, but not the diocesan Administrator, for diocesan associations, with the exception, however, of associations the right to whose establishment is reserved to others by apostolic privilege.

§2 The written consent of the diocesan Bishop is required for the valid establishment of an association or branch of an association in the diocese, even though it is done in virtue of an apostolic privilege. Permission, however, which is given by the diocesan Bishop for the foundation of a house of a religious institute, is valid also for the establishment in the same house, or in a church attached to it, of an association which is proper to that institute.

Can. 313 A public association or a confederation of public associations is constituted a juridical person by the very decree by which it is established by the authority competent in accordance with can. 312. Moreover, insofar as is required, it thereby receives its mission to pursue, in the name of the Church, those ends which it proposes for itself.

Can. 314 The statutes of any public association require the approval of the authority which, in accordance with can. 312 §1, is competent to establish the association; this approval is also required for a revision of, or a change in, the statutes.

Can. 315 Public associations can, on their own initiative, undertake projects which are appropriate to their character, and they are governed by the statutes, but under the overall direction of the ecclesiastical authority mentioned in can. 312 §1.

Can. 316   §1 A person who has publicly rejected the catholic faith, or has defected from ecclesiastical communion, or upon whom an excommunication has been imposed or declared, cannot validly be received into public associations.

§2 Those who have been lawfully enrolled but who fall into one of the categories mentioned in §1, having been previously warned, are to be dismissed, in accordance with the statutes of the association, without prejudice to their right of recourse to the ecclesiastical authority mentioned in can. 312 §1.

Can. 317   §1 Unless the statutes provide otherwise, it belongs to the ecclesiastical authority mentioned in can. 312 §1 to confirm the moderator of a public association on election, or to appoint the moderator on presentation, or by his own right to appoint the moderator. The same authority appoints the chaplain or ecclesiastical assistant, after consulting the senior officials of the association, wherever this is expedient.

§2 The norm of §1 is also valid for associations which members of religious institutes, by apostolic privilege, establish outside their own churches or houses. In associations which members of religious institutes establish in their own church or house, the appointment or confirmation of the moderator and chaplain belongs to the Superior of the institute, in accordance with the statutes.

§3 The laity can be moderators of associations which are not clerical. The chaplain or ecclesiastical assistant is not to be the moderator, unless the statutes provide otherwise.

§4 Those who hold an office of direction in political parties are not to be moderators in public associations of the faithful[†] which are directly ordered to the exercise of the apostolate.

Can. 318   §1 In special circumstances, when serious reasons so require, the ecclesiastical authority mentioned in can. 312 §1 can appoint a commissioner to direct the association in his name for the time being.

§2 The moderator of a public association may be removed for a just reason, by the person who made the appointment or the confirmation, but the Moderator himself and the senior officials of the association must be consulted, in accordance with the statutes. The chaplain can, however, be removed by the person who appointed him, in accordance with cann. 192–195.

Can. 319   §1 Unless otherwise provided, a lawfully established public association administers the goods it possesses, in accordance with the statutes, and under the overall direction of the ecclesiastical authority mentioned in can. 312 §1. It must give a yearly account to this authority.

§2 The association must also faithfully account to the same authority for the disbursement of contributions and alms which it has collected.

Can. 320   §1 Associations established by the Holy See can be suppressed only by the Holy See.

§2 For grave reasons, associations established by the Episcopal Conference can be suppressed by it. The diocesan Bishop can suppress those he has established, and also those which members of religious institutes have established by apostolic indult with the consent of the diocesan Bishop.

§3 A public association is not to be suppressed by the competent authority unless the moderator and other senior officials have been consulted.

Chapter III

PRIVATE ASSOCIATIONS OF CHRIST'S FAITHFUL

Can. 321   Christ's faithful direct and moderate private associations according to the provisions of the statutes.

Can. 322   §1 A private association of Christ's faithful can acquire juridical personality by a formal decree of the competent ecclesiastical authority mentioned in can. 312.

§2 No private association of Christ's faithful can acquire juridical personality unless its statutes are approved by the ecclesiastical authority mentioned in can. 312 §1. The approval of the statutes does not, however, change the private nature of the association.

Can. 323   §1 Although private associations of Christ's faithful enjoy their own autonomy in accordance with can. 321, they are subject to the supervision of ecclesiastical authority, in accordance with can. 305, and also to the governance of the same authority.

§2 It is also the responsibility of ecclesiastical authority, with due respect for the autonomy of private associations, to oversee and ensure that there is no dissipation of their forces, and that the exercise of their apostolate is directed to the common good.

Can. 324   §1 A private association of Christ's faithful can freely designate for itself a moderator and officers, in accordance with the statutes.

§2 If a private association of Christ's faithful wishes to have a spiritual counsellor, it can freely choose one for itself from among the priests who lawfully exercise a ministry in the diocese, but the priest requires the confirmation of the local Ordinary.

Can. 325   §1 A private association of Christ's faithful is free to administer any goods it possesses, according to the provisions of the statutes, but the competent ecclesiastical authority has the right to ensure that the goods are applied to the purposes of the association.

§2 In accordance with can. 1301, the association is subject to the authority of the local Ordinary in whatever concerns the administration and distribution of goods which are donated or left to it for pious purposes.

Can. 326   §1 A private association of Christ's faithful is extinguished in accordance with the norms of the statutes. It can also be suppressed by the competent authority if its activity gives rise to grave harm to ecclesiastical teaching or discipline, or is a scandal to the faithful.

§2 The fate of the goods of a private association which ceases to exist is to be determined in accordance with the statutes, without prejudice to acquired rights and to the wishes of donors.

Chapter IV

SPECIAL NORMS FOR LAY ASSOCIATIONS

Can. 327   Lay members of Christ's faithful are to hold in high esteem associations established for the spiritual purposes mentioned in can. 298. They should especially esteem those associations whose aim is to animate the temporal order with the christian spirit, and thus greatly foster an intimate union between faith and life.

Can. 328   Those who head lay associations, even those established by apostolic privilege, are to ensure that their associations cooperate with other associations of Christ's faithful, where this is expedient. They are to give their help freely to various christian works, especially those in the same territory.

Can. 329   Moderators of lay associations are to ensure that the members receive due formation, so that they may carry out the apostolate which is proper to the laity.

Part II
THE HIERARCHICAL CONSTITUTION OF THE CHURCH

Section I: The Supreme Authority of the Church

Chapter I
THE ROMAN PONTIFF AND THE COLLEGE OF BISHOPS

Can. 330 Just as, by the decree of the Lord, Saint Peter and the rest of the Apostles form one College, so for a like reason the Roman Pontiff, the successor of Peter, and the Bishops, the successors of the Apostles, are united together in one.

Article 1: The Roman Pontiff

Can. 331 The office uniquely committed by the Lord to Peter, the first of the Apostles, and to be transmitted to his successors, abides in the Bishop of the Church of Rome. He is the head of the College of Bishops, the Vicar of Christ, and the Pastor of the universal Church here on earth. Consequently, by virtue of his office, he has supreme, full, immediate and universal ordinary power in the Church, and he can always freely exercise this power.

Can. 332 §1 The Roman Pontiff acquires full and supreme power in the Church when, together with episcopal consecration, he has been lawfully elected and has accepted the election. Accordingly, if he already has the episcopal character, he receives this power from the moment he accepts election to the supreme pontificate. If he does not have the episcopal character, he is immediately to be ordained Bishop.

§2 Should it happen that the Roman Pontiff resigns from his office, it is required for validity that the resignation be freely made and properly manifested, but it is not necessary that it be accepted by anyone.

Can. 333 §1 By virtue of his office, the Roman Pontiff not only has power over the universal Church, but also has pre-eminent ordinary power over all particular Churches and their groupings. This reinforces and defends the proper, ordinary and immediate power which the Bishops have in the particular Churches entrusted to their care.

§2 The Roman Pontiff, in fulfilling his office as supreme Pastor of the Church, is always joined in full communion with the other Bishops, and indeed with the whole Church. He has the right, however, to determine, according to the needs of the Church, whether this office is to be exercised in a personal or in a collegial manner.

§3 There is neither appeal nor recourse against a judgement or a decree of the Roman Pontiff.

Can. 334 The Bishops are available to the Roman Pontiff in the exercise of his office, to cooperate with him in various ways, among which is the synod of Bishops. Cardinals also assist him, as do other persons and, according to the needs of the time, various institutes; all these persons and institutes fulfil their offices in his name and by his authority, for the good of all the Churches, in accordance with the norms determined by law.

Can. 335 When the Roman See is vacant, or completely impeded, no innovation is to be made in the governance of the universal Church. The special laws enacted for these circumstances are to be observed.

Article 2: The College of Bishops

Can. 336 The head of the College of Bishops is the Supreme Pontiff, and its members are the Bishops by virtue of their sacramental consecration and hierarchical communion with the head of the College and its members. This College of Bishops, in which the apostolic body abides in an unbroken manner, is, in union with its head and never without this head, also the subject of supreme and full power over the universal Church.

Can. 337 §1 The College of Bishops exercises its power over the universal Church in solemn form in an Ecumenical Council.

§2 It exercises this same power by the united action of the Bishops dispersed throughout the world, when this action is as such proclaimed or freely accepted by the Roman Pontiff, so that it becomes a truly collegial act.

§3 It belongs to the Roman Pontiff to select and promote, according to the needs of the Church, ways in which the College of Bishops can exercise its office in respect of the universal Church in a collegial manner.

Can. 338 §1 It is the prerogative of the Roman Pontiff alone to summon an Ecumenical Council, to preside over it personally or through others, to transfer, suspend or dissolve the Council, and to approve its decrees.

§2 It is also the prerogative of the Roman Pontiff to determine the matters to be dealt with in the Council, and to establish the order to be observed. The Fathers of the Council may add other matters to those proposed by the Roman Pontiff, but these must be approved by the Roman Pontiff.

Can. 339 §1 All Bishops, but only Bishops, who are members of the College of Bishops, have the right and the obligation to be present at an Ecumenical Council with a deliberative vote.

§2   Some others besides, who do not have the episcopal dignity, can be summoned to an Ecumenical Council by the supreme authority in the Church, to whom it belongs to determine what part they take in the Council.

Can. 340   If the Apostolic See should become vacant during the celebration of the Council, it is by virtue of the law itself suspended until the new Supreme Pontiff either orders it to continue or dissolves it.

Can. 341   §1   The decrees of an Ecumenical Council do not oblige unless they are approved by the Roman Pontiff as well as by the Fathers of the Council, confirmed by the Roman Pontiff and promulgated by his direction.

§2   If they are to have binding force, the same confirmation and promulgation is required for decrees which the College of Bishops issues by truly collegial actions in another manner introduced or freely accepted by the Roman Pontiff.

Chapter II

THE SYNOD OF BISHOPS

Can. 342   The synod of Bishops is a group of Bishops selected from different parts of the world, who meet together at specified times to promote the close relationship between the Roman Pontiff and the Bishops. These Bishops, by their counsel, assist the Roman Pontiff in the defence and development of faith and morals and in the preservation and strengthening of ecclesiastical discipline. They also consider questions concerning the mission of the Church in the world.

Can. 343   The function of the synod of Bishops is to discuss the matters proposed to it and set forth recommendations. It is not its function to settle matters or to draw up decrees, unless the Roman Pontiff has given it deliberative power in certain cases; in this event, it rests with the Roman Pontiff to ratify the decisions of the synod.

Can. 344   The synod of Bishops is directly under the authority of the Roman Pontiff, whose prerogative it is:

1° to convene the synod, as often as this seems opportune to him, and to designate the place where the meetings are to be held;
2° to ratify the election of those who, in accordance with the special law of the synod, are to be elected, and to designate and appoint other members;
3° at a suitable time before the celebration of the synod, to prescribe the outlines of the questions to be discussed, in accordance with the special law;
4° to determine the agenda;
5° to preside over the synod personally or through others;
6° to conclude, transfer, suspend or dissolve the synod.

Can. 345 The synod of Bishops can meet in general assembly, in which matters are dealt with which directly concern the good of the universal Church; such an assembly is either ordinary or extraordinary. It can also meet in special assembly, to deal with matters directly affecting a determined region or regions.

Can. 346 §1 The synod of Bishops meeting in ordinary general assembly is comprised, for the most part, of Bishops elected for each assembly by the Episcopal Conferences, in accordance with the norms of the special law of the synod. Other members are designated according to the same law; others are directly appointed by the Roman Pontiff. Added to these are some members of clerical religious institutes, elected in accordance with the same special law.

§2 The synod of Bishops meeting in extraordinary general assembly for the purpose of dealing with matters which require speedy resolution, is comprised, for the most part, of Bishops who, by reason of the office they hold, are designated by the special law of the synod; others are appointed directly by the Roman Pontiff. Added to these are some members of clerical religious institutes, elected in accordance with the same law.

§3 The synod of Bishops which meets in special assembly is comprised of members chosen principally from those regions for which the synod was convened, in accordance with the special law by which the synod is governed.

Can. 347 §1 When the meeting of the synod of Bishops is concluded by the Roman Pontiff, the function entrusted in it to the Bishops and other members ceases.

§2 If the Apostolic See becomes vacant after the synod has been convened or during its celebration, the meeting of the synod, and the function entrusted in it to the members, is by virtue of the law itself suspended, until the new Pontiff decrees either that the assembly is to be dissolved or that it is to continue.

Can. 348 §1 There is to be a permanent general secretariat of the synod, presided over by a Secretary general appointed by the Roman Pontiff. The Secretary is to have the assistance of a council of the secretariat, composed of Bishops, some elected by the synod of Bishops itself in accordance with the special law, others appointed by the Roman Pontiff. The function of all these persons ceases with the beginning of a new general assembly.

§2 For each assembly of the synod of Bishops there are one or more special secretaries, who are appointed by the Roman Pontiff. They remain in office only until the end of the synod assembly.

Chapter III
THE CARDINALS OF THE HOLY ROMAN CHURCH

Can. 349 The Cardinals of the Holy Roman Church constitute a special College, whose prerogative it is to elect the Roman Pontiff in accordance with the norms of a special law. The Cardinals are also available to the Roman Pontiff, either acting collegially, when they are summoned together to deal with questions of major importance, or acting individually, that is, in the offices which they hold in assisting the Roman Pontiff especially in the daily care of the universal Church.

Can. 350 §1 The College of Cardinals is divided into three orders: the episcopal order, to which belong those Cardinals to whom the Roman Pontiff assigns the title of a suburbicarian Church, and eastern-rite Patriarchs who are made members of the College of Cardinals; the presbyteral order, and the diaconal order.

§2 Cardinal priests and Cardinal deacons are each assigned a title or a deaconry in Rome by the Roman Pontiff.

§3 Eastern Patriarchs within the College of Cardinals have their patriarchal see as a title.

§4 The Cardinal Dean has the title of the diocese of Ostia, together with that of any other Church to which he already has a title.

§5 By a choice made in Consistory and approved by the Supreme Pontiff, Cardinal priests may transfer to another title; Cardinal deacons may transfer to another deaconry and, if they have been a full ten years in the diaconal order, to the presbyteral order: priority of order and of promotion is to be observed.

§6 A Cardinal who by choice transfers from the diaconal to the presbyteral order, takes precedence over all Cardinal priests who were promoted to the Cardinalate after him.

Can. 351 §1 Those to be promoted Cardinals are men freely selected by the Roman Pontiff, who are at least in the order of priesthood and are truly outstanding in doctrine, virtue, piety and prudence in practical matters; those who are not already Bishops must receive episcopal consecration.

§2 Cardinals are created by decree of the Roman Pontiff, which in fact is published in the presence of the College of Cardinals. From the moment of publication, they are bound by the obligations and they enjoy the rights defined in the law.

§3 A person promoted to the dignity of Cardinal, whose creation the Roman Pontiff announces, but whose name he reserves in petto, is not at that time bound by the obligations nor does he enjoy the rights of a Cardinal. When his name is published by the Roman Pontiff, however, he is bound by these obligations and enjoys these rights, but his right of precedence dates from the day of the reservation in petto.

Can. 352 §1 The Dean presides over the College of Cardinals. When he is unable to do so, the sub-Dean takes his place. The Dean, or the sub-Dean, has no power of governance over the other Cardinals, but is considered as first among equals.

§2 When the office of Dean is vacant, those Cardinals who have a suburbicarian title, and only those, under the presidency of the sub-Dean if he is present, or of the oldest member, elect one of their number to act as Dean of the College. They are to submit his name to the Roman Pontiff, to whom it belongs to approve the person elected.

§3 In the same way as set out in §2, the sub-Dean is elected, with the Dean presiding. It belongs to the Roman Pontiff to approve also the election of the sub-Dean.

§4 If the Dean and sub-Dean do not already have a domicile in Rome, they acquire it there.

Can. 353 §1 Cardinals assist the Supreme Pastor of the Church in collegial fashion particularly in Consistories, in which they are gathered by order of the Roman Pontiff and under his presidency. Consistories are either ordinary or extraordinary.

§2 In an ordinary Consistory all Cardinals, or at least those who are in Rome, are summoned for consultation on certain grave matters of more frequent occurrence, or for the performance of especially solemn acts.

§3 All Cardinals are summoned to an extraordinary Consistory, which takes place when the special needs of the Church and more serious matters suggest it.

§4 Only an ordinary Consistory in which certain solemnities are celebrated, can be public, that is when, in addition to the Cardinals, Prelates, representatives of civil states and other invited persons are admitted.

Can. 354 Cardinals who head the departments and other permanent sections of the Roman Curia and of Vatican City, who have completed their seventy-fifth year, are requested to offer their resignation from office to the Roman Pontiff, who will consider all the circumstances and make provision accordingly.

Can. 355 §1 It belongs to the Cardinal Dean to ordain the elected Roman Pontiff a Bishop, if he is not already ordained. If the Dean is prevented from doing so, the same right belongs to the sub-Dean or, if he is prevented, to the senior Cardinal of the episcopal order.

§2 The senior Cardinal Deacon announces the name of the newly elected Supreme Pontiff to the people. Acting in place of the Roman Pontiff, he also confers the pallium on metropolitan Bishops or gives the pallium to their proxies.

Can. 356 Cardinals have the obligation of cooperating closely with the Roman Pontiff. For this reason, Cardinals who have any office in the Curia and are not diocesan Bishops, are obliged to reside in Rome. Cardinals who are in charge of a diocese as diocesan Bishops, are to go to Rome whenever summoned by the Roman Pontiff.

Can. 357 §1 When a Cardinal has taken possession of a suburbicarian Church or of a titular Church in Rome, he is to further the good of the diocese or church by counsel and patronage. However, he has no power of governance over it, and he should not for any reason interfere in matters concerning the administration of its goods, or its discipline, or the service of the church.

§2   Cardinals living outside Rome and outside their own diocese, are exempt in what concerns their person from the power of governance of the Bishop of the diocese in which they are residing.

Can. 358   A Cardinal may be deputed by the Roman Pontiff to represent him in some solemn celebration or assembly of persons as a 'Legatus a latere', that is, as his alter ego; or he may, as a special emissary, be entrusted with a particular pastoral task. A Cardinal thus nominated is entitled to deal only with those affairs which have been entrusted to him by the Roman Pontiff himself.

Can. 359   When the Apostolic See is vacant, the College of Cardinals has only that power in the Church which is granted to it by special law.

Chapter IV

THE ROMAN CURIA

Can. 360   The Supreme Pontiff usually conducts the business of the universal Church through the Roman Curia, which acts in his name and with his authority for the good and for the service of the Churches. The Curia is composed of the Secretariat of State or Papal Secretariat, the Council for the public affairs of the Church, the Congregations, the Tribunals and other Institutes. The constitution and competence of all these is defined by special law.

Can. 361   In this Code the terms Apostolic See or Holy See mean not only the Roman Pontiff, but also, unless the contrary is clear from the nature of things or from the context, the Secretariat of State, the Council for the public affairs of the Church, and the other Institutes of the Roman Curia.

Chapter V

PAPAL LEGATES

Can. 362   The Roman Pontiff has an inherent and independent right to appoint Legates and to send them either to particular Churches in various countries or regions, or at the same time to States and to public Authorities. He also has the right to transfer or recall them, in accordance with the norms of international law concerning the mission and recall of representatives accredited to States.

Can. 363   §1   To Legates of the Roman Pontiff is entrusted the office of representing in a stable manner the person of the Roman Pontiff in the particular Churches, or also in the States and public Authorities, to whom they are sent.

§2   Those also represent the Apostolic See who are appointed to pontifical Missions as Delegates or Observers at international Councils or at Conferences and Meetings.

Can. 364   The principal task of a Papal Legate is continually to make more firm and effective the bonds of unity which exist between the Holy See and the particular Churches. Within the territory assigned to him, it is therefore the responsibility of a Legate:

1° to inform the Apostolic See about the conditions in which the particular Churches find themselves, as well as about all matters which affect the life of the Church and the good of souls;

2° to assist the Bishops by action and advice, while leaving intact the exercise of their lawful power;

3° to foster close relations with the Episcopal Conference, offering it every assistance;

4° in connection with the appointment of Bishops, to send or propose names of candidates to the Apostolic See, as well as to prepare the informative process about those who may be promoted, in accordance with the norms issued by the Apostolic See;

5° to take pains to promote whatever may contribute to peace, progress and the united efforts of peoples;

6° to work with the Bishops to foster appropriate exchanges between the Catholic Church and other Churches or ecclesial communities, and indeed with non-christian religions;

7° to work with the Bishops to safeguard, so far as the rulers of the State are concerned, those things which relate to the mission of the Church and of the Apostolic See;

8° to exercise the faculties and carry out the other instructions which are given to him by the Apostolic See.

Can. 365   §1 A papal Legate who at the same time acts as envoy to the State according to international law, has in addition the special role:

1° of promoting and fostering relationships between the Apostolic See and the Authorities of the State;

2° of dealing with questions concerning relations between Church and State; especially, of drawing up concordats and other similar agreements, and giving effect to them.

§2   As circumstances suggest, in the matters mentioned in §1, the papal Legate is not to omit to seek the opinion and counsel of the Bishops of the ecclesiastical jurisdiction and to keep them informed of the course of events.

Can. 366   Given the special nature of a Legate's role:

1° the papal Legation is exempt from the power of governance of the local Ordinary, except for the celebration of marriages;

2° the papal Legate has the right to perform liturgical celebrations, even in pontificalia, in all churches of the territory of his legation; as far as it is possible, he is to give prior notice to the local Ordinary.

Can. 367 The office of papal Legate does not cease when the Apostolic See is vacant, unless otherwise specified in the pontifical Letters; it does cease, however, on the expiry of the mandate, on receipt by him of notification of recall, and on acceptance of his resignation by the Roman Pontiff.

Section II
Particular Churches and their Groupings

TITLE I
PARTICULAR CHURCHES AND THE AUTHORITY · CONSTITUTED WITHIN THEM

Chapter I
PARTICULAR CHURCHES

Can. 368 Particular Churches, in which and from which the one and only catholic Church exists, are principally dioceses. Unless the contrary is clear, the following are equivalent to a diocese: a territorial prelature, a territorial abbacy, a vicariate apostolic, a prefecture apostolic and a permanently established apostolic administration.

Can. 369 A diocese is a portion of the people of God, which is entrusted to a Bishop to be nurtured by him, with the cooperation of the *presbyterium*, in such a way that, remaining close to its pastor and gathered by him through the Gospel and the Eucharist in the Holy Spirit, it constitutes a particular Church. In this Church, the one, holy, catholic and apostolic Church of Christ truly exists and functions.

Can. 370 A territorial prelature or abbacy is a certain portion of the people of God, territorially defined, the care of which is for special reasons entrusted to a Prelate or an Abbot, who governs it, in the manner of a diocesan Bishop, as its proper pastor.

Can. 371 §1 A vicariate apostolic or a prefecture apostolic is a certain portion of the people of God, which for special reasons is not yet constituted a diocese, and which is entrusted to the pastoral care of a Vicar apostolic or a Prefect apostolic, who governs it in the name of the Supreme Pontiff.

§2 An apostolic administration is a certain portion of the people of God which, for special and particularly serious reasons, is not yet established by the Supreme Pontiff as a diocese, and whose pastoral care is entrusted to an apostolic Administrator, who governs it in the name of the Supreme Pontiff.

Can. 372   §1 As a rule, that portion of the people of God which constitutes a diocese or other particular Church is to have a defined territory, so that it comprises all the faithful who live in that territory.

§2 If however, in the judgement of the supreme authority in the Church, after consultation with the Episcopal Conferences concerned, it is thought to be helpful, there may be established in a given territory particular Churches distinguished by the rite of the faithful or by some other similar quality.

Can. 373   It is within the competence of the supreme authority alone to establish particular Churches; once they are lawfully established, the law itself gives them juridical personality.

Can. 374   §1 Each diocese or other particular Church is to be divided into distinct parts or parishes.

§2 To foster pastoral care by means of common action, several neighbouring parishes can be joined together in special groups, such as vicariates forane.

Chapter II

BISHOPS

Article 1: Bishops in General

Can. 375   §1 By divine institution, Bishops succeed the Apostles through the Holy Spirit who is given to them. They are constituted Pastors in the Church, to be the teachers of doctrine, the priests of sacred worship and the ministers of governance.

§2 By their episcopal consecration, Bishops receive, together with the office of sanctifying, the offices also of teaching and of ruling, which however, by their nature, can be exercised only in hierarchical communion with the head of the College and its members.

Can. 376   Bishops to whom the care of a given diocese is entrusted are called diocesan Bishops; the others are called titular Bishops.

Can. 377   §1 The Supreme Pontiff freely appoints Bishops or confirms those lawfully elected.

§2 At least every three years, the Bishops of an ecclesiastical province or, if circumstances suggest it, of an Episcopal Conference, are to draw up, by common accord and in secret, a list of priests, even of members of institutes of consecrated life, who are suitable for the episcopate; they are to send this list to the Apostolic See. This is without prejudice to the right of every Bishop individually to make known to the Apostolic See the names of priests whom he thinks are worthy and suitable for the episcopal office.

§3 Unless it has been lawfully prescribed otherwise, for the appointment of a diocesan Bishop or a coadjutor Bishop, a ternus, as it is called, is to be proposed to the Apostolic See. In the preparation of this list, it is the responsibility of the papal Legate to seek individually the suggestions of the Metropolitan and of the Suffragans of the province to which the diocese in question belongs or with which it is joined in some grouping, as well as the suggestions of the president of the Episcopal Conference. The papal Legate is, moreover, to hear the views of some members of the college of consultors and of the cathedral chapter. If he judges it expedient, he is also to seek individually, and in secret, the opinions of other clerics, both secular and religious, and of lay persons of outstanding wisdom. He is then to send these suggestions, together with his own opinion, to the Apostolic See.

§4 Unless it has been lawfully provided otherwise, the diocesan Bishop who judges that his diocese requires an auxiliary Bishop, is to propose to the Apostolic See a list of the names of at least three priests suitable for this office.

§5 For the future, no rights or privileges of election, appointment, presentation or designation of Bishops are conceded to civil authorities.

Can. 378 §1 To be a suitable candidate for the episcopate, a person must:

  1° be outstanding in strong faith, good morals, piety, zeal for souls, wisdom, prudence and human virtues, and possess those other gifts which equip him to fulfil the office in question;

  2° be held in good esteem;

  3° be at least 35 years old;

  4° be a priest ordained for at least five years;

  5° hold a doctorate or at least a licentiate in sacred Scripture, theology or canon law, from an institute of higher studies approved by the Apostolic See, or at least be well versed in these disciplines.

§2 The definitive judgement on the suitability of the person to be promoted rests with the Apostolic See.

Can. 379 Unless prevented by a lawful reason, one who is promoted to the episcopate must receive episcopal consecration within three months of receiving the apostolic letters, and in fact before he takes possession of his office.

Can. 380 Before taking canonical possession of his office, he who has been promoted is to make the profession of faith and take the oath of fidelity to the Apostolic See, in acordance with the formula approved by the same Apostolic See.

Article 2: Diocesan Bishops

Can. 381 §1 In the diocese entrusted to his care, the diocesan Bishop has all the ordinary, proper and immediate power required for the exercise of his pastoral office, except in those matters which the law or a decree of the Supreme Pontiff reserves to the supreme or to some other ecclesiastical authority.

§2 Those who are at the head of the other communities of the faithful mentioned in can. 368, are equivalent in law to the diocesan Bishop, unless the contrary is clear from the nature of things or from a provision of the law.

Can. 382 §1 A person who is promoted to the episcopate cannot become involved in the exercise of the office entrusted to him before he has taken canonical possession of the diocese. However, he is able to exercise offices which he already held in the same diocese at the time of his promotion, without prejudice to can. 409 §2.

§2 Unless he is lawfully impeded, one who is not already consecrated a Bishop and is now promoted to the office of diocesan Bishop, must take canonical possession of his diocese within four months of receiving the apostolic letters. If he is already consecrated, he must take possession within two months of receiving the apostolic letters.

§3 A Bishop takes canonical possession of his diocese when, personally or by proxy, he shows the apostolic letters to the college of consultors, in the presence of the chancellor of the curia, who makes a record of the fact. This must take place within the diocese. In dioceses which are newly established he takes possession when he communicates the same letters to the clergy and the people in the cathedral church, with the senior of the priests present making a record of the fact.

§4 It is strongly recommended that the taking of canonical possession be performed with a liturgical act in the cathedral church, in the presence of the clergy and the people.

Can. 383 §1 In exercising his pastoral office, the diocesan Bishop is to be solicitous for all Christ's faithful entrusted to his care, whatever their age, condition or nationality, whether they live in the territory or are visiting there. He is to show an apostolic spirit also to those who, because of their condition of life, are not sufficiently able to benefit from ordinary pastoral care, and to those who have lapsed from religious practice.

§2 If he has faithful of a different rite in his diocese, he is to provide for their spiritual needs either by means of priests or parishes of the same rite, or by an episcopal Vicar.

§3 He is to act with humanity and charity to those who are not in full communion with the catholic Church; he should also foster ecumenism as it is understood by the Church.

§4 He is to consider the non-baptised as commended to him in the Lord, so that the charity of Christ, of which the Bishop must be a witness to all, may shine also on them.

Can. 384 He is to have a special concern for the priests, to whom he is to listen as his helpers and counsellors. He is to defend their rights and ensure that they fulfil the obligations proper to their state. He is to see that they have the means and the institutions needed for the development of their spiritual and intellectual life. He is to ensure that they are provided with adequate means of livelihood and social welfare, in accordance with the law.

Can. 385   He must in a very special way foster vocations to the various ministries and to consecrated life, having a special care for priestly and missionary vocations.

Can. 386   §1 The diocesan Bishop is bound to teach and illustrate to the faithful the truths of faith which are to be believed and applied to behaviour. He is himself to preach frequently. He is also to ensure that the provisions of the canons on the ministry of the word, especially on the homily and catechetical instruction, are faithfully observed, so that the whole of christian teaching is transmitted to all.

§2 By whatever means seem most appropriate, he is firmly to defend the integrity and unity of the faith to be believed. However, he is to acknowledge a just freedom in the further investigation of truths.

Can. 387   Mindful that he is bound to give an example of holiness, charity, humility and simplicity of life, the diocesan Bishop is to seek in every way to promote the holiness of Christ's faithful according to the special vocation of each. Since he is the principal dispenser of the mysteries of God, he is to strive constantly that Christ's faithful entrusted to his care may grow in grace through the celebration of the sacraments, and may know and live the paschal mystery.

Can. 388   §1 After he has taken possession of the diocese, the diocesan Bishop must apply the Mass for the people entrusted to him on each Sunday and on each holyday of obligation in his region.

§2 The Bishop must himself celebrate and apply the Mass for the people on the days mentioned in §1; if, however, he is lawfully impeded from so doing, he is to have someone else do so on those days, or do so himself on other days.

§3 A Bishop who, in addition to his own, is given another diocese, even as administrator, satisfies the obligation by applying one Mass for all the people entrusted to him.

§4 A Bishop who has not satisfied the obligation mentioned in §§1–3, is to apply as soon as possible as many Masses for the people as he has omitted.

Can. 389   He is frequently to preside at the Eucharistic celebration in the cathedral church or in some other church of his diocese, especially on holydays of obligation and on other solemnities.

Can. 390   The diocesan Bishop may use pontificalia throughout his diocese. He may not do so outside his diocese without the consent of the local Ordinary, either expressly given or at least reasonably presumed.

Can. 391   §1 The diocesan Bishop governs the particular Church entrusted to him with legislative, executive and judicial power, in accordance with the law.

§2 The Bishop exercises legislative power himself. He exercises executive power either personally or through Vicars general or episcopal Vicars, in accordance with the law. He exercises judicial power either personally or through a judicial Vicar and judges, in accordance with the law.

Can. 392 §1 Since the Bishop must defend the unity of the universal Church, he is bound to foster the discipline which is common to the whole Church, and so press for the observance of all ecclesiastical laws.

§2 He is to ensure that abuses do not creep into ecclesiastical discipline, especially concerning the ministry of the word, the celebration of the sacraments and sacramentals, the worship of God and the cult of the saints, and the administration of goods.

Can. 393 In all juridical transactions of the diocese, the diocesan Bishop acts in the person of the diocese.

Can. 394 §1 The Bishop is to foster various forms of the apostolate in his diocese and is to ensure that throughout the entire diocese, or in its particular districts, all works of the apostolate are coordinated under his direction, with due regard for the character of each apostolate.

§2 He is to insist on the faithful's obligation to exercise the apostolate according to the condition and talents of each. He is to urge them to take part in or assist various works of the apostolate, according to the needs of place and time.

Can. 395 §1 The diocesan Bishop is bound by the law of personal residence in his diocese, even if he has a coadjutor or auxiliary Bishop.

§2 Apart from the visit 'ad limina', attendance at councils or at the synod of Bishops or at the Episcopal Conference, at which he must be present, or by reason of another office lawfully entrusted to him, he may be absent from the diocese, for a just reason, for not longer than one month, continuously or otherwise, provided he ensures that the diocese is not harmed by this absence.

§3 He is not to be absent from his diocese on Christmas Day, during Holy Week, or on Easter Sunday, Pentecost and Corpus Christi, except for a grave and urgent reason.

§4 If the Bishop is unlawfully absent from the diocese for more than six months, the Metropolitan is to notify the Holy See. If it is the Metropolitan who is absent, the senior suffragan is to do the same.

Can. 396 §1 The Bishop is bound to visit his diocese in whole or in part each year, so that at least every five years he will have visited the whole diocese, either personally or, if he is lawfully impeded, through the coadjutor or auxiliary Bishop, the Vicar general, an episcopal Vicar or some other priest.

§2 The Bishop has a right to select any clerics he wishes as his companions and helpers in a visitation, any contrary privilege or custom being reprobated.

Can. 397 §1 Persons, catholic institutes, pious objects and places within the boundaries of the diocese, are subject to ordinary episcopal visitation.

§2 The Bishop may visit the members of religious institutes of pontifical right and their houses only in the cases stated in the law.

Can. 398 The Bishop is to endeavour to make his pastoral visitation with due diligence. He is to ensure that he is not a burden to anyone on the ground of undue expense.

Can. 399 §1 Every five years the diocesan Bishop is bound to submit to the Supreme Pontiff a report on the state of the diocese entrusted to him, in the form and at the time determined by the Apostolic See.

§2 If the year assigned for submitting this report coincides in whole or in part with the first two years of his governance of the diocese, for that occasion the Bishop need not draw up and submit the report.

Can. 400 §1 Unless the Apostolic See has decided otherwise, in the year in which he is bound to submit the report to the Supreme Pontiff, the diocesan Bishop is to go to Rome to venerate the tombs of the Blessed Apostles Peter and Paul, and to present himself to the Roman Pontiff.

§2 The Bishop is to satisfy this obligation personally, unless he is lawfully impeded; in which case he is to satisfy the obligation through the coadjutor, if he has one, or the auxiliary, or a suitable priest of his *presbyterium* who resides in his diocese.

§3 A Vicar apostolic can satisfy this obligation through a proxy, even through one residing in Rome. A Prefect apostolic is not bound by this obligation.

Can. 401 §1 A diocesan Bishop who has completed his seventy-fifth year of age is requested to offer his resignation from office to the Supreme Pontiff, who, taking all the circumstances into account, will make provision accordingly.

§2 A diocesan Bishop who, because of illness or some other grave reason, has become unsuited for the fulfilment of his office, is earnestly requested to offer his resignation from office.

Can. 402 §1 A Bishop whose resignation from office has been accepted, acquires the title 'emeritus' of his diocese. If he so wishes, he may have a residence in the diocese unless, because of special circumstances in certain cases, the Apostolic See provides otherwise.

§2 The Episcopal Conference must ensure that suitable and worthy provision is made for the upkeep of a Bishop who has resigned, bearing in mind the primary obligation which falls on the diocese which he served.

Article 3: Coadjutor and Auxiliary Bishops

Can. 403 §1 When the pastoral needs of the diocese require it, one or more auxiliary Bishops are to be appointed at the request of the diocesan Bishop. An auxiliary Bishop does not have the right of succession.

§2 In more serious circumstances, even of a personal nature, the diocesan Bishop may be given an auxiliary Bishop with special faculties.

§3 If the Holy See considers it more opportune, it can ex officio appoint a coadjutor Bishop, who also has special faculties. A coadjutor Bishop has the right of succession.

Can. 404 §1 The coadjutor Bishop takes possession of his office when, either personally or by proxy, he shows the apostolic letters of appointment to the diocesan Bishop and the college of consultors, in the presence of the chancellor of the curia, who makes a record of the fact.

§2 An auxiliary Bishop takes possession of his office when he shows his apostolic letters of appointment to the diocesan Bishop, in the presence of the chancellor of the curia, who makes a record of the fact.

§3 If the diocesan Bishop is wholly impeded, it is sufficient that either the coadjutor Bishop or the auxiliary Bishop show their apostolic letters of appointment to the college of consultors, in the presence of the chancellor of the curia.

Can. 405 §1 The coadjutor Bishop and the auxiliary Bishop have the obligations and the rights which are determined by the provisions of the following canons and defined in their letters of appointment.

§2 The coadjutor Bishop, or the auxiliary Bishop mentioned in can. 403 §2, assists the diocesan Bishop in the entire governance of the diocese, and takes his place when he is absent or impeded.

Can. 406 §1 The coadjutor Bishop, and likewise the auxiliary Bishop mentioned in can. 403 §2, is to be appointed a Vicar general by the diocesan Bishop. The diocesan Bishop is to entrust to him, in preference to others, those things which by law require a special mandate.

§2 Unless the apostolic letters provide otherwise, and without prejudice to the provision of §1, the diocesan Bishop is to appoint his auxiliary or auxiliaries as Vicar general or at least episcopal Vicar, in dependence solely on his authority, or on that of the coadjutor Bishop or of the auxiliary Bishop mentioned in can. 403 §2.

Can. 407 §1 For the greatest present and future good of the diocese, the diocesan Bishop, the coadjutor and the auxiliary Bishop mentioned in can. 403 §2, are to consult with each other on matters of greater importance.

§2 In assessing matters of greater importance, particularly those of a pastoral nature, the diocesan Bishop is to consult the auxiliary Bishop before all others.

§3 The coadjutor Bishop and the auxiliary Bishop, since they are called to share in the cares of the diocesan Bishop, should so exercise their office that they act and think in accord with him.

Can. 408   §1 As often as they are requested to do so by the diocesan Bishop, a coadjutor Bishop and an auxiliary Bishop who are not lawfully impeded, are obliged to perform those pontifical and other functions to which the diocesan Bishop is bound.

§2 Those episcopal rights and functions which the coadjutor can exercise are not habitually to be entrusted to another by the diocesan Bishop.

Can. 409   §1 When the episcopal see falls vacant, the coadjutor immediately becomes the Bishop of the diocese for which he was appointed, provided he has lawfully taken possession.

§2 Unless the competent authority has provided otherwise, when the episcopal see is vacant and until the new Bishop takes possession of the see, the auxiliary Bishop retains all and only those powers and faculties which he had as Vicar general or as episcopal Vicar when the see was occupied. If he is not appointed to the office of diocesan Administrator, he is to exercise this same power of his, conferred by the law, under the authority of the diocesan Administrator, who governs the diocese.

Can. 410   The coadjutor Bishop and the auxiliary Bishop are bound, like the diocesan Bishop, to reside in the diocese. Other than for the fulfilment of some duty outside the diocese, or for holidays, which are not to be longer than one month, they may not be away from the diocese except for a brief period.

Can. 411   The provisions of cann. 401 and 402 §2, concerning resignation from office, apply also to a coadjutor and an auxiliary Bishop.

Chapter III
THE IMPEDED OR VACANT SEE

Article 1: *The Impeded See*

Can. 412   The episcopal see is understood to be impeded if the diocesan Bishop is completely prevented from exercising the pastoral office in the diocese by reason of imprisonment, banishment, exile or incapacity, so that he is unable to communicate, even by letter, with the people of his diocese.

Can. 413   §1 Unless the Holy See has provided otherwise, when a see is impeded, the governance of the diocese devolves on the coadjutor Bishop, if there is one. If there is no coadjutor, or if he is impeded, it devolves upon the auxiliary Bishop, or the Vicar general, or the episcopal Vicar, or another priest: the order of persons to be followed is to be that determined in the list which the diocesan Bishop is to draw up as soon as possible after taking possession of his diocese. This list, which is to be communicated to the Metropolitan, is to be revised at least every three years, and kept under secrecy by the chancellor.

§2 If there is no coadjutor Bishop or if he is impeded, and the list mentioned in §1 is not at hand, it is the responsibility of the college of consultors to elect a priest who will govern the diocese.

§3 The person who undertakes the governance of the diocese according to the norms of §§1 or 2, is to notify the Holy See as soon as possible that the see is impeded and that he has undertaken the office.

Can. 414   Whoever is called, in accordance with can. 413, to exercise the pastoral care of the diocese for the time being, that is, only for the period during which the see is impeded, is in his pastoral care of the diocese bound by the obligations, and has the power, which by law belong to the diocesan Administrator.

Can. 415   If the diocesan Bishop is prohibited from exercising his office by reason of an ecclesiastical penalty, the Metropolitan is to refer the matter at once to the Holy See, so that it may make provision; if there is no Metropolitan, or if he is the one affected by the penalty, it is the suffragan senior by promotion who is to refer the matter.

Article 2: The Vacant See

Can. 416   The episcopal see becomes vacant by the death of the diocesan Bishop, by his resignation accepted by the Holy See, by transfer, or by deprivation notified to the Bishop.

Can. 417   Until they have received certain notification of the Bishop's death, all actions taken by the Vicar general or the episcopal Vicar have effect. Until they have received certain notification of the aforementioned papal acts, the same is true of actions taken by the diocesan Bishop, the Vicar general or the episcopal Vicar.

Can. 418   §1 Within two months of receiving certain notification of transfer, the Bishop must proceed to the diocese to which he has been transferred and take canonical possession of it. On the day on which he takes possession of the new diocese, the diocese from which he has been transferred becomes vacant.

§2 In the period between receiving certain notification of the transfer and taking possession of the new diocese, in the diocese from which he is being transferred the Bishop:

1° has the power, and is bound by the obligations, of a diocesan Administrator; all powers of the Vicar general and of the episcopal Vicar cease, without prejudice to can. 409 §2;
2° receives the full remuneration proper to the office.

Can. 419   While the see is vacant and until the appointment of a diocesan Administrator, the governance of the diocese devolves upon the auxiliary Bishop. If there are a number of auxiliary Bishops, it devolves upon the senior by promotion. If there is no auxiliary Bishop, it devolves upon the college of consultors, unless the Holy See has provided otherwise. The one who thus assumes the governance of the diocese must without delay convene the college which is competent to appoint a diocesan Administrator.

Can. 420 Unless the Holy See has prescribed otherwise, when the see is vacant in a vicariate or a prefecture apostolic, the governance is assumed by the Pro-Vicar or Pro-Prefect who was designated for this sole purpose by the Vicar or Prefect immediately upon taking possession.

Can. 421 §1 Within eight days of receiving notification of the vacancy of an episcopal see, a diocesan Administrator is to be elected by the college of consultors, to govern the diocese for the time being, without prejudice to the provisions of can. 502 §3.

§2 If, for any reason, the diocesan Administrator is not lawfully elected within the prescribed time, his appointment devolves upon the Metropolitan. If the metropolitan see is itself vacant, or if both the metropolitan see and a suffragan see are vacant, the appointment devolves on the suffragan who is senior by promotion.

Can. 422 The auxiliary Bishop or, if there is none, the college of consultors, must as soon as possible notify the Apostolic See of the death of the Bishop. The person elected as diocesan Administrator must as soon as possible notify the Apostolic See of his election.

Can. 423 §1 Only one diocesan Administrator is to be appointed, contrary customs being reprobated; otherwise the election is invalid.

§2 The diocesan Administrator is not to be at the same time the financial administrator. Accordingly, if the financial administrator of the diocese is elected Administrator, the finance committee is to elect another temporary financial administrator.

Can. 424 The diocesan Administrator is to be elected according to the norms of cann. 165–178.

Can. 425 §1 Only a priest who has completed his thirty-fifth year of age, and has not already been elected, appointed or presented for the same see, can validly be deputed to the office of diocesan Administrator.

§2 As diocesan Administrator a priest is to be elected who is outstanding for doctrine and prudence.

§3 If the conditions prescribed in §1 have not been oberved, the Metropolitan or, if the metropolitan see itself is vacant, the suffragan senior by promotion, having verified the truth of the matter, is to appoint an Administrator for that occasion. The acts of a person elected contrary to the provisions of §1 are by virtue of the law itself invalid.

Can. 426 Whoever governs the diocese before the appointment of the diocesan Administrator, has the power which the law gives to a Vicar general.

Can. 427 §1 The diocesan Administrator is bound by the obligations and enjoys the power of a diocesan Bishop, excluding those matters which are excepted by the nature of things or by the law itself.

§2 The diocesan Administrator obtains his power on his acceptance of the election, without the need of confirmation from anyone, but without prejudice to the provision of can. 833, n. 4.

Can. 428 §1 While the see is vacant, no innovation is to be made.

§2 Those who have the interim governance of the diocese are forbidden to do anything which could in any way prejudice the rights of the diocese or of the Bishop. Both they, and in like manner any other persons, are specifically forbidden to remove, destroy or in any way alter documents of the diocesan curia, either personally or through another.

Can. 429 The diocesan Administrator is bound by the obligations of residing in the diocese, and of applying the Mass for the people in accordance with can. 388.

Can. 430 §1 The office of the diocesan Administrator ceases when the new Bishop takes possession of the diocese.

§2 Removal of the diocesan Administrator is reserved to the Holy See. Should he perchance resign, the resignation is to be submitted in authentic form to the college which is competent to elect, but it does not require acceptance by the college. If the diocesan Administrator is removed, resigns or dies, another diocesan Administrator is to be elected in accordance with can. 421.

TITLE II: GROUPINGS OF PARTICULAR CHURCHES

Chapter I

ECCLESIASTICAL PROVINCES AND ECCLESIASTICAL REGIONS

Can. 431 Neighbouring particular Churches are to be grouped into ecclesiastical provinces, with a certain defined territory. The purpose of this grouping is to promote, according to the circumstances of persons and place, a common pastoral action of various neighbouring dioceses, and the more closely to foster relations between diocesan Bishops.

§2 From now onwards, as a rule, there are to be no exempt dioceses. Accordingly, individual dioceses and other particular Churches which exist within the territory of an ecclesiastical province, must be included in that ecclesiastical province.

§3 It is the exclusive prerogative of the supreme authority in the Church, after consulting the Bishops concerned, to establish, suppress or alter ecclesiastical provinces.

Can. 432   §1 The provincial council and the Metropolitan have authority over the ecclesiastical province, in accordance with the law.

§2 By virtue of the law, an ecclesiastical province has juridical personality.

Can. 433   §1 If it seems advantageous, especially in countries where there are very many particular Churches, the Holy See can, on the proposal of the Episcopal Conference, join together neighbouring provinces into ecclesiastical regions.

§2 An ecclesiastical region can be constituted a juridical person.

Can. 434   It is for a meeting of the Bishops of an ecclesiastical region to foster cooperation and common pastoral action in the region. However, the powers given to Episcopal Conferences in the canons of this Code do not belong to such a meeting, unless some of these powers have been specially granted to it by the Holy See.

Chapter II

METROPOLITANS

Can. 435   An ecclesiastical province is presided over by a Metropolitan, who is Archbishop in his own diocese. The office of Metropolitan is linked to an episcopal see, determined or approved by the Roman Pontiff.

Can. 436   §1 Within the suffragan dioceses, the Metropolitan is competent:

1° to see that faith and ecclesiastical discipline are carefully observed and to notify the Roman Pontiff if there be any abuses;

2° for a reason approved beforehand by the Apostolic See, to conduct a canonical visitation if the suffragan Bishop has neglected it;

3° to appoint a diocesan Administrator in accordance with cann. 421 §2 and 425 §3.

§2 Where circumstances require it, the Apostolic See can give the Metropolitan special functions and power, to be determined in particular law.

§3 The Metropolitan has no other power of governance over suffragan dioceses. He can, however, celebrate sacred functions in all churches as if he were a Bishop in his own diocese, provided, if it is the cathedral church, the diocesan Bishop has been previously notified.

Can. 437   §1 The Metropolitan is obliged to request the pallium from the Roman Pontiff, either personally or by proxy, within three months of his episcopal consecration or, if he has already been consecrated, of his canonical appointment. The pallium signifies the power which, in communion with the Roman Church, the Metropolitan possesses by law in his own province.

§2 The Metropolitan can wear the pallium, in accordance with the liturgical laws, in any church of the ecclesiastical province over which he presides, but not outside the province, not even with the assent of the diocesan Bishop.

§3 If the Metropolitan is transferred to another metropolitan see, he requires a new pallium.

Can. 438   The title of Patriarch or Primate gives a prerogative of honour, but in the latin Church does not carry with it any power of governance, except in certain matters where an apostolic privilege or approved custom establishes otherwise.

Chapter III
PARTICULAR COUNCILS

Can. 439   §1 A plenary council for all the particular Churches of the same Episcopal Conference is to be celebrated as often as the Episcopal Conference, with the approval of the Apostolic See, considers it necessary or advantageous.

§2 The norm laid down in §1 is valid also for a provincial council to be celebrated in an ecclesiastical province whose boundaries coincide with the boundaries of the country.

Can. 440   §1 A provincial council, for the various particular Churches of the same ecclesiastical province, is celebrated as often as, in the judgement of the majority of the diocesan Bishops of the province, it is considered opportune, without prejudice to can. 439 §2.

§2 A provincial council may not be called while the metropolitan see is vacant.

Can. 441   It is the responsibility of the Episcopal Conference:
1° to convene a plenary council;
2° to choose a place within the territory of the Episcopal Conference for the celebration of the council;
3° to elect from among the diocesan Bishops a president of the plenary council, who is to be approved by the Apostolic See;
4° to determine the order of business and the matters to be considered, to announce when the plenary council is to begin and how long it is to last, and to transfer, prorogue and dissolve it.

Can. 442   §1 It is the responsibility of the Metropolitan, with the consent of the majority of the suffragan Bishops:
1° to convene a provincial council;
2° to choose a place within the territory of the province for the celebration of the provincial council;
3° to determine the order of business and the matters to be considered, to announce when the provincial council is to begin and how long it is to last, and to transfer, prorogue and dissolve it.

§2 It is the prerogative of the Metropolitan to preside over the provincial council. If he is lawfully impeded from doing so, it is the prerogative of a suffragan Bishop elected by the other suffragan Bishops.

Can. 443 §1 The following have the right to be summoned to particular councils and have the right to a deliberative vote:

1° diocesan Bishops;

2° coadjutor and auxiliary Bishops;

3° other titular Bishops who have been given a special function in the territory, either by the Apostolic See or by the Episcopal Conference.

§2 Other titular Bishops who are living in the territory, even if they are retired, may be invited to particular councils; they have the right to a deliberative vote.

§3 The following are to be invited to particular councils, but with only a consultative vote:

1° Vicars general and episcopal Vicars of all the particular Churches in the territory;

2° the major Superiors of religious institutes and societies of apostolic life. Their number, for both men and women, is to be determined by the Episcopal Conference or the Bishops of the province, and they are to be elected respectively by all the major Superiors of institutes and societies which have a centre in the territory;

3° the rectors of ecclesiastical and catholic universities which have a centre in the territory, together with the deans of their faculties of theology and canon law;

4° some rectors of major seminaries, their number being determined as in no. 2; they are to be elected by the rectors of seminaries situated in the territory.

§4 Priests and others of Christ's faithful may also be invited to particular councils, but have only a consultative vote; their number is not to exceed half of those mentioned in §§1–3.

§5 The cathedral chapter, the council of priests and the pastoral council of each particular Church are to be invited to provincial councils, but in such a way that each is to send two members, designated in a collegial manner. They have only a consultative vote.

§6 Others may be invited to particular councils as guests, if this is judged expedient by the Episcopal Conference for a plenary council, or by the Metropolitan with the suffragan Bishops for a provincial council.

Can. 444 §1 All who are summoned to particular councils must attend, unless they are prevented by a just impediment, of whose existence they are obliged to notify the president of the council.

§2 Those who are summoned to a particular council in which they have a deliberative vote, but who are prevented from attending because of a just impediment, can send a proxy. The proxy, however, has only a consultative vote.

Can. 445   A particular council is to ensure that the pastoral needs of the people of God in its territory are provided for. While it must always respect the universal law of the Church, it has power of governance, especially legislative power. It can, therefore, determine whatever seems opportune for an increase of faith, for the ordering of common pastoral action, for the direction of morality and for the preservation, introduction and defence of a common ecclesiastical discipline.

Can. 446   When a particular council has concluded, the president is to ensure that all the acts of the council are sent to the Apostolic See. The decrees drawn up by the council are not to be promulgated until they have been reviewed by the Apostolic See. The council has the responsibility of defining the manner in which the decrees will be promulgated and the time when the promulgated decrees will begin to oblige.

Chapter IV

EPISCOPAL CONFERENCES

Can. 447   The Episcopal Conference, a permanent institution, is the assembly of the Bishops of a country or of a certain territory, exercising together certain pastoral offices for Christ's faithful of that territory. By forms and means of apostolate suited to the circumstances of time and place, it is to promote, in accordance with the law, that greater good which the Church offers to all people.

Can. 448   §1 As a general rule, the Episcopal Conference includes those who preside over all the particular Churches of the same country, in accordance with can. 450.

§2 An Episcopal Conference can, however, be established for a territory of greater or less extent if the Apostolic See, after consultation with the diocesan Bishops concerned, judges that circumstances suggest this. Such a Conference would include only the Bishops of some particular Churches in a certain territory, or those who preside over particular Churches in different countries. It is for the Apostolic See to lay down special norms for each case.

Can. 449   §1 It is for the supreme authority of the Church alone, after consultation with the Bishops concerned, to establish, suppress, or alter Episcopal Conferences.

§2 An Episcopal Conference lawfully established has juridical personality by virtue of the law itself.

Can. 450   §1 By virtue of the law, the following persons in the territory belong to the Episcopal Conference: all diocesan Bishops and those equivalent to them in law; all coadjutor Bishops, auxiliary Bishops and other titular Bishops who exercise in the territory a special office assigned to them by the Apostolic See or by the Episcopal Conference. Ordinaries   of   another   rite   may   be   invited,   but   have only a consultative vote, unless the statutes of the Episcopal Conference decree otherwise.

§2 The other titular Bishops and the Legate of the Roman Pontiff are not by law members of the Episcopal Conference.

Can. 451 Each Episcopal Conference is to draw up its own statutes, to be reviewed by the Apostolic See. In these, among other things, arrangements for the plenary meetings of the Conference are to be set out, and provision is to be made for a permanent committee of Bishops, and a general secretary of the Conference, and for other offices and commissions by which, in the judgement of the Conference, its purpose can more effectively be achieved.

Can. 452 §1 Each Episcopal Conference is to elect its president and determine who, in the lawful absence of the president, will exercise the function of vice-president. It is also to designate a general secretary, in accordance with the statutes.

§2 The president of the Conference or, when he is lawfully impeded, the vice-president, presides not only over the general meetings of the Conference but also over the permanent committee.

Can. 453 Plenary meetings of the Episcopal Conference are to be held at least once a year, and moreover as often as special circumstances require, in accordance with the provisions of the statutes.

Can. 454 §1 By virtue of the law diocesan Bishops, those equivalent to them in law and coadjutor Bishops have a deliberative vote in plenary meetings of the Episcopal Conference.

§2 Auxiliary Bishops and other titular Bishops who belong to the Episcopal Conference have a deliberative or consultative vote according to the provisions of the statutes of the Conference. Only those mentioned in §1, however, have a deliberative vote in the making or changing of the statutes.

Can. 455 §1 The Episcopal Conference can make general decrees only in cases where the universal law has so prescribed, or by special mandate of the Apostolic See, either on its own initiative or at the request of the Conference itself.

§2 For the decrees mentioned in §1 validly to be enacted at a plenary meeting, they must receive two thirds of the votes of those who belong to the Conference with a deliberative vote. These decrees do not oblige until they have been reviewed by the Apostolic See and lawfully promulgated.

§3 The manner of promulgation and the time they come into force are determined by the Episcopal Conference.

§4 In cases where neither the universal law nor a special mandate of the Apostolic See gives the Episcopal Conference the power mentioned in §1, the competence of each diocesan Bishop remains intact. In such cases, neither the Conference nor its president can act in the name of all the Bishops unless each and every Bishop has given his consent.

Can. 456   When a plenary meeting of the Episcopal Conference has been concluded, its minutes are to be sent by the president to the Apostolic See for information, and its decrees, if any, for review.

Can. 457   The permanent committee of Bishops is to prepare the agenda for the plenary meetings of the Conference, and it is to ensure that the decisions taken at those meetings are duly executed. It is also to conduct whatever other business is entrusted to it in accordance with the statutes.

Can. 458   The general secretary is to:
   1° prepare an account of the acts and decrees of the plenary meetings of the Conference, as well as the acts of the permanent committee of Bishops and to communicate these to all members of the Conference; also to record whatever other acts are entrusted to him by the president or the permanent committee;
   2° to communicate to neighbouring Episcopal Conferences such acts and documents as the Conference at a plenary meeting or the permanent committee of Bishops decides to send to them.

Can. 459   §1 Relations are to be fostered between Episcopal Conferences, especially neighbouring ones, in order to promote and defend whatever is for the greater good.
   §2 The Apostolic See must be consulted whenever actions or affairs undertaken by Conferences have an international character.

TITLE III
THE INTERNAL ORDERING OF PARTICULAR CHURCHES

Chapter I
THE DIOCESAN SYNOD

Can. 460   The diocesan synod is an assembly of selected priests and other members of Christ's faithful of a particular Church which, for the good of the whole diocesan community, assists the diocesan Bishop, in accordance with the following canons.

Can. 461   §1 The diocesan synod is to be held in each particular Church when the diocesan Bishop, after consulting the council of priests, judges that the circumstances suggest it.
   §2 If a Bishop is responsible for a number of dioceses, or has charge of one as his own and of another as Administrator, he may convene one diocesan synod for all the dioceses entrusted to him.

Can. 462   §1   Only the diocesan Bishop can convene a diocesan synod. A person who has interim charge of a diocese cannot do so.

§2   The diocesan Bishop presides over the diocesan synod. He may, however, delegate a Vicar general or an episcopal Vicar to fulfil this office at individual sessions of the synod.

Can. 463   §1   The following are to be summoned to the diocesan synod as members and they are obliged to participate in it:

1° the coadjutor Bishop and the auxiliary Bishops;

2° the Vicars general and episcopal Vicars, and the judicial Vicar;

3° the canons of the cathedral church;

4° the members of the council of priests;

5° lay members of Christ's faithful, not excluding members of institutes of consecrated life, to be elected by the pastoral council in the manner and the number to be determined by the diocesan Bishop or, where this council does not exist, on a basis determined by the diocesan Bishop;

6° the rector of the major seminary of the diocese;

7° the vicars forane;

8° at least one priest from each vicariate forane to be elected by all those who have the care of souls there; another priest is also to be elected, to take the place of the first if he is prevented from attending;

9° some Superiors of religious institutes and of societies of apostolic life which have a house in the diocese: these are to be elected in the number and the manner determined by the diocesan Bishop.

§2   The diocesan Bishop may also invite others to be members of the diocesan synod, whether clerics or members of institutes of consecrated life or lay members of the faithful†.

§3   If the diocesan Bishop considers it opportune, he may invite to the diocesan Synod as observers some ministers or members of Churches or ecclesial communities which are not in full communion with the catholic Church.

Can. 464   A member of the synod who is lawfully impeded from attending, cannot send a proxy to attend in his or her place, but is to notify the diocesan Bishop of the reason for not attending.

Can. 465   All questions proposed are to be subject to the free discussion of the members in the sessions of the synod.

Can. 466   The diocesan Bishop is the sole legislator in the diocesan synod. Other members of the synod have only a consultative vote. The diocesan Bishop alone signs the synodal declarations and decrees, and only by his authority may these be published.

Can. 467   The diocesan Bishop is to communicate the text of the declarations and decrees of the synod to the Metropolitan and to the Episcopal Conference.

Can. 468   §1 If he judges it prudent, the diocesan Bishop can suspend or dissolve the diocesan synod.

§2 Should the episcopal see become vacant or impeded, the diocesan synod is by virtue of the law itself suspended, until such time as the diocesan Bishop who succeeds to the see decrees that it be continued or declares it terminated.

Chapter II

THE DIOCESAN CURIA

Can. 469   The diocesan curia is composed of those institutes and persons who assist the Bishop in governing the entire diocese, especially in directing pastoral action, in providing for the administration of the diocese, and in exercising judicial power.

Can. 470   The appointment of those who fulfil an office in the diocesan curia belongs to the diocesan Bishop.

Can. 471   All who are admitted to an office in the curia must:

1° promise to fulfil their office faithfully, as determined by law or by the Bishop;

2° observe secrecy within the limits and according to the manner determined by law or by the Bishop.

Can. 472   The provisions of Book VII on 'Processes' are to be observed concerning cases and persons involved in the exercise of judicial power in the curia. The following canons are to be observed in what concerns the administration of the diocese.

Can. 473   §1 The diocesan Bishop must ensure that everything concerning the administration of the whole diocese is properly coordinated and is directed in the way that will best achieve the good of that portion of the people of God entrusted to his care.

§2 The diocesan Bishop has the responsibility of coordinating the pastoral action of the Vicars general and episcopal Vicars. Where it is useful, he may appoint a Moderator of the curia, who must be a priest. Under the Bishop's authority, the Moderator is to coordinate activities concerning administrative matters and to ensure that the others who belong to the curia properly fulfil the offices entrusted to them.

§3 Unless in the Bishop's judgement local conditions suggest otherwise, the Vicar general is to be appointed Moderator of the curia or, if there are several Vicars general, one of them.

§4 Where the Bishop judges it useful for the better promotion of pastoral action, he can establish an episcopal council, comprising the Vicars general and episcopal Vicars.

Can. 474   Acts of the curia which of their nature are designed to have a juridical effect must, as a requirement for validity, be signed by the

Ordinary from whom they emanate. They must also be signed by the chancellor of the curia or a notary. The chancellor is bound to notify the Moderator of the curia about these acts.

Article 1: Vicars General and Episcopal Vicars

Can. 475   §1 In each diocese the diocesan Bishop is to appoint a Vicar general to assist him in the governance of the whole diocese. The Vicar general has ordinary power, in accordance with the following canons.

§2 As a general rule, one Vicar general is to be appointed, unless the size of the diocese, the number of inhabitants, or other pastoral reasons suggest otherwise.

Can. 476   As often as the good governance of the diocese requires it, the diocesan Bishop can also appoint one or more episcopal Vicars. These have the same ordinary power as the universal law gives to a Vicar general, in accordance with the following canons. The competence of an episcopal Vicar, however, is limited to a determined part of the diocese, or to a specific type of activity, or to the faithful of a particular rite, or to certain groups of people.

Can. 477   §1 The Vicar general and the episcopal Vicar are freely appointed by the diocesan Bishop, and can be freely removed by him, without prejudice to can. 406. An episcopal Vicar who is not an auxiliary Bishop, is to be appointed for a period of time, which is to be specified in the act of appointment.

§2 If the Vicar general is absent or lawfully impeded, the diocesan Bishop can appoint another to take his place. The same norm applies in the case of an episcopal Vicar.

Can. 478   §1 The Vicar general and the episcopal Vicar are to be priests of not less than thirty years of age, with a doctorate or licentiate in canon law or theology, or at least well versed in these disciplines. They are to be known for their sound doctrine, integrity, prudence and practical experience.

§2 The office of Vicar general or episcopal Vicar may not be united with the office of canon penitentiary, nor may the office be given to blood relations of the Bishop up to the fourth degree.

Can. 479   §1 In virtue of his office, the Vicar general has the same executive power throughout the whole diocese as that which belongs by law to the diocesan Bishop: that is, he can perform all administrative acts, with the exception however of those which the Bishop has reserved to himself, or which by law require a special mandate of the Bishop.

§2 By virtue of the law itself, the episcopal Vicar has the same power as that mentioned in §1, but only for the determined part of the territory or type of activity, or for the faithful of the determined rite or group, for which he was appointed; matters which the Bishop reserves to himself or to the Vicar general, or which by law require a special mandate of the Bishop, are excepted.

§3 Within the limits of their competence, the Vicar general and the episcopal Vicar have also those habitual faculties which the Apostolic See has granted to the Bishop. They may also execute rescripts, unless it is expressly provided otherwise, or unless the execution was entrusted to the Bishop on a personal basis.

Can. 480 The Vicar general and episcopal Vicar must give a report to the diocesan Bishop concerning more important matters, both those yet to be attended to and those already dealt with. They are never to act against the will and mind of the diocesan Bishop.

Can. 481 §1 The power of the Vicar general or episcopal Vicar ceases when the period of their mandate expires, or by resignation. In addition, but without prejudice to cann. 406 and 409, it ceases when they are notified of their removal by the diocesan Bishop, or when the episcopal see falls vacant.

§2 When the office of the diocesan Bishop is suspended, the power of the Vicar general and of the episcopal Vicar is suspended, unless they are themselves Bishops.

Article 2: The Chancellor, other Notaries and the Archives

Can. 482 §1 In each curia a chancellor is to be appointed, whose principal office, unless particular law states otherwise, is to ensure that the acts of the curia are drawn up and dispatched, and that they are kept safe in the archive of the curia.

§2 If it is considered necessary, the chancellor may be given an assistant, who is to be called the vice-chancellor.

§3 The chancellor and vice-chancellor are automatically notaries and secretaries of the curia.

Can. 483 §1 Besides the chancellor, other notaries may be appointed, whose writing or signature authenticates public documents. These notaries may be appointed for all acts, or for judicial acts alone, or only for acts concerning a particular issue or business.

§2 The chancellor and notaries must be of unblemished reputation and above suspicion. In cases which could involve the reputation of a priest, the notary must be a priest.

Can. 484 The office of notary involves:

1° writing acts and documents concerning decrees, arrangements, obligations, and other matters which require their intervention;

2° faithfully recording in writing what is done, and signing the document, with a note of the place, the day, the month and the year;

3° while observing all that must be observed, showing acts or documents from the archives to those who lawfully request them, and verifying that copies conform to the original.

Can. 485   The chancellor and the other notaries can be freely removed by the diocesan Bishop. They can be removed by a diocesan Administrator only with the consent of the college of consultors.

Can. 486   §1 All documents concerning the diocese or parishes must be kept with the greatest of care.

§2 In each curia there is to be established in a safe place a diocesan archive where documents and writings concerning both the spiritual and the temporal affairs of the diocese are to be properly filed and carefully kept under lock and key.

§3 An inventory or catalogue is to be made of documents kept in the archive, with a short synopsis of each document.

Can. 487   §1 The archive must be locked, and only the Bishop and the chancellor are to have the key; no one may be allowed to enter unless with the permission of the Bishop, or with the permission of both the Moderator of the curia and the chancellor.

§2 Persons concerned have the right to receive, personally or by proxy, an authentic written or photostat copy of documents which are of their nature public and which concern their own personal status.

Can. 488   It is not permitted to remove documents from the archive, except for a short time and with the permission of the Bishop or of both the Moderator of the curia and the chancellor.

Can. 489   §1 In the diocesan curia there is also to be a secret archive, or at least in the ordinary archive there is to be a safe or cabinet, which is securely closed and bolted and which cannot be removed. In this archive documents which are to be kept under secrecy are to be most carefully guarded.

§2 Each year documents of criminal cases concerning moral matters are to be destroyed whenever the guilty parties have died, or ten years have elapsed since a condemnatory sentence concluded the affair. A short summary of the facts is to be kept, together with the text of the definitive judgement.

Can. 490   §1 Only the Bishop is to have the key of the secret archive.

§2 When the see is vacant, the secret archive or safe is not to be opened except in a case of real necessity, and then by the diocesan Administrator personally.

§3 Documents are not to be removed from the secret archive or safe.

Can. 491   §1 The diocesan Bishop is to ensure that the acts and documents of the archives of cathedral, collegiate, parochial and other churches in his territory are carefully kept and that two copies are made of inventories or catalogues. One of these copies is to remain in its own archive, the other is to be kept in the diocesan archive.

§2 The diocesan Bishop is to ensure that there is an historical archive in the diocese, and that documents which have an historical value are carefully kept in it and systematically filed.

§3 In order that the acts and documents mentioned in §§1 and 2 may be inspected or removed, the norms laid down by the diocesan Bishop are to be observed.

Article 3: The Finance Committee and the Financial Administrator

Can. 492 §1 In each diocese a finance committee is to be established, presided over by the diocesan Bishop or his delegate. It is to be composed of at least three of the faithful[†], expert in financial affairs and civil law, of outstanding integrity, and appointed by the Bishop.

§2 The members of the finance committee are appointed for five years, but when this period has expired they may be appointed for further terms of five years.

§3 Persons related to the Bishop up to the fourth degree of consanguinity or affinity are excluded from the finance committee.

Can. 493 Besides the functions entrusted to it in Book V on 'The Temporal Goods of the Church', it is the responsibility of the finance committee to prepare each year a budget of income and expenditure over the coming year for the governance of the whole diocese, in accordance with the direction of the diocesan Bishop. It is also the responsibility of the committee to account at the end of the year for income and expenditure.

Can. 494 §1 In each diocese a financial administrator is to be appointed by the Bishop, after consulting the college of consultors and the finance committee. The financial administrator is to be expert in financial matters and of truly outstanding integrity.

§2 The financial administrator is to be appointed for five years, but when this period has expired, may be appointed for further terms of five years. While in office he or she is not to be removed except for a grave reason, to be estimated by the Bishop after consulting the college of consultors and the finance committee.

§3 It is the responsibility of the financial administrator, under the authority of the Bishop, to administer the goods of the diocese in accordance with the plan of the finance committee, and to make those payments from diocesan funds which the Bishop or his delegates have lawfully authorised.

§4 At the end of the year the financial administrator must give the finance committee an account of income and expenditure.

Chapter III

THE COUNCIL OF PRIESTS AND THE COLLEGE OF CONSULTORS

Can. 495 §1 In each diocese there is to be established a council of priests, that is, a group of priests who represent the *presbyterium* and who are to be, as it were, the Bishop's senate. The council's role is to assist the Bishop, in accordance with the law, in the governance of the diocese, so that the pastoral welfare of that portion of the people of God entrusted to the Bishop may be most effectively promoted.

§2 In vicariates and prefectures apostolic, the Vicar or Prefect is to appoint a council composed of at least three missionary priests, whose opinion, even by letter, he is to hear in the more serious affairs.

Can. 496 The council of priests is to have its own statutes. These are to be approved by the diocesan Bishop, having taken account of the norms laid down by the Episcopal Conference.

Can. 497 As far as the designation of the members of the council of priests is concerned:

1° about half are to be freely elected by the priests themselves in accordance with the canons which follow and with the statutes;

2° some priests must, in accordance with the statutes, be members ex officio, that is belong to the council by reason of the office they hold;

3° the diocesan Bishop may freely appoint some others.

Can. 498 §1 The following have the right to both an active and a passive voice in an election to the council of priests:

1° all secular priests incardinated in the diocese;

2° priests who are living in the diocese and exercise some useful office there, whether they be secular priests not incardinated in the diocese, or priest members of religious institutes or of societies of apostolic life.

§2 Insofar as the statutes so provide, the same right of election may be given to other priests who have a domicile or quasi-domicile in the diocese.

Can. 499 The manner of electing the members of the council of priests is to be determined by the statutes, and in such a way that as far as possible the priests of the *presbyterium* are represented, with special regard to the diversity of ministries and to the various regions of the diocese.

Can. 500 §1 It is the prerogative of the diocesan Bishop to convene the council of priests, to preside over it, and to determine the matters to be discussed in it or to accept items proposed by the members.

§2 The council of priests has only a consultative vote. The diocesan Bishop is to consult it in matters of more serious moment, but he requires its consent only in the cases expressly defined in the law.

§3 The council of priests can never act without the diocesan Bishop. He alone can make public those things which have been decided in accordance with §2.

Can. 501 §1 The members of the council of priests are to be designated for a period specified in the statutes, subject however to the condition that over a five year period the council is renewed in whole or in part.

§2 When the see is vacant, the council of priests lapses and its functions are fulfilled by the college of consultors. The Bishop must reconstitute the council of priests within a year of taking possession.

§3 If the council of priests does not fulfil the office entrusted to it for the welfare of the diocese, or if it gravely abuses that office, it can be dissolved by the diocesan Bishop, after consultation with the Metropolitan; in the case of a metropolitan see, the Bishop must first consult with the suffragan Bishop who is senior by promotion. Within a year, however, the diocesan Bishop must reconstitute the council.

Can. 502   §1 From among the members of the council of priests, the diocesan Bishop freely appoints not fewer than six and not more than twelve priests, who are for five years to constitute the college of consultors. To it belong the functions determined by law; on the expiry of the five year period, however, it continues to exercise its functions until the new college is constituted.

§2 The diocesan Bishop presides over the college of consultors. If, however, the see is impeded or vacant, that person presides who in the interim takes the Bishop's place or, if he has not yet been appointed, then the priest in the college of consultors who is senior by ordination.

§3 The Episcopal Conference can determine that the functions of the college of consultors be entrusted to the cathedral chapter.

§4 Unless the law provides otherwise, in a vicariate or prefecture apostolic the functions of the college of consultors belong to the council of the mission mentioned in can. 495 §2.

Chapter IV
THE CHAPTER OF CANONS

Can. 503   A chapter of canons, whether cathedral or collegiate, is a college of priests, whose role is to celebrate the more solemn liturgical functions in a cathedral or a collegiate church. It is for the cathedral chapter, besides, to fulfil those roles entrusted to it by law or by the diocesan Bishop.

Can. 504   The establishment, alteration or suppression of a cathedral chapter is reserved to the Apostolic See.

Can. 505   Every chapter, whether cathedral or collegiate, is to have its own statutes, established by lawful capitular act and approved by the diocesan Bishop. These statutes are not to be changed or abrogated except with the approval of the diocesan Bishop.

Can. 506   §1 The statutes of a chapter, while preserving always the laws of the foundation, are to determine the nature of the chapter and the number of canons. They are to define what the chapter and the individual canons are to do in carrying out divine worship and their ministry. They are to decide the meetings at which chapter business is conducted and, while observing the provisions of the universal law, they are to prescribe the conditions required for the validity and for the lawfulness of the proceedings.

§2 In the statutes the remuneration is also to be defined, both the fixed salary and the amounts to be paid on the occasion of discharging the office; so too, having taken account of the norms laid down by the Holy See, the insignia of the canons.

Can. 507   §1 Among the canons there is to be one who presides over the chapter. In accordance with the statutes other offices are also to be established, account having been taken of the practice prevailing in the region.

§2 Other offices may be allotted to clerics not belonging to the chapter, so that, in accordance with the statutes, they may provide assistance to the canons.

Can. 508   §1 The canon penitentiary both of a cathedral church and of a collegiate church has by law ordinary faculties, which he cannot however delegate to others, to absolve in the sacramental forum from *latae sententiae* censures which have not been declared and are not reserved to the Holy See. Within the diocese he can absolve not only diocesans but outsiders also, whereas he can absolve diocesans even outside the diocese.

§2 Where there is no chapter, the diocesan Bishop is to appoint a priest to fulfil this office.

Can. 509   §1 It belongs to the diocesan Bishop, after consultation with the chapter, but not to the diocesan Administrator, to bestow each and every canonry both in the cathedral church and in a collegiate church; any privilege to the contrary is revoked. It is also for the diocesan Bishop to confirm the person elected by the chapter to preside over it.

§2 The diocesan Bishop is to appoint to canonries only priests who are of sound doctrine and life and who have exercised a praiseworthy ministry.

Can. 510   §1 Parishes are no longer to be united with chapters of canons. Those which are united to a chapter are to be separated from it by the diocesan Bishop.

§2 In a church which is at the same time a parochial and a capitular church, a parish priest is to be appointed, whether chosen from the chapter or not. He is bound by all the obligations and he enjoys all the rights and faculties which by law belong to a parish priest.

§3 The diocesan Bishop is to establish certain norms whereby the pastoral duties of the parish priest and the roles proper to the chapter are duly harmonised, so that the parish priest is not a hindrance to capitular functions, nor the chapter to those of the parish. Any conflicts which may arise are to be settled by the diocesan Bishop, who is to ensure above all that the pastoral needs of the faithful are suitably provided for.

§4 Alms given to a church which is at the same time a parochial and a capitular church, are presumed to be given to the parish, unless it is otherwise established.

Chapter V
THE PASTORAL COUNCIL

Can. 511 In each diocese, in so far as pastoral circumstances suggest, a pastoral council is to be established. Its function, under the authority of the Bishop, is to study and weigh those matters which concern the pastoral works in the diocese, and to propose practical conclusions concerning them.

Can. 512 §1 A pastoral council is composed of members of Christ's faithful who are in full communion with the catholic Church: clerics, members of institutes of consecrated life, and especially lay people. They are designated in the manner determined by the diocesan Bishop.

§2 The members of Christ's faithful assigned to the pastoral council are to be selected in such a way that the council truly reflects the entire portion of the people of God which constitutes the diocese, taking account of the different regions of the diocese, of social conditions and professions, and of the part played in the apostolate by the members, whether individually or in association with others.

§3 Only those members of Christ's faithful who are outstanding in firm faith, high moral standards and prudence are to be assigned to the pastoral council.

Can. 513 §1 The pastoral council is appointed for a determinate period, in accordance with the provisions of the statutes drawn up by the Bishop.

§2 When the see is vacant, the pastoral council lapses.

Can. 514 §1 The pastoral council has only a consultative vote. It is for the diocesan Bishop alone to convene it, according to the needs of the apostolate, and to preside over it. He alone has the right to make public the matters dealt with in the council.

§2 It is to be convened at least once a year.

Chapter VI
PARISHES, PARISH PRIESTS AND ASSISTANT PRIESTS

Can. 515 §1 A parish is a certain community of Christ's faithful stably established within a particular Church, whose pastoral care, under the authority of the diocesan Bishop, is entrusted to a parish priest as its proper pastor.

§2 The diocesan Bishop alone can establish, suppress or alter parishes. He is not to establish, suppress or notably alter them unless he has consulted the council of priests.

§3 A lawfully established parish has juridical personality by virtue of the law itself.

Can. 516   §1 Unless the law provides otherwise, a quasi-parish is equivalent to a parish. A quasi-parish is a certain community of Christ's faithful within a particular Church, entrusted to a priest as its proper pastor, but because of special circumstances not yet established as a parish.

§2 Where some communities cannot be established as parishes or quasi-parishes, the diocesan Bishop is to provide for their spiritual care in some other way.

Can. 517   §1 Where circumstances so require, the pastoral care of a parish, or of a number of parishes together, can be entrusted to several priests jointly, but with the stipulation that one of the priests is to be the moderator of the pastoral care to be exercised. This moderator is to direct the joint action and to be responsible for it to the Bishop.

§2 If, because of a shortage of priests, the diocesan Bishop has judged that a deacon, or some other person who is not a priest, or a community of persons, should be entrusted with a share in the exercise of the pastoral care of a parish, he is to appoint some priest who, with the powers and faculties of a parish priest, will direct the pastoral care.

Can. 518   As a general rule, a parish is to be territorial, that is, it is to embrace all Christ's faithful of a given territory. Where it is useful, however, personal parishes are to be established, determined by reason of the rite, language or nationality of the faithful[†] of a certain territory, or on some other basis.

Can. 519   The parish priest is the proper pastor of the parish entrusted to him. He exercises the pastoral care of the community entrusted to him under the authority of the diocesan Bishop, whose ministry of Christ he is called to share, so that for this community he may carry out the offices of teaching, sanctifying and ruling with the cooperation of other priests or deacons and with the assistance of lay members of Christ's faithful, in accordance with the law.

Can. 520   §1 A juridical person may not be a parish priest. However, the diocesan Bishop, but not the diocesan Administrator, can, with the consent of the competent Superior, entrust a parish to a clerical religious institute or to a clerical society of apostolic life, even by establishing it in the church of the institute or society, subject however to the rule that one priest be the parish priest or, if the pastoral care is entrusted to several priests jointly, that there be a moderator as mentioned in can. 517 §1.

§2 The entrustment of a parish, as in §1, may be either in perpetuity or for a specified time. In either case this is to be done by means of a written agreement made between the diocesan Bishop and the competent Superior of the institute or society. This agreement must expressly and accurately define, among other things, the work to be done, the persons to be assigned to it and the financial arrangements.

Can. 521   §1   To be validly appointed a parish priest, one must be in the sacred order of priesthood.

§2   He is also to be outstanding in sound doctrine and uprightness of character, endowed with zeal for souls and other virtues, and possessed of those qualities which by universal or particular law are required for the care of the parish in question.

§3   In order that one be appointed to the office of parish priest, his suitability must be clearly established, in a manner determined by the diocesan Bishop, even by examination.

Can. 522   It is necessary that a parish priest have the benefit of stability, and therefore he is to be appointed for an indeterminate period of time. The diocesan Bishop may appoint him for a specified period of time only if the Episcopal Conference has by decree allowed this.

Can. 523   Without prejudice to can. 682, appointment to the office of parish priest belongs to the diocesan Bishop, who is free to confer it on whomsoever he wishes, unless someone else has a right of presentation or election.

Can. 524   The diocesan Bishop is to confer a vacant parish on the one whom, after consideration of all the circumstances, he judges suitable for the parochial care of that parish, without any preference of persons. In order to assess suitability, he is to consult the vicar forane, conduct suitable enquiries and, if it is appropriate, seek the view of some priests and lay members of Christ's faithful.

Can. 525   When a see is vacant or impeded, it is for the diocesan Administrator or whoever governs the diocese in the interim:

1°   to institute priests lawfully presented for a parish or to confirm those lawfully elected to one;

2°   to appoint parish priests if the see has been vacant or impeded for a year.

Can. 526   §1   A parish priest is to have the parochial care of one parish only. However, because of a shortage of priests or other circumstances, the care of a number of neighbouring parishes can be entrusted to the one parish priest.

§2   In any one parish there is to be only one parish priest, or one moderator in accordance with can. 517 §1; any contrary custom is reprobated and any contrary privilege revoked.

Can. 527   §1   One who is promoted to exercise the pastoral care of a parish obtains this care and is bound to exercise it from the moment he takes possession.

§2 The local Ordinary or a priest delegated by him puts the parish priest into possession, in accordance with the procedure approved by particular law or by lawful custom. For a just reason, however, the same Ordinary can dispense from this procedure, in which case the communication of the dispensation to the parish replaces the taking of possession.

§3 The local Ordinary is to determine the time within which the parish priest must take possession of the parish. If, in the absence of a lawful impediment, he has not taken possession within this time, the local Ordinary can declare the parish vacant.

Can. 528 §1 The parish priest has the obligation of ensuring that the word of God is proclaimed in its entirety to those living in the parish. He is therefore to see to it that the lay members of Christ's faithful are instructed in the truths of faith, especially by means of the homily on Sundays and holydays of obligation and by catechetical formation. He is to foster works which promote the spirit of the Gospel, including its relevance to social justice. He is to have a special care for the catholic education of children and young people. With the collaboration of the faithful[†], he is to make every effort to bring the gospel message to those also who have given up religious practice or who do not profess the true faith.

§2 The parish priest is to take care that the blessed Eucharist is the centre of the parish assembly of the faithful. He is to strive to ensure that the faithful[†] are nourished by the devout celebration of the sacraments, and in particular that they frequently approach the sacraments of the blessed Eucharist and penance. He is to strive to lead them to prayer, including prayer in their families, and to take a live and active part in the sacred liturgy. Under the authority of the diocesan Bishop, the parish priest must direct this liturgy in his own parish, and he is bound to be on guard against abuses.

Can. 529 §1 So that he may fulfil his office of pastor diligently, the parish priest is to strive to know the faithful entrusted to his care. He is therefore to visit their families, sharing in their cares and anxieties and, in a special way, their sorrows, comforting them in the Lord. If in certain matters they are found wanting, he is prudently to correct them. He is to help the sick and especially the dying in great charity, solicitously restoring them with the sacraments and commending their souls to God. He is to be especially diligent in seeking out the poor, the suffering, the lonely, those who are exiled from their homeland, and those burdened with special difficulties. He is to strive also to ensure that spouses and parents are sustained in the fulfilment of their proper duties, and to foster the growth of christian life in the family.

§2 The parish priest is to recognise and promote the specific role which the lay members of Christ's faithful have in the mission of the Church, fostering their associations which have religious purposes. He is to co-operate with his proper Bishop and with the *presbyterium* of the diocese. Moreover, he is to endeavour to ensure that the faithful are concerned for the community of the parish, that they feel themselves to be members both of the diocese and of the universal Church, and that they take part in and sustain works which promote this community.

Can. 530   The functions especially entrusted to the parish priest are as follows:

1° the administration of baptism;

2° the administration of the sacrament of confirmation to those in danger of death, in accordance with can. 883, n. 3;

3° the administration of Viaticum and of the anointing of the sick, without prejudice to can. 1003 §§2 and 3, and the imparting of the apostolic blessing;

4° the assistance at marriages and the nuptial blessing;

5° the conducting of funerals;

6° the blessing of the baptismal font at paschal time, the conduct of processions outside the church, and the giving of solemn blessings outside the church;

7° the more solemn celebration of the Eucharist on Sundays and holydays of obligation.

Can. 531   Even though another person has performed some parochial function, he is to give the offering he receives from the faithful[†] on that occasion to the parish fund unless, in respect of voluntary offerings, there is a clear contrary intention on the donor's part; it is for the diocesan Bishop, after consulting the council of priests, to prescribe regulations concerning the destination of these offerings and to provide for the remuneration of clerics who fulfil such a parochial function.

Can. 532   In all juridical matters, the parish priest acts in the person of the parish, in accordance with the law. He is to ensure that the parish goods are administered in accordance with cann. 1281–1288.

Can. 533   §1 The parish priest is obliged to reside in the parochial house, near the church. In particular cases, however, where there is a just reason, the local Ordinary may permit him to reside elsewhere, especially in a house common to several priests, provided the carrying out of the parochial duties is properly and suitably catered for.

§2 Unless there is a grave reason to the contrary, the parish priest may each year be absent on holiday from his parish for a period not exceeding one month, continuous or otherwise. The days which the parish priest spends on the annual spiritual retreat are not reckoned in this period of vacation. For an absence from the parish of more than a week, however, the parish priest is bound to advise the local Ordinary.

§3 It is for the diocesan Bishop to establish norms by which, during the parish priest's absence, the care of the parish is provided for by a priest with the requisite faculties.

Can. 534   §1 When he has taken possession of his parish, the parish priest is bound on each Sunday and holyday of obligation in his diocese to apply the Mass for the people entrusted to him. If he is lawfully impeded from this celebration, he is to have someone else apply the Mass on these days or apply it himself on other days.

§2   A parish priest who has the care of several parishes is bound to apply only one Mass on the days mentioned in §1, for all the people entrusted to him.

§3   A parish priest who has not discharged the obligations mentioned in §§1 and 2, is as soon as possible to apply for the people as many Masses as he has omitted.

Can. 535   §1   In each parish there are to be parochial registers, that is, of baptisms, of marriages and of deaths, and any other registers prescribed by the Episcopal Conference or by the diocesan Bishop. The parish priest is to ensure that entries are accurately made and that the registers are carefully preserved.

§2   In the register of baptisms, a note is to be made of confirmation and of matters pertaining to the canonical status of the faithful[†] by reason of marriage, without prejudice to the provision of can. 1133, and by reason of adoption, the reception of sacred order, the making of perpetual profession in a religious institute, or a change of rite. These annotations are always to be reproduced on a baptismal certificate.

§3   Each parish is to have its own seal. Certificates concerning the canonical status of the faithful[†], and all acts which can have juridical significance, are to be signed by the parish priest or his delegate and secured with the parochial seal.

§4   In each parish there is to be an archive, in which the parochial books are to be kept, together with episcopal letters and other documents which it may be necessary or useful to preserve. On the occasion of visitation or at some other opportune time, the diocesan Bishop or his delegate is to inspect all of these matters. The parish priest is to take care that they do not fall into unauthorised hands.

§5   Older parochial registers are also to be carefully safeguarded, in accordance with the provisions of particular law.

Can. 536   §1   If, after consulting the council of priests, the diocesan Bishop considers it opportune, a pastoral council is to be established in each parish. In this council, which is presided over by the parish priest, Christ's faithful, together with those who by virtue of their office are engaged in pastoral care in the parish, give their help in fostering pastoral action.

§2   The pastoral council has only a consultative vote, and it is regulated by the norms laid down by the diocesan Bishop.

Can. 537   In each parish there is to be a finance committee to help the parish priest in the administration of the goods of the parish, without prejudice to can. 532. It is ruled by the universal law and by the norms laid down by the diocesan Bishop, and it is comprised of members of the faithful[†] selected according to these norms.

Can. 538   §1   A parish priest ceases to hold office by removal or transfer effected by the diocesan Bishop in accordance with the law; by his personal resignation, for a just reason, which for validity requires that it be accepted by the diocesan Bishop; and by the lapse of time if, in accordance with the particular law mentioned in can. 522, he was appointed for a specified period of time.

§2 A parish priest who is a member of a religious institute or is incardinated in a society of apostolic life, is removed in accordance with can. 682 §2.

§3 A parish priest who has completed his seventy fifth year of age is requested to offer his resignation from office to the diocesan Bishop who, after considering all the circumstances of person and place, is to decide whether to accept or defer it. Having taken account of the norms laid down by the Episcopal Conference, the diocesan Bishop must make provision for the appropriate maintenance and residence of the priest who has resigned.

Can. 539 When a parish is vacant, or when the parish priest is prevented from exercising his pastoral office in the parish by reason of imprisonment, exile or banishment, or by reason of incapacity or ill health or some other cause, the diocesan Bishop is as soon as possible to appoint a parochial administrator, that is, a priest who will take the place of the parish priest in accordance with can. 540.

Can. 540 §1 The parochial administrator is bound by the same obligations and has the same rights as a parish priest, unless the diocesan Bishop prescribes otherwise.

§2 The parochial administrator may not do anything which could prejudice the rights of the parish priest or could do harm to parochial property.

§3 When he has discharged his office, the parochial administrator is to give an account to the parish priest.

Can. 541 §1 When a parish is vacant, or when the parish priest is impeded from exercising his pastoral office, pending the appointment of a parochial administrator the interim governance of the parish is to be undertaken by the assistant priest; if there are a number of assistants, by the senior by appointment; if there are none, by the parish priest determined by particular law.

§2 The one who has undertaken the governance of the parish in accordance with §1, is at once to inform the local Ordinary of the parish vacancy.

Can. 542 The priests to whom, in accordance with can. 516 § 1*, is jointly entrusted the pastoral care of a parish or of a number of parishes together:

    1° must possess the qualities mentioned in can. 521;
    2° are to be appointed in accordance with cann. 522 and 524;

---

*Translators' note: It would appear that this reference should read 'can. 517 §1'.

3° obtain the pastoral care only from the moment of taking possession: their moderator is put into possession in accordance with can. 527 §2; for the other priests, the profession of faith lawfully made replaces the taking of possession.

Can. 543   §1 Each of the priests to whom the care of a parish or of a number of parishes together is jointly entrusted, is bound to fulfil the duties and functions of a parish priest mentioned in cann. 528, 529 and 530. They are to do this according to a plan determined among themselves. The faculty to assist at marriages, and all the faculties to dispense which are given to a parish priest by virtue of the law itself, belong to all, but are to be exercised under the direction of the moderator.

§2 All the priests who belong to the group:

1° are bound by the obligation of residence;
2° are by common counsel to establish an arrangement by which one of them celebrates the Mass for the people, in accordance with can. 534.
3° *in juridical affairs, only the moderator acts in the person of the parish or parishes entrusted to the group.

Can. 544   When one of the priests, or the moderator, of the group mentioned in can. 517 §1 ceases to hold office, or when any member of it becomes incapable of exercising his pastoral office, the parish or parishes whose care is entrusted to the group do not become vacant. It is for the diocesan Bishop to appoint another moderator; until he is appointed by the Bishop, the priest of the group who is senior by appointment is to fulfil this office.

Can. 545   §1 Whenever it is necessary or opportune for the due pastoral care of the parish, one or more assistant priests can be joined with the parish priest. As cooperators with the parish priest and sharers in his concern, they are, by common counsel and effort with the parish priest and under his authority, to labour in the pastoral ministry.

§2 An assistant priest may be appointed either to help in exercising the entire pastoral ministry, whether in the whole parish or in a part of it or for a particular group of the faithful within it, or even to help in carrying out a specific ministry in a number of parishes at the same time.

Can. 546   To be validly appointed an assistant priest, one must be in the sacred order of priesthood.

Can. 547   The diocesan Bishop freely appoints an assistant priest; if he has judged it opportune, he will have consulted the parish priest or parish priests of the parishes to which the assistant is appointed, and the Vicar forane, without prejudice to can. 682 §1.

---

*Translators' note: It would appear that n. 3 should read '§3'.

Can. 548   §1 The obligations and rights of assistant priests are defined not only by the canons of this chapter, but also by the diocesan statutes, and by the letter of the diocesan Bishop; they are more specifically determined by the directions of the parish priest.

§2   Unless it is otherwise expressly provided in the letter of the diocesan Bishop, the assistant priest is by virtue of his office bound to help the parish priest in the entire parochial ministry, with the exception of the application of the Mass for the people. Likewise, if the matter should arise in accordance with the law, he is bound to take the place of the parish priest.

§3   The assistant priest is to report regularly to the parish priest on pastoral initiatives, both those planned and those already undertaken. In this way the parish priest and the assistant or assistants can by their joint efforts provide a pastoral care of the parish for which they are together answerable.

Can. 549   When the parish priest is absent, the norms of can. 541 §1 are to be observed, unless the diocesan Bishop has provided otherwise in accordance with can. 533 §3, or unless a parochial administrator has been appointed. If can. 541 §1 is applied, the assistant priest is bound by all the obligations of the parish priest, with the exception of the obligation to apply the Mass for the people.

Can. 550   §1 The assistant priest is bound to reside in the parish or, if he is appointed for a number of parishes at the same time, in one of them. For a just reason, however, the local Ordinary may permit him to reside elsewhere, especially in a house common to several priests, provided the carrying out of the pastoral duties does not in any way suffer thereby.

§2   The local Ordinary is to see to it that, where it is possible, some manner of common life in the parochial house be encouraged between the parish priest and the assistants.

§3   As far as holidays are concerned, the assistant priest has the same rights as the parish priest.

Can. 551   The provisions of can. 531 are to be observed in respect of offerings which Christ's faithful make to the assistant priest on the occasion of his exercise of the pastoral ministry.

Can. 552   Without prejudice to can. 682 §2, an assistant priest may for a just reason be removed by the diocesan Bishop or the diocesan Administrator.

Chapter VII
VICARS FORANE

Can. 553   §1 The Vicar forane, known also as the dean or the archpriest or by some other title, is the priest who is placed in charge of a vicariate forane.

§2 Unless it is otherwise prescribed by particular law, the Vicar forane is appointed by the diocesan Bishop; if he has considered it prudent to do so, he will have consulted the priests who are exercising the ministry in the vicariate.

Can. 554 §1 For the office of Vicar forane, which is not tied to the office of parish priest of any given parish, the Bishop is to choose a priest whom, in view of the circumstances of place and time, he has judged to be suitable.

§2 The Vicar forane is to be appointed for a certain period of time, determined by particular law.

§3 For a just reason, the diocesan Bishop may in accordance with his prudent judgement freely remove the Vicar forane from office.

Can. 555 §1 Apart from the faculties lawfully given to him by particular law, the Vicar forane has the duty and the right:

1° to promote and coordinate common pastoral action in the vicariate;

2° to see that the clerics of his district lead a life befitting their state, and discharge their obligations carefully;

3° to ensure that religious functions are celebrated according to the provisions of the sacred liturgy; that the elegance and neatness of the churches and sacred furnishings are properly maintained, particularly in regard to the celebration of the Eucharist and the custody of the blessed Sacrament; that the parish registers are correctly entered and duly safeguarded; that ecclesiastical goods are carefully administered; finally, that the parochial house is looked after with care.

§2 In the vicariate entrusted to him, the Vicar forane:

1° is to encourage the clergy, in accordance with the provisions of particular law, to attend at the prescribed time lectures and theological meetings or conferences, in accordance with can. 272 §2*.

2° is to see to it that spiritual assistance is available to the priests of his district, and he is to show a particular solicitude for those who are in difficult circumstances or are troubled by problems.

§3 When he has come to know that parish priests of his district are seriously ill, the Vicar forane is to ensure that they do not lack spiritual and material help. When they die, he is to ensure that their funerals are worthily celebrated. Moreover, should any of them fall ill or die, he is to see to it that books, documents, sacred furnishings and other items belonging to the Church are not lost or removed.

§4 The Vicar forane is obliged to visit the parishes of his district in accordance with the arrangement made by the diocesan Bishop.

---

*Translators' note: It would appear that this reference should read 'can. 279 §2'.

Chapter VIII

RECTORS OF CHURCHES AND CHAPLAINS

Article 1: Rectors of Churches

Can. 556 Rectors of churches are here understood to be priests to whom is entrusted the care of some church which is neither a parochial nor a capitular church, nor a church attached to the house of a religious community or a society of apostolic life which holds services in it.

Can. 557 §1 The rector of a church is freely appointed by the diocesan Bishop, without prejudice to a right of election or presentation to which someone may lawfully have claim: in which case the diocesan Bishop has the right to confirm or to appoint the rector.

§2 Even if the church belongs to some clerical religious institute of pontifical right, it is for the diocesan Bishop to appoint the rector presented by the Superior.

§3 The rector of a church which is attached to a seminary or to a college governed by clerics, is the rector of the seminary or college, unless the diocesan Bishop has determined otherwise.

Can. 558 Without prejudice to can. 262, the rector of a church may not perform in his church the parochial functions mentioned in can. 530 nn. 1–6, without the consent or, where the matter requires it, the delegation of the parish priest.

Can. 559 The rector can conduct liturgical celebrations, even solemn ones, in the church entrusted to him, without prejudice to the legitimate laws of a foundation, and on condition that in the judgement of the local Ordinary these celebrations do not in any way harm the parochial ministry.

Can. 560 Where he considers it opportune, the local Ordinary may direct the rector to celebrate in his church certain functions for the people, even parochial functions, and also to open the church to certain groups of the faithful so that they may hold liturgical celebrations there.

Can. 561 Without the permission of the rector or some other lawful superior, no one may celebrate the Eucharist, administer the sacraments, or perform other sacred functions in the church. This permission is to be given or refused in accordance with the law.

Can. 562 Under the authority of the local Ordinary, having observed the lawful statutes and respected acquired rights, the rector of a church is obliged to see that sacred functions are worthily celebrated in the church, in accordance with liturgical and canon law, that obligations are faithfully fulfilled, that the property is carefully administered, and that the maintenance and adornment of the furnishings and buildings are assured.

He must also ensure that nothing is done which is in any way unbecoming to the holiness of the place and to the reverence due to the house of God.

Can. 563   For a just reason, the local Ordinary may in accordance with his prudent judgement remove the rector of a church from office, even if he had been elected or presented by others, but without prejudice to can. 682 §2.

Article 2: Chaplains

Can. 564   A chaplain is a priest to whom is entrusted in a stable manner the pastoral care, at least in part, of some community or special group of Christ's faithful, to be exercised in accordance with universal and particular law.

Can. 565   Unless the law provides otherwise or unless special rights lawfully belong to someone, a chaplain is appointed by the local Ordinary, to whom also it belongs to appoint one who has been presented or to confirm one elected.

Can. 566   §1 A chaplain must be given all the faculties which due pastoral care demands. Besides those which are given by particular law or by special delegation, a chaplain has by virtue of his office the faculty to hear the confessions of the faithful entrusted to his care, to preach to them the word of God, to administer Viaticum and the anointing of the sick, and to confer the sacrament of confirmation when they are in danger of death.

§2 In hospitals and prisons and on sea voyages, a chaplain has the further facility, to be exercised only in those places, to absolve from *latae sententiae* censures which are neither reserved nor declared, without prejudice to can. 976.

Can. 567   §1 The local Ordinary is not to proceed to the appointment of a chaplain to a house of a lay religious institute without consulting the Superior. The Superior has the right, after consulting the community, to propose a particular priest.

§2 It is the responsibility of the chaplain to celebrate or to direct liturgical functions; he may not, however, involve himself in the internal governance of the institute.

Can. 568   As far as possible, chaplains are to be appointed for those who, because of their condition of life, are not able to avail themselves of the ordinary care of parish priests, as for example, migrants, exiles, fugitives, nomads and sea-farers.

Can. 569   Chaplains to the armed forces are governed by special laws.

Can. 570   If a non-parochial church is attached to a centre of a community or group, the rector of the church is to be the chaplain, unless the care of the community or of the church requires otherwise.

Can. 571   In the exercise of his pastoral office a chaplain is to maintain the due relationship with the parish priest.

Can. 572   In regard to the removal of a chaplain, the provisions of can. 563 are to be observed.

Part III
INSTITUTES OF CONSECRATED LIFE AND SOCIETIES OF APOSTOLIC LIFE

Section I: Institutes of Consecrated Life

TITLE I: NORMS COMMON TO ALL INSTITUTES OF CONSECRATED LIFE

Can. 573 §1 Life consecrated through profession of the evangelical counsels is a stable form of living, in which the faithful follow Christ more closely under the action of the Holy Spirit, and are totally dedicated to God, who is supremely loved. By a new and special title they are dedicated to seek the perfection of charity in the service of God's Kingdom, for the honour of God, the building up of the Church and the salvation of the world. They are a splendid sign in the Church, as they foretell the heavenly glory.

§2 Christ's faithful freely assume this manner of life in institutes of consecrated life which are canonically established by the competent ecclesiastical authority. By vows or by other sacred bonds, in accordance with the laws of their own institutes, they profess the evangelical counsels of chastity, poverty and obedience. Because of the charity to which these counsels lead, they are linked in a special way to the Church and its mystery.

Can. 574 §1 The state of persons who profess the evangelical counsels in these institutes belongs to the life and holiness of the Church. It is therefore to be fostered and promoted by everyone in the Church.

§2 Some of Christ's faithful are specially called by God to this state, so that they may benefit from a special gift in the life of the Church and contribute to its saving mission according to the purpose and spirit of each institute.

Can. 575 The evangelical counsels, based on the teaching and example of Christ the Master, are a divine gift which the Church received from the Lord and which by His grace it preserves always.

Can. 576 It is the prerogative of the competent authority in the Church to interpret the evangelical counsels, to legislate for their practice and, by canonical approval, to constitute the stable forms of living which arise from them. The same authority has the responsibility to do what is in its power to ensure that institutes grow and flourish according to the spirit of their founders and to their sound traditions.

Can. 577   In the Church there are many institutes of consecrated life, with gifts that differ according to the graces given them: they more closely follow Christ praying, or Christ proclaiming the Kingdom of God, or Christ doing good to people, or Christ in dialogue with the people of this world, but always Christ doing the will of the Father.

Can. 578   The whole patrimony of an institute must be faithfully preserved by all. This patrimony is comprised of the intentions of the founders, of all that the competent ecclesiastical authority has approved concerning the nature, purpose, spirit and character of the institute, and of its sound traditions.

Can. 579   Provided the Apostolic See has been consulted, diocesan Bishops can, by formal decree, establish institutes of consecrated life in their own territories.

Can. 580   The aggregation of one institute of consecrated life to another is reserved to the competent authority of the aggregating institute, always safeguarding the canonical autonomy of the other institute.

Can. 581   It is for the competent authority of the institute to divide the institute into parts, by whatever name these may be called, to establish new parts, or to unite or otherwise modify those in existence, in accordance with the constitutions.

Can. 582   Fusions and unions of institutes of consecrated life are reserved to the Apostolic See alone. To it are likewise reserved confederations or federations.

Can. 583   Changes in institutes of consecrated life which affect elements previously approved by the Apostolic See, cannot be made without the permission of the same See.

Can. 584   Only the Apostolic See can suppress an institute and dispose of its temporal goods.

Can. 585   The competent authority of an institute can suppress parts of the same institute.

Can. 586   §1   A true autonomy of life, especially of governance, is recognised for each institute. This autonomy means that each institute has its own discipline in the Church and can preserve whole and entire the patrimony described in can. 578.

§2 Local Ordinaries have the responsibility of preserving and safeguarding this autonomy.

Can. 587 §1 To protect more faithfully the vocation and identity of each institute, the fundamental code or constitutions of the institute are to contain, in addition to those elements which are to be preserved in accordance with can. 578, basic norms about the governance of the institute, the discipline of the members, the admission and formation of members, and the proper object of their sacred bonds.

§2 This code is approved by the competent ecclesiastical authority, and can be changed only with the consent of the same.

§3 In the constitutions, the spiritual and juridical elements are to be aptly harmonised. Norms, however, are not to be multiplied without necessity.

§4 Other norms which are established by the competent authority of the institute are to be properly collected in other codes, but these can be conveniently reviewed and adapted according to the needs of time and place.

Can. 588 §1 In itself, the state of consecrated life is neither clerical nor lay.

§2 A clerical institute is one which, by reason of the end or purpose intended by the founder, or by reason of lawful tradition, is under the governance of clerics, presupposes the exercise of sacred orders, and is recognised as such by ecclesiastical authority.

§3 A lay institute is one which is recognised as such by ecclesiastical authority because, by its nature, character and purpose, its proper role, defined by its founder or by lawful tradition, does not include the exercise of sacred orders.

Can. 589 An institute of consecrated life is of pontifical right if it has been established by the Apostolic See, or approved by it by means of a formal decree. An institute is of diocesan right if it has been established by the diocesan Bishop and has not obtained a decree of approval from the Apostolic See.

Can. 590 §1 Institutes of consecrated life, since they are dedicated in a special way to the service of God and of the whole Church, are in a particular manner subject to its supreme authority.

§2 The individual members are bound to obey the Supreme Pontiff as their highest Superior, by reason also of their sacred bond of obedience.

Can. 591 The better to ensure the welfare of institutes and the needs of the apostolate, the Supreme Pontiff, by virtue of his primacy in the universal Church, and with a view to the common good, can withdraw institutes of consecrated life from the governance of local Ordinaries, and subject them to himself alone, or to some other ecclesiastical authority.

Can. 592 §1 To promote closer union between institutes and the Apostolic See, each supreme Moderator is to send a brief account of the state and life of the institute to the same Apostolic See, in the manner and at the time it lays down.

§2 Moderators of each institute are to promote a knowledge of the documents issued by the Holy See which affect the members entrusted to them, and are to ensure that these documents are observed.

Can. 593 In their internal governance and discipline, institutes of pontifical right are subject directly and exclusively to the authority of the Apostolic See, without prejudice to can. 586.

Can. 594 An institute of diocesan right remains under the special care of the diocesan Bishop, without prejudice to can. 586.

Can. 595 §1 It is the Bishop of the principal house who approves the constitutions, and confirms any changes lawfully introduced into them, except for those matters which the Apostolic See has taken in hand. He also deals with major affairs which exceed the power of the internal authority of the institute. If the institute had spread to other dioceses, he is in all these matters to consult with the other diocesan Bishops concerned.

§2 The diocesan Bishop can grant a dispensation from the constitutions in particular cases.

Can. 596 §1 Superiors and Chapters of institutes have that authority over the members which is defined in the universal law and in the constitutions.

§2 In clerical religious institutes of pontifical right, Superiors have in addition the ecclesiastical power of governance, for both the external and the internal forum.

§3 The provisions of cann. 131, 133 and 137–144 apply to the authority mentioned in §1.

Can. 597 §1 Every catholic with a right intention and the qualities required by universal law and the institute's own law, and who is without impediment, may be admitted to an institute of consecrated life.

§2 No one may be admitted without suitable preparation.

Can. 598 §1 Each institute, taking account of its own special character and purposes, is to define in its constitutions the manner in which the evangelical counsels of chastity, poverty and obedience are to be observed in its way of life.

§2 All members must not only observe the evangelical counsels faithfully and fully, but also direct their lives according to the institute's own law, and so strive for the perfection of their state.

Can. 599 The evangelical counsel of chastity embraced for the sake of the Kingdom of heaven, is a sign of the world to come, and a source of greater fruitfulness in an undivided heart. It involves the obligation of perfect continence observed in celibacy.

Can. 600   The evangelical counsel of poverty in imitation of Christ, who for our sake was made poor when he was rich, entails a life which is poor in reality and in spirit, sober and industrious, and a stranger to earthly riches. It also involves dependence and limitation in the use and the disposition of goods, in accordance with each institute's own law.

Can. 601   The evangelical counsel of obedience, undertaken in the spirit of faith and love in the following of Christ, who was obedient even unto death, obliges submission of one's will to lawful Superiors, who act in the place of God when they give commands that are in accordance with each institute's own constitutions.

Can. 602   The fraternal life proper to each institute unites all the members into, as it were, a special family in Christ. It is to be so defined that for all it proves of mutual assistance to fulfil their vocation. The fraternal union of the members, rooted and based in charity, is to be an example of universal reconciliation in Christ.

Can. 603   §1 Besides institutes of consecrated life, the Church recognises the life of hermits or anchorites, in which Christ's faithful withdraw further from the world and devote their lives to the praise of God and the salvation of the world through the silence of solitude and through constant prayer and penance.
   §2 Hermits are recognised by law as dedicated to God in consecrated life if, in the hands of the diocesan Bishop, they publicly profess, by a vow or some other sacred bond, the three evangelical counsels, and then lead their particular form of life under the guidance of the diocesan Bishop.

Can. 604   §1 The order of virgins is also to be added to these forms of consecrated life. Through their pledge to follow Christ more closely, virgins are consecrated to God, mystically espoused to Christ and dedicated to the service of the Church, when the diocesan Bishop consecrates them according to the approved liturgical rite.
   §2 Virgins can be associated together to fulfil their pledge more faithfully, and to assist each other to serve the Church in a way that befits their state.

Can. 605   The approval of new forms of consecrated life is reserved to the Apostolic See. Diocesan Bishops, however, are to endeavour to discern new gifts of consecrated life which the Holy Spirit entrusts to the Church. They are also to assist promotors to express their purposes in the best possible way, and to protect these purposes with suitable statutes, especially by the application of the general norms contained in this part of the Code.

Can. 606   Provisions concerning institutes of consecrated life and their members are equally valid in law for both sexes, unless it is otherwise clear from the context or from the nature of things.

TITLE II: RELIGIOUS INSTITUTES

Can. 607   §1 Religious life, as a consecration of the whole person, manifests in the Church the marvellous marriage established by God as a sign of the world to come. Religious thus consummate a full gift of themselves as a sacrifice offered to God, so that their whole existence becomes a continuous worship of God in charity.

§2 A religious institute is a society in which, in accordance with their own law, the members pronounce public vows and live a fraternal life in common. The vows are either perpetual or temporary; if the latter, they are to be renewed when the time elapses.

§3 The public witness which religious are to give to Christ and the Church involves that separation from the world which is proper to the character and purpose of each institute.

Chapter I

RELIGIOUS HOUSES AND THEIR ESTABLISHMENT AND SUPPRESSION

Can. 608   A religious community is to live in a lawfully constituted house, under the authority of a Superior designated according to the norms of law. Each house is to have at least an oratory, in which the Eucharist is celebrated and reserved, so that it may truly be the centre of the community.

Can. 609   §1 A house of a religious institute is established, with the prior written consent of the diocesan Bishop, by the authority competent according to the constitutions.

§2 For the establishment of a monastery of cloistered nuns, the permission of the Apostolic See is also required.

Can. 610   §1 In establishing religious houses, the welfare of the Church and of the institute are to be kept in mind, and care must be taken to safeguard everything that is necessary for the members to lead their religious life in accordance with the purposes and spirit proper to the institute.

§2 No house is to be established unless it is prudently foreseen that the needs of the members can be suitably provided for.

Can. 611   The consent of the diocesan Bishop for the establishment of a religious house carries with it the right:

1° to lead a life according to the character and purposes proper to the institute;

2° to engage in the works which are proper to the institute, in accordance with the law, and subject to any conditions attached to the consent;

3° for clerical religious institutes to have a church, subject to the provisions of can. 1215 §3, and to conduct the sacred ministries, with due observance of the law.

Can. 612   The consent of the diocesan Bishop is required if a religious house is to be used for apostolic works other than those for which it was established. This permission is not required for a change which, while observing the laws of the foundation, concerns only internal governance and discipline.

Can. 613   §1 A religious house of canons regular or of monks under the governance and care of their own Moderator is autonomous, unless the constitutions decree otherwise.

§2 The Moderator of an autonomous house is by law a major Superior.

Can. 614   Monasteries of cloistered nuns which are associated with an institute of men, have their own rule of life and governance, in accordance with the constitutions. The mutual rights and obligations are to be defined in such a way that spiritual good may come from the association.

Can. 615   If an autonomous monastery has no major Superior other than its own Moderator, and is not associated with any institute of religious in such a way that the Superior of that institute has over the monastery a real authority determined by the constitutions, it is entrusted, in accordance with the norms of law, to the special vigilance of the diocesan Bishop.

Can. 616   §1 After consultation with the diocesan Bishop, a supreme Moderator can suppress a lawfully established religious house, in accordance with the constitutions. The institute's own law is to make provision for the disposal of the goods of the suppressed house, with due regard for the wishes of founders or benefactors and for lawfully acquired rights.

§2 The Holy See alone can suppress the sole house of an institute, in which case it is also reserved to the Holy See to prescribe concerning the property of the house.

§3 Unless the constitutions enact otherwise, the suppression of the autonomous houses mentioned in can. 613 belongs to the general chapter.

§4 The suppression of an autonomous monastery of cloistered nuns pertains to the Apostolic See; the provisions of the constitutions are to be observed concerning the property of the monastery.

Chapter II

THE GOVERNANCE OF INSTITUTES

Article 1: Superiors and Councils

Can. 617 Superiors are to fulfil their office and exercise their authority in accordance with the norms of the universal law and of their own law.

Can. 618 The authority which Superiors receive from God through the ministry of the Church is to be exercised by them in a spirit of service. In fulfilling their office they are to be docile to the will of God, and are to govern those subject to them as children of God. By their reverence for the human person, they are to promote voluntary obedience. They are to listen willingly to their subjects and foster their cooperation for the good of the institute and the Church, without prejudice however to their authority to decide and to command what is to be done.

Can. 619 Superiors are to devote themselves to their office with diligence. Together with the members entrusted to them, they are to strive to build in Christ a fraternal community, in which God is sought and loved above all. They are therefore frequently to nourish their members with the food of God's word and lead them to the celebration of the liturgy. They are to be an example to the members in cultivating virtue and in observing the laws and traditions proper to the institute. They are to give the members opportune assistance in their personal needs. They are to be solicitous in caring for and visiting the sick; they are to chide the restless, console the fainthearted and be patient with all.

Can. 620 Major Superiors are those who govern an entire institute, or a province or a part equivalent to a province, or an autonomous house; the vicars of the above are also major Superiors. To these are added the Abbot Primate and the Superior of a monastic congregation, though these do not have all the authority which the universal law gives to major Superiors.

Can. 621 A province is a union of several houses which, under one superior, constitutes an immediate part of the same institute, and is canonically established by lawful authority.

Can. 622 The supreme Moderator has authority over all provinces, houses and members of the institute, to be exercised in accordance with the institute's own law. Other Superiors have authority within the limits of their office.

Can. 623 To be validly appointed or elected to the office of Superior, members must have been perpetually or definitively professed for an appropriate period of time, to be determined by their own law or, for major Superiors, by the constitutions.

Can. 624 §1 Superiors are to be constituted for a certain and appropriate period of time, according to the nature and needs of the institute, unless the constitutions establish otherwise for the supreme Moderator and for Superiors of an autonomous house.

§2 An institute's own law is to make suitable provisions so that Superiors constituted for a defined time do not continue in offices of governance for too long a period of time without an interval.

§3 During their period in office, however, Superiors may be removed or transferred to another office, for reasons prescribed in the institute's own law.

Can. 625 The supreme Moderator of the institute is to be designated by canonical election, in accordance with the constitutions.

§2 The Bishop of the principal house of the institute presides at the election of the Superior of the autonomous monastery mentioned in can. 615, and at the election of the supreme Moderator of an institute of diocesan right.

§3 Other Superiors are to be constituted in accordance with the constitutions, but in such a way that if they are elected, they require the confirmation of the competent major Superior; if they are appointed by the Superior, the appointment is to be preceded by suitable consultation.

Can. 626 Superiors in conferring offices, and members in electing to office, are to observe the norms of the universal law and the institute's own law, avoiding any abuse or preference of persons. They are to have nothing but God and the good of the institute before their eyes, and appoint or elect those whom, in the Lord, they know to be worthy and fitting. In elections, besides, they are to avoid directly or indirectly lobbying for votes, either for themselves or for others.

Can. 627 §1 Superiors are to have their own council, in accordance with the constitutions, and they must make use of it in the exercise of their office.

§2 Apart from the cases prescribed in the universal law, an institute's own law is to determine the cases in which the validity of an act depends upon consent or advice being sought in accordance with can. 127.

Can. 628 §1 Superiors who are designated for this office by the institute's own law are at stated times to visit the houses and the members entrusted to them, in accordance with the norms of the same law.

§2 The diocesan Bishop has the right and the duty to visit the following, even in respect of religious discipline:

    1° the autonomous monasteries mentioned in can. 615;

    2° the individual houses of an institute of diocesan right situated in his territory.

§3 The members are to act with confidence towards the visitator, to whom when lawfully questioning they are bound to reply truthfully and with charity. It is not lawful for anyone in any way to divert the members from this obligation or otherwise to hinder the scope of the visitation.

Can. 629 Superiors are to reside each in his or her own house, and they are not to leave it except in accordance with the institute's own law.

Can. 630 §1 While safeguarding the discipline of the institute, Superiors are to acknowledge the freedom due to the members concerning the sacrament of penance and the direction of conscience.

§2 Superiors are to take care, in accordance with the institute's own law, that the members have suitable confessors available, to whom they may confess frequently.

§3 In monasteries of cloistered nuns, in houses of formation, and in large lay communities, there are to be ordinary confessors, approved by the local Ordinary after consultation with the community. There is, however, no obligation to approach these confessors.

§4 Superiors are not to hear the confessions of their subjects unless the members spontaneously request them to do so.

§5 The members are to approach their superiors with trust and be able to open their minds freely and spontaneously to them. Superiors, however, are forbidden in any way to induce the members to make a manifestation of conscience to themselves.

Article 2: Chapters

Can. 631 §1 In an institute the general chapter has supreme authority in accordance with the constitutions. It is to be composed in such a way that it represents the whole institute and becomes a true sign of its unity in charity. Its principal functions are to protect the patrimony of the institute mentioned in can. 578 and to foster appropriate renewal in accord with that patrimony. It also elects the supreme Moderator, deals with matters of greater importance, and issues norms which all are bound to obey.

§2 The composition of the general chapter and the limits of its powers are to be defined in the constitutions. The institute's own law is to determine in further detail the order to be observed in the celebration of the chapter, especially regarding elections and the matters to be treated.

§3 According to the norms determined in the institute's own law, not only provinces and local communities, but also any individual member may freely submit their wishes and suggestions to the general chapter.

Can. 632 The institute's own law is to determine in greater detail matters concerning other chapters and other similar assemblies of the institute, that is, concerning their nature, authority, composition, procedure and time of celebration.

Can. 633 §1 Participatory and consultative bodies are faithfully to carry out the task entrusted to them, in accordance with the universal law and the institute's own law. In their own way they are to express the care and participation of all the members for the good of the whole institute or community.

§2 In establishing and utilising these means of participation and consultation, a wise discernment is to be observed, and the way in which they operate is to be in conformity with the character and purpose of the institute.

Article 3: Temporal Goods and their Administration

Can. 634 §1 Since they are by virtue of the law juridical persons, institutes, provinces and houses have the capacity to acquire, possess, administer and alienate temporal goods, unless this capacity is excluded or limited in the constitutions.

§2 They are, however, to avoid all appearance of luxury, excessive gain and the accumulation of goods.

Can. 635 §1 Since the temporal goods of religious institutes are ecclesiastical goods, they are governed by the provisions of Book V on 'The Temporal Goods of the Church', unless there is express provision to the contrary.

§2 Each institute, however, is to establish suitable norms for the use and administration of goods, so that the poverty proper to the institute may be fostered, defended and expressed.

Can. 636 §1 In each institute, and in each province ruled by a major Superior, there is to be a financial administrator, distinct from the major Superior and constituted in accordance with the institute's own law. The financial administrator is to administer the goods under the direction of the respective Superior. Even in local communities a financial administrator, distinct from the local Superior, is in so far as possible to be constituted.

§2 At the time and in the manner determined in the institute's own law, the financial administrator and others with financial responsibilities are to render an account of their administration to the competent authority.

Can. 637 Once a year, the autonomous monasteries mentioned in can. 615 are to render an account of their administration to the local Ordinary. The local Ordinary also has the right to be informed about the financial affairs of a religious house of diocesan right.

Can. 638 §1 It is for an institute's own law, within the limits of the universal law, to define the acts which exceed the purpose and the manner of ordinary administration, and to establish what is needed for the validity of an act of extraordinary administration.

§2 Besides Superiors, other officials designated for this task in the institute's own law may, within the limits of their office, validly make payments and perform juridical acts of ordinary administration.

§3 For the validity of alienation, and of any transaction by which the patrimonial condition of the juridical person could be adversely affected, there is required the written permission of the competent Superior, given with the consent of his or her council. Moreover, the permission of the Holy See is required if the transaction involves a sum exceeding that which the Holy See has determined for each region, or if it concerns things donated to the Church as a result of a vow, or objects which are precious by reason of their artistic or historical value.

§4 For the autonomous monasteries mentioned in can. 615, and for institutes of diocesan right, the written consent of the diocesan Bishop is necessary.

Can. 639   §1 If a juridical person has contracted debts and obligations, even with the permission of the Superior, it is responsible for them.

§2 If individual members have, with the permission of the Superior, entered into contracts concerning their own property, they are responsible. If, however, they have conducted business for the institute on the mandate of a Superior, the institute is responsible.

§3 If a religious has entered into a contract without any permission of Superiors, the religious is responsible, not the juridical person.

§4 However, an action can always be brought against a person who has gained from a contract entered into.

§5 Superiors are to be careful not to allow debts to be contracted unless they are certain that normal income can service the interest on the debt, and by lawful amortization repay the capital over a period which is not unduly extended.

Can. 640   Taking into account the circumstances of the individual places, institutes are to make a special effort to give, as it were, a collective testimony of charity and poverty. They are to do all in their power to donate something from their own resources to help the needs of the Church and the support of the poor.

Chapter III

THE ADMISSION OF CANDIDATES AND THE FORMATION OF MEMBERS

Article 1: Admission to the Novitiate

Can. 641   The right to admit candidates to the novitiate belongs to the major Superiors, in accordance with the norms of the institute's own law.

Can. 642   Superiors are to exercise a vigilant care to admit only those who, besides being of required age, are healthy, have a suitable disposition, and have sufficient maturity to undertake the life which is proper to the institute. If necessary, the health, disposition and maturity are to be established by experts, without prejudice to can. 220.

Can. 643   §1 The following are invalidly admitted to the novitiate:
   1° One who has not yet completed the seventeenth year of age;
   2° a spouse, while the marriage lasts;
   3° one who is currently bound by a sacred bond to some institute of consecrated life, or is incorporated in some society of apostolic life, without prejudice to can. 684;

4° one who enters the institute through force, fear or deceit, or whom the Superior accepts under the same influences;

5° one who has concealed his or her incorporation in an institute of consecrated life or society of apostolic life.

§2 An institute's own law can constitute other impediments even for the validity of admission, or attach other conditions.

Can. 644 Superiors are not to admit secular clerics to the novitiate without consulting their proper Ordinary; nor those who have debts which they are unable to meet.

Can. 645 §1 Before candidates are admitted to the novitiate they must produce proof of baptism and confirmation, and of their free status.

§2 The admission of clerics or others who had been admitted to another institute of consecrated life, to a society of apostolic life, or to a seminary, requires in addition the testimony of, respectively, the local Ordinary, or the major Superior of the institute or society, or the rector of the seminary.

§3 An institute's own law can demand further proofs concerning the suitability of candidates and their freedom from any impediment.

§4 The Superiors can seek other information, even under secrecy, if this seems necessary to them.

Article 2: The Novitiate and the Formation of Novices

Can. 646 The purpose of the novitiate, by which life in an institute begins, is to give the novices a greater understanding of their divine vocation, and of their vocation to that institute. During the novitiate the novices are to experience the manner of life of the institute and form their minds and hearts in its spirit. At the same time their resolution and suitability are to be tested.

Can. 647 §1 The establishment, transfer and suppression of a novitiate house are to take place by a written decree of the supreme Moderator of the institute, given with the consent of the council.

§2 To be valid, a novitiate must take place in a house which is duly designated for this purpose. In particular cases and by way of exception, and with the permission of the supreme Moderator given with the consent of the council, a candidate can make the novitiate in another house of the institute, under the direction of an approved religious who takes the place of the director of novices.

§3 A major Superior can allow a group of novices to reside, for a certain period of time, in another specified house of the institute.

Can. 648 §1 For validity, the novitiate must comprise twelve months spent in the novitiate community, without prejudice to the provision of can. 647 §3.

§2 To complete the formation of the novices, the constitutions can prescribe, in addition to the time mentioned in §1, one or more periods of apostolic activity, to be performed outside the novitiate community.

§3 The novitiate is not to be extended beyond two years.

Can. 649   §1 Without prejudice to the provisions of can. 647 §3, and can. 648 §2, a novitiate is invalidated by an absence from the novitiate house of more than three months, continuous or broken. Any absence of more than fifteen days must be made good.

§2 With the permission of the competent major Superior, first profession may be anticipated, though not by more than fifteen days.

Can. 650   §1 The object of the novitiate demands that novices be formed under the supervision of the director of novices, in a manner of formation to be defined by the institute's own law.

§2 The governance of the novices is reserved to the director of novices alone, under the authority of the major Superiors.

Can. 651   §1 The director of novices is to be a member of the institute who has taken perpetual vows and has been lawfully designated.

§2 If need be, directors of novices may be given assistants, who are subject to them in regard to the governance of the novitiate and the manner of formation.

§3 Those in charge of the formation of novices are to be members who have been carefully prepared, and who are not burdened with other tasks, so that they may discharge their office fruitfully and in a stable fashion.

Can. 652   §1 It is the responsibility of the directors of novices and their assistants to discern and test the vocation of the novices, and gradually to form them to lead the life of perfection which is proper to the institute.

§2 Novices are to be led to develop human and christian virtues. Through prayer and self-denial they are to be introduced to a fuller way of perfection. They are to be instructed in contemplating the mystery of salvation, and in reading and meditating on the sacred Scriptures. Their preparation is to enable them to develop their worship of God in the sacred liturgy. They are to learn how to lead a life consecrated to God and their neighbour in Christ through the evangelical counsels. They are to learn about the character and spirit of the institute, its purpose and discipline, its history and life, and be imbued with a love for the Church and its sacred Pastors.

§3 Novices, conscious of their own responsibility, are to cooperate actively with the director of novices, so that they may faithfully respond to the grace of their divine vocation.

§4 By the example of their lives and by prayer, the members of the institute are to ensure that they do their part in assisting the work of formation of the novices.

§5 The period of novitiate mentioned in can. 648 §1, is to be set aside exclusively for the work of formation. The novices are therefore not to be engaged in studies or duties which do not directly serve this formation.

Can. 653   §1 A novice may freely leave the institute. The competent authority of the institute may also dismiss a novice.

§2   On the completion of the novitiate, a novice, if judged suitable, is to be admitted to temporary profession; otherwise the novice is to be dismissed. If a doubt exists concerning suitability, the time of probation may be prolonged by the major Superior, in accordance with the institute's own law, but for a period not exceeding six months.

Article 3: Religious Profession

Can. 654   By religious profession members make a public vow to observe the three evangelical counsels. Through the ministry of the Church they are consecrated to God, and are incorporated into the institute, with the rights and duties defined by law.

Can. 655   Temporary profession is to be made for the period defined by the institute's own law. This period may not be less than three years nor longer than six years.

Can. 656   The validity of temporary profession requires:
    1° that the person making it has completed at least the eighteenth year of age;
    2° that the novitiate has been made validly;
    3° that admission has been granted, freely and in accordance with the norms of law, by the competent Superior, after a vote of his or her council;
    4° that the profession be explicit and made without force, fear or deceit;
    5° that the profession be received by the lawful Superior, personally or through another.

Can. 657   §1   When the period of time for which the profession was made has been completed, a religious who freely asks, and is judged suitable, is to be admitted to a renewal of profession or to perpetual profession; otherwise, the religious is to leave.
§2   If it seems opportune, the period of temporary profession can be extended by the competent Superior in accordance with the institute's own law. The total time during which the member is bound by temporary vows may not, however, extend beyond nine years.
§3   Perpetual profession can for a just reason be anticipated, but not by more than three months.

Can. 658   Besides the conditions mentioned in can. 656, nn. 3, 4 and 5, and others attached by the institute's own law, the validity of perpetual profession requires:
    1° that the person has completed at least the twenty-first year of age;
    2° that there has been previous temporary profession for at least three years, without prejudice to the provision of can. 657 §3.

Article 4: The Formation of Religious

Can. 659   §1 After first profession, the formation of all members in each institute is to be completed, so that they may lead the life proper to the institute more fully, and fulfil its mission more effectively.

§2 The institute's own law is, therefore, to define the nature and duration of this formation. In this, the needs of the Church and the conditions of people and times are to be kept in mind, insofar as this is required by the purpose and the character of the institute.

§3 The formation of members who are being prepared for sacred orders is governed by the universal law and the institute's own program of studies.

Can. 660   §1 Formation is to be systematic, adapted to the capacity of the members, spiritual and apostolic, both doctrinal and practical. Suitable ecclesiastical and civil degrees are to be obtained as opportunity offers.

§2 During the period of formation members are not to be given offices and undertakings which hinder their formation.

Can. 661   Religious are to be diligent in continuing their spiritual, doctrinal and practical formation throughout their lives. Superiors are to ensure that they have the assistance and the time to do this.

Chapter IV

THE OBLIGATIONS AND RIGHTS OF INSTITUTES AND OF THEIR MEMBERS

Can. 662   Religious are to find their supreme rule of life in the following of Christ as proposed in the Gospel and as expressed in the constitutions of their own institute.

Can. 663   §1 The first and principal duty of all religious is to be the contemplation of things divine and constant union with God in prayer.

§2 Each day the members are to make every effort to participate in the Eucharistic sacrifice, receive the most holy Body of Christ and adore the Lord himself present in the Sacrament.

§3 They are to devote themselves to reading the sacred Scriptures and to mental prayer. In accordance with the provisions of their own law, they are to celebrate the liturgy of the hours worthily, without prejudice to the obligation of clerics mentioned in can. 276, §2, n. 3. They are also to perform other exercises of piety.

§4 They are to have a special devotion to the Virgin Mother of God, the example and protectress of all consecrated life, including by way of the rosary.

§5 They are faithfully to observe the period of annual retreat.

Can. 664   Religious are earnestly to strive for the conversion of soul to God. They are to examine their consciences daily, and to approach the sacrament of penance frequently.

Can. 665 §1 Religious are to reside in their own religious house and observe the common life; they are not to stay elsewhere except with the permission of the Superior. For a lengthy absence from the religious house, the major Superior, for a just reason and with the consent of the council, can authorise a member to live outside a house of the institute; such an absence is not to exceed one year, unless it be for reasons of health, studies or an apostolate to be exercised in the name of the institute.

§2 Members who unlawfully absent themselves from a religious house with the intention of withdrawing from the authority of Superiors, are to be carefully sought out and helped to return and to persevere in their vocation.

Can. 666 In using the means of social communication, a necessary discretion is to be observed. Members are to avoid whatever is harmful to their vocation and dangerous to the chastity of a consecrated person.

Can. 667 §1 In accordance with the institute's own law, there is to be in all houses an enclosure appropriate to the character and mission of the institute. Some part of the house is always to be reserved to the members alone.

§2 A stricter discipline of enclosure is to be observed in monasteries which are devoted to the contemplative life.

§3 Monasteries of cloistered nuns who are wholly devoted to the contemplative life, must observe papal enclosure, that is, in accordance with the norms given by the Apostolic See. Other monasteries of cloistered nuns are to observe an enclosure which is appropriate to their nature and is defined in the constitutions.

§4 The diocesan Bishop has the faculty of entering, for a just reason, the enclosure of cloistered nuns whose monasteries are situated in his diocese. For a grave reason and with the assent of the Abbess, he can permit others to be admitted to the enclosure, and permit the nuns to leave the enclosure for whatever time is truly necessary.

Can. 668 §1 Before their first profession, members are to cede the administration of their goods to whomsoever they wish and, unless the constitutions provide otherwise, they are freely to make dispositions concerning the use and enjoyment of these goods. At least before perpetual profession, they are to make a will which is valid also in civil law.

§2 To change these dispositions for a just reason, and to take any action concerning temporal goods, there is required the permission of the Superior who is competent in accordance with the institute's own law.

§3 Whatever a religious acquires by personal labour, or on behalf of the institute, belongs to the institute. Whatever comes to a religious in any way through pension, grant or insurance also passes to the institute, unless the institute's own law decrees otherwise.

§4 When the nature of an institute requires members to renounce their goods totally, this renunciation is to be made before perpetual profession and, as far as possible, in a form that is valid also in civil law; it shall come into effect from the day of profession. The same procedure is to be followed by a perpetually professed religious who, in accordance with the norms of the institute's own law and with the permission of the supreme Moderator, wishes to renounce goods, in whole or in part.

§5 Professed religious who, because of the nature of their institute, totally renounce their goods, lose the capacity to acquire and possess goods; actions of theirs contrary to the vow of poverty are therefore invalid. Whatever they acquire after renunciation belongs to the institute, in accordance with the institute's own law.

Can. 669 §1 As a sign of their consecration and as a witness to poverty, religious are to wear the habit of their institute, determined in accordance with the institute's own law.

§2 Religious of a clerical institute who do not have a special habit are to wear clerical dress, in accordance with can. 284.

Can. 670 The institute must supply the members with everything that, in accordance with the constitutions, is necessary to fulfil the purpose of their vocation.

Can. 671 Religious are not to undertake tasks and offices outside their own institute without the permission of the lawful Superior.

Can. 672 Religious are bound by the provisions of cann. 277, 285, 286, 287 and 289. Religious who are clerics are also bound by the provisions of can. 279 §2. In lay institutes of pontifical right, the permission mentioned in can. 285 §4 can be given by the major Superior.

Chapter V

THE APOSTOLATE OF INSTITUTES

Can. 673 The apostolate of all religious consists primarily in the witness of their consecrated life, which they are bound to foster through prayer and penance.

Can. 674 Institutes which are wholly directed to contemplation always have an outstanding part in the mystical Body of Christ. They offer to God an exceptional sacrifice of praise. They embellish the people of God with very rich fruits of holiness, move them by their example, and give them increase by a hidden apostolic fruitfulness. Because of this, no matter how urgent the needs of the active apostolate, the members of these institutes cannot be called upon to assist in the various pastoral ministries.

Can. 675   §1 Apostolic action is of the very nature of institutes dedicated to apostolic works. The whole life of the members is, therefore, to be imbued with an apostolic spirit, and the whole of their apostolic action is to be animated by a religious spirit.

§2 Apostolic action is always to proceed from intimate union with God, and is to confirm and foster this union.

§3 Apostolic action exercised in the name of the Church and by its command is to be performed in communion with the Church.

Can. 676   Lay institutes of men and women participate in the pastoral mission of the Church through the spiritual and corporal works of mercy, performing very many different services for people. They are therefore to remain faithful to the grace of their vocation.

Can. 677   §1 Superiors and members are faithfully to hold fast to the mission and works which are proper to their institute. According to the needs of time and place, however, they are prudently to adapt them, making use of new and appropriate means.

§2 Institutes which have associations of Christ's faithful joined to them are to have a special care that these associations are imbued with the genuine spirit of their family.

Can. 678   §1 In matters concerning the care of souls, the public exercise of divine worship and other works of the apostolate, religious are subject to the authority of the Bishops, whom they are bound to treat with sincere obedience and reverence.

§2 In the exercise of an apostolate towards persons outside the institute, religious are also subject to their own Superiors and must remain faithful to the discipline of the institute. If the need arises, Bishops themselves are not to fail to insist on this obligation.

§3 In directing the apostolic works of religious, diocesan Bishops and religious Superiors must proceed by way of mutual consultation.

Can. 679   For a very grave reason a diocesan Bishop can forbid a member of a religious institute to remain in his diocese, provided the person's major Superior has been informed and has failed to act; the matter must immediately be reported to the Holy See.

Can. 680   Organised cooperation is to be fostered among different institutes, and between them and the secular clergy. Under the direction of the Bishop, there is to be a coordination of all apostolic works and actions, with due respect for the character and purpose of each institute and the laws of its foundation.

Can. 681   §1 Works which the diocesan Bishop entrusts to religious are under the authority and direction of the Bishop, without prejudice to the rights of religious Superiors in accordance with can. 678 §§2 and 3.

§2 In these cases a written agreement is to be made between the diocesan Bishop and the competent Superior of the institute. This agreement must expressly and accurately define, among other things, the work to be done, the members to be assigned to it and the financial arrangements.

Can. 682   §1 If an ecclesiastical office in a diocese is to be conferred on a member of a religious institute, the religious is appointed by the diocesan Bishop on presentation by, or at least with the consent of, the competent Superior.

§2 The religious can be removed from the office at the discretion of the authority who made the appointment, with prior notice being given to the religious Superior; or by the religious Superior, with prior notice being given to the appointing authority. Neither requires the other's consent.

Can. 683   §1 Either personally or through a delegate, the diocesan Bishop can visit churches or oratories to which Christ's faithful have habitual access, schools other than those open only to the institute's own members, and other works of religion and charity entrusted to religious, whether these works be spiritual or temporal. He can do this at the time of pastoral visitation, or in a case of necessity.

§2 If the diocesan Bishop becomes aware of abuses, and a warning to the religious Superior having been in vain, he can by his own authority deal with the matter.

Chapter VI
THE SEPARATION OF MEMBERS FROM THE INSTITUTE

Article 1: *Transfer to another Institute*

Can. 684   §1 Perpetually professed members cannot transfer from their own religious institute to another, except by permission of the supreme Moderators of both institutes, given with the consent of their respective councils.

§2 On completion of a probationary period of at least three years, the member can be admitted to perpetual profession in the new institute. A member who refuses to make this profession, or is not admitted to do so by the competent Superiors, is to return to the original institute, unless an indult of secularisation has been obtained.

§3 For a religious to transfer from one autonomous monastery to another monastery of the same institute, federation or confederation, the consent of the major Superior of both monasteries and of the chapter of the receiving monastery is required and is sufficient, unless the institute's own law has established further conditions. A new profession is not required.

§4 The institute's own law is to determine the time and manner of the probation which must precede the member's profession in the new institute.

§5 To transfer to a secular institute or to a society of apostolic life, or to transfer from these to a religious institute, the permission of the Holy See is required and its instructions are to be followed.

Can. 685 §1 Until profession is made in the new institute, the rights and obligations of the member in the previous institute are suspended, but the vows remain. From the beginning of probation, the member is bound to observe the laws of the new institute.

§2 By profession in the new institute the member is incorporated into it, and the earlier vows, rights and obligations cease.

Article 2: Departure from the Institute

Can. 686 §1 With the consent of his or her council, the supreme Moderator can for a grave reason grant an indult of exclaustration to a perpetually professed member for a period not exceeding three years. In the case of a cleric, the indult requires the prior consent of the Ordinary of the place where the clerics must reside. To extend this indult, or to grant one for more than three years, is reserved to the Holy See or, in an institute of diocesan right, to the diocesan Bishop.

§2 Only the Apostolic See can grant an indult of exclaustration for cloistered nuns.

§3 At the request of the supreme Moderator acting with the consent of his or her council, exclaustration can be imposed by the Holy See on a member of an institute of pontifical right, or by a diocesan Bishop on a member of an institute of diocesan right. In either case a grave reason is required, and equity and charity are to be observed.

Can. 687 Members who are exclaustrated are considered as dispensed from those obligations which are incompatible with their new condition of life. They remain dependent on and under the care of their Superiors and, particularly in the case of a cleric, of the local Ordinary. They may wear the religious habit, unless the indult specifies otherwise, but they lack active and passive voice.

Can. 688 §1 A person who, on completion of the time of temporary profession, wishes to leave the institute, is free to do so.

§2 A person who, during the time of temporary profession, for a grave reason asks to leave the institute, can obtain an indult to leave. In an institute of pontifical right, this indult can be given by the supreme Moderator with the consent of his or her council. In institutes of diocesan right and in the monasteries mentioned in can. 615, the indult must, for validity, be confirmed by the Bishop in whose diocese is located the house to which the person is assigned.

Can. 689 §1 The competent major Superior, after consulting his or council, can for just reasons exclude a member from making further profession on the completion of temporary profession.

§2 Even though contracted after profession, a physical or psychological infirmity which, in the judgement of experts, renders the member mentioned in §1 unsuited to lead a life in the institute, constitutes a reason for not admitting the member to renewal of profession or to perpetual profession, unless the infirmity was contracted through the negligence of the institute or because of work performed in the institute.

§3 A religious who becomes insane during the period of temporary vows cannot be dismissed from the institute, even though unable to make a new profession.

Can. 690   §1 A person who lawfully leaves the institute after completing the novitiate or after profession, can be re-admitted by the supreme Moderator, with the consent of his or her council, without the obligation of repeating the novitiate. The same Moderator is to determine an appropriate probation prior to temporary profession, and the length of time in vows before making perpetual profession, in accordance with the norms of can. 655 and 657.

§2 The Superior of an autonomous monastery, acting with the consent of his or her council, has the same faculty.

Can. 691   §1 A perpetually professed religious is not to seek an indult to leave the institute, except for very grave reasons, weighed before the Lord. The petition is to be presented to the supreme Moderator of the institute, who will forward it to the competent authority with his or her own opinon and that of the council.

§2 In institutes of pontifical right this indult is reserved to the Apostolic See. In institutes of diocesan right the indult can be granted by the Bishop in whose diocese is located the house to which the religious is assigned.

Can. 692   An indult to leave the institute, which is lawfully granted and notified to the member, by virtue of the law itself carries with it, unless it has been rejected by the member in the act of notification, a dispensation from the vows and from all obligations arising from profession.

Can. 693   If the member is a cleric, the indult is not granted until he has found a Bishop who will incardinate him in his diocese or at least receive him there on probation. If he is received on probation, he is by virtue of the law itself incardinated in the diocese after five years, unless the Bishop has rejected him.

Article 3: The Dismissal of Members

Can. 694   §1 A member is to be considered automatically dismissed if he or she:

    1° has notoriously defected from the catholic faith;

    2° has contracted marriage or attempted to do so, even civilly.

§2 In these cases the major Superior with his or her council must, after collecting the evidence, without delay make a declaration of the fact, so that the dismissal is juridically established.

Can. 695 §1 A member must be dismissed for the offences mentioned in cann. 1397, 1398 and 1395, unless, for the offences mentioned in can. 1395 §2, the Superior judges that dismissal is not absolutely necessary; and that sufficient provision can be made in some other way for the amendment of the member, the restoration of justice and the reparation of scandal.

§2 In these cases the major Superior is to collect the evidence concerning the facts and the imputability of the offence. The accusation and the evidence are then to be presented to the member, who shall be given the opportunity for defence. All the acts, signed by the major Superior and the notary, are to be forwarded, together with the written and signed replies of the member, to the supreme Moderator.

Can. 696 §1 A member can be dismissed for other causes, provided they are grave, external, imputable and juridically proven. Among such causes are: habitual neglect of the obligations of consecrated life; repeated violations of the sacred bonds; obstinate disobedience to the lawful orders of Superiors in grave matters; grave scandal arising from the culpable behaviour of the member; obstinate attachment to, or diffusion of, teachings condemned by the *magisterium* of the Church; public adherence to materialistic or atheistic ideologies; the unlawful absence mentioned in can. 665 §2, if it extends for a period of six months; other reasons of similar gravity which are perhaps defined in the institute's own law.

§2 A member in temporary vows can be dismissed even for less grave reasons determined in the institute's own law.

Can. 697 §1 In the cases mentioned in can. 696, if the major Superior, after consulting his or her council, judges that the process of dismissal should be commenced:

1° the major Superior is to collect or complete the evidence;

2° the major Superior is to warn the member in writing, or before two witnesses, with an explicit caution that dismissal will follow unless the member reforms. The reasons for dismissal are to be clearly expressed and the member is to be given every opportunity for defence. If the warning has no effect, another warning is to be given after an interval of at least fifteen days;

3° if this latter warning is also ineffectual, and the major Superior with his or her council judges that there is sufficient proof of incorrigibility, and that the defence by the member is insufficient, after fifteen days from the last warning have passed in vain all the acts, signed by the major Superior and the notary, are to be forwarded, together with the signed replies of the member, to the supreme Moderator.

Can. 698 In all the cases mentioned in cann. 695 and 696, the member always retains the right to communicate with, and send replies directly to, the supreme Moderator.

Can. 699 §1 The supreme Moderator and his or her council are to proceed in collegial fashion in accurately weighing the evidence, the arguments, and the defence. For validity, the council must comprise at least four members. If by a secret vote it is decided to dismiss the religious, a decree of dismissal is to be drawn up, which for validity must express at least in summary form the reasons in law and in fact.

§2 In the autonomous monasteries mentioned in can. 615, the judgement about dismissal belongs to the diocesan Bishop. The Superior is to submit the acts to him after they have been reviewed by the council.

Can. 700   The decree of dismissal has no effect unless it is confirmed by the Holy See, to whom the decree and all the acts are to be forwarded. If the matter concerns an institute of diocesan right, the confirmation belongs to the Bishop in whose diocese is located the house to which the religious belongs. For validity the decree must indicate the right of the person dismissed to have recourse to the competent authority within ten days of receiving notification of the decree. The recourse has a suspensive effect.

Can. 701   By lawful dismissal, both the vows and the rights and duties deriving from profession automatically cease. If the member is a cleric, he may not exercise sacred orders until he finds a Bishop who will, after a suitable probation, receive him into his diocese in accordance with can. 693, or who will at least allow him to exercise his sacred orders.

Can. 702   §1 Whoever lawfully leaves a religious institute or is lawfully dismissed from one, cannot claim anything from the institute for any work done in it.

§2 The institute, however, is to show equity and evangelical charity towards the member who is separated from it.

Can. 703   §1 In a case of grave external scandal, or of extremely grave and imminent harm to the institute, a member can be expelled forthwith from the house by the major Superior. If there is danger in delay, this can be done by the local Superior with the consent of his or her council. The major Superior, if need be, is to introduce a process of dismissal in accordance with the norms of law, or refer the matter to the Apostolic See.

Can. 704   In the report to be sent to the Apostolic See in accordance with can. 592, §1, mention is to be made of members who have been separated in any way from the institute.

Chapter VII

RELIGIOUS RAISED TO THE EPISCOPATE

Can. 705   A religious who is raised to the episcopate remains a member of his institute, but is subject only to the Roman Pontiff by his vow of obedience. He is not bound by obligations which he prudently judges are not compatible with his condition.

Can. 706   In the case of the religious mentioned above:

1° if he has lost the ownership of his goods through his profession, he now has the use and enjoyment and the administration of the goods which he acquires. In the case of a diocesan Bishop and of those mentioned in can. 381 §2, the particular Church acquires their ownership; in the case of others, they belong to the institute or the Holy See, depending on whether the institute is or is not capable of possessing goods;

2° if he has not lost the ownership of his goods through his profession, he recovers the use and enjoyment and the administration of the goods he possessed; what he obtains later, he acquires fully;

3° in both cases any goods he receives which are not personal gifts must be disposed of according to the intention of the donors.

Can. 707   §1 A religious Bishop 'emeritus' may choose to reside outside the house of his institute, unless the Apostolic See disposes otherwise.

§2 If he has served a diocese, can. 402 §2 is to be observed concerning his suitable and worthy maintenance, unless his own institute wishes to provide such maintenance. Otherwise, the Apostolic See is to make other provision.

Chapter VIII
CONFERENCES OF MAJOR SUPERIORS

Can. 708   Major Superiors can usefully meet together in conferences and councils, so that by combined effort they may work to achieve more fully the purpose of each institute, while respecting the autonomy, nature and spirit of each. They can also deal with affairs which are common to all, and work to establish suitable coordination and cooperation with Episcopal Conferences and with individual Bishops.

Can. 709   Conferences of major Superiors are to have their own statutes, which must be approved by the Holy See. Only the Holy See can establish them or give them juridical personality. They remain under the ultimate direction of the Holy See.

TITLE III: SECULAR INSTITUTES

Can. 710   A secular institute is an institute of consecrated life in which Christ's faithful, living in the world, strive for the perfection of charity and endeavour to contribute to the sanctification of the world, especially from within.

Can. 711   Without prejudice to the provisions of the law concerning institutes of consecrated life, consecration as a member of a secular institute does not change the member's canonical status among the people of God, be it lay or clerical.

Can. 712 Without prejudice to the provisions of can. 598–601, the constitutions are to establish the sacred bonds by which the evangelical counsels are undertaken in the institute. They are to define the obligations which these bonds entail, while always preserving in the manner of life the secular character proper to the institute.

Can. 713 §1 Members of these institutes express and exercise their special consecration in apostolic activity. Like a leaven, they endeavour to permeate everything with an evangelical spirit for the strengthening and growth of the Body of Christ.

§2 Lay members participate in the evangelising mission of the Church in the world and from within the world. They do this by their witness of christian life and of fidelity to their consecration, and by the assistance they give in directing temporal affairs to God and in animating the world by the power of the Gospel. They also offer their cooperation to serve the ecclesial community in accordance with the secular manner of life proper to them.

§3 Clerical members, by the witness of their consecrated life, especially in the *presbyterium*, support their colleagues by a distinctive apostolic charity, and in the people of God they further the sanctification of the world by their sacred ministry.

Can. 714 Members are to live their lives in the ordinary conditions of the world, either alone, in their families or in fraternal groups, in accordance with the constitutions.

Can. 715 §1 Clerical members incardinated in a diocese are subject to the diocesan Bishop, except for whatever concerns the consecrated life of their own institutes.

§2 Those who, in accordance with the norms of can. 266 §3, are incardinated in the institute, and who are appointed to works proper to the institute or to the governance of the institute, are subject to the Bishop in the same way as religious.

Can. 716 §1 All members are to take an active part in the life of the institute, in accordance with the institute's own law.

§2 Members of the same institute are to preserve a rapport with one another, carefully fostering a unity of spirit and a genuine fraternity.

Can. 717 §1 The constitutions are to determine the institute's own form of governance. They are to define the period of time for which Moderators exercise their office and the manner in which they are to be designated.

§2 No one is to be designated supreme Moderator unless definitively incorporated into the institute.

§3 Those entrusted with the governance of the institute are to ensure that its unity of spirit is maintained, and that the active participation of the members is developed.

Can. 718 The administration of the goods of the institute must express and foster evangelical poverty. It is governed by the norms of Book V on 'The Temporal Goods of the Church', and by the institute's own law. This same law of the institute is also to define the obligations, especially the financial obligations, of the institute towards the members engaged in its work.

Can. 719 §1 Members are to respond faithfully to their vocation, and their apostolic action is to proceed from their union with Christ. They are therefore to devote themselves assiduously to prayer and engage in a suitable way in the reading of the sacred Scriptures. They are to make an annual retreat and perform other spiritual exercises in accordance with their own law.

§2 The celebration of the Eucharist, daily where possible, is to be the source and strength of their whole consecrated life.

§3 They are to go freely to the sacrament of penance and receive it frequently.

§4 They are to be free to obtain the necessary spiritual direction. Should they so desire, they may seek such counsel even from their Moderators.

Can. 720 The right of admitting a person to the institute, or to probation, or to the taking of sacred bonds, both temporary and perpetual or definitive, belongs to the major Moderators with their council, in accordance with the constitutions.

Can. 721 §1 The following are invalidly admitted to initial probation:

1° one who has not yet attained majority;

2° one who is currently bound by a sacred bond in another institute of consecrated life, or incorporated in a society of apostolic life;

3° a spouse, while the marriage lasts.

§2 The constitutions can establish other impediments to admission, even for validity, or attach conditions to it.

§3 For a person to be received into the institute, that degree of maturity is required which is necessary to live the life of the institute properly.

Can. 722 §1 The initial probation is to be so arranged that the candidates can better recognise their divine vocation and their vocation to that institute, and be trained in the spirit and manner of life of the institute.

§2 Candidates are to be properly formed to live a life according to the evangelical counsels. They are to be taught how to translate this life completely into their apostolate, applying those forms of evangelisation which best correspond to the purpose, spirit and character of the institute.

§3 The constitutions are to define the manner and time of the probation to be made before the first sacred bonds are undertaken in the institute; this time is to be not less than two years.

Can. 723 §1 When the time of the initial probation has been completed, a candidate who is judged suitable is either to undertake the three evangelical counsels, sealed with a sacred bond, or to leave the institute.

§2 This first incorporation is to be temporary, in accordance with the constitutions, but is to be for not less than five years.

§3 When this period of incorporation has been completed, a member who is judged suitable is to be admitted to perpetual, or definitive incorporation, that is, by temporary bonds always to be renewed.

§4 Definitive incorporation is equivalent to perpetual incorporation in respect of defined juridical effects, which are to be established in the constitutions.

Can. 724 §1 After the first acceptance of the sacred bonds, formation is to continue without interruption in accordance with the constitutions.

§2 Members are to be formed simultaneously in matters human and divine. The Moderators of the institute are to have a serious concern for the continued spiritual formation of the members.

Can. 725 The institute can associate with itself, by some form of bond determined in the constitutions, other members of Christ's faithful who seek evangelical perfection according to the spirit of the institute and who share in its mission.

Can. 726 §1 When the time of temporary incorporation is completed, the member can freely leave the institute, or can for a just cause be excluded from renewing the sacred bonds by the major Moderator, after consultation with his or her council.

§2 A temporarily incorporated member who freely requests it, can for a grave reason be granted an indult to leave the institute by the supreme Moderator, with the consent of the council.

Can. 727 §1 A perpetually incorporated member who wishes to leave the institute must, after seriously weighing the matter before the Lord, petition the Apostolic See through the supreme Moderator, if the institute is of pontifical right; otherwise, the indult can also be obtained from the diocesan Bishop, as determined in the constitutions.

§2 For a cleric who is incardinated in the institute, the provision of can. 693 is to be observed.

Can. 728 When an indult to leave the institute has been lawfully granted, all bonds, rights and obligations deriving from incorporation cease.

Can. 729 A member is dismissed from the institute in accordance with the norms of cann. 694 and 695. The constitutions are also to determine other reasons for dismissal, provided they are proportionately grave, external, imputable and juridically proven. The procedure established in cann. 697–700 is to be observed, and the provisions of can. 701 apply to the person who is dismissed.

Can. 730 For a member to transfer from one secular institute to another, the provisions of can. 684 §§1, 2, 4 and 685, are to be observed. A transfer to or from another kind of institute of consecrated life requires the permission of the Apostolic See, whose instructions must be followed.

Section II: Societies of Apostolic Life

Can. 731 §1 Societies of apostolic life resemble institutes of consecrated life. Their members, without taking religious vows, pursue the apostolic purpose proper to each society. Living a fraternal life in common in their own special manner, they strive for the perfection of charity through the observance of the constitutions.

§2 Among these societies are some in which the members, through a bond defined in the constitutions, undertake to live the evangelical counsels.

Can. 732 Cann. 578–597 and 606 apply to societies of apostolic life, with due regard, however, for the nature of each society. For the societies mentioned in can. 731 §2, cann. 598–602 also apply.

Can. 733 §1 A house is established and a local community is constituted by the competent authority of the society, with the prior written consent of the diocesan Bishop. The Bishop must also be consulted when there is question of its suppression.

§2 Consent to establish a house carries with it the right to have at least an oratory in which the blessed Eucharist is celebrated and reserved.

Can. 734 The governance of the society is determined by the constitutions, without prejudice, in accordance with the nature of each society, to cann. 617–633.

Can. 735 §1 The admission, probation, incorporation and formation of members are determined by each society's own law.

§2 For admission into the society, the conditions prescribed in cann. 642–645 are to be observed.

§3 The society's own law must determine a programme of doctrinal, spiritual and apostolic probation and formation that is adapted to the purpose and character of the society. In this way members can recognise their divine vocation and be suitably prepared for the mission and way of life of the society.

Can. 736 §1 In clerical societies, the clerics are incardinated into the society, unless the constitutions determine otherwise.

§2 The norms concerning the secular clergy apply to the programme of studies and reception of orders, without prejudice to §1.

Can. 737   For the members, incorporation carries with it the rights and obligations defined in the constitutions. On the part of the society, it implies a responsibility to lead the members towards the purpose of their vocation, in accordance with the constitutions.

Can. 738   §1 All members are subject to their own Moderators in matters concerning the internal life and discipline of the society, in accordance with the constitutions.

§2 They are also subject to the diocesan Bishop in matters concerning public worship, the care of souls and other works of the apostolate, with due regard to cann. 679–683.

§3 The relationship between a member who is incardinated in a diocese and his proper Bishop is to be defined in the constitutions or in particular agreements.

Can. 739   Apart from the obligations which derive from their constitutions, members are bound by the common obligations of clerics, unless the nature of things or the context indicates otherwise.

Can. 740   Members must live in a lawfully constituted house or community and observe a common life, in accordance with their own law. This same law also governs their absence from the house or community.

Can. 741   §1 Societies and, unless the constitutions provide otherwise, their constituent parts and their houses, are juridical persons. As such, they are capable of acquiring, possessing, administering and alienating temporal goods in accordance with the provisions of Book V on 'The Temporal Goods of the Church', of cann. 636, 638 and 639, and of their own law.

§2 Members are also capable, in accordance with their own law, of acquiring, possessing, administering and disposing of temporal goods, but whatever comes to them in view of the society is acquired for the society.

Can. 742   The departure and dismissal of a member who is not definitively incorporated are governed by the constitutions of each society.

Can. 743   A member who is definitively incorporated can obtain an indult to leave the society from the supreme Moderator with the consent of the council, unless the constitutions reserve this to the Apostolic See. This indult means that the rights and obligations deriving from definitive incorporation cease, without prejudice to can. 693.

Can. 744   §1 Permission for a member who is definitively incorporated to transfer to another society of apostolic life is likewise reserved to the supreme Moderator with the consent of his or her council. The rights and obligations of the member's own society are suspended for the time being, but the member has the right to return to it before definitive incorporation into the new society.

§2 To transfer to an institute of consecrated life or from such an institute to a society of apostolic life, the permission of the Holy See is required, and its instructions are to be followed.

Can. 745 The supreme Moderator, with the consent of his or her council, can grant a definitively incorporated member an indult to live outside the society for a period not exceeding three years. Rights and obligations which are not compatible with this new condition are suspended, but the member remains under the care of the Moderators. If the member is a cleric, the consent of the Ordinary of the place where he must reside is also required, and the member remains under the care of the Ordinary and dependent upon him.

Can. 746 For the dismissal of a member who is definitively incorporated, the provisions of cann. 694–704 are to be observed, making the appropriate adjustments.

Book III
THE TEACHING OFFICE OF THE CHURCH

Can. 747   §1 It is the obligation and inherent right of the Church, independent of any human authority, to preach the Gospel to all peoples, using for this purpose even its own means of social communication; for it is to the Church that Christ the Lord entrusted the deposit of faith, so that by the assistance of the Holy Spirit, it might conscientiously guard revealed truth, more intimately penetrate it, and faithfully proclaim and expound it.

§2   The Church has the right always and everywhere to proclaim moral principles, even in respect of the social order, and to make judgements about any human matter in so far as this is required by fundamental human rights or the salvation of souls.

Can. 748   §1 All are bound to seek the truth in the matters which concern God and his Church; when they have found it, then by divine law they are bound, and they have the right, to embrace and keep it.

§2   It is never lawful for anyone to force others to embrace the catholic faith against their conscience.

Can. 749   §1 In virtue of his office the Supreme Pontiff is infallible in his teaching when, as chief Shepherd and Teacher of all Christ's faithful, with the duty of strengthening his brethren in the faith, he proclaims by definitive act a doctrine to be held concerning faith or morals.

§2   The College of Bishops also possesses infallibility in its teaching when the Bishops, gathered together in an Ecumenical Council and exercising their *magisterium* as teachers and judges of faith and morals, definitively declare for the universal Church a doctrine to be held concerning faith or morals; likewise, when the Bishops, dispersed throughout the world but maintaining the bond of union among themselves and with the successor of Peter, together with the same Roman Pontiff authentically teach matters of faith or morals, and are agreed that a particular teaching is definitively to be held.

§3   No doctrine is understood to be infallibly defined unless this is manifestly demonstrated.

Can. 750   Those things are to be believed by divine and catholic faith which are contained in the word of God as it has been written or handed down by tradition, that is, in the single deposit of faith entrusted to the Church, and which are at the same time proposed as divinely revealed either by the solemn *magisterium* of the Church, or by its ordinary and universal *magisterium*, which is manifested by the common adherence of Christ's faithful under the guidance of the sacred *magisterium*. All are therefore bound to shun any contrary doctrines.

Can. 751   Heresy is the obstinate denial or doubt, after baptism, of a truth which must be believed by divine and catholic faith. Apostasy is the total repudiation of the christian faith. Schism is the withdrawal of submission to the Supreme Pontiff or from communion with the members of the Church subject to him.

Can. 752   While the assent of faith is not required, a religious submission of intellect and will is to be given to any doctrine which either the Supreme Pontiff or the College of Bishops, exercising their authentic *magisterium*, declare upon a matter of faith or morals, even though they do not intend to proclaim that doctrine by definitive act. Christ's faithful are therefore to ensure that they avoid whatever does not accord with that doctrine.

Can. 753   Whether they teach individually, or in Episcopal Conferences, or gathered together in particular councils, Bishops in communion with the head and the members of the College, while not infallible in their teaching, are the authentic instructors and teachers of the faith for Christ's faithful entrusted to their care. The faithful[†] are bound to adhere, with a religious submission of mind, to this authentic *magisterium* of their Bishops.

Can. 754   All Christ's faithful are obliged to observe the constitutions and decrees which lawful ecclesiastical authority issues for the purpose of proposing doctrine or of proscribing erroneous opinions; this is particularly the case of those published by the Roman Pontiff or by the College of Bishops.

Can. 755   §1 It pertains especially to the entire College of Bishops and to the Apostolic See to foster and direct among catholics the ecumenical movement, the purpose of which is the restoration of unity between all christians which, by the will of Christ, the Church is bound to promote.

§2 It is a matter likewise for Bishops and, in accordance with the law, for Episcopal Conferences, to promote this same unity and, in line with the various needs and opportunities of the circumstances, to issue practical norms which accord with the provisions laid down by the supreme authority of the Church.

TITLE I: THE MINISTRY OF THE DIVINE WORD

Can. 756   §1 The office of preaching the Gospel to the whole Church has been committed principally to the Roman Pontiff and to the College of Bishops.

§2 For the particular Churches entrusted to them, that office is exercised by the individual Bishops, who are the moderators of the entire ministry of the word in their Churches. Sometimes, however, in accordance with the law, a number of Bishops simultaneously carry out that office together in respect of a number of different Churches.

Can. 757   It belongs to priests, as co-operators of the Bishops, to proclaim the Gospel of God. For the people entrusted to their care, this task rests especially on parish priests, and on other priests entrusted with the care of souls. Deacons also are to serve the people of God in the ministry of the word, in union with the Bishop and his *presbyterium*.

Can. 758   By reason of their consecration to God, members of institutes of consecrated life bear particular witness to the Gospel, and so are fittingly called upon by the Bishop to help in proclaiming the Gospel.

Can. 759   The lay members of Christ's faithful, by reason of their baptism and confirmation, are witnesses to the good news of the Gospel, by their words and by the example of their christian life. They can also be called upon to cooperate with Bishops and priests in the exercise of the ministry of the word.

Can. 760   The mystery of Christ is to be faithfully and fully presented in the ministry of the word, which must be founded upon sacred Scripture, Tradition, liturgy and the *magisterium* and life of the Church.

Can. 761   While pride of place must always be given to preaching and catechetical instruction, all the available means of proclaiming christian doctrine are to be used: the exposition of doctrine in schools, in institutes of higher learning, at conferences and meetings of all kinds; public declarations by lawful authority on the occasion of certain events; the printed word and other means of social communication.

Chapter I

PREACHING THE WORD OF GOD

Can. 762   The people of God are first united through the word of the living God, and are fully entitled to seek this word from their priests. For this reason sacred ministers are to consider the office of preaching as of great importance, since proclaiming the Gospel of God to all is among their principal duties.

Can. 763   Bishops have the right to preach the word of God everywhere, even in churches and oratories of religious institutes of pontifical right, unless the local Bishop has expressly forbidden it in particular cases.

Can. 764   Without prejudice to the provisions of can. 765, priests and deacons, with the at least presumed consent of the rector of a church, have the faculty to preach everywhere, unless this faculty has been restricted or removed by the competent Ordinary, or unless particular law requires express permission.

Can. 765   To preach to religious in their churches or oratories, permission is required of the Superior who is competent according to their constitutions.

Can. 766   The laity may be allowed to preach in a church or oratory if in certain circumstances it is necessary, or in particular cases it would be advantageous, according to the provisions of the Episcopal Conference and without prejudice to can. 767 §1.

Can. 767   §1 The most important form of preaching is the homily, which is part of the liturgy, and is reserved to a priest or deacon. In the course of the liturgical year, the mysteries of faith and the rules of christian living are to be expounded in the homily from the sacred text.

§2 At all Masses on Sundays and holydays of obligation, celebrated with a congregation, there is to be a homily and, except for a grave reason, this may not be omitted.

§3 It is strongly recommended that, if a sufficient number of people are present, there be a homily at weekday Masses also, especially during Advent and Lent, or on a feast day or an occasion of grief.

§4 It is the responsibility of the parish priest or the rector of a church to ensure that these provisions are carefully observed.

Can. 768   §1 Those who announce the word of God to Christ's faithful are first and foremost to set out those things which it is necessary to believe and to practise for the glory of God and the salvation of all.

§2 They are also to explain to the faithful the teaching of the *magister-ium* of the Church concerning the dignity and freedom of the human person; the unity, stability and duties of the family; people's social obligations and the ordering of temporal affairs according to the plan established by God.

Can. 769   Christian teaching is to be explained in a manner that is suited to the condition of the hearers and adapted to the circumstances of the times.

Can. 770   At certain times, according to the regulations of the diocesan Bishop, parish priests are to arrange for sermons in the form of retreats and missions, as they are called, or in other forms adapted to requirements.

Can. 771   §1 Pastors of souls, especially Bishops and parish priests, are to be solicitous that the word of God is preached to those also of the faithful who, because of the circumstances of their lives, cannot sufficiently avail themselves of the ordinary pastoral care or are even totally deprived of it.

§2 They are also to take care that the good news of the Gospel reaches those living in their territory who are non-believers, since these too, no less than the faithful, must be included in the care of souls.

Can. 772   §1 In the exercise of the office of preaching, everyone is moreover to observe the norms laid down by the Bishop of the diocese.

§2 In expounding christian teaching on radio or television, the provisions of the Episcopal Conference are to be observed.

Chapter II
CATECHICAL FORMATION

Can. 773 It is pastors of souls especially who have the serious duty of attending to the catechesis of the christian people, so that, through doctrinal formation and the experience of the christian life, the living faith of the people may be manifest and active.

Can. 774 §1 The care for catechesis, under the direction of lawful ecclesiastical authority, extends to all members of the Church, to each according to his or her role.

§2 Before all others, parents are bound to form their children, by word and example, in faith and in christian living. The same obligation binds godparents and those who take the place of parents.

Can. 775 §1 While observing provisions made by the Apostolic See, it is the responsibility of diocesan Bishops to issue norms concerning catechetical matters; to ensure that appropriate means of catechesis are available, even by preparing a catechism, if this seems opportune; to foster and to coordinate catechetical initiatives.

§2 If it is thought to be useful, the Episcopal Conference may, with the prior approval of the Apostolic See, publish catechisms for its territory.

§3 The Episcopal Conference may establish a catechetical office, whose principal purpose is to assist individual dioceses in catechetical matters.

Can. 776 By virtue of his office, the parish priest is bound to ensure the catechetical formation of adults, young people and children. To this end, he is to avail himself of the help of clerics attached to the parish, as well as of members of institutes of consecrated life and of societies of apostolic life, being mindful of the character of each institute; and the assistance of lay members of Christ's faithful, especially catechists. All of these, unless they are lawfully impeded, are not to refuse to give their labours willingly. The parish priest is also to promote and to foster the role of parents in the family catechesis mentioned in can. 774, §2.

Can. 777 In a special way, the parish priest is to ensure, in accordance with the norms laid down by the diocesan Bishop, that:

    1° an adequate catechesis is given for the celebration of the sacraments;

    2° children are properly prepared for first confession and first holy communion, and for the sacrament of confirmation, by means of catechetical formation over an appropriate period of time;

    3° children, after they have made their first holy communion, are given a richer and deeper catechetial formation;

    4° as far as their condition allows, catechetical formation is given to the mentally and physically handicapped;

    5° the faith of young people and of adults is strengthened, enlightened and developed by various catechetical methods and initiatives.

Can. 778   Religious Superiors and Superiors of societies of apostolic life are to ensure that catechetical formation is diligently given in their churches and schools, and in other works in any way entrusted to their care.

Can. 779   Catechetical formation is to be given by employing all those aids, educational resources and means of communication which seem the more effective in securing that the faithful, according to their character, capability, age and circumstances of life, may be more fully steeped in catholic teaching and prepared to put it into practice.

Can. 780   Local Ordinaries are to ensure that catechists are duly trained to carry out their office properly, namely, that continuing formation is available to them, that they have an appropriate knowledge of the teaching of the Church, and that they learn both the theory and the practice of the principles of pedagogy.

TITLE II: THE MISSIONARY ACTIVITY OF THE CHURCH

Can. 781   Because the whole Church is of its nature missionary and the work of evangelisation is to be considered a fundamental duty of the people of God, all Christ's faithful must be conscious of the responsibility to play their part in missionary activity.

Can. 782   §1 The Roman Pontiff and the College of Bishops have the responsibility for the overall direction and coordination of the initiatives and activities which concern missionary work and cooperation.
  §2 As the sponsors of the universal Church and of all the Churches, all Bishops are to have a special solicitude for missionary activity, especially by arousing, fostering and sustaining missionary initiatives in their own particular Churches.

Can. 783   Members of institutes of consecrated life, because of the dedication to the service of the Church deriving from their very consecration, have an obligation to play a zealous and special part in missionary activity, in a manner appropriate to their institute.

Can. 784   Missionaries, that is, those who have been sent by the competent ecclesiastical authority to engage in missionary activity, may be chosen from the indigenous population or from others, be they secular clergy, or members of institutes of consecrated life or of a society of apostolic life, or other lay members of Christ's faithful.

Can. 785   §1 Catechists are to be given a role in missionary work. These are lay members of Christ's faithful who have received proper formation and are outstanding in their living of the christian life. Under the direction of missionaries, they are to present the Gospel teaching and engage in liturgical worship and in works of charity.

§2 Catechists are to receive their formation in schools founded for this purpose. If there are no such schools, they are to be formed under the direction of the missionaries.

Can. 786 Missionary activity properly so called, whereby the Church is founded amongst peoples or groups where it has not taken root before, is performed principally by the Church sending heralds of the Gospel, until such time as the new Churches are fully constituted, that is, have their own resources and sufficient means, so that they themselves can carry on the work of evangelisation.

Can. 787 §1 By the testimony of their words and of their lives, missionaries are to establish a sincere dialogue with those who do not believe in Christ, so that, taking their native character and culture into account, ways may be opened up by which they can be led to know the good news of the Gospel.

§2 Missionaries are to ensure that they teach the truths of the faith to those whom they judge to be ready to receive the good news of the Gospel, so that, if they freely request it, they may be admitted to the reception of baptism.

Can. 788 §1 Those who have expressed the wish to embrace faith in Christ, and who have completed the period of their preliminary catechumenate, are to be admitted to the catechumenate proper in a liturgical ceremony; and their names are to be inscribed in the book which is kept for this purpose.

§2 By formation and their first steps in christian living, catechumens are to be initiated into the mysteries of salvation, and introduced into the life of faith, liturgy and charity of the people of God, as well as into the apostolate.

§3 It is the responsibility of the Episcopal Conference to establish norms concerning the arrangement of the catechumenate, determining what should be done by catechumens and what should be their prerogatives.

Can. 789 By means of appropriate formation, neophytes are to be led to a deeper knowledge of the Gospel truths, and to the fulfilment of the duties undertaken in baptism. They are also to be imbued with a sincere love of Christ and his Church.

Can. 790 §1 In mission territories, it is the responsibility of the diocesan Bishop:

1° to promote, regulate and coordinate both new initiatives and established works concerning missionary activity;

2° to ensure that there are proper agreements with the Moderators of those institutes which dedicate themselves to missionary activities, and that relationships with them are for the good of the mission.

§2 The provisions made by the diocesan Bishop in accordance with §1, n. 1 are binding on all missionaries, including religious and their helpers residing in his territory.

Can. 791   In order to foster missionary cooperation, in each diocese:

1° vocations to the mission are to be promoted;

2° a priest is to be appointed to promote missionary initiatives, especially the 'Pontifical Missionary Works';

3° a day for the missions is to be celebrated annually;

4° each year an appropriate financial contribution for the missions is to be sent to the Holy See.

Can. 792   The Episcopal Conference is to establish and promote means by which those who come to their territory from the missions, for the purpose of work or study, are to be given a fraternal welcome and helped with suitable pastoral care.

TITLE III: CATHOLIC EDUCATION

Can. 793   §1 Parents, and those who take their place, have both the obligation and the right to educate their children. Catholic parents have also the duty and the right to choose those means and institutes which, in their local circumstances, can best promote the catholic education of their children.

§2 Parents have moreover the right to avail themselves of that assistance from civil society which they need to provide a catholic education for their children.

Can. 794   §1 The Church has in a special way the duty and the right of educating, for it has a divine mission of helping all to arrive at the fullness of christian life.

§2 Pastors of souls have the duty of making all possible arrangements so that all the faithful may avail themselves of a catholic education.

Can. 795   Education must pay regard to the formation of the whole person, so that all may attain their eternal destiny and at the same time promote the common good of society. Children and young persons are therefore to be cared for in such a way that their physical, moral and intellectual talents may develop in a harmonious manner, so that they may attain a greater sense of responsibility and a right use of freedom, and be formed to take an active part in social life.

Chapter I

SCHOOLS

Can. 796 §1 Among the means of advancing education, Christ's faithful are to consider schools as of great importance, since they are the principal means of helping parents to fulfil their role in education.

§2 There must be the closest cooperation between parents and the teachers to whom they entrust their children to be educated. In fulfilling their task, teachers are to collaborate closely with the parents and willingly listen to them; assocations and meetings of parents are to be set up and held in high esteem.

Can. 797 Parents must have a real freedom in their choice of schools. For this reason Christ's faithful must be watchful that the civil society acknowledges this freedom of parents and, in accordance with the requirements of distributive justice, even provides them with assistance.

Can. 798 Parents are to send their children to those schools which will provide for their catholic education. If they cannot do this, they are bound to ensure the proper catholic education of their children outside the school.

Can. 799 Christ's faithful are to strive to secure that in the civil society the laws which regulate the formation of the young, also provide a religious and moral education in the schools that is in accord with the conscience of the parents.

Can. 800 §1 The Church has the right to establish and to direct schools for any field of study or of any kind and grade.

§2 Christ's faithful are to promote catholic schools, doing everything possible to help in establishing and maintaining them.

Can. 801 Religious institutes which have education as their mission are to keep faithfully to this mission and earnestly strive to devote themselves to catholic education, providing this also through their own schools which, with the consent of the diocesan Bishop, they have established.

Can. 802 §1 If there are no schools in which an education is provided that is imbued with a christian spirit, the diocesan Bishop has the responsibility of ensuring that such schools are established.

§2 Where it is suitable, the diocesan Bishop is to provide for the establishment of professional and technical schools, and of other schools catering for special needs.

Can. 803 §1 A catholic school is understood to be one which is under the control of the competent ecclesiastical authority or of a public ecclesiastical juridical person, or one which in a written document is acknowledged as catholic by the ecclesiastical authority.

§2 Formation and education in a catholic school must be based on the principles of catholic doctrine, and the teachers must be outstanding in true doctrine and uprightness of life.

§3 No school, even if it is in fact catholic, may bear the title 'catholic school' except by the consent of the competent ecclesiastical authority.

Can. 804 §1 The formation and education in the catholic religion provided in any school, and through various means of social communication, is subject to the authority of the Church. It is for the Episcopal Conference to issue general norms concerning this field of activity and for the diocesan Bishop to regulate and watch over it.

§2 The local Ordinary is to be careful that those who are appointed as teachers of religion in schools, even non-catholic ones, are outstanding in true doctrine, in the witness of their christian life, and in their teaching ability.

Can. 805 In his own diocese, the local Ordinary has the right to appoint or to approve teachers of religion and, if religious or moral considerations require it, the right to remove them or to demand that they be removed.

Can. 806 §1 The diocesan Bishop has the right to watch over and inspect the catholic schools situated in his territory, even those established or directed by members of religious institutes. He has also the right to issue directives concerning the general regulation of catholic schools; these directives apply also to schools conducted by members of a religious institute, although they retain their autonomy in the internal management of their schools.

§2 Those who are in charge of catholic schools are to ensure, under the supervision of the local Ordinary, that the formation given in them is, in its academic standards, at least as outstanding as that in other schools in the area.

Chapter II

CATHOLIC UNIVERSITIES
AND OTHER INSTITUTES OF HIGHER STUDIES

Can. 807 The Church has the right to establish and to govern universities, which serve to promote the deeper culture and fuller development of the human person, and to complement the Church's own teaching office.

Can. 808 No university, even if it is in fact catholic, may bear the title 'catholic university' except by the consent of the competent ecclesiastical authority.

Can. 809 If it is possible and appropriate, Episcopal Conferences are to take care to have within their territories suitably located universities or at least faculties, in which the various disciplines, while retaining their own scientific autonomy, may be researched and taught in the light of catholic doctrine.

Can. 810   §1 In catholic universities it is the duty of the competent statutory authority to ensure that there be appointed teachers who are not only qualified in scientific and pedagogical expertise, but are also outstanding in their integrity of doctrine and uprightness of life. If these requirements are found to be lacking, it is also that authority's duty to see to it that these teachers are removed from office, in accordance with the procedure determined in the statutes.

§2   The Episcopal Conference and the diocesan Bishops concerned have the duty and the right of seeing to it that, in these universities, the principles of catholic doctrine are faithfully observed.

Can. 811   §1 The competent ecclesiastical authority is to ensure that in catholic universities there is established a faculty or an institute or at least a chair of theology, in which lectures are given to lay students also.

§2   In every catholic university there are to be lectures which principally treat of those theological questions connected with the studies of each faculty.

Can. 812   Those who teach theological subjects in any institute of higher studies must have a mandate from the competent ecclesiastical authority.

Can. 813   The diocesan Bishop is to be zealous in his pastoral care of students, even by the creation of a special parish, or at least by appointing priests with a stable assignment to this care. In all universities, even in those which are not catholic, the diocesan Bishop is to provide catholic university centres, to be of assistance to the young people, especially in spiritual matters.

Can. 814   The provisions which are laid down for universities apply equally to other institutes of higher studies.

Chapter III

ECCLESIASTICAL UNIVERSITIES AND FACULTIES

Can. 815   By virtue of its office to announce revealed truth, it belongs to the Church to have its own ecclesiastical universities and faculties to study the sacred sciences and subjects related to them, and to teach these disciplines to students in a scientific manner.

Can. 816   §1 Ecclesiastical universities and faculties may be constituted only by the Apostolic See or with its approval. Their overall direction also belongs to the Apostolic See.

§2   Each ecclesiastical university and faculty must have its own statutes and program of studies, approved by the Apostolic See.

Can. 817   Only a university or a faculty established or approved by the Apostolic See may confer academic degrees which have canonical effects in the Church.

Can. 818   The provisions of cann. 810, 812 and 813 concerning catholic universities apply also to ecclesiastical universities and faculties.

Can. 819   In so far as the good of a diocese or religious institute or indeed even of the universal Church requires it, young persons, clerics and members of institutes, outstanding in character, intelligence and virtue, must be sent to ecclesiastical universities or faculties by their diocesan Bishops or the Superiors of their institutes.

Can. 820   Moderators and professors of ecclesiastical universities and faculties are to ensure that the various faculties of the university cooperate with each other, to the extent that their aims permit. They are also to ensure that between their own university or faculty and other universities and faculties, even non-ecclesiastical ones, there be a mutual cooperation in which, through conferences, coordinated scientific research and other means, they work together for the greater increase of scientific knowledge.

Can. 821   Where it is possible, the Episcopal Conference and the diocesan Bishop are to provide for the establishment of institutes for higher religious studies, in which are taught theological and other subjects pertaining to christian culture.

TITLE IV
THE MEANS OF SOCIAL COMMUNICATION AND BOOKS IN PARTICULAR

Can. 822   §1 In exercising their office the pastors of the Church, availing themselves of a right which belongs to the Church, are to make an ample use of the means of social communication.

§2 Pastors are also to teach the faithful that they have the duty of working together so that the use of the means of social communication may be imbued with a human and christian spirit.

§3 All Christ's faithful, especially those who in any way take part in the management or use of the media, are to be diligent in assisting pastoral action, so that the Church can more effectively exercise its office through these means.

Can. 823   §1 In order to safeguard the integrity of faith and morals, pastors of the Church have the duty and the right to ensure that in writings or in the use of the means of social communication there should be no ill effect on the faith and morals of Christ's faithful. They also have the duty and the right to demand that where writings of the faithful[†] touch upon matters of faith and morals, these be submitted to their judgement. Moreover, they have the duty and the right to condemn writings which harm true faith or good morals.

§2 For Christ's faithful entrusted to their care, the duty and the right mentioned in §1 belong to the Bishops, both as individuals and in particular councils or Episcopal Conferences; for the whole people of God, they belong to the supreme authority in the Church.

Can. 824 §1 Unless it is otherwise provided, the local Ordinary whose permission or approval for publishing a book is to be sought according to the canons of this title, is the author's proper local Ordinary, or the Ordinary of the place in which the book is published.

§2 Unless the contrary is clear, what is said in the canons of this title about books, applies also to any writings intended for publication.

Can. 825 §1 Books of the sacred Scriptures may not be published unless they are approved by the Apostolic See or the Episcopal Conference. The publication of translations of the sacred Scriptures requires the approval of the same authority, and they must have necessary and sufficient explanatory notes.

§2 With the permission of the Episcopal Conference, catholic members of Christ's faithful, in cooperation with separated brethren, may prepare and publish versions of the Scriptures, with appropriate explanatory notes.

Can. 826 §1 For liturgical books, the provisions of can. 838 are to be observed.

§2 To republish liturgical books or to publish translations of all or part of them, it must be established, by an attestation of the Ordinary of the place in which they are published, that they accord with an approved edition.

§3 Prayer books, for either the public or the private use of the faithful, are not to be published except by permission of the local Ordinary.

Can. 827 §1 Without prejudice to the provisions of can. 775 §2, the publication of catechisms and other writings pertaining to catechetical formation, as well as their translations, requires the approval of the local Ordinary.

§2 Books dealing with matters concerning sacred Scripture, theology, canon law, church history, or religious or moral subjects may not be used as textbooks on which the instruction is based, in elementary, intermediate or higher schools, unless they were published with the approbation of the competent ecclesiastical authority or were subsequently approved by that authority.

§3 It is recommended that books dealing with the subjects mentioned in §2, even though not used as basic textbooks, and any writings which specially concern religion or good morals, be submitted to the judgement of the local Ordinary.

§4 Books or other written material dealing with religion or morals may not be displayed, sold or given away in churches or oratories, unless they were published with the permission of the competent ecclesiastical authority or were subsequently approved by that authority.

Can. 828 Collections of decrees or acts published by any ecclesiastical authority may not be republished without first seeking the permission of the same authority and observing the conditions which it lays down.

Can. 829 Approval or permission to publish a work is valid only for the first edition, but not for new editions or translations.

Can. 830 §1 Every local Ordinary retains the right to appoint persons whom he considers competent to give a judgement about books. The Episcopal Conference, however, may draw up a list of censors who are outstanding for their knowledge, right doctrine and prudence, to be available to diocesan curias; it may even establish a commission of censors whom the local Ordinary can consult.
§2 In carrying out this task, a censor must put aside all preference of persons and look only to the teaching of the Church concerning faith and morals, as declared by its *magisterium*.
§3 The censor must give an opinion in writing. If it is favourable, the Ordinary may, in his prudent judgement, give his permission for the work to be published, adding his own name and the date and place of the permission. If he does not give this permission, the Ordinary must inform the author of the reasons for the refusal.

Can. 831 §1 Unless there is a just and reasonable cause, no member of Christ's faithful may write in newspapers, pamphlets or periodicals which clearly are accustomed to attack the catholic religion or good morals. Clerics and members of religious institutes may write in them only with the permission of the local Ordinary.
§2 It is for the Episcopal Conference to lay down norms determining the requirements for clerics and members of religious institutes to take part in radio and television programmes which concern catholic doctrine or morals.

Can. 832 To publish writings on matters of religion or morals, members of religious institutes require also the permission of their major Superior, in accordance with the constitutions.

TITLE V: THE PROFESSION OF FAITH

Can. 833 The following are personally bound to make a profession of faith, according to the formula approved by the Apostolic See:
1° in the presence of the president or his delegate: all who, with a

deliberative or a consultative vote, take part in an Ecumenical Council, a particular council, the synod of Bishops, or a diocesan synod; in the presence of the council or synod: the president himself;

2° in accordance with the statutes of the sacred College: those promoted to the dignity of Cardinal;

3° in the presence of a delegate of the Apostolic See: all who are promoted to the episcopate, and all those who are equivalent to a diocesan Bishop;

4° in the presence of the college of consultors: the diocesan Administrator;

5° in the presence of the diocesan Bishop or his delegate: Vicars general, episcopal Vicars and judicial Vicars;

6° in the presence of the local Ordinary or his delegate: parish priests; the rector, professors of theology and philosophy in seminaries, at the beginning of their term of office; and those who are to be promoted to the order of diaconate;

7° in the presence of the Chancellor or, in the absence of the Chancellor, the local Ordinary, or the delegates of either: the rector of an ecclesiastical or catholic university, at the beginning of the term of office; in the presence of the rector if he is a priest, or of the local Ordinary or the delegates of either: those who in any universities teach subjects which deal with faith or morals, at the beginning of their term of office;

8° in accordance with the constitutions: Superiors in religious institutes and clerical societies of apostolic life.

Book IV
THE SANCTIFYING
OFFICE OF THE CHURCH

Can. 834   §1 The Church carries out its office of sanctifying in a special way in the sacred liturgy, which is an exercise of the priestly office of Jesus Christ. In the liturgy, by the use of signs perceptible to the senses, our sanctification is symbolised and, in a manner appropriate to each sign, is brought about. Through the liturgy a complete public worship is offered to God by the head and members of the mystical body of Christ.

§2 This worship takes place when it is offered in the name of the Church, by persons lawfully deputed and through actions approved by ecclesiastical authority.

Can. 835   §1 The sanctifying office is exercised principally by Bishops, who are the high priests, the principal dispensers of the mysteries of God and the moderators, promoters and guardians of the entire liturgical life in the Churches entrusted to their care.

§2 This office is also exercised by priests. They, too, share in the priesthood of Christ and, as his ministers under the authority of the Bishop, are consecrated to celebrate divine worship and to sanctify the people.

§3 Deacons have a share in the celebration of divine worship in accordance with the provisions of law.

§4 The other members of Christ's faithful have their own part in this sanctifying office, each in his or her own way actively sharing in liturgical celebrations, particlarly in the Eucharist. Parents have a special share in this office when they live their married lives in a christian spirit and provide for the christian education of their children.

Can. 836   Since christian worship, in which the common priesthood of Christ's faithful is exercised, must proceed from and rest upon faith, sacred ministers are to strive diligently to arouse and enlighten this faith, especially by the ministry of the word by which faith is born and nourished.

Can. 837   §1 Liturgical actions are not private but are celebrations of the Church itself as the 'sacrament of unity', that is, the holy people united and ordered under the Bishops. Accordingly, they concern the whole body of the Church, making it known and influencing it. They affect individual members of the Church in ways that vary according to orders, role and actual participation.

§2 Since liturgical matters by their very nature call for a community celebration, they are, as far as possible, to be celebrated in the presence of Christ's faithful and with their active participation.

Can. 838   §1 The ordering and guidance of the sacred liturgy depends solely upon the authority of the Church, namely, that of the Apostolic See and, as provided by law, that of the diocesan Bishop.

§2 It is the prerogative of the Apostolic See to regulate the sacred liturgy of the universal Church, to publish liturgical books and review their vernacular translations, and to be watchful that liturgical regulations are everywhere faithfully observed.

§3 It pertains to Episcopal Conferences to prepare vernacular translations of liturgical books, with appropriate adaptations as allowed by the books themselves and, with the prior review of the Holy See, to publish these translations.

§4 Within the limits of his competence, it belongs to the diocesan Bishop to lay down for the Church entrusted to his care, liturgical regulations which are binding on all.

Can. 839 §1 The Church carries out its sanctifying office by other means also, that is by prayer, in which it asks God to make Christ's faithful holy in the truth, and by works of penance and charity, which play a large part in establishing and strengthening in souls the Kingdom of Christ, and so contribute to the salvation of the world.

§2 Local Ordinaries are to ensure that the prayers and the pious and sacred practices of the christian people are in full harmony with the laws of the Church.

Part I
THE SACRAMENTS

Can. 840 The sacraments of the New Testament were instituted by Christ the Lord and entrusted to the Church. As actions of Christ and of the Church, they are signs and means by which faith is expressed and strengthened, worship is offered to God and our sanctification is brought about. Thus they contribute in the most effective manner to establishing, strengthening and manifesting ecclesiastical communion. Accordingly, in the celebration of the sacraments both the sacred ministers and all the other members of Christ's faithful must show great reverence and due care.

Can. 841 Since the sacraments are the same throughout the universal Church, and belong to the divine deposit of faith, only the supreme authority in the Church can approve or define what is needed for their validity. It belongs to the same authority, or to another competent authority in accordance with can. 838 §§3 and 4, to determine what is required for their lawful celebration, administration and reception and for the order to be observed in their celebration.

Can. 842 §1 A person who has not received baptism cannot validly be admitted to the other sacraments.

§2 The sacraments of baptism, confirmation and the blessed Eucharist so complement one another that all three are required for full christian initiation.

Can. 843 §1 Sacred ministers may not deny the sacraments to those who opportunely ask for them, are properly disposed and are not prohibited by law from receiving them.

§2 According to their respective offices in the Church, both pastors of souls and all other members of Christ's faithful have a duty to ensure that those who ask for the sacraments are prepared for their reception. This should be done through proper evangelisation and catechetical instruction, in accordance with the norms laid down by the competent authority.

Can. 844 §1 Catholic ministers may lawfully administer the sacraments only to catholic members of Christ's faithful, who equally may lawfully receive them only from catholic ministers, except as provided in §§2, 3 and 4 of this canon and in can. 861 §2.

§2 Whenever necessity requires or a genuine spiritual advantage commends it, and provided the danger of error or indifferentism is avoided, Christ's faithful for whom it is physically or morally impossible to approach a catholic minister, may lawfully receive the sacraments of penance, the Eucharist and anointing of the sick from non-catholic ministers in whose Churches these sacraments are valid.

§3 Catholic ministers may lawfully administer the sacraments of penance, the Eucharist and anointing of the sick to members of the eastern Churches not in full communion with the catholic Church, if they spontaneously ask for them and are properly disposed. The same applies to members of other Churches which the Apostolic See judges to be in the same position as the aforesaid eastern Churches so far as the sacraments are concerned.

§4 If there is a danger of death or if, in the judgement of the diocesan Bishop or of the Episcopal Conference, there is some other grave and pressing need, catholic ministers may lawfully administer these same sacraments to other christians not in full communion with the catholic Church, who cannot approach a minister of their own community and who spontaneously ask for them, provided that they demonstrate the catholic faith in respect of these sacraments and are properly disposed.

§5 In respect of the cases dealt with in §§2, 3 and 4, the diocesan Bishop or the Episcopal Conference is not to issue general norms except after consultation with the competent authority, at least at the local level, of the non-catholic Church or community concerned.

Can. 845   §1 Because they imprint a character, the sacraments of baptism, confirmation and order cannot be repeated.

§2 If after diligent enquiry a prudent doubt remains as to whether the sacraments mentioned in §1 have been conferred at all, or conferred validly, they are to be conferred conditionally.

Can. 846   §1 The liturgical books, approved by the competent authority, are to be faithfully followed in the celebration of the sacraments. Accordingly, no one may on a personal initiative add to or omit or alter anything in those books.

§2 The ministers are to celebrate the sacraments according to their own rite.

Can. 847   §1 In administering sacraments in which holy oils are to be used, the minister must use oil made from olives or other plants, which, except as provided in can. 999, n. 2, has recently been consecrated or blessed by a Bishop. Older oil is not to be used except in a case of necessity.

§2 The parish priest is to obtain the holy oils from his own Bishop and keep them carefully in fitting custody.

Can. 848   For the administration of the sacraments the minister may not ask for anything beyond the offerings which are determined by the competent authority, and he must always ensure that the needy are not deprived of the help of the sacraments by reason of poverty.

TITLE I: BAPTISM

Can. 849 Baptism, the gateway to the sacraments, is necessary for salvation, either by actual reception or at least by desire. By it people are freed from sins, are born again as children of God and, made like to Christ by an indelible character, are incorporated into the Church. It is validly conferred only by a washing in real water with the proper form of words.

Chapter I

THE CELEBRATION OF BAPTISM

Can. 850 Baptism is administered according to the rite prescribed in the approved liturgical books, except in a case of urgent necessity when only those elements which are required for the validity of the sacrament must be observed.

Can. 851 The celebration of baptism should be properly prepared. Accordingly:

1° an adult who intends to receive baptism is to be admitted to the catechumenate and, as far as possible, brought through the various stages to sacramental initiation, in accordance with the rite of initiation as adapted by the Episcopal Conference and with the particular norms issued by it;

2° the parents of a child who is to be baptised, and those who are to undertake the office of sponsors, are to be suitably instructed on the meaning of this sacrament and the obligations attaching to it. The parish priest is to see to it that either he or others duly prepare the parents, by means of pastoral advice and indeed by prayer together; a number of families might be brought together for this purpose and, where possible, each family visited.

Can. 852 §1 The provisions of the canons on adult baptism apply to all those who, being no longer infants, have reached the use of reason.

§2 One who is incapable of personal responsibility is regarded as an infant even in regard to baptism.

Can. 853 Apart from a case of necessity, the water to be used in conferring baptism is to be blessed, in accordance with the provisions of the liturgical books.

Can. 854 Baptism is to be conferred either by immersion or by pouring, in accordance with the provisions of the Episcopal Conference.

Can. 855 Parents, sponsors and parish priests are to take care that a name is not given which is foreign to christian sentiment.

Can. 856 Though baptism may be celebrated on any day, it is recommended that normally it be celebrated on a Sunday or, if possible, on the vigil of Easter.

Can. 857 §1 Apart from a case of necessity, the proper place for baptism is a church or an oratory.

§2 As a rule and unless a just reason suggests otherwise, an adult is to be baptised in his or her proper parish church, and an infant in the proper parish church of the parents.

Can. 858 §1 Each parish church is to have a baptismal font, without prejudice to the same right already acquired by other churches.

§2 The local Ordinary, after consultation with the local parish priest, may for the convenience of the faithful permit or order that a baptismal font be placed also in another church or oratory within the parish.

Can. 859 If, because of distance or other circumstances, the person to be baptised cannot without grave inconvenience go or be brought to the parish church or the oratory mentioned in can. 858 §2, baptism may and must be conferred in some other church or oratory which is nearer, or even in some other fitting place.

Can. 860 §1 Apart from a case of necessity, baptism is not to be conferred in private houses, unless the local Ordinary should for a grave reason permit it.

§2 Unless the diocesan Bishop has decreed otherwise, baptism is not to be conferred in hospital, except in a case of necessity or for some other pressing pastoral reason.

Chapter II

THE MINISTER OF BAPTISM

Can. 861 §1 The ordinary minister of baptism is a Bishop, a priest or a deacon, without prejudice to the provision of can. 530, n. 1.

§2 If the ordinary minister is absent or impeded, a catechist or some other person deputed to this office by the local Ordinary, may lawfully confer baptism; indeed, in a case of necessity, any person who has the requisite intention may do so. Pastors of souls, especially parish priests, are to be diligent in ensuring that Christ's faithful are taught the correct way to baptise.

Can. 862 Except in a case of necessity, it is unlawful for anyone without due permission to confer baptism outside his own territory, not even upon his own subjects.

Can. 863 The baptism of adults, at least of those who have completed their fourteenth year, is to be referred to the Bishop, so that he himself may confer it if he judges this appropriate.

Chapter III

THE PERSONS TO BE BAPTISED

Can. 864   Every unbaptised person, and only such a person, can be baptised.

Can. 865   §1 To be admitted to baptism, an adult must have manifested the intention to receive baptism, must be adequately instructed in the truths of the faith and in the duties of a christian, and tested in the christian life over the course of the catechumenate. The person must moreover be urged to have sorrow for personal sins.

§2 An adult in danger of death may be baptised if, with some knowledge of the principal truths of the faith, he or she has in some manner manifested the intention to receive baptism and promises to observe the requirements of the christian religion.

Can. 866   Unless there is a grave reason to the contrary, immediately after receiving baptism an adult is to be confirmed, to participate in the celebration of the Eucharist and to receive holy communion.

Can. 867   §1 Parents are obliged to see that their infants are baptised within the first few weeks. As soon as possible after the birth, indeed even before it, they are to approach the parish priest to ask for the sacrament for their child, and to be themselves duly prepared for it.

§2 If the infant is in danger of death, it is to be baptised without any delay.

Can. 868   §1 For an infant to be baptised lawfully it is required:
    1° that the parents, or at least one of them, or the person who lawfully holds their place, give their consent;
    2° that there be a well-founded hope that the child will be brought up in the catholic religion. If such hope is truly lacking, the baptism is, in accordance with the provisions of particular law, to be deferred and the parents advised of the reason for this.

§2 An infant of catholic parents, indeed even of non-catholic parents, may in danger of death be baptised even if the parents are opposed to it.

Can. 869   §1 If there is doubt as to whether a person was baptised or whether a baptism was conferred validly, and after serious enquiry this doubt persists, the person is to be baptised conditionally.

§2 Those baptised in a non-catholic ecclesial community are not to be baptised conditionally unless there is a serious reason for doubting the validity of their baptism, on the ground of the matter or the form of words used in the baptism, or of the intention of the adult being baptised or of that of the baptising minister.

§3 If in the cases mentioned in §§1 and 2 a doubt remains about the conferring of the baptism or its validity, baptism is not to be conferred until the doctrine of the sacrament of baptism is explained to the person to be baptised, if that person is an adult. Moreover, the reasons for doubting the validity of the earlier baptism should be given to the person or, where an infant is concerned, to the parents.

Can. 870 An abandoned infant or a foundling is to be baptised unless diligent enquiry establishes that it has already been baptised.

Can. 871 Aborted foetuses, if they are alive, are to be baptised, in so far as this is possible.

Chapter IV
SPONSORS

Can. 872 In so far as possible, a person being baptised is to be assigned a sponsor. In the case of an adult baptism, the sponsor's role is to assist the person in christian initiation. In the case of an infant baptism, the role is together with the parents to present the child for baptism, and to help it to live a christian life befitting the baptised and faithfully to fulfil the duties inherent in baptism.

Can. 873 One sponsor, male or female, is sufficient; but there may be two, one of each sex.

Can. 874 §1 To be admitted to undertake the office of sponsor, a person must:
　　1° be appointed by the candidate for baptism, or by the parents or whoever stands in their place, or failing these, by the parish priest or the minister; to be appointed the person must be suitable for this role and have the intention of fulfilling it;
　　2° be not less than sixteen years of age, unless a different age has been stipulated by the diocesan Bishop, or unless the parish priest or the minister considers that there is a just reason for an exception to be made;
　　3° be a catholic who has been confirmed and has received the blessed Eucharist, and who lives a life of faith which befits the role to be undertaken;
　　4° not labour under a canonical penalty, whether imposed or declared;
　　5° not be either the father or the mother of the person to be baptised.
　§2 A baptised person who belongs to a non-catholic ecclesial community may be admitted only in company with a catholic sponsor, and then simply as a witness to the baptism.

Chapter V

PROOF AND REGISTRATION OF BAPTISM

Can. 875 Whoever administers baptism is to take care that if there is not a sponsor present, there is at least one witness who can prove that the baptism was conferred.

Can. 876 To prove that baptism has been conferred, if there is no conflict of interest, it is sufficient to have either one unexceptionable witness or, if the baptism was conferred upon an adult, the sworn testimony of the baptised person.

Can. 877 §1 The parish priest of the place in which the baptism was conferred must carefully and without delay record in the register of baptism the names of the baptised, the minister, the parents, the sponsors and, if there were such, the witnesses, and the place and date of baptism. He must also enter the date and place of birth.

§2 In the case of a child of an unmarried mother, the mother's name is to be entered if her maternity is publicly known or if, either in writing or before two witnesses, she freely asks that this be done. Similarly, the name of the father is to be entered, if his paternity is established either by some public document or by his own declaration in the presence of the parish priest and two witnesses. In all other cases, the name of the baptised person is to be registered, without any indication of the name of the father or of the parents.

§3 In the case of an adopted child, the names of the adopting parents are to be registered and, at least if this is done in the local civil registration, the names of the natural parents in accordance with §§1 and 2, subject however to the rulings of the Episcopal Conference.

Can. 878 If baptism was administered neither by the parish priest nor in his presence, the minister of baptism, whoever that was, must notify the parish priest of the parish in which the baptism was administered, so that he may register the baptism in accordance with can. 877 §1.

TITLE II: THE SACRAMENT OF CONFIRMATION

Can. 879 The sacrament of confirmation confers a character. By it the baptised continue their path of christian initiation. They are enriched with the gift of the Holy Spirit, and are more closely linked to the Church. They are made strong and more firmly obliged by word and deed to witness to Christ and to spread and defend the faith.

Part I   The Sacraments

Chapter I

THE CELEBRATION OF CONFIRMATION

Can. 880 §1 The sacrament of confirmation is conferred by anointing with chrism on the forehead in a laying on of hands, and by the words prescribed in the approved liturgical books.

§2 The chrism to be used in the sacrament of confirmation must have been consecrated by a Bishop, even when the sacrament is administered by a priest.

Can. 881 It is desirable that the sacrament of confirmation be celebrated in a church and indeed during Mass. However, for a just and reasonable cause it may be celebrated apart from Mass and in any fitting place.

Chapter II

THE MINISTER OF CONFIRMATION

Can. 882 The ordinary minister of confirmation is a Bishop. A priest can also validly confer this sacrament if he has the faculty to do so, either from the general law or by way of a special grant from the competent authority.

Can. 883 The following have, by law, the faculty to administer confirmation:

    1° within the confines of their jurisdiction, those who in law are equivalent to a diocesan Bishop;

    2° in respect of the person to be confirmed, the priest who by virtue of his office or by mandate of the diocesan Bishop baptises an adult or admits a baptised adult into full communion with the catholic Church;

    3° in respect of those in danger of death, the parish priest or indeed any priest.

Can. 884 §1 The diocesan Bishop is himself to administer confirmation or to ensure that it is administered by another Bishop. If necessity so requires, he may grant to one or several specified priests the faculty to administer this sacrament.

§2 For a grave reason the Bishop, or the priest who by law or by special grant of the competent authority has the faculty to confirm, may in individual cases invite other priests to join with him in administering the sacrament.

Can. 885 §1 The diocesan Bishop is bound to ensure that the sacrament of confirmation is conferred upon his subjects who duly and reasonably request it.

§2 A priest who has this faculty must use it for those in whose favour it was granted.

Can. 886 §1 A Bishop in his own diocese may lawfully administer the sacrament of confirmation even to the faithful who are not his subjects, unless there is an express prohibition by their own Ordinary.

§2 In order lawfully to administer confirmation in another diocese, unless it be to his own subjects, a Bishop needs the permission, at least reasonably presumed, of the diocesan Bishop.

Can. 887 A priest who has the faculty to administer confirmation may, within the territory assigned to him, lawfully administer this sacrament even to those from outside the territory, unless there is a prohibition by their own Ordinary. He cannot, however, validly confirm anyone in another territory, without prejudice to the provision of can. 883, n. 3.

Can. 888 Within the territory in which they can confer confirmation, ministers may confirm even in exempt places.

Chapter III

THE PERSONS TO BE CONFIRMED

Can. 889 §1 Every baptised person who is not confirmed, and only such a person, is capable of receiving confirmation.

§2 Apart from the danger of death, to receive confirmation lawfully a person who has the use of reason must be suitably instructed, properly disposed and able to renew the baptismal promises.

Can. 890 The faithful are bound to receive this sacrament at the proper time. Parents and pastors of souls, especially parish priests, are to see that the faithful are properly instructed to receive the sacrament and come to it at the opportune time.

Can. 891 The sacrament of confirmation is to be conferred on the faithful at about the age of discretion, unless the Episcopal Conference has decided on a different age, or there is a danger of death or, in the judgement of the minister, a grave reason suggests otherwise.

Chapter IV

SPONSORS

Can. 892 As far as possible the person to be confirmed is to have a sponsor. The sponsor's function is to take care that the person confirmed behaves as a true witness of Christ and faithfully fulfils the duties inherent in this sacrament.

Can. 893 §1 A person who would undertake the office of sponsor must fulfil the conditions mentioned in can.874.

§2 It is desirable that the sponsor chosen be the one who undertook this role at baptism.

Chapter V
PROOF AND REGISTRATION OF CONFIRMATION

Can. 894   To establish that confirmation has been conferred, the provisions of can. 876 are to be observed.

Can. 895   The names of those confirmed, the minister, the parents, the sponsors and the place and date of the confirmation are to be recorded in the confirmation register of the diocesan curia or, wherever this has been prescribed by the Episcopal Conference or by the diocesan Bishop, in the register to be kept in the parochial archive. The parish priest must notify the parish priest of the place of the baptism that the confirmation was conferred, so that it be recorded in the baptismal register, in accordance with can. 535 §2.

Can. 896   If the parish priest of the place was not present, the minister, personally or through someone else, is to notify him as soon as possible that the confirmation was conferred.

TITLE III: THE BLESSED EUCHARIST

Can. 897   The most venerable sacrament is the blessed Eucharist, in which Christ the Lord himself is contained, offered and received, and by which the Church continually lives and grows. The eucharistic Sacrifice, the memorial of the death and resurrection of the Lord, in which the Sacrifice of the cross is forever perpetuated, is the summit and the source of all worship and christian life. By means of it the unity of God's people is signified and brought about, and the building up of the body of Christ is perfected. The other sacraments and all the apostolic works of Christ are bound up with, and directed to, the blessed Eucharist.

Can. 898   Christ's faithful are to hold the blessed Eucharist in the highest honour. They should take an active part in the celebration of the most august Sacrifice of the Mass; they should receive the sacrament with great devotion and frequently, and should reverence it with the greatest adoration. In explaining the doctrine of this sacrament, pastors of souls are assiduously to instruct the faithful about their obligation in this regard.

Chapter I

THE CELEBRATION OF THE EUCHARIST

Can. 899   §1 The celebration of the Eucharist is an action of Christ himself and of the Church. In it Christ the Lord, through the ministry of the priest, offers himself, substantially present under the appearances of bread and wine, to God the Father, and gives himself as spiritual nourishment to the faithful who are associated with him in his offering.

§2 In the eucharistic assembly the people of God are called together under the presidency of the Bishop or of a priest authorised by him, who acts in the person of Christ. All the faithful present, whether clerics or lay people, unite to participate in their own way, according to their various orders and liturgical roles.

§3 The eucharistic celebration is to be so ordered that all the participants derive from it the many fruits for which Christ the Lord instituted the eucharistic Sacrifice.

Article 1: The Minister of the Blessed Eucharist

Can. 900   §1 The only minister who, in the person of Christ, can bring into being the sacrament of the Eucharist, is a validly ordained priest.

§2 Any priest who is not debarred by canon law may lawfully celebrate the Eucharist, provided the provisions of the following canons are observed.

Can. 901   A priest is entitled to offer Mass for anyone, living or dead.

Can. 902   Unless the benefit of Christ's faithful requires or suggests otherwise, priests may concelebrate the Eucharist; they are, however, fully entitled to celebrate the Eucharist individually, but not while a celebration is taking place in the same church or oratory.

Can. 903   A priest is to be permitted to celebrate the Eucharist, even if he is not known to the rector of the church, provided either that he presents commendatory letters, not more than a year old, from his own Ordinary or Superior, or that it can be prudently judged that he is not debarred from celebrating.

Can. 904   Remembering always that in the mystery of the eucharistic Sacrifice the work of redemption is continually being carried out, priests are to celebrate frequently. Indeed, daily celebration is earnestly recommended, because, even if it should not be possible to have the faithful present, it is an action of Christ and of the Church in which priests fulfil their principal role.

Can. 905   §1 Apart from those cases in which the law allows him to celebrate or concelebrate the Eucharist a number of times on the same day, a priest may not celebrate more than once a day.

§2 If there is a scarcity of priests, the local Ordinary may for a good reason allow priests to celebrate twice in one day or even, if pastoral need requires it, three times on Sundays or holydays of obligation.

Can. 906   A priest may not celebrate the eucharistic Sacrifice without the participation of at least one of the faithful, unless there is a good and reasonable cause for doing so.

Can. 907   In the celebration of the Eucharist, deacons and lay persons are not permitted to say the prayers, especially the eucharistic prayer, nor to perform the actions which are proper to the celebrating priest.

Can. 908   Catholic priests are forbidden to concelebrate the Eucharist with priests or ministers of Churches or ecclesial communities which are not in full communion with the catholic Church.

Can. 909   A priest is not to omit dutifully to prepare himself by prayer before the celebration of the Eucharist, nor afterwards to omit to make thanksgiving to God.

Can. 910   §1 The ordinary minister of holy communion is a Bishop, a priest or a deacon.

§2 The extraordinary minister of holy communion is an acolyte, or another of Christ's faithful deputed in accordance with can. 230 §3.

Can. 911   §1 The duty and right to bring the blessed Eucharist to the sick as Viaticum belongs to the parish priest, to assistant priests, to chaplains and, in respect of all who are in the house, to the community Superior in clerical religious institutes or societies of apostolic life.

§2 In a case of necessity, or with the permission at least presumed of the parish priest, chaplain or Superior, who must subsequently be notified, any priest or other minister of holy communion must do this.

Article 2: Participation in the Blessed Eucharist

Can. 912   Any baptised person who is not forbidden by law may and must be admitted to holy communion.

Can. 913   §1 For holy communion to be administered to children, it is required that they have sufficient knowledge and be accurately prepared, so that according to their capacity they understand what the mystery of Christ means, and are able to receive the Body of the Lord with faith and devotion.

§2 The blessed Eucharist may, however, be administered to children in danger of death if they can distinguish the Body of Christ from ordinary food and receive communion with reverence.

Can. 914   It is primarily the duty of parents and of those who take their place, as it is the duty of the parish priest, to ensure that children who have reached the use of reason are properly prepared and, having made their sacramental confession, are nourished by this divine food as soon as possible. It is also the duty of the parish priest to see that children who have not reached the use of reason, or whom he has judged to be insufficiently disposed, do not come to holy communion.

Can. 915   Those upon whom the penalty of excommunication or interdict has been imposed or declared, and others who obstinately persist in manifest grave sin, are not to be admitted to holy communion.

Can. 916   Anyone who is conscious of grave sin may not celebrate Mass or receive the Body of the Lord without previously having been to sacramental confession, unless there is a grave reason and there is no opportunity to confess; in this case the person is to remember the obligation to make an act of perfect contrition, which includes the resolve to go to confession as soon as possible.

Can. 917   One who has received the blessed Eucharist may receive it again on the same day only within a eucharistic celebration in which that person participates, without prejudice to the provision of can. 921 §2.

Can. 918   It is most strongly recommended that the faithful receive holy communion in the course of a eucharistic celebration. If, however, for good reason they ask for it apart from the Mass, it is to be administered to them, observing the liturgical rites.

Can. 919   §1 Whoever is to receive the blessed Eucharist is to abstain for at least one hour before holy communion from all food and drink, with the sole exception of water and medicine.
§2 A priest who, on the same day, celebrates the blessed Eucharist twice or three times may consume something before the second or third celebration, even though there is not an hour's interval.
§3 The elderly and those who are suffering from some illness, as well as those who care for them, may receive the blessed Eucharist even if within the preceding hour they have consumed something.

Can. 920   §1 Once admitted to the blessed Eucharist, each of the faithful is obliged to receive holy communion at least once a year.
§2 This precept must be fulfilled during paschal time, unless for a good reason it is fulfilled at another time during the year.

Can. 921   §1 Christ's faithful who are in danger of death, from whatever cause, are to be strengthened by holy communion as Viaticum.
§2 Even if they have already received holy communion that same day, it is nevertheless strongly suggested that in danger of death they should communicate again.
§3 While the danger of death persists, it is recommended that holy communion be administered a number of times, but on separate days.

Can. 922 Holy Viaticum for the sick is not to be unduly delayed. Those who have the care of souls are to take assiduous care that the sick are strengthened by it while they are in full possession of their faculties.

Can. 923 Christ's faithful may participate in the eucharistic Sacrifice and receive holy communion in any catholic rite, without prejudice to the provisions of can. 844.

Article 3: The Rites and Ceremonies of the Eucharistic Celebration

Can. 924 §1 The most holy Sacrifice of the Eucharist must be celebrated in bread, and in wine to which a small quantity of water is to be added.

§2 The bread must be wheaten only, and recently made, so that there is no danger of corruption.

§3 The wine must be natural, made from grapes of the vine, and not corrupt.

Can. 925 Holy communion is to be given under the species of bread alone or, in accordance with the liturgical laws, under both species or, in case of necessity, even under the species of wine alone.

Can. 926 In the eucharistic celebration, in accordance with the ancient tradition of the latin Church, the priest is to use unleavened bread wherever he celebrates Mass.

Can. 927 It is absolutely wrong, even in urgent and extreme necessity, to consecrate one element without the other, or even to consecrate both outside the eucharistic celebration.

Can. 928 The eucharistic celebration is to be carried out either in the latin language or in another language, provided the liturgical texts have been lawfully approved.

Can. 929 In celebrating and administering the Eucharist, priests and deacons are to wear the sacred vestments prescribed by the rubrics.

Can. 930 §1 A priest who is ill or elderly, if he is unable to stand, may celebrate the eucharistic Sacrifice sitting but otherwise observing the liturgical laws; he may not, however, do so in public except by permission of the local Ordinary.

§2 A priest who is blind or suffering from some other infirmity, may lawfully celebrate the eucharistic Sacrifice by using the text of any approved Mass, with the assistance, if need be, of another priest or deacon or even a properly instructed lay person.

Article 4: The Time and Place of the Eucharistic Celebration

Can. 931 The celebration and distribution of the Eucharist may take place on any day and at any hour, except those which are excluded by the liturgical laws.

Can. 932   §1 The eucharistic celebration is to be carried out in a sacred place, unless in a particular case necessity requires otherwise; in which case the celebration must be in a fitting place.

§2 The eucharistic Sacrifice must be carried out at an altar that is dedicated or blessed. Outside a sacred place an appropriate table may be used, but always with an altar cloth and a corporal.

Can. 933   For a good reason, with the express permission of the local Ordinary and provided scandal has been eliminated, a priest may celebrate the Eucharist in a place of worship of any Church or ecclesial community which is not in full communion with the catholic Church.

Chapter II

THE RESERVATION AND VENERATION OF THE BLESSED EUCHARIST

Can. 934   §1 The blessed Eucharist:

  1° must be reserved in the cathedral church or its equivalent, in every parish church, and in the church or oratory attached to the house of a religious institute or society of apostolic life;

  2° may be reserved in a Bishop's chapel and, by permission of the local Ordinary, in other churches, oratories and chapels.

§2 In sacred places where the blessed Eucharist is reserved there must always be someone who is responsible for it, and as far as possible a priest is to celebrate Mass there at least twice a month.

Can. 935   It is not lawful for anyone to keep the blessed Eucharist in personal custody or to carry it around, unless there is an urgent pastoral need and the prescriptions of the diocesan Bishop are observed.

Can. 936   In a house of a religious institute or other house of piety, the blessed Eucharist is to be reserved only in the church or principal oratory attached to the house. For a just reason, however, the Ordinary can permit it to be reserved also in another oratory of the same house.

Can. 937   Unless there is a grave reason to the contrary, a church in which the blessed Eucharist is reserved is to be open to the faithful for at least some hours every day, so that they can pray before the blessed Sacrament.

Can. 938   §1 The blessed Eucharist is to be reserved habitually in only one tabernacle of a church or oratory.

§2 The tabernacle in which the blessed Eucharist is reserved should be sited in a distinguished place in the church or oratory, a place which is conspicuous, suitably adorned and conducive to prayer.

§3 The tabernacle in which the blessed Eucharist is habitually reserved is to be immovable, made of solid and non-transparent material, and so locked as to give the greatest security against any danger of profanation.

§4 For a grave reason, especially at night, it is permitted to reserve the blessed Eucharist in some other safer place, provided it is fitting.

§5 The person in charge of a church or oratory is to see to it that the key of the tabernacle in which the blessed Eucharist is reserved, is in maximum safe keeping.

Can. 939 Consecrated hosts, in a quantity sufficient for the needs of the faithful, are to be kept in a pyx or ciborium, and are to be renewed frequently, the older hosts having been duly consumed.

Can. 940 A special lamp is to burn continuously before the tabernacle in which the blessed Eucharist is reserved, to indicate and to honour the presence of Christ.

Can. 941 §1 In churches or oratories which are allowed to reserve the blessed Eucharist, there may be exposition, either with the pyx or with the monstrance, in accordance with the norms prescribed in the liturgical books.

§2 Exposition of the blessed Sacrament may not take place while Mass is being celebrated in the same area of the church or oratory.

Can. 942 It is recommended that in these churches or oratories, there is to be each year a solemn exposition of the blessed Sacrament for an appropriate, even if not for a continuous time, so that the local community may more attentively meditate on and adore the eucharistic mystery. This exposition is to take place only if a fitting attendance of the faithful is foreseen, and the prescribed norms are observed.

Can. 943 The minister of exposition of the blessed Sacrament and of the eucharistic blessing is a priest or deacon. In special circumstances the minister of exposition and deposition alone, but without the blessing, is an acolyte, and extraordinary minister of holy communion, or another person deputed by the local Ordinary, in accordance with the regulations of the diocesan Bishop.

Can. 944 §1 Wherever in the judgement of the diocesan Bishop it can be done, a procession through the streets is to be held, especially on the solemnity of the Body and Blood of Christ, as a public witness of veneration of the blessed Eucharist.

§2 It is for the diocesan Bishop to establish such regulations about processions as will provide for participation in them and for their being carried out in a dignified manner.

Chapter III

THE OFFERING MADE FOR THE CELEBRATION OF MASS

Can. 945   §1 In accordance with the approved custom of the Church, any priest who celebrates or concelebrates a Mass may accept an offering to apply the Mass for a specific intention.

§2 It is earnestly recommended to priests that, even if they do not receive an offering, they celebrate Mass for the intentions of Christ's faithful, especially of those in need.

Can. 946   The faithful[†] who make an offering so that Mass can be celebrated for their intention, contribute to the good of the Church, and by that offering they share in the Church's concern for the support of its ministers and its activities.

Can. 947   Even the semblance of trafficking or trading is to be entirely excluded from Mass offerings.

Can. 948   Separate Masses must be applied for the intentions of those for whom an individual offering, even if small, has been made and accepted.

Can. 949   One who is obliged to celebrate and apply Mass for the intentions of those who made an offering, is bound by this obligation even if the offering received is lost through no fault of his.

Can. 950   If a sum of money is offered for the application of Masses, but with no indication of the number of Masses to be celebrated, their number is to be calculated on the basis of the offering prescribed in the place where the donor resides, unless the donor's intention must lawfully be presumed to have been otherwise.

Can. 951   §1 A priest who celebrates a number of Masses on the same day may apply each Mass for the intention for which an offering was made, subject however to the rule that, apart from Christmas Day, he may retain for himself the offering for only one Mass; the others he is to transmit to purposes prescribed by the Ordinary, while allowing for some compensation on the ground of an extrinsic title.

§2 A priest who on the same day concelebrates a second Mass may not under any title accept an offering for that Mass.

Can. 952   §1 The provincial council or the provincial Bishops' meeting is to determine by decree, for the whole of the province, what offering is to be made for the celebration and application of Mass. Nonetheless, it is permitted to accept, for the application of a Mass, an offering voluntarily made, which is greater, or even less, than that which has been determined.

§2 Where there is no such decree, the custom existing in the diocese is to be observed.

§3 Members of religious institutes of all kinds must abide by the decree or the local custom mentioned in §§1 and 2.

Can. 953 No one may accept more offerings for Masses to be celebrated by himself than he can discharge within a year.

Can. 954 If in certain churches or oratories more Masses are requested than can be celebrated there, these may be celebrated elsewhere, unless the donors have expressly stipulated otherwise.

Can. 955 §1 One who intends to transfer to others the celebration of Masses to be applied, is to transfer them as soon as possible to priests of his own choice, provided he is certain that they are of proven integrity. He must transfer the entire offering received, unless it is quite certain that an amount in excess of the diocesan offering was given as a personal gift. Moreover, it is his obligation to see to the celebration of the Masses until such time as he has received evidence that the obligation has been undertaken and the offering received.

§2 Unless it is established otherwise, the time within which Masses are to be celebrated begins from the day the priest who is to celebrate them receives them.

§3 Those who transfer to others Masses to be celebrated are without delay to record in a book both the Masses which they have accepted and those which they have passed on, noting also the offerings for these Masses.

§4 Each priest must accurately record the Masses which he has accepted to celebrate and those which he has in fact celebrated.

Can. 956 Each and every administrator of pious causes and those, whether clerics or lay persons, who are in any way obliged to provide for the celebration of Masses, are to transfer to their Ordinaries, in a manner to be determined by the latter, such Mass obligations as have not been discharged within a year.

Can. 957 The duty and the right to see that Mass obligations are fulfilled belongs, in the case of churches of the secular clergy, to the local Ordinary; in the case of churches of religious institutes or societies of apostolic life, to their Superiors.

Can. 958 §1 The parish priest, as well as the rector of a church or other pious place in which Mass offerings are usually received, is to have a special book in which he is accurately to record the number, the intention and the offering of the Masses to be celebrated, and the fact of their celebration.

§2 The Ordinary is obliged to inspect these books each year, either personally or through others.

TITLE IV: THE SACRAMENT OF PENANCE

Can. 959 In the sacrament of penance the faithful who confess their sins to a lawful minister, are sorry for those sins and have a purpose of amendment, receive from God, through the absolution given by that minister, forgiveness of sins they have committed after baptism, and at the same time they are reconciled with the Church, which by sinning they wounded.

Chapter I

THE CELEBRATION OF THE SACRAMENT

Can. 960 Individual and integral confession and absolution constitute the sole ordinary means by which a member of the faithful who is conscious of grave sin is reconciled with God and with the Church. Physical or moral impossibility alone excuses from such confession, in which case reconciliation may be attained by other means also.

Can. 961 §1 General absolution, without prior individual confession, cannot be given to a number of penitents together, unless:
    1° danger of death threatens and there is not time for the priest or priests to hear the confessions of the individual penitents;
    2° there exists a grave necessity, that is, given the number of penitents, there are not enough confessors available properly to hear the individual confessions within an appropriate time, so that without fault of their own the penitents are deprived of the sacramental grace or of holy communion for a lengthy period of time. A sufficient necessity is not, however, considered to exist when confessors cannot be available merely because of a great gathering of penitents, such as can occur on some major feastday or pilgrimage.
    §2 It is for the diocesan Bishop to judge whether the conditions required in §1, n. 2 are present; mindful of the criteria agreed with the other members of the Episcopal Conference, he can determine the cases of such necessity.

Can. 962 §1 For a member of Christ's faithful to benefit validly from a sacramental absolution given to a number of people simultaneously, it is required not only that he or she be properly disposed, but be also at the same time personally resolved to confess in due time each of the grave sins which cannot for the moment be thus confessed.
    §2 Christ's faithful are to be instructed about the requirements set out in §1, as far as possible even on the occasion of general absolution being received. An exhortation that each person should make an act of contrition is to precede a general absolution, even in the case of danger of death if there is time.

Can. 963 Without prejudice to the obligation mentioned in can. 989, a person whose grave sins are forgiven by a general absolution, is as soon as possible, when the opportunity occurs, to make an individual confession before receiving another general absolution, unless a just reason inter venes.

Can. 964 §1 The proper place for hearing sacramental confessions is a church or oratory.

§2 As far as the confessional is concerned, norms are to be issued by the Episcopal Conference, with the proviso however that confessionals, which the faithful who so wish may freely use, are located in an open place, and fitted with a fixed grille between the penitent and the confessor.

§3 Except for a just reason, confessions are not to be heard elsewhere than in a confessional.

Chapter II
THE MINISTER OF THE SACRAMENT OF PENANCE

Can. 965 Only a priest is the minister of the sacrament of penance.

Can. 966 §1 For the valid absolution of sins, it is required that, in addition to the power of order, the minister has the faculty to exercise that power in respect of the faithful to whom he gives absolution.

§2 A priest can be given this faculty either by the law itself, or by a concession issued by the competent authority in accordance with can. 969.

Can. 967 §1 Besides the Roman Pontiff, Cardinals by virtue of the law itself have the faculty to hear the confessions of Christ's faithful everywhere. Likewise, Bishops have this faculty, which they may lawfully use everywhere, unless in a particular case the diocesan Bishop has refused.

§2 Those who have the faculty habitually to hear confessions, whether by virtue of their office or by virtue of a concession by the Ordinary of either the place of incardination or that in which they have a domicile, can exercise that faculty everywhere, unless in a particular case the local Ordinary has refused, without prejudice to the provisions of can. 974 §§2 and 3.

§3 In respect of the members and of those others who live day and night in a house of an institute or society, this same faculty is by virtue of the law itself possessed everywhere by those who have the faculty to hear confessions, whether by virtue of their office or by virtue of a special concession of the competent Superior in accordance with cann. 968 §2 and 969 §2. They may lawfully use this faculty, unless in a particular case some major Superior has, in respect of his own subjects, refused.

Can. 968 §1 By virtue of his office, for each within the limits of his jurisdiction, the faculty to hear confessions belongs to the local Ordinary, to the canon penitentiary, to the parish priest, and to those others who are in the place of the parish priest.

§2 By virtue of their office, the faculty to hear the confessions of their own subjects and of those others who live day and night in the house, belongs to the Superiors of religious institutes or of societies of apostolic life, if they are clerical and of pontifical right, who in accordance with the constitutions have executive power of governance, without prejudice however to the provision of can. 630 §4.

Can. 969   §1 Only the local Ordinary is competent to give to any priests whomsoever the faculty to hear the confessions of any whomsoever of the faithful. Priests who are members of religious institutes may not, however, use this faculty without the permission, at least presumed, of their Superior.

§2 The Superior of a religious institute or of a society of apostolic life, mentioned in can. 968 §2, is competent to give to any priests whomsoever the faculty to hear the confessions of his own subjects and of those others who live day and night in the house.

Can. 970   The faculty to hear confessions is not to be given except to priests whose suitability has been established, either by examination or by some other means.

Can. 971   The local Ordinary is not to give the faculty habitually to hear confessions to a priest, even to one who has a domicile or quasi-domicile within his jurisdiction, without first, as far as possible, consulting that priest's own Ordinary.

Can. 972   The faculty to hear confessions may be given by the competent authority mentioned in can. 969, for either an indeterminate or a determinate period of time.

Can. 973   The faculty habitually to hear confessions is to be given in writing.

Can. 974   §1 Neither the local Ordinary nor the competent Superior may, except for a grave reason, revoke the grant of a faculty habitually to hear confessions.

§2 If the faculty to hear confessions granted by the local Ordinary mentioned in can. 967, §2, is revoked by that Ordinary, the priest loses the faculty everywhere. If the faculty is revoked by another local Ordinary, the priest loses it only in the territory of the Ordinary who revokes it.

§3 Any local Ordinary who has revoked a priest's faculty to hear confessions is to notify the Ordinary who is proper to that priest by reason of incardination or, if the priest is a member of a religious institute, his competent Superior.

§4 If the faculty to hear confessions is revoked by his own major Superior, the priest loses everywhere the faculty to hear the confessions of the members of the institute. But if the faculty is revoked by another competent Superior, the priest loses it only in respect of those subjects who are in that Superior's jurisdiction.

Can. 975   Apart from revocation, the faculty mentioned in can. 967 §2 ceases by loss of office, by excardination, or by loss of domicile.

Can. 976   Any priest, even though he lacks the faculty to hear confessions, can validly and lawfully absolve any penitents who are in danger of death, from any censures and sins, even if an approved priest is present.

Can. 977   The absolution of a partner in a sin against the sixth commandment of the Decalogue is invalid, except in danger of death.

Can. 978   §1 In hearing confessions the priest is to remember that he is at once both judge and healer, and that he is constituted by God as a minister of both divine justice and divine mercy, so that he may contribute to the honour of God and the salvation of souls.

§2 In administering the sacrament, the confessor, as a minister of the Church, is to adhere faithfully to the teaching of the *magisterium* and to the norms laid down by the competent authority.

Can. 979   In asking questions the priest is to act with prudence and discretion, taking into account the condition and the age of the penitent, and he is to refrain from enquiring the name of a partner in sin.

Can. 980   If the confessor is in no doubt about the penitent's disposition and the penitent asks for absolution, it is not to be denied or delayed.

Can. 981   The confessor is to impose salutary and appropriate penances, in proportion to the kind and number of sins confessed, taking into account, however, the condition of the penitent. The penitent is bound personally to fulfil these penances.

Can. 982   A person who confesses to having falsely denounced to ecclesiastical authority a confessor innocent of the crime of solicitation to a sin against the sixth commandment of the Decalogue, is not to be absolved unless that person has first formally withdrawn the false denunciation and is prepared to make good whatever harm may have been done.

Can. 983   §1 The sacramental seal is inviolable. Accordingly, it is absolutely wrong for a confessor in any way to betray the penitent, for any reason whatsoever, whether by word or in any other fashion.

§2 An interpreter, if there is one, is also obliged to observe this secret, as are all others who in any way whatever have come to a knowledge of sins from a confession.

Can. 984   §1 The confessor is wholly forbidden to use knowledge acquired in confession to the detriment of the penitent, even when all danger of disclosure is excluded.

§2 A person who is in authority may not in any way, for the purpose of external governance, use knowledge about sins which has at any time come to him from the hearing of confession.

Can. 985 The director and assistant director of novices, and the rector of a seminary or of any other institute of education, are not to hear the sacramental confessions of their students resident in the same house, unless in individual instances the students of their own accord request it.

Can. 986 §1 All to whom by virtue of office the care of souls is committed, are bound to provide for the hearing of the confessions of the faithful entrusted to them, who reasonably request confession, and they are to provide these faithful with an opportunity to make individual confession on days and at times arranged to suit them.

§2 In an urgent necessity, every confessor is bound to hear the confessions of Christ's faithful, and in danger of death every priest is so obliged.

Chapter III

THE PENITENT

Can. 987 In order that the faithful may receive the saving remedy of the sacrament of penance, they must be so disposed that, repudiating the sins they have committed and having the purpose of amending their lives, they turn back to God.

Can. 988 §1 The faithful are bound to confess, in kind and in number, all grave sins committed after baptism, of which after careful examination of conscience they are aware, which have not yet been directly pardoned by the keys of the Church, and which have not been confessed in an individual confession.

§2 The faithful are recommended to confess also venial sins.

Can. 989 All the faithful who have reached the age of discretion are bound faithfully to confess their grave sins at least once a year.

Can. 990 No one is forbidden to confess through an interpreter, provided however that abuse and scandal are avoided, and without prejudice to the provision of can. 983 §2.

Can. 991 All Christ's faithful are free to confess their sins to lawfully approved confessors of their own choice, even to one of another rite.

Chapter IV
INDULGENCES

Can. 992   An indulgence is the remission in the sight of God of the temporal punishment due for sins, the guilt of which has already been forgiven. A member of Christ's faithful who is properly disposed and who fulfils certain specific conditions, may gain an indulgence by the help of the Church which, as the minister of redemption, authoritatively dispenses and applies the treasury of the merits of Christ and the Saints.

Can. 993   An indulgence is partial or plenary according as it partially or wholly frees a person from the temporal punishment due for sins.

Can. 994   All members of the faithful can gain indulgences, partial or plenary, for themselves, or they can apply them by way of suffrage to the dead.

Can. 995   §1 Apart from the supreme authority in the Church, only those can grant indulgences to whom this power is either acknowledged in the law, or given by the Roman Pontiff.
   §2 No authority below the Roman Pontiff can give to others the faculty of granting indulgences, unless this authority has been expressly given to the person by the Apostolic See.

Can. 996   §1 To be capable of gaining indulgences a person must be baptised, not excommunicated, and in the state of grace at least on the completion of the prescribed work.
   §2 To gain them, however, the person who is capable must have at least the intention of gaining them, and must fulfil the prescribed works at the time and in the manner determined by the terms of the grant.

Can. 997   As far as the granting and the use of indulgences is concerned, the other provisions contained in the special laws of the Church must also be observed.

TITLE VI
THE SACRAMENT OF ANOINTING OF THE SICK

Can. 998   The anointing of the sick, by which the Church commends to the suffering and glorified Lord the faithful who are dangerously ill so that he may support and save them, is conferred by anointing them with oil and pronouncing the words prescribed in the liturgical books.

Chapter I

THE CELEBRATION OF THE SACRAMENT

Can. 999   The oil to be used in the anointing of the sick can be blessed not only by a Bishop but also by:
1° those who are in law equivalent to the diocesan Bishop;
2° in a case of necessity, any priest but only in the actual celebration of the sacrament.

Can. 1000   §1 The anointings are to be carried out accurately, with the words and in the order and manner prescribed in the liturgical books. In a case of necessity, however, a single anointing on the forehead, or even on another part of the body, is sufficient while the full formula is recited.
§2 The minister is to anoint with his own hand, unless a grave reason indicates the use of an instrument.

Can. 1001   Pastors of souls and those who are close to the sick are to ensure that the sick are helped by this sacrament in good time.

Can. 1002   The communal celebration of anointing of the sick, for a number of the sick together, who have been appropriately prepared and are rightly disposed, may be held in accordance with the regulations of the diocesan Bishop.

Chapter II

THE MINISTER OF ANOINTING OF THE SICK

Can. 1003   §1 Every priest, but only a priest, can validly administer the anointing of the sick.
§2 All priests to whom has been committed the care of souls, have the obligation and the right to administer the anointing of the sick to those of the faithful entrusted to their pastoral care. For a reasonable cause, any other priest may administer this sacrament if he has the consent, at least presumed, of the aforementioned priest.
§3 Any priest may carry the holy oil with him, so that in a case of necessity he can administer the sacrament of anointing of the sick.

Chapter III

THOSE TO BE ANOINTED

Can. 1004   §1 The anointing of the sick can be administered to any member of the faithful who, having reached the use of reason, begins to be in danger of death by reason of illness or old age.
§2 This sacrament can be repeated if the sick person, having recovered, again becomes seriously ill or if, in the same illness, the danger becomes more serious.

Can. 1005   If there is any doubt as to whether the sick person has reached the age of reason, or is dangerously ill, or is dead, this sacrament is to be administered.

Can. 1006 This sacrament is to be administered to the sick who, when they were in possession of their faculties, at least implicitly asked for it.

Can. 1007 The anointing of the sick is not to be conferred upon those who obstinately persist in a manifestly grave sin.

TITLE VI: ORDERS

Can. 1008 By divine institution some among Christ's faithful are, through the sacrament of order, marked with an indelible character and are thus constituted sacred ministers; thereby they are consecrated and deputed so that, each according to his own grade, they fulfil, in the person of Christ the Head, the offices of teaching, sanctifying and ruling, and so they nourish the people of God.

Can. 1009 §1 The orders are the episcopate, the priesthood and the diaconate.

§2 They are conferred by the imposition of hands and the prayer of consecration which the liturgical books prescribe for each grade.

Chapter I

THE CELEBRATION OF ORDINATION AND THE MINISTER

Can. 1010 An ordination is to be celebrated during Mass, on a Sunday or holyday of obligation. For pastoral reasons, however, it may take place on other days also, even on ferial days.

Can. 1011 §1 An ordination is normally to be celebrated in the cathedral church. For pastoral reasons, however, it may be celebrated in another church or oratory.

§2 Clerics and other members of Christ's faithful are to be invited to attend an ordination, so that the greatest possible number may be present at the celebration.

Can. 1012 The minister of sacred ordination is a consecrated Bishop.

Can. 1013 No Bishop is permitted to consecrate anyone as Bishop, unless it is first established that a pontifical mandate has been issued.

Can. 1014 Unless a dispensation has been granted by the Apostolic See, the principal consecrating Bishop at an episcopal consecration is to have at least two other consecrating Bishops with him. It is, however, entirely appropriate that all the Bishops present should join with these in consecrating the Bishop-elect.

Can. 1015   §1 Each candidate is to be ordained to the priesthood or to the diaconate by his proper Bishop, or with lawful dimissorial letters granted by that Bishop.

§2 If not impeded from doing so by a just reason, a Bishop is himself to ordain his own subjects. He may not, however, without an apostolic indult lawfully ordain a subject of an oriental rite.

§3 Anyone who is entitled to give dimissorial letters for the reception of orders may also himself confer these orders, if he is a Bishop.

Can. 1016   In what concerns the ordination to the diaconate of those who intend to enrol themselves in the secular clergy, the proper Bishop is the Bishop of the diocese in which the aspirant has a domicile, or the Bishop of the diocese to which he intends to devote himself. In what concerns the priestly ordination of the secular clergy, it is the Bishop of the diocese in which the aspirant was incardinated by the diaconate.

Can. 1017   A Bishop may not confer orders outside his own jurisdiction except with the permission of the diocesan Bishop.

Can. 1018   §1 The following can give dimissorial letters for the secular clergy:
    1° the proper Bishop mentioned in can. 1016;
    2° the apostolic Administrator; with the consent of the college of consultors, the diocesan Administrator; with the consent of the council mentioned in can. 495 §2, the Pro-vicar and Pro-prefect apostolic.

§2 The diocesan Administrator, the Pro-vicar and Pro-prefect apostolic are not to give dimissorial letters to those to whom admission to orders was refused by the diocesan Bishop or by the Vicar or Prefect apostolic.

Can. 1019   §1 It belongs to the major Superior of a clerical religious institute of pontifical right or of a clerical society of apostolic life of pontifical right to grant dimissorial letters for the diaconate and for the priesthood to his subjects who are, in accordance with the constitutions, perpetually or definitively enrolled in the institute or society.

§2 The ordination of all other candidates of whatever institute or society, is governed by the law applying to the secular clergy, any indult whatsoever granted to Superiors being revoked.

Can. 1020   Dimissorial letters are not to be granted unless all the testimonials and documents required by the law in accordance with cann. 1050 and 1051 have first been obtained.

Can. 1021   Dimissorial letters may be sent to any Bishop in communion with the Apostolic See, but not to a Bishop of a rite other than that of the ordinand, unless there is an apostolic indult.

Can. 1022   When the ordaining Bishop has received the prescribed dimissorial letters, he may proceed to the ordination only when the authenticity of these letters is established beyond any doubt whatever.

Can. 1023   Dimissorial letters can be limited or can be revoked by the person granting them or by his successor; once granted, they do not lapse on the expiry of the grantor's authority.

Chapter II
THOSE TO BE ORDAINED

Can. 1024   Only a baptised man can validly receive sacred ordination.

Can. 1025   §1 In order lawfully to confer the orders of priesthood or diaconate, it must have been established, in accordance with the proofs laid down by law, that in the judgement of the proper Bishop or competent major Superior, the candidate possesses the requisite qualities, that he is free of any irregularity or impediment, and that he has fulfilled the requirements set out in can. 1033–1039. Moreover, the documents mentioned in can. 1050 must be to hand, and the investigation mentioned in can. 1051 must have been carried out.

§2 It is further required that, in the judgement of the same lawful Superior, the candidate is considered beneficial to the ministry of the Church.

§3 A Bishop ordaining his own subject who is destined for the service of another diocese, must be certain that the ordinand will in fact be attached to that other diocese.

Article 1: The Requirements in those to be Ordained

Can. 1026   For a person to be ordained, he must enjoy the requisite freedom. It is absolutely wrong to compel anyone, in any way or for any reason whatsoever, to receive orders, or to turn away from orders anyone who is canonically suitable.

Can. 1027   Aspirants to the diaconate and the priesthood are to be formed by careful preparation in accordance with the law.

Can. 1028   The diocesan Bishop or the competent Superior must ensure that before they are promoted to any order, candidates are properly instructed concerning the order itself and its obligations.

Can. 1029   Only those are to be promoted to orders who, in the prudent judgement of the proper Bishop or the competent major Superior, all things considered, have sound faith, are motivated by the right intention, are endowed with the requisite knowledge, enjoy a good reputation, and have moral probity, proven virtue and the other physical and psychological qualities appropriate to the order to be received.

Can. 1030   The proper Bishop or the competent major Superior may, but only for a canonical reason, even one which is occult, forbid admission to the priesthood to deacons subject to them who were destined for the priesthood, without prejudice to recourse in accordance with the law.

Can. 1031 §1 The priesthood may be conferred only upon those who have completed their twenty-fifth year of age, and possess a sufficient maturity; moreover, an interval of at least six months between the diaconate and the priesthood must have been observed. Those who are destined for the priesthood are to be admitted to the order of diaconate only when they have completed their twenty-third year.

§2 A candidate for the permanent diaconate who is not married may be admitted to the diaconate only when he has completed at least his twenty-fifth year; if he is married, not until he has completed at least his thirty-fifth year, and then with the consent of his wife.

§3 Episcopal Conferences may issue a regulation which requires a later age for the priesthood and for the permanent diaconate.

§4 A dispensation of more than a year from the age required by §§1 and 2 is reserved to the Apostolic See.

Can. 1032 §1 Aspirants to the priesthood may be promoted to the diaconate only when they have completed the fifth year of the curriculum of philosophical and theological studies.

§2 After completing the curriculum of studies and before being promoted to the priesthood, deacons are to spend an appropriate time, to be determined by the Bishop or by the competent major Superior, exercising the diaconal order and taking part in the pastoral ministry.

§3 An aspirant to the permanent diaconate is not to be promoted to this order until he has completed the period of formation.

Article 2: Prerequisites for Ordination

Can. 1033 Only one who has received the sacrament of sacred confirmation may lawfully be promoted to orders.

Can. 1034 §1 An aspirant to the diaconate or to the priesthood is not to be ordained unless he has first, through the liturgical rite of admission, secured enrolment as a candidate from the authority mentioned in cann. 1016 and 1019. He must previously have submitted a petition in his own hand and signed by him, which has been accepted in writing by the same authority.

§2 One who has by vows become a member of a clerical institute is not obliged to obtain this admission.

Can. 1035 §1 Before anyone may be promoted to the diaconate, whether permanent or transitory, he must have received the ministries of lector and acolyte, and have exercised them for an appropriate time.

§2 Between the conferring of the ministry of acolyte and the diaconate there is to be an interval of at least six months.

Can. 1036 For a candidate to be promoted to the order of diaconate or priesthood, he must submit to the proper Bishop or to the competent major Superior a declaration written in his own hand and signed by him, in which he attests that he will spontaneously and freely receive the sacred order and will devote himself permanently to the ecclesiastical ministry, asking at the same time that he be admitted to receive the order.

Can. 1037   A candidate for the permanent diaconate who is not married, and likewise a candidate for the priesthood, is not to be admitted to the order of diaconate unless he has, in the prescribed rite, publicly before God and the Church undertaken the obligation of celibacy, or unless he has taken perpetual vows in a religious institute.

Can. 1038   A deacon who refuses to be promoted to the priesthood may not be forbidden the exercise of the order he has received, unless he is constrained by a canonical impediment, or unless there is some other grave reason, to be estimated by the diocesan Bishop or the competent major Superior.

Can. 1039   All who are to be promoted to any order must make a retreat for at least five days, in a place and in the manner determined by the Ordinary. Before he proceeds to the ordination, the Bishop must have assured himself that the candidates have duly made the retreat.

Article 3: Irregularities and other Impediments

Can. 1040   Those bound by an impediment are to be barred from the reception of orders. An impediment may be simple; or it may be perpetual, in which case it is called an irregularity. No impediment is contracted which is not contained in the following canons.

Can. 1041   The following persons are irregular for the reception of orders:

1° one who suffers from any form of insanity, or from any other psychological infirmity, because of which he is, after experts have been consulted, judged incapable of being able to fulfil the ministry;

2° one who has committed the offence of apostasy, heresy or schism;

3° one who has attempted marriage, even a civil marriage, either while himself prevented from entering marriage whether by an existing marriage bond or by a sacred order or by a public and perpetual vow of chastity, or with a woman who is validly married or is obliged by the same vow;

4° one who has committed wilful homicide, or one who has actually procured an abortion, and all who have positively co-operated;

5° one who has gravely and maliciously mutilated himself or another, or who has attempted suicide;

6° one who has carried out an act of order which is reserved to those in the order of the episcopate or priesthood, while himself

185

either not possessing that order or being barred from its exercise by some canonical penalty, declared or imposed.

Can. 1042   The following are simply impeded from receiving orders:
1° a man who has a wife, unless he is lawfully destined for the permanent diaconate;
2° one who exercises an office or administration forbidden to clerics, in accordance with cann. 285 and 286, of which he must render an account; the impediment binds until such time as, having relinquished the office and administration and rendered the account, he has been freed;
3° a neophyte, unless, in the judgement of the Ordinary, he has been sufficiently tested.

Can. 1043   Christ's faithful are bound to reveal, before ordination, to the Ordinary or to the parish priest, such impediments to sacred orders as they may know about.

Can. 1044   §1 The following are irregular for the exercise of orders already received:
1° one who, while bound by an irregularity for the reception of orders, unlawfully received orders;
2° one who committed the offence mentioned in can. 1041, n. 2, if the offence is public;
3° one who committed any of the offences mentioned in can. 1041, nn. 3, 4, 5, 6.
§2 The following are impeded from the exercise of orders:
1° one who, while bound by an impediment to the reception of orders, unlawfully received orders;
2° one who suffers from insanity or from some other psychological infirmity mentioned in can. 1041, n. 1, until such time as the Ordinary, having consulted an expert, has allowed the exercise of the order in question.

Can. 1045   Ignorance of irregularities and impediments does not exempt from them.

Can. 1046   Irregularities and impediments are multiplied if they arise from different causes, not however from the repetition of the same cause, unless it is a question of the irregularity arising from the commission of wilful homicide or from having actually procured an abortion.

Can. 1047   §1 If the fact on which they are based has been brought to the judicial forum, dispensation from all irregularities is reserved to the Apostolic See alone.
§2 Dispensation from the following irregularities and impediments to the reception of orders is also reserved to the Apostolic See:
1° irregularities arising from the offences mentioned in can. 1041, nn. 2 and 3, if they are public;

2° an irregularity arising from the offence, whether public or occult, mentioned in can. 1041, n. 4;

3° the impediment mentioned in can. 1042, n. 1.

§3 To the Apostolic See is also reserved the dispensation from the irregularities for the exercise of an order received mentioned in can. 1041, n. 3 but only in public cases, and in n. 4 of the same canon even in occult cases.

§4 The Ordinary can dispense from irregularities and impediments not reserved to the Holy See.

Can. 1048 In the more urgent occult cases, if the Ordinary or, in the case of the irregularities mentioned in can. 1041, nn. 3 and 4, the Penitentiary cannot be approached, and if there is imminent danger of serious harm or loss of reputation, the person who is irregular for the exercise of an order may exercise it. There remains, however, the obligation of his having recourse as soon as possible to the Ordinary or the Penitentiary, without revealing his name, and through a confessor.

Can. 1049 §1 In a petition to obtain a dispensation from irregularities or impediments, all irregularities and impediments are to be mentioned. However, a general dispensation is valid also for those omitted in good faith, with the exception of the irregularities mentioned in can. 1041, n. 4, or of others which have been brought to the judicial forum; it is not, however, valid for those concealed in bad faith.

§2 If it is question of an irregularity arising from wilful homicide or from a procured abortion, for the validity of the dispensation even the number of offences must be stated.

§3 A general dispensation from irregularities and impediments to the reception of orders is valid for all orders.

Article 4: Documents required and the Investigation

Can. 1050 For a person to be promoted to sacred orders, the following documents are required:

1° a certificate of studies duly completed in accordance with can. 1032;

2° for those to be ordained to the priesthood, a certificate of the reception of the diaconate;

3° for those to be promoted to the diaconate, certificates of the reception of baptism, of confirmation and of the ministries mentioned in can. 1035, and a certificate that the declaration mentioned in can. 1036 has been made; if an ordinand to be promoted to the permanent diaconate is married, a certificate of his marriage and testimony of his wife's consent.

Can. 1051 In the investigation of the requisite qualities of one who is to be ordained, the following provisions are to be observed:

1° there is to be a certificate from the rector of the seminary or of the house of formation, concerning the qualities required in the candidate for the reception of the order, namely sound doctrine, genuine piety, good moral behaviour, fitness for the exercise of the ministry; likewise, after proper investigation, a certificate of the candidate's state of physical and psychological health;

2° the diocesan Bishop or the major Superior may, in order properly to complete the investigation, use other means which, taking into account the circumstances of time and place, may seem useful, such as testimonial letters, public notices or other sources of information.

Can. 1052 §1 For a Bishop to proceed to an ordination which he is to confer by his own right, he must be satisfied that the documents mentioned in can. 1050 are at hand and that, as a result of the investigations prescribed by law, the suitability of the candidate has been positively established.

§2 For a Bishop to proceed to the ordination of someone not his own subject, it is sufficient that the dimissorial letters state that those documents are at hand, that the investigation has been conducted in accordance with the law, and that the candidate's suitability has been established. If the ordinand is a member of a religious institute or a society of apostolic life, these letters must also testify that he has been definitively enrolled in the institute or society and that he is a subject of the Superior who gives the letters.

§3 If, not withstanding all this, the Bishop has definite reasons for doubting that the candidate is suitable to receive orders, he is not to promote him.

Chapter III

THE REGISTRATION AND EVIDENCE OF ORDINATION

Can. 1053 §1 After an ordination, the names of the individuals ordained, the name of the ordaining minister, and the place and date of ordination are to be entered in a special register which is to be carefully kept in the curia of the place of ordination. All the documents of each ordination are to be accurately preserved.

§2 The ordaining Bishop is to give to each person ordained an authentic certificate of the ordination received. Those who, with dimissorial letters, have been promoted by a Bishop other than their own, are to submit the certificate to their proper Ordinary for the registration of the ordination in a special register, to be kept in the archive.

Can. 1054 The local Ordinary, if it concerns the secular clergy, or the competent major Superior, if it concerns his subjects, is to send a notification of each ordination to the parish priest of the place of baptism. The parish priest is to record the ordination in the baptismal register in accordance with can. 535 §2.

TITLE VII: MARRIAGE

Can. 1055 §1 The marriage covenant, by which a man and a woman establish between themselves a partnership of their whole life, and which of its own very nature is ordered to the well-being of the spouses and to the procreation and upbringing of children, has, between the baptised, been raised by Christ the Lord to the dignity of a sacrament.

§2 Consequently, a valid marriage contract cannot exist between baptised persons without its being by that very fact a sacrament.

Can. 1056 The essential properties of marriage are unity and indissolubility; in christian marriage they acquire a distinctive firmness by reason of the sacrament.

Can. 1057 §1 A marriage is brought into being by the lawfully manifested consent of persons who are legally capable. This consent cannot be supplied by any human power.

§2 Matrimonial consent is an act of will by which a man and a woman by an irrevocable covenant mutually give and accept one another for the purpose of establishing a marriage.

Can. 1058 All can contract marriage who are not prohibited by law.

Can. 1059 The marriage of catholics, even if only one party is baptised, is governed not only by divine law but also by canon law, without prejudice to the competence of the civil authority in respect of the merely civil effects of the marriage.

Can. 1060 Marriage enjoys the favour of law. Consequently, in doubt the validity of a marriage must be upheld until the contrary is proven.

Can. 1061 §1 A valid marriage between baptised persons is said to be merely ratified, if it is not consummated; ratified and consummated, if the spouses have in a human manner engaged together in a conjugal act in itself apt for the generation of offspring. To this act marriage is by its nature ordered and by it the spouses become one flesh.

§2 If the spouses have lived together after the celebration of their marriage, consummation is presumed until the contrary is proven.

§3 An invalid marriage is said to be putative if it has been celebrated in good faith by at least one party. It ceases to be such when both parties become certain of its nullity.

Can. 1062 §1 A promise of marriage, whether unilateral or bilateral, called an engagement, is governed by the particular law which the Episcopal Conference has enacted, after consideration of such customs and civil laws as may exist.

§2 No right of action to request the celebration of marriage arises from a promise of marriage, but there does arise an action for such reparation of damages as may be due.

Chapter I

PASTORAL CARE AND THE PREREQUISITES FOR THE CELEBRATION OF MARRIAGE

Can. 1063 Pastors of souls are obliged to ensure that their own church community provides for Christ's faithful the assistance by which the married state is preserved in its christian character and develops in perfection. This assistance is to be given principally:

1° by preaching, by catechetical instruction adapted to children, young people and adults, indeed by the use of the means of social communication, so that Christ's faithful are instructed in the meaning of christian marriage and in the role of christian spouses and parents;

2° by personal preparation for entering marriage, so that the spouses are disposed to the holiness and the obligations of their new state;

3° by the fruitful celebration of the marriage liturgy, so that it clearly emerges that the spouses manifest, and participate in, the mystery of the unity and fruitful love between Christ and the Church;

4° by the help given to those who have entered marriage, so that by faithfully observing and protecting their conjugal covenant, they may day by day achieve a holier and a fuller family life.

Can. 1064 It is the responsibility of the local Ordinary to ensure that this assistance is duly organised. If it is considered opportune, he should consult with men and women of proven experience and expertise.

Can. 1065 §1 Catholics who have not yet received the sacrament of confirmation are to receive it before being admitted to marriage, if this can be done without grave inconvenience.

§2 So that the sacrament of marriage may be fruitfully received, spouses are earnestly recommended that they approach the sacraments of penance and the blessed Eucharist.

Can. 1066 Before a marriage takes place, it must be established that nothing stands in the way of its valid and lawful celebration.

Can. 1067 The Episcopal Conference is to lay down norms concerning the questions to be asked of the parties, the publication of marriage banns, and the other appropriate means of enquiry to be carried out before marriage. Only when he has carefully observed these norms may the parish priest assist at a marriage.

Can. 1068   In danger of death, if other proofs are not available, it suffices, unless there are contrary indications, to have the assertion of the parties, sworn if need be, that they are baptised and free of any impediment.

Can. 1069   Before the celebration of a marriage, all the faithful are bound to reveal to the parish priest or the local Ordinary such impediments as they may know about.

Can. 1070   If someone other than the parish priest whose function it is to assist at the marriage has made the investigations, he is by an authentic document to inform that parish priest of the outcome of these enquiries as soon as possible.

Can. 1071   §1 Except in a case of necessity, no one is to assist without the permission of the local Ordinary at:
1° a marriage of *vagi*;
2° a marriage which cannot be recognised by the civil law or celebrated in accordance with it;
3° a marriage of a person for whom a previous union has created natural obligations towards a third party or towards children;
4° a marriage of a person who has notoriously rejected the catholic faith;
5° a marriage of a person who is under censure;
6° a marriage of a minor whose parents are either unaware of it or are reasonably opposed to it;
7° a marriage to be entered by proxy, as mentioned in can. 1105.
§2 The local Ordinary is not to give permission to assist at the marriage of a person who has notoriously rejected the Catholic faith unless, with the appropriate adjustments, the norms of can. 1125 have been observed.

Can. 1072   Pastors of souls are to see to it that they dissuade young people from entering marriage before the age customarily accepted in the region.

Chapter II
DIRIMENT IMPEDIMENTS IN GENERAL

Can. 1073   A diriment impediment renders a person incapable of validly contracting a marriage.

Can. 1074   An impediment is said to be public, when it can be proved in the external forum; otherwise, it is occult.

Can. 1075   §1 Only the supreme authority in the Church can authentically declare when the divine law prohibits or invalidates a marriage.

§2 Only the same supreme authority has the right to establish other impediments for those who are baptised.

Can. 1076   A custom which introduces a new impediment, or is contrary to existing impediments, is to be reprobated.

Can. 1077   §1 The local Ordinary can in a specific case forbid a marriage of his own subjects, wherever they are residing, or of any person actually present in his territory; he can do this only for a time, for a grave reason and while that reason persists.

§2 Only the supreme authority in the Church can attach an invalidating clause to a prohibition.

Can. 1078   §1 The local Ordinary can dispense his own subjects wherever they are residing, and all who are actually present in his territory, from all impediments of ecclesiastical law, except for those whose dispensation is reserved to the Apostolic See.

§2 The impediments whose dispensation is reserved to the Apostolic See are:

1° the impediment arising from sacred orders or from a public perpetual vow of chastity in a religious institute of pontifical right;

2° the impediment of crime mentioned in can. 1090.

§3 A dispensation is never given from the impediment of consanguinity in the direct line or in the second degree of the collateral line.

Can. 1079   §1 When danger of death threatens, the local Ordinary can dispense his own subjects, wherever they are residing, and all who are actually present in his territory, both from the form to be observed in the celebration of marriage, and from each and every impediment of ecclesiastical law, whether public or occult, with the exception of the impediment arising from the sacred order of priesthood.

§2 In the same circumstances mentioned in §1, but only for cases in which not even the local Ordinary can be approached, the same faculty of dispensation is possessed by the parish priest, by a properly delegated sacred minister, and by the priest or deacon who assists at the marriage in accordance with can. 1116 §2.

§3 In danger of death, the confessor has the power to dispense from occult impediments for the internal forum, whether within the act of sacramental confession or outside it.

§4 In the case mentioned in §2, the local Ordinary is considered unable to be approached if he can be reached only by telegram or by telephone.

Can. 1080   §1 Whenever an impediment is discovered after everything has already been prepared for a wedding and the marriage cannot without probable danger of grave harm be postponed until a dispensation is obtained from the competent authority, the power to dispense from all impediments, except those mentioned in can. 1078 §2, n. 1, is possessed by the local Ordinary and, provided the case is occult, by all those mentioned in can. 1079 §§2–3, the conditions prescribed therein having been observed.

§2 This power applies also to the validation of a marriage when there is the same danger in delay and there is no time to have recourse to the Apostolic See or, in the case of impediments from which he can dispense, to the local Ordinary.

Can. 1081 The parish priest or the priest or deacon mentioned in can. 1079 §2, should inform the local Ordinary immediately of a dispensation granted for the external forum, and this dispensation is to be recorded in the marriage register.

Can. 1082 Unless a rescript of the Penitentiary provides otherwise, a dispensation from an occult impediment granted in the internal non-sacramental forum, is to be recorded in the book to be kept in the secret archive of the curia. No other dispensation for the external forum is necessary if at a later stage the occult impediment becomes public.

Chapter III

INDIVIDUAL DIRIMENT IMPEDIMENTS

Can. 1083 §1 A man cannot validly enter marriage before the completion of his sixteenth year of age, nor a woman before the completion of her fourteenth year.

§2 The Episcopal Conference may establish a higher age for the lawful celebration of marriage.

Can. 1084 §1 Antecedent and perpetual impotence to have sexual intercourse, whether on the part of the man or on that of the woman, whether absolute or relative, by its very nature invalidates marriage.

§2 If the impediment of impotence is doubtful, whether the doubt be one of law or one of fact, the marriage is not to be prevented nor, while the doubt persists, is it to be declared null.

§3 Without prejudice to the provisions of can. 1098, sterility neither forbids nor invalidates a marriage.

Can. 1085 §1 A person bound by the bond of a previous marriage, even if not consummated, invalidly attempts marriage.

§2 Even though the previous marriage is invalid or for any reason dissolved, it is not thereby lawful to contract another marriage before the nullity or the dissolution of the previous one has been established lawfully and with certainty.

Can. 1086 §1 A marriage is invalid when one of the two persons was baptised in the catholic Church or received into it and has not by a formal act defected from it, and the other was not baptised.

§2 This impediment is not to be dispensed unless the conditions mentioned in cann. 1125 and 1126 have been fulfilled.

§3 If at the time the marriage was contracted one party was commonly understood to be baptised, or if his or her baptism was doubtful, the validity of the marriage is to be presumed in accordance with can. 1060, until it is established with certainty that one party was baptised and the other was not.

Can. 1087   Those who are in sacred orders invalidly attempt marriage.

Can. 1088   Those who are bound by a public perpetual vow of chastity in a religious institute invalidly attempt marriage.

Can. 1089   No marriage can exist between a man and a woman who has been abducted, or at least detained, with a view to contracting a marriage with her, unless the woman, after she has been separated from her abductor and established in a safe and free place, chooses marriage of her own accord.

Can. 1090   §1 One who, with a view to entering marriage with a particular person, has killed that person's spouse, or his or her own spouse, invalidly attempts this marriage.
§2 They also invalidly attempt marriage with each other who, by mutual physical or moral action, brought about the death of either's spouse.

Can. 1091   §1 Marriage is invalid between those related by consanguinity in all degrees of the direct line, whether ascending or descending, legitimate or natural.
§2 In the collateral line, it is invalid up to the fourth degree inclusive.
§3 The impediment of consanguinity is not multiplied.
§4 A marriage is never to be permitted if a doubt exists as to whether the parties are related by consanguinity in any degree of the direct line, or in the second degree of the collateral line.

Can. 1092   Affinity in any degree of the direct line invalidates marriage.

Can. 1093   The impediment of public propriety arises when a couple live together after an invalid marriage, or from a notorious or public concubinage. It invalidates marriage in the first degree of the direct line between the man and those related by consanguinity to the woman, and vice versa.

Can. 1094   Those who are legally related by reason of adoption cannot validly marry each other if their relationship is in the direct line or in the second degree of the collateral line.

Chapter IV

MATRIMONIAL CONSENT

Can. 1095   The following are incapable of contracting marriage:
1° those who lack sufficient use of reason;
2° those who suffer from a grave lack of discretionary judgement concerning the essential matrimonial rights and obligations to be mutually given and accepted;
3° those who, because of causes of a psychological nature, are unable to assume the essential obligations of marriage.

Can. 1096   §1 For matrimonial consent to exist, it is necessary that the contracting parties be at least not ignorant of the fact that marriage is a permanent partnership between a man and a woman, ordered to the procreation of children through some form of sexual cooperation.
§2 This ignorance is not presumed after puberty.

Can. 1097   §1 Error about a person renders a marriage invalid.
§2 Error about a quality of the person, even though it be the reason for the contract, does not render a marriage invalid unless this quality is directly and principally intended.

Can. 1098   A person contracts invalidly who enters marriage inveigled by deceit, perpetrated in order to secure consent, concerning some quality of the other party, which of its very nature can seriously disrupt the partnership of conjugal life.

Can. 1099   Provided it does not determine the will, error concerning the unity or the indissolubility or the sacramental dignity of marriage does not vitiate matrimonial consent.

Can. 1100   Knowledge of or opinion about the nullity of a marriage does not necessarily exclude matrimonial consent.

Can. 1101   §1 The internal consent of the mind is presumed to conform to the words or the signs used in the celebration of a marriage.
§2 If, however, either or both of the parties should by a positive act of will exclude marriage itself or any essential element of marriage or any essential property, such party contracts invalidly.

Can. 1102   §1 Marriage cannot be validly contracted subject to a condition concerning the future.
§2 Marriage entered into subject to a condition concerning the past or the present is valid or not, according as whatever is the basis of the condition exists or not.
§3 However, a condition as mentioned in §2 may not lawfully be attached except with the written permission of the local Ordinary.

Can. 1103   A marriage is invalid which was entered into by reason of force or of grave fear imposed from outside, even if not purposely, from which the person has no escape other than by choosing marriage.

Can. 1104 §1 To contract marriage validly it is necessary that the contracting parties be present together, either personally or by proxy.

§2 The spouses are to express their matrimonial consent in words; if, however, they cannot speak, then by equivalent signs.

Can. 1105 §1 For a marriage by proxy to be valid, it is required:
1° that there be a special mandate to contract with a specific person;
2° that the proxy be designated by the mandator and personally discharge this function;

§2 For the mandate to be valid, it is to be signed by the mandator, and also by the parish priest or local Ordinary of the place in which the mandate is given or by a priest delegated by either of them or by at least two witnesses, or it is to be drawn up in a document which is authentic according to the civil law.

§3 If the mandator cannot write, this is to be recorded in the mandate and another witness added who is also to sign the document; otherwise, the mandate is invalid.

§4 If the mandator revokes the mandate, or becomes insane, before the proxy contracts in his or her name, the marriage is invalid, even though the proxy or the other contracting party is unaware of the fact.

Can. 1106 Marriage can be contracted through an interpreter, but the parish priest may not assist at such a marriage unless he is certain of the trustworthiness of the interpreter.

Can. 1107 Even if a marriage has been entered into invalidly by reason of an impediment or defect of form, the consent given is presumed to persist until its withdrawal has been established.

Chapter V

THE FORM OF THE CELEBRATION OF MARRIAGE

Can. 1108 §1 Only those marriages are valid which are contracted in the presence of the local Ordinary or parish priest or of the priest or deacon delegated by either of them, who, in the presence of two witnesses, assists, in accordance however with the rules set out in the following canons, and without prejudice to the exceptions mentioned in cann. 144, 1112 §1, 1116 and 1127 §§2–3.

§2 Only that person who, being present, asks the contracting parties to manifest their consent and in the name of the Church receives it, is understood to assist at a marriage.

Can. 1109 Within the limits of their territory, the local Ordinary and the parish priest by virtue of their office validly assist at the marriages not only of their subjects, but also of non-subjects, provided one or other of the parties is of the latin rite. They cannot assist if by sentence or decree they have been excommunicated, placed under interdict or suspended from office, or been declared to be such.

Can. 1110   A personal Ordinary and a personal parish priest by virtue of their office validly assist, within the confines of their jurisdiction, at the marriages only of those of whom at least one party is their subject.

Can. 1111   §1 As long as they validly hold office, the local Ordinary and the parish priest can delegate to priests and deacons the faculty, even the general faculty, to assist at marriages within the confines of their territory.

§2 In order that the delegation of the faculty to assist at marriages be valid, it must be expressly given to specific persons; if there is question of a special delegation, it is to be given for a specific marriage; if however there is question of a general delegation, it is to be given in writing.

Can. 1112   §1 Where there are no priests and deacons, the diocesan Bishop can delegate lay persons to assist at marriages, if the Episcopal Conference has given its prior approval and the permission of the Holy See has been obtained.

§2 A suitable lay person is to be selected, capable of giving instruction to those who are getting married, and fitted to conduct the marriage liturgy properly.

Can. 1113   §1 Before a special delegation is granted, provision is to be made for all those matters which the law prescribes to establish the freedom to marry.

Can. 1114   One who assists at a marriage acts unlawfully unless he has satisfied himself of the parties' freedom to marry in accordance with the law and, whenever he assists by virtue of a general delegation, has satisfied himself of the parish priest's permission, if this is possible.

Can. 1115   Marriages are to be celebrated in the parish in which either of the contracting parties has a domicile or a quasi-domicile or a month's residence or, if there is question of *vagi*, in the parish in which they are actually residing. With the permission of the proper Ordinary or the proper parish priest, marriages may be celebrated elsewhere.

Can. 1116   §1 If one who, in accordance with the law, is competent to assist, cannot be present or be approached without grave inconvenience, those who intend to enter a true marriage can validly and lawfully contract in the presence of witnesses only:

1° in danger of death;
2° apart from danger of death, provided it is prudently foreseen that this state of affairs will continue for a month.

§2 In either case, if another priest or deacon is at hand who can be present, he must be called upon and, together with the witnesses, be present at the celebration of the marriage, without prejudice to the validity of the marriage in the presence of only the witnesses.

Can. 1117   The form prescribed above is to be observed if at least one of the parties contracting marriage was baptised in the catholic Church or received into it and has not by a formal act defected from it, without prejudice to the provisions of can. 1127 §2.

Can. 1118   §1 A marriage between catholics, or between a catholic party and a baptised non-catholic, is to be celebrated in the parish church. By permission of the local Ordinary or of the parish priest, it may be celebrated in another church or oratory.

§2 The local Ordinary can allow a marriage to be celebrated in another suitable place.

§3 A marriage between a catholic party and an unbaptised party may be celebrated in a church or in another suitable place.

Can. 1119   Apart from a case of necessity, in the celebration of marriage those rites are to be observed which are prescribed in the liturgical books approved by the Church, or which are acknowledged by lawful customs.

Can. 1120   The Episcopal Conference can draw up its own rite of marriage, in keeping with those usages of place and people which accord with the christian spirit; it is to be reviewed by the Holy See, and it is without prejudice to the law that the person who is present to assist at the marriage is to ask for and receive the expression of the consent of the contracting parties.

Can. 1121   §1 As soon as possible after the celebration of a marriage, the parish priest of the place of celebration or whoever takes his place, even if neither has assisted at the marriage, is to record in the marriage register the names of the spouses, of the person who assisted and of the witnesses, and the place and date of the celebration of the marriage; this is to be done in the manner prescribed by the Episcopal Conference or by the diocesan Bishop.

§2 Whenever a marriage is contracted in accordance with can. 1116, the priest or deacon, if he was present at the celebration, otherwise the witnesses, are bound jointly with the contracting parties as soon as possible to inform the parish priest or the local Ordinary about the marriage entered into.

§3 In regard to a marriage contracted with a dispensation from the canonical form, the local Ordinary who granted the dispensation is to see to it that the dispensation and the celebration are recorded in the marriage register both of the curia, and of the proper parish of the catholic party whose parish priest carried out the inquiries concerning the freedom to marry. The catholic spouse is obliged as soon as possible to notify that same Ordinary and parish priest of the fact that the marriage was celebrated, indicating also the place of celebration and the public form which was observed.

Can. 1122   §1 A marriage which has been contracted is to be recorded also in the baptismal registers in which the baptism of the spouses was entered.

§2 If a spouse contracted marriage elsewhere than in the parish of baptism, the parish priest of the place of celebration is to send a notification of the marriage as soon as possible to the parish priest of the place of baptism.

Can. 1123   Whenever a marriage is validated for the external forum, or declared invalid, or lawfully dissolved other than by death, the parish priest of the place of the celebration of the marriage must be informed, so that an entry may be duly made in the registers of marriage and of baptism.

Chapter VI
MIXED MARRIAGES

Can. 1124   Without the express permission of the competent authority, marriage is prohibited between two baptised persons, one of whom was baptised in the catholic Church or received into it after baptism and has not defected from it by a formal act, the other of whom belongs to a Church or ecclesial community not in full communion with the catholic Church.

Can. 1125   The local Ordinary can grant this permission if there is a just and reasonable cause. He is not to grant it unless the following conditions are fulfilled:

1° the catholic party is to declare that he or she is prepared to remove dangers of defecting from the faith, and is to make a sincere promise to do all in his or her power in order that all the children be baptised and brought up in the catholic Church;
2° the other party is to be informed in good time of these promises to be made by the catholic party, so that it is certain that he or she is truly aware of the promise and of the obligation of the catholic party;
3° both parties are to be instructed about the purposes and essential properties of marriage, which are not to be excluded by either contractant.

Can. 1126   It is for the Episcopal Conference to prescribe the manner in which these declarations and promises, which are always required, are to be made, and to determine how they are to be established in the external forum, and how the non-catholic party is to be informed of them.

Can. 1127   §1 The provisions of can. 1108 are to be observed in regard to the form to be used in a mixed marriage. If, however, the catholic party contracts marriage with a non-catholic party of oriental rite, the canonical form of celebration is to be observed for lawfulness only; for validity, however, the intervention of a sacred minister is required, while observing the other requirements of law.

§2 If there are grave difficulties in the way of observing the canonical form, the local Ordinary of the catholic party has the right to dispense from it in individual cases, having however consulted the Ordinary of the place of the celebration of the marriage; for validity, however, some public form of celebration is required. It is for the Episcopal Conference to establish norms whereby this dispensation may be granted in a uniform manner.

§3 It is forbidden to have, either before or after the canonical celebration in accordance with §1, another religious celebration of the same marriage for the purpose of giving or renewing matrimonial consent. Likewise, there is not to be a religious celebration in which the catholic assistant and a non-catholic minister, each performing his own rite, ask for the consent of the parties.

Can. 1128   Local Ordinaries and other pastors of souls are to see to it that the catholic spouse and the children born of a mixed marriage are not without the spiritual help needed to fulfil their obligations; they are also to assist the spouses to foster the unity of conjugal and family life.

Can. 1129   The provisions of cann. 1127 and 1128 are to be applied also to marriages which are impeded by the impediment of disparity of worship mentioned in can. 1086 §1.

Chapter VII

THE SECRET CELEBRATION OF MARRIAGE

Can. 1130   For a grave and urgent reason, the local Ordinary may permit that a marriage be celebrated in secret.

Can. 1131   Permission to celebrate a marriage in secret involves:
   1° that the investigations to be made before the marriage are carried out in secret;
   2° that the secret in regard to the marriage which has been celebrated is observed by the local Ordinary, by whoever assists, by the witnesses and by the spouses.

Can. 1132   The obligation of observing the secret mentioned in can. 1131 n. 2 ceases for the local Ordinary if from its observance a threat arises of grave scandal or of grave harm to the sanctity of marriage. This fact is to be made known to the parties before the celebration of the marriage.

Can. 1133   A marriage celebrated in secret is to be recorded only in a special register which is to be kept in the secret archive of the curia.

Chapter VIII
THE EFFECTS OF MARRIAGE

Can. 1134   From a valid marriage there arises between the spouses a bond which of its own nature is permanent and exclusive. Moreover, in christian marriage the spouses are by a special sacrament strengthened and, as it were, consecrated for the duties and the dignity of their state.

Can. 1135   Each spouse has an equal obligation and right to whatever pertains to the partnership of conjugal life.

Can. 1136   Parents have the most grave obligation and the primary right to do all in their power to ensure their children's physical, social, cultural, moral and religious upbringing.

Can. 1137   Children who are conceived or born of a valid or of a putative marriage are legitimate.

Can. 1138   §1   The father is he who is identified by a lawful marriage, unless by clear arguments the contrary is proven.
§2   Children are presumed legitimate who are born at least 180 days after the date the marriage was celebrated, or within 300 days from the date of the dissolution of conjugal life.

Can. 1139   Illegitimate children are legitimated by the subsequent marriage of their parents, whether valid or putative, or by a rescript of the Holy See.

Can. 1140   As far as canonical effects are concerned, legitimated children are equivalent to legitimate children in all respects, unless it is otherwise expressly provided by the law.

Chapter IX
THE SEPARATION OF THE SPOUSES

Article 1: The Dissolution of the Bond

Can. 1141   A marriage which is ratified and consummated cannot be dissolved by any human power or by any cause other than death.

Can. 1142   A non-consummated marriage between baptised persons or between a baptised party and an unbaptised party can be dissolved by the Roman Pontiff for a just reason, at the request of both parties or of either party, even if the other is unwilling.

Can. 1143 §1 In virtue of the pauline privilege, a marriage entered into by two unbaptised persons is dissolved in favour of the faith of the party who received baptism, by the very fact that a new marriage is contracted by that same party, provided the unbaptised party departs.

§2 The unbaptised party is considered to depart if he or she is unwilling to live with the baptised party, or to live peacefully without offence to the Creator, unless the baptised party has, after the reception of baptism, given the other just cause to depart.

Can. 1144 §1 For the baptised person validly to contract a new marriage, the unbaptised party must always be interpellated whether:

1° he or she also wishes to receive baptism;
2° he or she at least is willing to live peacefully with the baptised party without offence to the Creator.

§2 This interpellation is to be done after baptism. However, the local Ordinary can for a grave reason permit that the interpellation be done before baptism; indeed he can dispense from it, either before or after baptism, provided it is established, by at least a summary and extrajudicial procedure, that it cannot be made or that it would be useless.

Can. 1145 As a rule, the interpellation is to be done on the authority of the local Ordinary of the converted party. A period of time for reply is to be allowed by this Ordinary to the other party, if indeed he or she asks for it, warning the person however that if the period passes without any reply, silence will be taken as a negative response.

§2 Even an interpellation made privately by the converted party is valid, and indeed it is lawful if the form prescribed above cannot be observed.

§3 In both cases there must be lawful proof in the external forum of the interpellation having been done and of its outcome.

Can. 1146 The baptised party has the right to contract a new marriage with a catholic:

1° if the other party has replied in the negative to the interpellation, or if the interpellation has been lawfully omitted;
2° if the unbaptised person, whether already interpellated or not, who at first persevered in peaceful cohabitation without offence to the Creator, has subsequently departed without just cause, without prejudice to the provisions of cann. 1144 and 1145.

Can. 1147 However, the local Ordinary can for a grave reason allow the baptised party, using the pauline privilege, to contract marriage with a non-catholic party, whether baptised or unbaptised; in this case, the provisions of the canons on mixed marriages must also be observed.

Can. 1148 §1 When an unbaptised man who simultaneously has a number of unbaptised wives, has received baptism in the catholic Church, if it would be a hardship for him to remain with the first of the wives, he may retain one of them, having dismissed the others. The same applies to an unbaptised woman who simultaneously has a number of unbaptised husbands.

§2   In the cases mentioned in §1, when baptism has been received, the marriage is to be contracted in the legal form, with due observance, if need be, of the provisions concerning mixed marriages and of other provisions of law.

§3   In the light of the moral, social and economic circumstances of place and person, the local Ordinary is to ensure that adequate provision is made, in accordance with the norms of justice, christian charity and natural equity, for the needs of the first wife and of the others who have been dismissed.

Can. 1149   An unbaptised person who, having received baptism in the catholic Church, cannot re-establish cohabitation with his or her un-baptised spouse by reason of captivity or persecution, can contract another marriage, even if the other party has in the meantime received baptism, without prejudice to the provisions of can.1141.

Can. 1150   In a doubtful matter the privilege of the faith enjoys the favour of law.

Article 2: Separation while the Bond remains

Can. 1151   Spouses have the obligation and the right to maintain their common conjugal life, unless a lawful reason excuses them.

Can. 1152   §1   It is earnestly recommended that a spouse, motivated by christian charity and solicitous for the good of the family, should not refuse to pardon an adulterous partner and should not sunder the conjugal life. Nevertheless, if that spouse has not either expressly or tacitly condoned the other's fault, he or she has the right to sever the common conjugal life, provided he or she has not consented to the adultery, nor been the cause of it, nor also committed adultery.

§2   Tacit condonation occurs if the innocent spouse, after becoming aware of the adultery, has willingly engaged in a marital relationship with the other spouse; it is presumed, however, if the innocent spouse has maintained the common conjugal life for six months, and has not had recourse to ecclesiastical or to civil authority.

§3   Within six months of having spontaneously terminated the common conjugal life, the innocent spouse is to bring a case for separation to the competent ecclesiastical authority. Having examined all the circumstances, this authority is to consider whether the innocent spouse can be brought to condone the fault and not prolong the separation permanently.

Can. 1153   §1   A spouse who occasions grave danger of soul or body to the other or to the children, or otherwise makes the common life unduly difficult, provides the other spouse with a reason to leave, either by a decree of the local Ordinary or, if there is danger in delay, even on his or her own authority.

§2 In all cases, when the reason for separation ceases, the common conjugal life is to be restored, unless otherwise provided by ecclesiastical authority.

Can. 1154   When a separation of spouses has taken place, provision is always, and in good time, to be made for the due maintenance and upbringing of the children.

Can. 1155   The innocent spouse may laudably readmit the other spouse to the conjugal life, in which case he or she renounces the right to separation.

Chapter X

THE VALIDATION OF MARRIAGE

Article 1: Simple Validation

Can. 1156   §1 To validate a marriage which is invalid because of a diriment impediment, it is required that the impediment cease or be dispensed, and that at least the party aware of the impediment renews consent.

§2 This renewal is required by ecclesiastical law for the validity of the validation, even if at the beginning both parties had given consent and had not afterwards withdrawn it.

Can. 1157   The renewal of consent must be a new act of will consenting to a marriage which the renewing party knows or thinks was invalid from the beginning.

Can. 1158   §1 If the impediment is public, consent is to be renewed by both parties in the canonical form, without prejudice to the provision of can. 1127 §3.

§2 If the impediment cannot be proved, it is sufficient that consent be renewed privately and in secret, specifically by the party who is aware of the impediment provided the other party persists in the consent given, or by both parties if the impediment is known to both.

Can. 1159   §1 A marriage invalid because of a defect of consent is validated if the party who did not consent, now does consent, provided the consent given by the other party persists.

§2 If the defect of the consent cannot be proven, it is sufficient that the party who did not consent, gives consent privately and in secret.

§3 If the defect of consent can be proven, it is necessary that consent be given in the canonical form.

Can. 1160   For a marriage which is invalid because of defect of form to become valid, it must be contracted anew in the canonical form, without prejudice to the provisions of can. 1127 §3*.

Article 2: Retroactive Validation

Can. 1161 §1 The retroactive validation of an invalid marriage is its validation without the renewal of consent, granted by the competent authority. It involves a dispensation from an impediment if there is one, and from the canonical form if it had not been observed, as well as a referral back to the past of the canonical effects.

§2 The validation takes place from the moment the favour is granted; the referral back, however, is understood to have been made to the moment the marriage was celebrated, unless it is otherwise expressly provided.

§3 A retroactive validation is not to be granted unless it is probable that the parties intend to persevere in conjugal life.

Can. 1162 §1 If consent is lacking in either or both of the parties, a marriage cannot be rectified by a retroactive validation, whether consent was absent from the beginning or, though given at the beginning, was subsequently revoked.

§2 If the consent was indeed absent from the beginning but was subsequently given, a retroactive validation can be granted from the moment the consent was given.

Can. 1163 §1 A marriage which is invalid because of an impediment or because of defect of the legal form, can be validated retroactively, provided the consent of both parties persists.

§2 A marriage which is invalid because of an impediment of the natural law or of the divine positive law, can be validated retroactively only after the impediment has ceased.

Can. 1164 A retroactive validation may validly be granted even if one or both of the parties is unaware of it; it is not, however, to be granted except for a grave reason.

Can. 1165 §1 Retroactive validation can be granted by the Apostolic See.

§2 It can be granted by the diocesan Bishop in individual cases, even if a number of reasons for nullity occur together in the same marriage, assuming that for a retroactive validation of a mixed marriage the conditions of can. 1125 will have been fulfilled. It cannot, however, be granted by him if there is an impediment whose dispensation is reserved to the Apostolic See in accordance with can. 1078 §2, or if there is question of an impediment of the natural law or of the divine positive law which has now ceased.

---

*Translators' note: It would appear that this reference should read 'Can. 1127 §2'.

Part II
THE OTHER ACTS OF DIVINE WORSHIP

TITLE I: SACRAMENTALS

Can. 1166 Sacramentals are sacred signs which in a sense imitate the sacraments. They signify certain effects, especially spiritual ones, and they achieve these effects through the intercession of the Church.

Can. 1167 §1 Only the Apostolic See can establish new sacramentals, or authentically interpret, suppress or change existing ones.

§2 The rites and the formulae approved by ecclesiastical authority are to be accurately observed when celebrating or administering sacramentals.

Can. 1168 The minister of the sacramentals is a cleric who has the requisite power. In accordance with the liturgical books and subject to the judgement of the local Ordinary, certain sacramentals can also be administered by lay people who possess the appropriate qualities.

Can. 1169 §1 Consecrations and dedications can be validly carried out by those who are invested with the episcopal character, and by priests who are permitted to do so by law or by legitimate grant.

§2 Any priest can impart blessings, except for those reserved to the Roman Pontiff or to Bishops.

§3 A deacon can impart only those blessings which are expressly permitted to him by law.

Can. 1170 While blessings are to be imparted primarily to catholics, they may be given also to catechumens and, unless there is a prohibition by the Church, even to non-catholics.

Can. 1171 Sacred objects, set aside for divine worship by dedication or blessing, are to be treated with reverence. They are not to be made over to secular or inappropriate use, even though they may belong to private persons.

Can. 1172 §1 No one may lawfully exorcise the possessed without the special and express permission of the local Ordinary.

§2 This permission is to be granted by the local Ordinary only to a priest who is endowed with piety, knowledge, prudence and integrity of life.

TITLE II: THE LITURGY OF THE HOURS

Can. 1173 In fulfilment of the priestly office of Christ, the Church celebrates the liturgy of the hours, wherein it listens to God speaking to his people and recalls the mystery of salvation. In this way, the Church praises God without ceasing, in song and prayer, and it intercedes with him for the salvation of the whole world.

Can. 1174 §1 Clerics are obliged to recite the liturgy of the hours, in accordance with can. 276, §2, n. 3; members of institutes of consecrated life and of societies of apostolic life are obliged in accordance with their constitutions.
§2 Others also of Christ's faithful are earnestly invited, according to circumstances, to take part in the liturgy of the hours as an action of the Church.

Can. 1175 In carrying out the liturgy of the hours, each particular hour is, as far as possible, to be recited at the time assigned to it.

TITLE III: CHURCH FUNERALS

Can. 1176 §1 Christ's faithful who have died are to be given a Church funeral according to the norms of law.
§2 Church funerals are to be celebrated according to the norms of the liturgical books. In these funeral rites the Church prays for the spiritual support of the dead, it honours their bodies, and at the same time it brings to the living the comfort of hope.
§3 The Church earnestly recommends that the pious custom of burial be retained; but it does not forbid cremation, unless this is chosen for reasons which are contrary to christian teaching.

Chapter I

THE CELEBRATION OF FUNERALS

Can. 1177 §1 The funeral of any deceased member of the faithful should normally be celebrated in the church of that person's proper parish.
§2 However, any member of the faithful, or those in charge of the

deceased person's funeral, may choose another church; this requires the consent of whoever is in charge of that church and a notification to the proper parish priest of the deceased.

§3 When death has occurred outside the person's proper parish, and the body is not returned there, and another church has not been chosen, the funeral rites are to be celebrated in the church of the parish where the death occurred, unless another church is determined by particular law.

Can. 1178   The funeral ceremonies of a diocesan Bishop are to be celebrated in his own cathedral church, unless he himself has chosen another church.

Can. 1179   Normally, the funerals of religious or of members of a society of apostolic life are to be celebrated in their proper church or oratory: by the Superior, if the institute or society is a clerical one; otherwise, by the chaplain.

Can. 1180   §1 If a parish has its own cemetery, the deceased faithful are to be buried there, unless another cemetery has lawfully been chosen by the deceased person, or by those in charge of that person's burial.

§2 All may, however, choose their cemetery of burial unless prohibited by law from doing so.

Can. 1181   The provisions of can. 1264 are to be observed in whatever concerns the offerings made on the occasion of funerals. Moreover, care is to be taken that at funerals there is to be no preference of persons, and that the poor are not deprived of proper funeral rites.

Can. 1182   After the burial an entry is to be made in the register of the dead, in accordance with particular law.

Chapter II

THOSE TO WHOM CHURCH FUNERALS ARE TO BE ALLOWED OR DENIED

Can. 1183   §1 As far as funeral rites are concerned, catechumens are to be reckoned among Christ's faithful.

§2 Children whose parents had intended to have them baptised but who died before baptism, may be allowed Church funeral rites by the local Ordinary.

§3 Provided their own minister is not available, baptised persons belonging to a non-catholic Church or ecclesial community may, in accordance with the prudent judgement of the local Ordinary, be allowed Church funeral rites, unless it is established that they did not wish this.

Can. 1184   §1 Church funeral rites are to be denied to the following, unless they gave some signs of repentance before death:
   1° notorious apostates, heretics and schismatics;

2° those who for anti-christian motives chose that their bodies be cremated;

3° other manifest sinners to whom a Church funeral could not be granted without public scandal to the faithful.

§2 If any doubt occurs, the local Ordinary is to be consulted and his judgement followed.

Can. 1185   Any form of funeral Mass is also to be denied to a person who has been excluded from a Church funeral.

TITLE IV
THE CULT OF THE SAINTS, OF SACRED IMAGES AND OF RELICS

Can. 1186   To foster the sanctification of the people of God, the Church commends to the special and filial veneration of Christ's faithful the Blessed Mary ever-Virgin, the Mother of God, whom Christ constituted the Mother of all. The Church also promotes the true and authentic cult of the other Saints, by whose example the faithful[†] are edified and by whose intercession they are supported.

Can. 1187   Only those servants of God may be venerated by public cult who have been numbered by ecclesiastical authority among the Saints or the Blessed.

Can. 1188   The practice of exposing sacred images in churches for the veneration of the faithful is to be retained. However, these images are to be displayed in moderate numbers and in suitable fashion, so that the christian people are not disturbed, nor is occasion given for less than appropriate devotion.

Can. 1189   The written permission of the Ordinary is required to restore precious images needing repair: that is, those distinguished by reason of age, art or cult, which are exposed in churches and oratories to the veneration of the faithful. Before giving such permission, the Ordinary is to seek the advice of experts.

Can. 1190   §1 It is absolutely wrong to sell sacred relics.

§2 Distinguished relics, and others which are held in great veneration by the people, may not validly be in any way alienated nor transferred on a permanent basis, without the permission of the Apostolic See.

§3 The provision of §2 applies to images which are greatly venerated in any church by the people.

TITLE V: VOWS AND OATHS

Chapter I
VOWS

Can. 1191 §1 A vow is a deliberate and free promise made to God, concerning some good which is possible and better. The virtue of religion requires that it be fulfilled.

§2 Unless they are prohibited by law, all who have an appropriate use of reason are capable of making a vow.

§3 A vow made as a result of grave and unjust fear or of deceit is by virtue of the law itself invalid.

Can. 1192 §1 A vow is public if it is accepted in the name of the Church by a lawful Superior; otherwise, it is private.

§2 It is solemn if it is recognised by the Church as such; otherwise, it is simple.

§3 It is personal if it promises an action by the person making the vow; real, if it promises some thing; mixed, if it has both a personal and a real aspect.

Can. 1193 Of its nature a vow obliges only the person who makes it.

Can. 1194 A vow ceases by lapse of the time specified for the fulfilment of the obligation, or by a substantial change in the matter promised, or by cessation of a condition upon which the vow depended or of the purpose of the vow, or by dispensation, or by commutation.

Can. 1195 A person who has power over the matter of a vow can suspend the obligation of the vow for such time as the fulfilment of the vow would affect that person adversely.

Can. 1196 Besides the Roman Pontiff, the following can dispense from private vows, provided the dispensation does not injure the acquired rights of others;

    1° the local Ordinary and the parish priest, in respect of all their own subjects and also of *peregrini*;

    2° the Superior of a religious institute or of a society of apostolic life, if these are clerical and of pontifical right, in respect of members, novices and those who reside day and night in a house of the institute or society;

    3° those to whom the faculty of dispensing has been delegated by the Apostolic See or by the local Ordinary.

Can. 1197 What has been promised by private vow can be commuted into something better or equally good by the person who made the vow. It can be commuted into something less good by one who has authority to dispense in accordance with can. 1196.

Can. 1198   Vows taken before religious profession are suspended as long as the person who made the vow remains in the religious institute.

Chapter II

OATHS

Can. 1199   §1   An oath is the invocation of the divine Name as witness to the truth. It cannot be taken except in truth, judgement and justice.

§2   An oath which is required or accepted by the canons cannot validly be taken by proxy.

Can. 1200   §1   A person who freely swears on oath to do something is specially obliged by the virtue of religion to fulfil that which he or she asserted by the oath.

§2   An oath extorted by deceit, force or grave fear is by virtue of the law itself invalid.

Can. 1201   §1   A promissory oath is determined by the nature and condition of the act to which it is attached.

§2   An act which directly threatens harm to others or is prejudicial to the public good or to eternal salvation, is in no way reinforced by an oath sworn to do that act.

Can. 1202   §1   The obligation of a promissory oath ceases:
　　1°　if it is remitted by the person in whose favour the oath was sworn;
　　2°　if what was sworn is substantially changed or, because of altered circumstances, becomes evil or completely irrelevant, or hinders a greater good;
　　3°　if the purpose or the condition ceases under which the oath may have been made;
　　4°　by dispensation or commutation in accordance with can. 1203.

Can. 1203   Those who can suspend, dispense or commute a vow have, in the same measure, the same power over a promissory oath. But if dispensation from an oath would tend to harm others and they refuse to remit the obligation, only the Apostolic See can dispense the oath.

Can. 1204   An oath is subject to strict interpretation, in accordance with the law and with the intention of the person taking the oath or, if that person acts deceitfully, in accordance with the intention of the person in whose presence the oath is taken.

Part III
SACRED PLACES AND TIMES

TITLE I: SACRED PLACES

Can. 1205 Sacred places are those which are assigned to divine worship or to the burial of the faithful by the dedication or blessing which the liturgical books prescribe for this purpose.

Can. 1206 The dedication of a place belongs to the diocesan Bishop and to those equivalent to him in law. For a dedication in their own territory they can depute any Bishop or, in exceptional cases, a priest.

Can. 1207 Sacred places are blessed by the Ordinary, but the blessing of churches is reserved to the diocesan Bishop. Both may, however, delegate another priest for the purpose.

Can. 1208 A document is to be drawn up to record the dedication or blessing of a church, or the blessing of a cemetery. One copy is to be kept in the diocesan curia, the other in the archive of the church.

Can. 1209 The dedication or the blessing of a place is sufficiently established even by a single unexceptionable witness, provided no one is harmed thereby.

Can. 1210 In a sacred place only those things are to be permitted which serve to exercise or promote worship, piety and religion. Anything out of harmony with the holiness of the place is forbidden. The Ordinary may however, for individual cases, permit other uses, provided they are not contrary to the sacred character of the place.

Can. 1211 Sacred places are desecrated by acts done in them which are gravely injurious and give scandal to the faithful when, in the judgement of the local Ordinary, these acts are so serious and so contrary to the sacred character of the place that worship may not be held there until the harm is repaired by means of the penitential rite which is prescribed in the liturgical books.

Can. 1212 Sacred places lose their dedication or blessing if they have been in great measure destroyed, or if they have been permanently made over to secular usage, whether by decree of the competent Ordinary or simply in fact.

Can. 1213   Ecclesiastical authority freely exercises its powers and functions in sacred places.

Chapter I

CHURCHES

Can. 1214   The term church means a sacred building intended for divine worship, to which the faithful have right of access for the exercise, especially the public exercise, of divine worship.

Can. 1215   §1   No church is to be built without the express and written consent of the diocesan Bishop.

§2   The diocesan Bishop is not to give his consent until he has consulted the council of priests and the rectors of neighbouring churches, and then decides that the new church can serve the good of souls and that the necessary means will be available to build the church and to provide for divine worship.

§3   Even though they have received the diocesan Bishop's consent to establish a new house in a diocese or city, religious institutes must obtain the same Bishop's permission before they may build a church in a specific and determined place.

Can. 1216   In the building and restoration of churches the advice of experts is to be used, and the principles and norms of liturgy and of sacred art are to be observed.

Can. 1217   §1   As soon as possible after completion of the building the new church is to be dedicated or at least blessed, following the laws of the sacred liturgy.

§2   Churches, especially cathedrals and parish churches, are to be dedicated by a solemn rite.

Can. 1218   Each church is to have its own title. Once the church has been dedicated this title cannot be changed.

Can. 1219   All acts of divine worship may be carried out in a church which has been lawfully dedicated or blessed, without prejudice to parochial rights.

Can. 1220   §1   Those responsible are to ensure that there is in churches such cleanliness and ornamentation as befits the house of God, and that anything which is discordant with the sacred character of the place is excluded.

§2   Ordinary concern for preservation and appropriate means of security are to be employed to safeguard sacred and precious goods.

Can. 1221   Entry to a church at the hours of sacred functions is to be open and free of charge.

Can. 1222 §1 If a church cannot in any way be used for divine worship and there is no possibility of its being restored, the diocesan Bishop may allow it to be used for some secular but not unbecoming purpose.

§2 Where other grave reasons suggest that a particular church should no longer be used for divine worship, the diocesan Bishop may allow it to be used for a secular but not unbecoming purpose. Before doing so, he must consult the council of priests; he must also have the consent of those who could lawfully claim rights over that church, and be sure that the good of souls would not be harmed by the transfer.

Chapter II

ORATORIES AND PRIVATE CHAPELS

Can. 1223 An oratory means a place which, by permission of the Ordinary, is set aside for divine worship, for the convenience of some community or group of the faithful who assemble there, to which however other members of the faithful may, with the consent of the competent Superior, have access.

Can. 1224 §1 The Ordinary is not to give the permission required for setting up an oratory unless he has first, personally or through another, inspected the place destined for the oratory and found it to be becomingly arranged.

§2 Once this permission has been given, the oratory cannot be converted to a secular usage without the authority of the same Ordinary.

Can. 1225 All sacred services may be celebrated in a lawfully constituted oratory, apart from those which are excluded by the law, by a provision of the local Ordinary, or by liturgical laws.

Can. 1226 The term private chapel means a place which, by permission of the local Ordinary, is set aside for divine worship, for the convenience of one or more individuals.

Can. 1227 Bishops can set up for their own use a private chapel which enjoys the same rights as an oratory.

Can. 1228 Without prejudice to the provision of can. 1227, the permission of the local Ordinary is required for the celebration of Mass and of other sacred functions in any private chapel.

Can. 1229 It is appropriate that oratories and private chapels be blessed according to the rite prescribed in the liturgical books. They must, however, be reserved for divine worship only and be freed from all domestic use.

Chapter III

SHRINES

Can. 1230 The term shrine means a church or other sacred place which, with the approval of the local Ordinary, is by reason of special devotion frequented by the faithful as pilgrims.

Can. 1231 For a shrine to be described as national, the approval of the Episcopal Conference is necessary. For it to be described as international, the approval of the Holy See is required.

Can. 1232 §1 The local Ordinary is competent to approve the statutes of a diocesan shrine; the Episcopal Conference, those of a national shrine; the Holy See alone, those of an international shrine.

§2 The statutes of a shrine are to determine principally its purpose, the authority of the rector, and the ownership and administration of its property.

Can. 1233 Certain privileges may be granted to shrines when the local circumstances, the number of pilgrims and especially the good of the faithful would seem to make this advisable.

Can. 1234 §1 At shrines the means of salvation are to be more abundantly made available to the faithful: by sedulous proclamation of the word of God, by suitable encouragement of liturgical life, especially by the celebration of the Eucharist and penance, and by the fostering of approved forms of popular devotion.

§2 In shrines or in places adjacent to them, votive offerings of popular art and devotion are to be displayed and carefully safeguarded.

Chapter IV

ALTARS

Can. 1235 §1 The altar or table on which the eucharistic Sacrifice is celebrated is termed fixed if it is so constructed that it is attached to the floor and therefore cannot be moved; it is termed movable, if it can be removed.

§2 It is proper that in every church there should be a fixed altar. In other places which are intended for the celebration of sacred functions, the altar may be either fixed or movable.

Can. 1236 §1 In accordance with the traditional practice of the Church, the table of a fixed altar is to be of stone, indeed of a single natural stone. However, even some other worthy and solid material may be used, if the Episcopal Conference so judges. The support or the base can be made from any material.

§2 A movable altar can be made of any solid material which is suitable for liturgical use.

Can. 1237 §1 Fixed altars are to be dedicated, movable ones either dedicated or blessed, according to the rites prescribed in the liturgical books.

§2 The ancient tradition of placing relics of Martyrs or of other Saints within a fixed altar is to be retained, in accordance with the rites prescribed in the liturgical books.

Can. 1238 §1 An altar loses its dedication or blessing in accordance with can. 1212.

§2 Altars, whether fixed or movable, do not lose their dedication or blessing as a result of a church or other sacred place being made over to secular usage.

Can. 1239 §1 An altar, whether fixed or movable, is to be reserved for divine worship alone, to the exclusion of any secular usage.

§2 No corpse is to be buried beneath an altar; otherwise, it is not lawful to celebrate Mass at that altar.

Chapter V

CEMETERIES

Can. 1240 §1 Where possible, the Church is to have its own cemeteries, or at least an area in public cemeteries which is duly blessed and reserved for the deceased faithful.

§2 If, however, this is not possible, then individual graves are to be blessed in due form on each occasion.

Can. 1241 §1 Parishes and religious institutes may each have their own cemetery.

§2 Other juridical persons or families may each have their own special cemetery or burial place which, if the local Ordinary judges accordingly, is to be blessed.

Can. 1242 Bodies are not to be buried in churches, unless it is a question of the Roman Pontiff or of Cardinals or, in their proper Churches, of diocesan Bishops even retired.

Can. 1243 Appropriate norms are to be enacted by particular law for the management of cemeteries, especially in what concerns the protection and the fostering of their sacred character.

TITLE II: SACRED TIMES

Can. 1244 §1 Only the supreme ecclesiastical authority can establish, transfer or suppress holydays or days of penance which are applicable to the universal Church, without prejudice to the provisions of can. 1246 §2.

§2 Diocesan Bishops can proclaim special holydays or days of penance for their own dioceses or territories, but only for individual occasions.

Can. 1245 Without prejudice to the right of diocesan Bishops as in can. 87, a parish priest, in individual cases, for a just reason and in accordance with the prescriptions of the diocesan Bishop, can give a dispensation from the obligation of observing a holyday or day of penance, or commute the obligation into some other pious works. The Superior of a pontifical clerical religious institute or society of apostolic life has the same power in respect of his own subjects and of those who reside day and night in a house of the institute or society.

Chapter I

FEAST DAYS

Can. 1246 §1 The Lord's Day, on which the paschal mystery is celebrated, is by apostolic tradition to be observed in the universal Church as the primary holyday of obligation. In the same way the following holydays are to be observed: the Nativity of Our Lord Jesus Christ, the Epiphany, the Ascension of Christ, the feast of the Body and Blood of Christ, the feast of Mary the Mother of God, her Immaculate Conception, her Assumption, the feast of St Joseph, the feast of the Apostles SS Peter and Paul, and the feast of All Saints.

§2 However, the Episcopal Conference may, with the prior approval of the Apostolic See, suppress certain holydays of obligation or transfer them to a Sunday.

Can. 1247 On Sundays and other holydays of obligation, the faithful are obliged to assist at Mass. They are also to abstain from such work or business that would inhibit the worship to be given to God, the joy proper to the Lord's Day, or the due relaxation of mind and body.

Can. 1248 §1 The obligation of assisting at Mass is satisfied wherever Mass is celebrated in a catholic rite either on a holyday itself or on the evening of the previous day.

§2 If it is impossible to assist at a eucharistic celebration, either because no sacred minister is available or for some other grave reason, the faithful are strongly recommended to take part in a liturgy of the Word, if there be such in the parish church or some other sacred place, which is celebrated in accordance with the provisions laid down by the diocesan Bishop; or to spend an appropriate time in prayer, whether personally or as a family or, as occasion presents, in a group of families.

Chapter II
DAYS OF PENANCE

Can. 1249   All Christ's faithful are obliged by divine law, each in his or her own way, to do penance. However, so that all may be joined together in a certain common practice of penance, days of penance are prescribed. On these days the faithful† are in a special manner to devote themselves to prayer, to engage in works of piety and charity, and to deny themselves, by fulfilling their obligations more faithfully and especially by observing the fast and abstinence which the following canons prescribe.

Can. 1250   The days and times of penance for the universal Church are each Friday of the whole year and the season of Lent.

Can. 1251   Abstinence from meat, or from some other food as determined by the Episcopal Conference, is to be observed on all Fridays, unless a solemnity should fall on a Friday. Abstinence and fasting are to be observed on Ash Wednesday and Good Friday.

Can. 1252   The law of abstinence binds those who have completed their fourteenth year. The law of fasting binds those who have attained their majority, until the beginning of their sixtieth year. Pastors of souls and parents are to ensure that even those who by reason of their age are not bound by the law of fasting and abstinence, are taught the true meaning of penance.

Can. 1253   The Episcopal Conference can determine more particular ways in which fasting and abstinence are to be observed. In place of abstinence or fasting it can substitute, in whole or in part, other forms of penance, especially works of charity and exercises of piety.

Book V
THE TEMPORAL GOODS
OF THE CHURCH

Can. 1254 §1 The catholic Church has the inherent right, independently of any secular power, to acquire, retain, administer and alienate temporal goods, in pursuit of its proper objectives.

§2 These proper objectives are principally the regulation of divine worship, the provision of fitting support for the clergy and other ministers, and the carrying out of works of the sacred apostolate and of charity, especially for the needy.

Can. 1255 The universal Church, as well as the Apostolic See, particular Churches and all other public and private juridical persons are capable of acquiring, retaining, administering and alienating temporal goods, in accordance with the law.

Can. 1256 Under the supreme authority of the Roman Pontiff, ownership of goods belongs to that juridical person which has lawfully acquired them.

Can. 1257 §1 All temporal goods belonging to the universal Church, to the Apostolic See or to other public juridical persons in the Church, are ecclesiastical goods and are regulated by the canons which follow, as well as by their own statutes.

§2 Unless it is otherwise expressly provided, temporal goods belonging to a private juridical person are regulated by its own statutes, not by these canons.

Can. 1258 In the canons which follow, the term Church signifies not only the universal Church or the Apostolic See, but also any public juridical person in the Church, unless the contrary is clear from the context or from the nature of the matter.

TITLE I: THE ACQUISITION OF GOODS

Can. 1259 The Church may acquire temporal goods in any way in which, by either natural or positive law, it is lawful for others to do this.

Can. 1260 The Church has the inherent right to require from the faithful whatever is necessary for its proper objectives.

Can. 1261 §1 The faithful have the right to donate temporal goods for the benefit of the Church.

§2 The diocesan Bishop is bound to remind the faithful of the obligation mentioned in can. 222 §1, and in an appropriate manner to urge it.

Can. 1262 The faithful are to give their support to the Church in response to appeals and in accordance with the norms laid down by the Episcopal Conference.

Can. 1263   The diocesan Bishop, after consulting the finance committee and the council of priests, has the right to levy on public juridical persons subject to his authority a tax for the needs of the diocese. This tax must be moderate and proportionate to their income. He may impose an extraordinary and moderate tax on other physical and juridical persons only in a grave necessity and under the same conditions, but without prejudice to particular laws and customs which may give him greater rights.

Can. 1264   Unless the law prescribes otherwise, it is for the provincial Bishops' meeting to:
      1° determine the taxes, to be approved by the Apostolic See, for acts of executive authority which grant a favour, or for the execution of rescripts from the Apostolic See;
      2° determine the offerings on the occasion of the administration of the sacraments and sacramentals.

Can. 1265   §1   Without prejudice to the right of mendicant religious, all private juridical or physical persons are forbidden to make a collection for any pious or ecclesiastical institute or purpose without the written permission of their proper Ordinary and of the local Ordinary.
    §2   The Episcopal Conference can draw up rules regarding collections, which must be observed by all, including those who from their foundation are called and are 'mendicants'.

Can. 1266   §1   In all churches and oratories regularly open to Christ's faithful, including those belonging to religious institutes, the local Ordinary may order that a special collection be taken up for specified parochial, diocesan, national or universal initiatives. The collection must afterwards be carefully forwarded to the diocesan curia.

Can. 1267   §1   Unless the contrary is clear, offerings made to Superiors or administrators of any ecclesiastical juridical person, even a private one, are presumed to have been made to the juridical person itself.
    §2   If there is question of a public juridical person, the offerings mentioned in §1 cannot be refused except for a just reason and, in matters of greater importance, with the permission of the Ordinary. Without prejudice to the provisions of can. 1295, the permission of the Ordinary is also required for the acceptance of offerings to which are attached some qualifying obligation or condition.
    §3   Offerings given by the faithful for a specified purpose may be used only for that purpose.

Can. 1268   The Church recognises prescription, in accordance with cann. 197–199, as a means both of acquiring temporal goods and of being freed from their obligations.

Can. 1269   Sacred objects in private ownership may be acquired by private persons by prescription, but they may not be used for secular purposes unless they have lost their dedication or blessing. If, however, they belong to a public ecclesiastical juridical person, they may be acquired only by another public ecclesiastical juridical person.

Can. 1270   Immovable goods, precious movable goods, rights and legal claims, whether personal or real, which belong to the Apostolic See, are prescribed after a period of one hundred years. For those goods which belong to another public ecclesiastical juridical person, the period for prescription is thirty years.

Can. 1271   By reason of their bond of unity and charity, and according to the resources of their dioceses, Bishops are to join together to produce those means which the Apostolic See may from time to time need to exercise properly its service of the universal Church.

Can. 1272   In those regions where benefices properly so called still exist, it is for the Episcopal Conference to regulate such benefices by appropriate norms, agreed with and approved by the Apostolic See. The purpose of these norms is that the income and as far as possible the capital itself of the benefice should by degrees be transferred to the fund mentioned in can. 1274 §1.

TITLE II: THE ADMINISTRATION OF GOODS

Can. 1273   The Roman Pontiff, by virtue of his primacy of governance, is the supreme administrator and steward of all ecclesiastical goods.

Can. 1274   §1 In every diocese there is to be a special fund which collects offerings and temporal goods for the purpose of providing, in accordance with can. 281, for the support of the clergy who serve the diocese, unless they are otherwise catered for.

§2 Where there is as yet no properly organised system of social provision for the clergy, the Episcopal Conference is to see that a fund is established which will furnish adequate social security for them.

§3 To the extent that it is required, a common reserve is to be established in every diocese by which the Bishop is enabled to fulfil his obligations towards other persons who serve the Church and to meet various needs of the diocese; this can also be the means by which wealthier dioceses may help poorer ones.

§4 Depending on differing local circumstances, the purposes described in §§2 and 3 might better be achieved by amalgamating various diocesan funds, or by cooperation between various dioceses, or even by setting up a suitable association for them, or indeed for the whole territory of the Episcopal Conference itself.

§5 If possible, these funds are to be established in such a manner that they will have standing also in the civil law.

Can. 1275   A reserve set up by a number of different dioceses is to be administered according to norms opportunely agreed upon by the Bishops concerned.

Can. 1276   §1 Ordinaries must carefully supervise the administration of all the goods which belong to public juridical persons subject to them, without prejudice to lawful titles which may give the Ordinary greater rights.

§2 Taking into account rights, lawful customs and the circumstances, Ordinaries are to regulate the whole matter of the administration of ecclesiastical goods by issuing special instructions, within the limits of universal and particular law.

Can. 1277   In carrying out acts of administration which, in the light of the financial situation of the diocese, are of major importance, the diocesan Bishop must consult the finance committee and the college of consultors. For acts of extraordinary administration, except in cases expressly provided for in the universal law or stated in the documents of foundation, the diocesan Bishop needs the consent of the committee and of the college of consultors. It is for the Episcopal Conference to determine what are to be regarded as acts of extraordinary administration.

Can. 1278   Besides the duties mentioned in can. 494 §§3 and 4, the diocesan Bishop may also entrust to the financial administrator the duties mentioned in can. 1276 §1 and can. 1279 §2.

Can. 1279   §1 The administration of ecclesiastical goods pertains to the one with direct power of governance over the person to whom the goods belong, unless particular law or statutes or legitimate custom state otherwise, and without prejudice to the right of the Ordinary to intervene where there is negligence on the part of the administrator.

§2 Where no administrators are appointed for a public juridical person by law or by the documents of foundation or by its own statutes, the Ordinary to which it is subject is to appoint suitable persons as administrators for a three-year term. The same persons can be re-appointed by the Ordinary.

Can. 1280   Every juridical person is to have its own finance committee, or at least two counsellors, who are to assist in the performance of the administrator's duties, in accordance with the statutes.

Can. 1281   §1 Without prejudice to the provisions of the statutes, administrators act invalidly when they go beyond the limits and manner of ordinary administration, unless they have first received in writing from the Ordinary the faculty to do so.

§2 The statutes are to determine what acts go beyond the limits and manner of ordinary administration. If the statutes are silent on this point, it is for the diocesan Bishop, after consulting the finance committee, to determine these acts for the persons subject to him.

§3 Except and insofar as it is to its benefit, a juridical person is not held responsible for the invalid actions of its administrators. The juridical person is, however, responsible when such actions are valid but unlawful, without prejudice to its right to bring an action or have recourse against the administrators who have caused it damage.

Can. 1282   All persons, whether clerics or laity, who lawfully take part in the administration of ecclesiastical goods, are bound to fulfil their duties in the name of the Church, in accordance with the law.

Can. 1283   Before administrators undertake their duties:

1° they must take an oath, in the presence of the Ordinary or his delegate, that they will well and truly perform their office;

2° they are to draw up a clear and accurate inventory, to be signed by themselves, of all immovable goods, of those movable goods which are precious or of a high cultural value, and of all other goods, with a description and an estimate of their value; when this has been compiled, it is to be certified as correct;

3° one copy of this inventory is to be kept in the administration office and another in the curial archive; any change which takes place in the property is to be noted on both copies.

Can. 1284   §1 All administrators are to perform their duties with the diligence of a good householder.

§2 Therefore they must:

1° be vigilant that no goods placed in their care in any way perish or suffer damage; to this end they are, to the extent necessary, to arrange insurance contracts;

2° ensure that the ownership of ecclesiastical goods is safeguarded in ways which are valid in civil law;

3° observe the provisions of canon and civil law, and the stipulations of the founder or donor or lawful authority; they are to take special care that damage will not be suffered by the Church through the non-observance of the civil law;

4° seek accurately and at the proper time the income and produce of the goods, guard them securely and expend them in accordance with the wishes of the founder or lawful norms;

5° at the proper time pay the interest which is due by reason of a loan or pledge, and take care that in due time the capital is repaid;

6° with the consent of the Ordinary make use of money which is surplus after payment of expenses and which can be profitably invested for the purposes of the juridical person;

7° keep accurate records of income and expenditure;

8° draw up an account of their administration at the end of each year;

9° keep in order and preserve in a convenient and suitable archive the documents and records establishing the rights of the Church or institute to its goods; where conveniently possible, authentic copies must be placed in the curial archives.

§3   It is earnestly recommended that administrators draw up each year a budget of income and expenditure. However, it is left to particular law to make this an obligation and to determine more precisely how it is to be presented.

Can. 1285   Solely within the limits of ordinary administration, administrators are allowed to make gifts for pious purposes or christian charity out of the movable goods which do not form part of the stable patrimony.

Can. 1286   Administrators of temporal goods:
  1° in making contracts of employment, are accurately to observe also, according to the principles taught by the Church, the civil laws relating to labour and social life;
  2° are to pay to those who work for them under contract a just and honest wage which will be sufficient to provide for their needs and those of their dependents.

Can. 1287   §1   Where ecclesiastical goods of any kind are not lawfully withdrawn from the power of governance of the diocesan Bishop, their administrators, both clerical and lay, are bound to submit each year to the local Ordinary an account of their administration, which he is to pass on to his finance committee for examination. Any contrary custom is reprobated.

§2   Administrators are to render accounts to the faithful concerning the goods they have given to the Church, in accordance with the norms to be laid down by particular law.

Can. 1288   Administrators are not to begin legal proceedings in the name of a public juridical person, nor are they to contest them in a secular court, without first obtaining the written permission of their proper Ordinary.

Can. 1289   Although they may not be bound to the work of administration by virtue of an ecclesiastical office, administrators may not arbitrarily relinquish the work they have undertaken. If they do so, and this occasions damage to the Church, they are bound to restitution.

TITLE III: CONTRACTS AND ESPECIALLY ALIENATION

Can. 1290   Without prejudice to can. 1547*, whatever the local civil law decrees about contracts, both generally and specifically, and about the voiding of contracts, is to be observed regarding goods which are subject to the power of governance of the Church, and with the same effect,

---

*Translators' note: It would appear that this reference should read 'can. 1259'.

provided that the civil law is not contrary to divine law, and that canon law does not provide otherwise.

Can. 1291   The permission of the authority competent by law is required for the valid alienation of goods which, by lawful assignment, constitute the stable patrimony of a public juridical person, whenever their value exceeds the sum determined by law.

Can. 1292   §1   Without prejudice to the provision of can. 638 §3, when the amount of the goods to be alienated is between the minimum and maximum sums to be established by the Episcopal Conference for its region, the competent authority in the case of juridical persons not subject to the diocesan Bishop is determined by the juridical person's own statutes. In other cases, the competent authority is the diocesan Bishop acting with the consent of the finance committee, of the college of consultors, and of any interested parties. The diocesan Bishop needs the consent of these same persons to alienate goods which belong to the diocese itself.

§2   The permission of the Holy See also is required for the valid alienation of goods whose value exceeds the maximum sum, or if it is a question of the alienation of something given to the Church by reason of a vow, or of objects which are precious by reason of their artistic or historical significance.

§3   When a request is made to alienate goods which are divisible, the request must state what parts have already been alienated; otherwise, the permission is invalid.

§4   Those who must give advice about or consent to the alienation of goods are not to give this advice or consent until they have first been informed precisely both about the economic situation of the juridical person whose goods it is proposed to alienate and about alienations which have already taken place.

Can. 1293   §1   To alienate goods whose value exceeds the determined minimum sum, it is also required that there be:

   1°   a just reason, such as urgent necessity, evident advantage, or a religious, charitable or other grave pastoral reason;

   2°   a written expert valuation of the goods to be alienated.

§2   To avoid harm to the Church, any other precautions drawn up by lawful authority are also to be followed.

Can. 1294   §1   Normally goods must not be alienated for a price lower than that given in the valuation.

§2   The money obtained from alienation must be carefully invested for the benefit of the Church, or prudently expended according to the purposes of the alienation.

Can. 1295   The provisions of cann. 1291–1294, to which the statutes of juridical persons are to conform, must be observed not only in alienation, but also in any dealings in which the patrimonial condition of the juridical person may be jeopardised.

Can. 1296 When alienation has taken place without the prescribed canonical formalities, but is valid in civil law, the competent authority must carefully weigh all the circumstances and decide whether, and if so what, action is to be taken, namely personal or real, by whom and against whom, to vindicate the rights of the Church.

Can. 1297 It is the duty of the Episcopal Conference, taking into account the local circumstances, to determine norms about the leasing of ecclesiastical goods, especially about permission to be obtained from the competent ecclesiastical authority.

Can. 1298 Unless they are of little value, ecclesiastical goods are not to be sold or leased to the administrators themselves or to their relatives up to the fourth degree of consanguinity or affinity, without the special written permission of the competent authority.

TITLE IV
PIOUS DISPOSITIONS IN GENERAL
AND PIOUS FOUNDATIONS

Can. 1299 §1 Those who by the natural law and by canon law can freely dispose of their goods may leave them to pious causes either by an act *inter vivos* or by an act *mortis causa*.

§2 In arrangements *mortis causa* in favour of the Church, the formalities of the civil law are as far as possible to be observed. If these formalities have been omitted, the heirs must be advised of their obligation to fulfil the intention of the testator.

Can. 1300 The intentions of the faithful who give or leave goods to pious causes, whether by an act *inter vivos* or by an act *mortis causa*, once lawfully accepted, are to be most carefully observed, even in the manner of the administration and the expending of the goods, without prejudice to the provisions of can. 1301 §3.

Can. 1301 §1 The Ordinary is the executor of all pious dispositions whether made *mortis causa* or *inter vivos*.

§2 By this right the Ordinary can and must ensure, even by making a visitation, that pious dispositions are fulfilled. Other executors are to render him an account when they have finished their task.

§3 Any clause contrary to this right of the Ordinary which is added to a last will, is to be regarded as non-existent.

Can. 1302 §1 Anyone who receives goods in trust for pious causes, whether by an act *inter vivos* or by last will, must inform the Ordinary about the trust, as well as about the goods in question, both movable and immovable, and about any obligations attached to them. If the donor has expressly and totally forbidden this, the trust is not to be accepted.

§2 The Ordinary must demand that goods left in trust be safely preserved and, in accordance with can. 1301, he must ensure that the pious disposition is executed.

§3 When goods given in trust to a member of a religious institute or society of apostolic life, are destined for a particular place or diocese or their inhabitants, or for pious causes, the Ordinary mentioned in §§1 and 2 is the local Ordinary. Otherwise, when the person is a member of a pontifical clerical institute or of a pontifical clerical society of apostolic life, it is the major Superior; when of other religious institutes, it is the member's proper Ordinary.

Can. 1303 §1 In law the term pious foundation comprises:

1° autonomous pious foundations, that is, aggregates of things destined for the purposes described in can. 114 §2, and established as juridical persons by the competent ecclesiastical authority.

2° non-autonomous pious foundations, that is, temporal goods given in any way to a public juridical person and carrying with them a long-term obligation, such period to be determined by particular law. The obligation is for the juridical person, from the annual income, to celebrate Masses, or to perform other determined ecclesiastical functions, or in some other way to fulfil the purposes mentioned in can. 114 §2.

§2 If the goods of a non-autonomous pious foundation are entrusted to a juridical person subject to the diocesan Bishop, they are, on the expiry of the time, to be sent to the fund mentioned in can. 1274 §1, unless some other intention was expressly manifested by the donor. Otherwise, the goods fall to the juridical person itself.

Can. 1304 §1 For the valid acceptance of a pious foundation by a juridical person, the written permission of the Ordinary is required. He is not to give this permission until he has lawfully established that the juridical person can satisfy not only the new obligations to be undertaken, but also any already undertaken. The Ordinary is to take special care that the revenue fully corresponds to the obligations laid down, taking into account the customs of the region or place.

§2 Other conditions for the establishment or acceptance of a pious foundation are to be determined by particular law.

Can. 1305 Money and movable goods which are assigned as a dowry are immediately to be put in a safe place approved by the Ordinary, so that the money or the value of the movable goods is safeguarded; as soon as possible, they are to be carefully and profitably invested for the good of the foundation, with an express and individual mention of the obligation undertaken, in accordance with the prudent judgement of the Ordinary when he has consulted those concerned and his own finance committee.

Can. 1306 §1 All foundations, even if made orally, are to be recorded in writing.

§2 One copy of the document is to be carefully preserved in the curial archive and another copy in the archive of the juridical person to which the foundation pertains.

Can. 1307 §1 When the provisions of cann. 1300–1302 and 1287 have been observed, a document showing the obligations arising from the pious foundations is to be drawn up. This is to be displayed in a conspicuous place, so that the obligations to be fulfilled are not forgotten.

§2 Apart from the book mentioned in can. 958 §1, another book is to be kept by the parish priest or rector, in which each of the obligations, their fulfilment and the offering given, is to be recorded.

Can. 1308 §1 The reduction of Mass obligations, for a just and necessary reason, is reserved to the Apostolic See, without prejudice to the provisions which follow.

§2 If this is expressly provided for in the document of foundation, the Ordinary may reduce Mass obligations on the ground of reduced income.

§3 In the cases of Masses given in legacies or in foundations of any kind, which are solely for the purpose of Masses, the diocesan Bishop has the power, because of the diminution of income and for as long as this persists, to reduce the obligations to the level of the offering lawfully current in the diocese. He may do this, however, only if there is no one who has an obligation to increase the offering and can actually be made to do so.

§4 The diocesan Bishop has the power to reduce the obligations or legacies of Masses which bind an ecclesiastical institute, if the revenue has become insufficient to achieve in a fitting manner the proper purpose of the institute.

§5 The supreme Moderator of a clerical religious institute of pontifical right has the powers given in §§3 and 4.

Can. 1309 Where a fitting reason exists, the authorities mentioned in can. 1308 have the power to transfer Mass obligations to days, churches or altars other than those determined in the foundation.

Can. 1310 §1 The intentions of the faithful in pious cases may be reduced, directed or changed by the Ordinary, if the donor has expressly conceded this power to him, but only for a just and necessary reason.

§2 If it has become impossible to carry out the obligations because of reduced income, or for any other reason arising without fault on the part of the administrators, the Ordinary can diminish these obligations in an equitable manner, with the exception of the reduction of Masses, which is governed by the provisions of can. 1308. He may do so only after consulting those concerned and his own finance committee, keeping in the best way possible to the intention of the donor.

§3 In all other cases, the Apostolic See is to be approached.

Book VI
SANCTIONS IN THE CHURCH

Part I
OFFENCES AND PUNISHMENTS IN GENERAL

TITLE I: THE PUNISHMENT OF OFFENCES IN GENERAL

Can. 1311 The Church has its own inherent right to constrain with penal sanctions Christ's faithful who commit offences.

Can. 1312 §1 The penal sanctions in the Church are:
1° medicinal penalties or censures, which are listed in cann. 1331–1333;
2° expiatory penalties, mentioned in can. 1336;
§2 The law may determine other expiatory penalties which deprive a member of Christ's faithful of some spiritual or temporal good, and are consistent with the Church's supernatural purpose.
§3 Use is also made of penal remedies and penances: the former primarily to prevent offences, the latter rather to substitute for or to augment a penalty.

TITLE II: PENAL LAW AND PENAL PRECEPT

Can. 1313 §1 If a law is changed after an offence has been committed, the law more favourable to the offender is to be applied.
§2 If a later law removes a law, or at least a penalty, the penalty immediately lapses.

Can. 1314 A penalty is for the most part *ferendae sententiae*, that is, not binding upon the offender until it has been imposed. It is, however, *latae sententiae*, so that it is incurred automatically upon the commission of an offence, if a law or precept expressly lays this down.

Can. 1315 §1 Whoever has legislative power can also make penal laws. A legislator can, however, by laws of his own, reinforce with a fitting penalty a divine law or an ecclesiastical law of a higher authority, observing the limits of his competence in respect of territory or persons.

§2   A law can either itself determine the penalty or leave its determination to the prudent decision of a judge.

§3   A particular law can also add other penalties to those laid down for a certain offence in a universal law; this is not to be done, however, except for the gravest necessity. If a universal law threatens an undetermined penalty or a discretionary penalty, a particular law can establish in its place a determined or an obligatory penalty.

Can. 1316   Diocesan Bishops are to take care that as far as possible any penalties which are to be imposed by law are uniform within the same city or region.

Can. 1317   Penalties are to be established only in so far as they are really necessary for the better maintenance of ecclesiastical discipline. Dismissal from the clerical state, however, cannot be laid down by particular law.

Can. 1318   A legislator is not to threaten *latae sententiae* penalties, except perhaps for some outstanding and malicious offences which may be either more grave by reason of scandal or such that they cannot be effectively punished by *ferendae sententiae* penalties. He is not, however, to constitute censures, especially excommunication, except with the greatest moderation, and only for the more grave offences.

Can. 1319   §1   To the extent to which a legislator can impose precepts by virtue of the power of governance in the external forum, to that extent can he also by precept threaten a determined penalty, other than a perpetual expiatory penalty.

§2   A precept to which a penalty is attached is not to be issued unless the matter has been very carefully considered, and unless the provisions of can. 1317 and 1318 concerning particular laws have been observed.

Can. 1320   In all matters in which they come under the authority of the local Ordinary, religious can be constrained by him with penalties.

TITLE III: THOSE WHO ARE LIABLE TO PENAL SANCTIONS

Can. 1321   §1   No one can be punished for the commission of an external violation of a law or precept unless it is gravely imputable by reason of malice or of culpability.

§2   A person who deliberately violated a law or precept is bound by the penalty prescribed in that law or precept. If, however, the violation was due to the omission of due diligence, the person is not punished unless the law or precept provides otherwise.

§3   Where there has been an external violation, imputability is presumed, unless it appears otherwise.

Can. 1322 Those who habitually lack the use of reason, even though they appeared sane when they violated a law or precept, are deemed incapable of committing an offence.

Can. 1323 No one is liable to a penalty who, when violating a law or precept:

1° has not completed the sixteenth year of age;

2° was, without fault, ignorant of violating the law or precept; inadvertence and error are equivalent to ignorance;

3° acted under physical force, or under the impetus of a chance occurrence which the person could not foresee or if foreseen could not avoid;

4° acted under the compulsion of grave fear, even if only relative, or by reason of necessity or grave inconvenience, unless, however, the act is intrinsically evil or tends to be harmful to souls;

5° acted, within the limits of due moderation, in lawful self-defence or defence of another against an unjust aggressor;

6° lacked the use of reason, without prejudice to the provisions of cann. 1324, §1, n. 2 and 1325;

7° thought, through no personal fault, that some one of the circumstances existed which are mentioned in nn. 4 or 5.

Can. 1324 §1 The perpetrator of a violation is not exempted from penalty, but the penalty prescribed in the law or precept must be diminished, or a penance substituted in its place, if the offence was committed by:

1° one who had only an imperfect use of reason;

2° one who was lacking the use of reason because of culpable drunkenness or other mental disturbance of a similar kind;

3° one who acted in the heat of passion which, while serious, nevertheless did not precede or hinder all mental deliberation and consent of the will, provided that the passion itself had not been deliberately stimulated or nourished;

4° a minor who has completed the sixteenth year of age;

5° one who was compelled by grave fear, even if only relative, or by reason of necessity or grave inconvenience, if the act is intrinsically evil or tends to be harmful to souls;

6° one who acted in lawful self-defence or defence of another against an unjust aggressor, but did not observe due moderation;

7° one who acted against another person who was gravely and unjustly provocative;

8° one who erroneously, but culpably, thought that some one of the circumstances existed which are mentioned in can. 1323, nn. 4 or 5;

9° one who through no personal fault was unaware that a penalty was attached to the law or precept;

10° one who acted without full imputability, provided it remained grave.

§2 A judge can do the same if there is any other circumstance present which would reduce the gravity of the offence.

§3 In the circumstances mentioned in §1, the offender is not bound by a *latae sententiae* penalty.

Can. 1325   Ignorance which is crass or supine or affected can never be taken into account when applying the provisions of cann. 1323 and 1324. Likewise, drunkenness or other mental disturbances cannot be taken into account if these have been deliberately sought so as to commit the offence or to excuse it; nor can passion which has been deliberately stimulated or nourished.

Can. 1326   §1 A judge may inflict a more serious punishment than that prescribed in the law or precept when:

    1° a person, after being condemned, or after the penalty has been declared, continues so to offend that obstinate ill-will may prudently be concluded from the circumstances;

    2° a person who is established in some position of dignity, or who has abused a position of authority or an office, in order to commit a crime;

    3° an offender who, after a penalty for a culpable offence was constituted, foresaw the event but nevertheless omitted to take the precautions to avoid it which any careful person would have taken.

§2 In the cases mentioned in §1, if the penalty constituted is *latae sententiae*, another penalty or a penance may be added.

Can. 1327   A particular law may, either as a general rule or for individual offences, determine excusing, attenuating or aggravating circumstances, over and above the cases mentioned in cann. 1323–1326. Likewise, circumstances may be determined in a precept which excuse from, attenuate or aggravate the penalty constituted in the precept.

Can. 1328   §1 One who in furtherance of an offence did something or failed to do something but then, involuntarily, did not complete the offence, is not bound by the penalty prescribed for the completed offence, unless the law or a precept provides otherwise.

§2 If the acts or the omissions of their nature lead to the carrying out of the offence, the person responsible may be subjected to a penance or to a penal remedy, unless he or she had spontaneously desisted from the offence which had been initiated. However, if scandal or other serious harm or danger has resulted, the perpetrator, even though spontaneously desisting, may be punished by a just penalty, but of a lesser kind than that determined for the completed crime.

Can. 1329   §1 Where a number of persons conspire together to commit an offence, and accomplices are not expressly mentioned in the law or precept, if *ferendae sententiae* penalties were constituted for the principal offender, then the others are subject to the same penalties or to other penalties of the same or a lesser gravity.

§2 In the case of a *latae sententiae* penalty attached to an offence, accomplices, even though not mentioned in the law or precept, incur the same penalty if, without their assistance, the crime would not have been committed, and if the penalty is of such a nature as to be able to affect them; otherwise, they can be punished with *ferendae sententiae* penalties.

Can. 1330 §1 An offence which consists in a declaration or in some other manifestation of doctrine or knowledge, is not to be regarded as effected if no one actually perceives the declaration or manifestation.

TITLE IV: PENALTIES AND OTHER PUNISHMENTS

Chapter I

CENSURES

Can. 1331 §1 An excommunicated person is forbidden:
   1° to have any ministerial part in the celebration of the Sacrifice of the Eucharist or in any other ceremonies of public worship;
   2° to celebrate the sacraments or sacramentals and to receive the sacraments;
   3° to exercise any ecclesiastical offices, ministries, functions or acts of governance.
  §2 If the excommunication has been imposed or declared, the offender:
   1° proposing to act in defiance of the provision of §1, n. 1 is to be removed, or else the liturgical action is to be suspended, unless there is a grave reason to the contrary;
   2° invalidly exercises any acts of governance which, in accordance with §1, n. 3, are unlawful;
   3° is forbidden to benefit from privileges already granted;
   4° cannot validly assume any dignity, office or other function in the Church;
   5° loses the title to the benefits of any dignity, office, function or pension held in the Church.

Can. 1332 One who is under interdict is obliged by the prohibition of can. 1331 §1, nn. 1 and 2; if the interdict was imposed or declared, the provision of can. 1331 §2, n. 1 is to be observed.

Can. 1333 §1 Suspension, which can affect only clerics, prohibits:
   1° all or some of the acts of the power of order;
   2° all or some of the acts of the power of governance;
   3° the exercise of all or some of the rights or functions attaching to an office.
  §2 In a law or a precept it may be prescribed that, after a judgement which imposes or declares the penalty, a suspended person cannot validly perform acts of the power of governance.

§3 The prohibition never affects:

1° any offices or power of governance which are not within the control of the Superior who establishes the penalty;

2° a right of residence which the offender may have by virtue of office;

3° the right to administer goods which may belong to an office held by the person suspended, if the penalty is *latae sententiae.*

§4 A suspension prohibiting the receipt of benefits, stipends, pensions or other such things, carries with it the obligation of restitution of whatever has been unlawfully received, even though this was in good faith.

Can. 1334   §1 The extent of a suspension, within the limits laid down in the preceding canon, is defined either by the law or precept, or by the judgement or decree whereby the penalty is imposed.

§2 A law, but not a precept, can establish a *latae sententiae* suspension without an added determination or limitation; such a penalty has all the effects enumerated in can. 1333 §1.

Can. 1335   If a censure prohibits the celebration of the sacraments or sacramentals or the exercise of a power of governance, the prohibition is suspended whenever this is necessary to provide for the faithful who are in danger of death. If a *latae sententiae* censure has not been declared, the prohibition is also suspended whenever one of the faithful requests a sacrament or sacramental or an act of the power of governance; for any just reason it is lawful to make such a request.

Chapter II

EXPIATORY PENALTIES

Can. 1336   §1 Expiatory penalties can affect the offender either forever or for a determinate or an indeterminate period. Apart from others which the law may perhaps establish, these penalties are as follows:

1° a prohibition against residence, or an order to reside, in a certain place or territory;

2° deprivation of power, office, function, right, privilege, faculty, favour, title or insignia, even of a merely honorary nature;

3° a prohibition on the exercise of those things enumerated in n. 2, or a prohibition on their exercise inside or outside a certain place; such a prohibition is never under pain of nullity;

4° a penal transfer to another office;

5° dismissal from the clerical state.

§2 Only those expiatory penalties may be *latae sententiae* which are enumerated in §1, n. 3.

Can. 1337   §1 A prohibition against residing in a certain place or territory can affect both clerics and religious. An order to reside in a certain place can affect secular clerics and, within the limits of their constitutions, religious.

§2 An order imposing residence in a certain place or territory must have the consent of the Ordinary of that place, unless there is question of a house set up for penance or rehabilitation of clerics, including extra-diocesans.

Can. 1338 §1 The deprivations and prohibitions enumerated in can. 1336 §1, nn. 2 and 3 never affect powers, offices, functions, rights, privileges, faculties, favours, titles or insignia, which are not within the control of the Superior who establishes the penalty.

§2 There can be no deprivation of the power of order, but only a prohibition against the exercise of it or of some of its acts; neither can there be a deprivation of academic degrees.

§3 The norm laid down for censures in can. 1335 is to be observed in regard to the prohibitions mentioned in can. 1336 §1, n. 3.

Chapter III
PENAL REMEDIES AND PENANCES

Can. 1339 §1 When someone is in a proximate occasion of committing an offence or when, after an investigation, there is a serious suspicion that an offence has been committed, the Ordinary either personally or through another can give that person warning.

§2 In the case of behaviour which gives rise to scandal or serious disturbance of public order, the Ordinary can also correct the person, in a way appropriate to the particular conditions of the person and of what has been done.

§3 The fact that there has been a warning or a correction must always be proven, at least from some document to be kept in the secret archive of the curia.

Can. 1340 §1 A penance, which is imposed in the external forum, is the performance of some work of religion or piety or charity.

§2 A public penance is never to be imposed for an occult transgression.

§3 According to his prudent judgement, the Ordinary may add penances to the penal remedy of warning or correction.

TITLE V: THE APPLICATION OF PENALTIES

Can. 1341 The Ordinary is to start a judicial or an administrative procedure for the imposition or the declaration of penalties only when he perceives that neither by fraternal correction or reproof, nor by any methods of pastoral care, can the scandal be sufficiently repaired, justice restored and the offender reformed.

Can. 1342 §1 Whenever there are just reasons against the use of a judicial procedure, a penalty can be imposed or declared by means of an extra-judicial decree; in every case, penal remedies and penances may be applied by a decree.

§2 Perpetual penalties cannot be imposed or declared by means of a decree; nor can penalties which the law or precept establishing them forbids to be applied by decree.

§3 What the law or decree says of a judge in regard to the imposition or declaration of a penalty in a trial, is to be applied also to a Superior who imposes or declares a penalty by an extra-judicial decree, unless it is otherwise clear, or unless there is question of provisions which concern only procedural matters.

Can. 1343 If a law or precept gives the judge the power to apply or not to apply a penalty, the judge may also, according to his own conscience and prudence, modify the penalty or in its place impose a penance.

Can. 1344 Even though the law may use obligatory words, the judge may, according to his own conscience and prudence:

  1° defer the imposition of the penalty to a more opportune time, if it is foreseen that greater evils may arise from a too hasty punishment of the offender;

  2° abstain from imposing the penalty or substitute a milder penalty or a penance, if the offender has repented and repaired the scandal, or if the offender has been or foreseeably will be sufficiently punished by the civil authority;

  3° may suspend the obligation of observing an expiatory penalty, if the person is a first-offender after a hitherto blameless life, and there is no urgent need to repair scandal; this is, however, to be done in such a way that if the person again commits an offence within a time laid down by the judge, then that person must pay the penalty for both offences, unless in the meanwhile the time for prescription of a penal action in respect of the former offence has expired.

Can. 1345 Whenever the offender had only an imperfect use of reason, or committed the offence out of fear or necessity or in the heat of passion or with a mind disturbed by drunkenness or a similar cause, the judge can refrain from inflicting any punishment if he considers that the person's reform may be better accomplished in some other way.

Can. 1346 Whenever the offender has committed a number of offences and the sum of penalties which should be imposed seems excessive, it is left to the prudent decision of the judge to moderate the penalties in an equitable fashion.

Can. 1347 §1 A censure cannot validly be imposed unless the offender has beforehand received at least one warning to purge the contempt, and has been allowed suitable time to do so.

§2 The offender is said to have purged the contempt if he or she has truly repented of the offence and has made, or at least seriously promised to make, reparation for the damage and scandal.

Can. 1348   When the person has been found not guilty of an accusation, or where no penalty has been imposed, the Ordinary may provide for the person's welfare or for the common good by opportune warnings or other solicitous means, and even, if the case calls for it, by the use of penal remedies.

Can. 1349   If a penalty is indeterminate, and if the law does not provide otherwise, the judge is not to impose graver penalties, especially censures, unless the seriousness of the case really demands it. He may not impose penalties which are perpetual.

Can. 1350   §1 In imposing penalties on a cleric, except in the case of dismissal from the clerical state, care must always be taken that he does not lack what is necessary for his worthy support.

§2 If a person is truly in need because he has been dismissed from the clerical state, the Ordinary is to provide in the best way possible.

Can. 1351   A penalty binds an offender everywhere, even when the one who established or imposed it has ceased from office, unless it is otherwise expressly provided.

Can. 1352   §1 If a penalty prohibits the reception of the sacraments or sacramentals, the prohibition is suspended for as long as the offender is in danger of death.

§2 The obligation of observing a *latae sententiae* penalty which has not been declared, and is not notorious in the place where the offender actually is, is suspended either in whole or in part to the extent that the offender cannot observe it without the danger of grave scandal or loss of good name.

Can. 1352   An appeal or a recourse against judgements of a court or against decrees which impose or declare any penalty, has a suspensive effect.

TITLE VI: THE CESSATION OF PENALTIES

Can. 1354   §1 Besides those who are enumerated in cann. 1355–56, all who can dispense from a law which is supported by a penalty, can also remit the penalty itself.

§2 Moreover, a law or precept which establishes a penalty can also grant to others the power of remitting the penalty.

§3 If the Apostolic See has reserved the remission of a penalty to itself or to others, the reservation is to be strictly interpreted.

Can. 1355 §1 Provided it is not reserved to the Apostolic See, a penalty which is established by law and has been imposed or declared, can be remitted by the following:

1° the Ordinary who initiated the judicial proceedings to impose or declare the penalty, or who by a decree, either personally or through another, imposed or declared it;

2° the Ordinary of the place where the offender actually is, after consulting the Ordinary mentioned in n. 1, unless because of extraordinary circumstances this is impossible.

§2 Provided it is not reserved to the Apostolic See, a *latae sententiae* penalty established by law but not yet declared, can be remitted by the Ordinary in respect of his subjects and of those actually in his territory or of those who committed the offence in his territory. Moreover, any Bishop can do this, but only in the course of sacramental confession.

Can. 1356 §1 A *ferendae* or a *latae sententiae* penalty established in a precept not issued by the Apostolic See, can be remitted by the following:

1° the Ordinary of the place where the offender actually is;

2° if the penalty has been imposed or declared, the Ordinary who initiated the judicial proceedings to impose or declare the penalty, or who by a decree, either personally or through another, imposed or declared it.

§2 Before the remission is granted, the author of the precept is to be consulted, unless because of extraordinary circumstance this is impossible.

Can. 1357 §1 Without prejudice to the provisions of cann. 508 and 976, a confessor can in the internal sacramental forum remit a *latae sententiae* censure of excommunication or interdict which has not been declared, if it is difficult for the penitent to remain in a state of grave sin for the time necessary for the competent Superior to provide.

§2 In granting the remission, the confessor is to impose upon the penitent, under pain of again incurring the censure, the obligation to have recourse within one month to the competent Superior or to a priest having the requisite faculty, and to abide by his instructions. In the meantime, the confessor is to impose an appropriate penance and, to the extent demanded, to require reparation of scandal and damage. The recourse, however, may be made even through the confessor, without mention of a name.

§3 The same duty of recourse, when they have recovered, binds those who in accordance with can. 976 have had remitted an imposed or declared censure or one reserved to the Holy See.

Can. 1358 §1 The remission of a censure cannot be granted except to an offender whose contempt has been purged in accordance with can. 1347 §2. However, once the contempt has been purged, the remission cannot be refused.

§2 The one who remits a censure can make provision in accordance with can. 1348, and can also impose a penance.

Can. 1359 If one is bound by a number of penalties, a remission is valid only for those penalties expressed in it. A general remission, however, removes all penalties, except those which in the petition have been concealed in bad faith.

Can. 1360 The remission of a penalty extorted by grave fear is invalid.

Can. 1361 §1 A remission can be granted even to a person who is not present, or conditionally.

§2 A remission in the external forum is to be granted in writing, unless a grave reason suggests otherwise.

§3 Care is to be taken that the petition for remission or the remission itself is not made public, except insofar as this would either be useful for the protection of the good name of the offender, or be necessary to repair scandal.

Can. 1362 §1 A criminal action is extinguished by prescription after three years, except for:

1° offences reserved to the Congregation for the Doctrine of the Faith;

2° an action arising from any of the offences mentioned in cann. 1394, 1395, 1397, 1398, which is extinguished after five years;

3° offences not punished by the universal law, where a particular law has prescribed a different period of prescription.

§2 Prescription runs from the day the offence was committed or, if the offence was enduring or habitual, from the day it ceased.

Can. 1363 §1 An action to execute a penalty is extinguished by prescription if the judge's decree of execution mentioned in can. 1651 was not notified to the offender within the periods mentioned in can. 1362; these periods are to be reckoned from the day the condemnatory judgement became an adjudged matter.

§2 The same applies, with the necessary adjustments, if the penalty was imposed by an extra-judicial decree.

Part II
PENALTIES FOR PARTICULAR OFFENCES

TITLE I: OFFENCES AGAINST RELIGION AND THE UNITY OF THE CHURCH

Can. 1364 §1 An apostate from the faith, a heretic or a schismatic incurs a *latae sententiae* excommunication, without prejudice to the provision of can. 194 §1, n. 2; a cleric, moreover, may be punished with the penalties mentioned in can. 1336 §1, nn. 1, 2 and 3.

§2 If a longstanding contempt or the gravity of scandal calls for it, other penalties may be added, not excluding dismissal from the clerical state.

Can. 1365 One who is guilty of prohibited participation in religious rites is to be punished with a just penalty.

Can. 1366 Parents, and those taking the place of parents, who hand over their children to be baptised or brought up in a non-catholic religion, are to be punished with a censure or other just penalty.

Can. 1367 One who throws away the consecrated species or, for a sacrilegious purpose, takes them away or keeps them, incurs a *latae sententiae* excommunication reserved to the Apostolic See; a cleric, moreover, may be punished with some other penalty, not excluding dismissal from the clerical state.

Can. 1368 A person who, in asserting or promising something before an ecclesiastical authority, commits perjury, is to be punished with a just penalty.

Can. 1369 A person is to be punished with a just penalty, who, at a public event or assembly, or in a published writing, or by otherwise using the means of social communication, utters blasphemy, or gravely harms public morals, or rails at or excites hatred of or contempt for religion or the Church.

TITLE II
OFFENCES AGAINST CHURCH AUTHORITIES AND THE FREEDOM OF THE CHURCH

Can. 1370 §1 A person who uses physical force against the Roman Pontiff incurs a *latae sententiae* excommunication reserved to the Apostolic See; if the offender is a cleric, another penalty, not excluding dismissal from the clerical state, may be added according to the gravity of the crime.

§2 One who does this against a Bishop incurs a *latae sententiae* interdict and, if a cleric, he incurs also a *latae sententiae* suspension.

§3 A person who uses physical force against a cleric or religious out of contempt for the faith, or the Church, or ecclesiastical authority or the ministry, is to be punished with a just penalty.

Can. 1371 The following are to be punished with a just penalty:
1° a person who, apart from the case mentioned in can. 1364 §1, teaches a doctrine condemned by the Roman Pontiff, or by an Ecumenical Council, or obstinately rejects the teaching mentioned in can. 752 and, when warned by the Apostolic See or by the Ordinary, does not retract;
2° a person who in any other way does not obey the lawful command or prohibition of the Apostolic See or the Ordinary or Superior and, after being warned, persists in disobedience.

Can. 1372 A person who appeals from an act of the Roman Pontiff to an Ecumenical Council or to the College of Bishops, is to be punished with a censure.

Can. 1373 A person who publicly incites his or her subjects to hatred or animosity against the Apostolic See or the Ordinary because of some act of ecclesiastical authority or ministry, or who provokes the subjects to disobedience against them, is to be punished by interdict or other just penalties.

Can. 1374 A person who joins an association which plots against the Church is to be punished with a just penalty; one who promotes or takes office in such an association is to be punished with an interdict.

Can. 1375 Those who hinder the freedom of the ministry or of an election or of the exercise of ecclesiastical power, or the lawful use of sacred or other ecclesiastical goods, or who intimidate either an elector or one who is elected or one who exercises ecclesiastical power or ministry, may be punished with a just penalty.

Can. 1376 A person who profanes a sacred object, moveable or immovable, is to be punished with a just penalty.

Can. 1377 A person who without the prescribed permission alienates ecclesiastical goods, is to be punished with a just penalty.

TITLE III
USURPATION OF ECCLESIASTICAL OFFICES
AND OFFENCES COMMITTED IN THEIR EXERCISE

Can. 1378 §1 A priest who acts against the prescription of can. 977 incurs a *latae sententiae* excommunication reserved to the Apostolic See.

§2 The following incur a *latae sententiae* interdict or, if a cleric, a *latae sententiae* suspension:

1° a person who, not being an ordained priest, attempts to celebrate Mass;

2° a person who, apart from the case mentioned in §1, though unable to give valid sacramental absolution, attempts to do so, or hears a sacramental confession.

§3 In the cases mentioned in §2, other penalties, not excluding excommunication, can be added, according to the gravity of the offence.

Can. 1379 A person who, apart from the cases mentioned in can. 1378, pretends to administer a sacrament, is to be punished with a just penalty.

Can. 1380 A person who through simony celebrates or receives a sacrament, is to be punished with an interdict or suspension.

Can. 1381 §1 Anyone who usurps an ecclesiastical office is to be punished with a just penalty.

§2 The unlawful retention of an ecclesiastical office after being deprived of it, or ceasing from it, is equivalent to usurpation.

Can. 1382 Both the Bishop who, without a pontifical mandate, consecrates a person a Bishop, and the one who receives the consecration from him, incur a *latae sententiae* excommunication reserved to the Apostolic See.

Can. 1383 A Bishop who, contrary to the provision of can. 1015, ordained someone else's subject without the lawful dimissorial letters, is prohibited from conferring orders for one year. The person who received the order is ipso facto suspended from the order received.

Can. 1384 A person who, apart from the cases mentioned in cann. 1378–1383, unlawfully exercises the office of a priest or another sacred ministry, may be punished with a just penalty.

Can. 1385 A person who unlawfully traffics in Mass offerings is to be punished with a censure or other just penalty.

Can. 1386 A person who gives or promises something so that some one who exercises an office in the Church would unlawfully act or fail to act, is to be punished with a just penalty; likewise, the person who accepts such gifts or promises.

Can. 1387 A priest who in confession, or on the occasion or under the pretext of confession, solicits a penitent to commit a sin against the sixth commandment of the Decalogue, is to be punished, according to the gravity of the offence, with suspension, prohibitions and deprivations; in the more serious cases he is to be dismissed from the clerical state.

Can. 1388 §1 A confessor who directly violates the sacramental seal, incurs a *latae sententiae* excommunication reserved to the Apostolic See; he who does so only indirectly is to be punished according to the gravity of the offence.

§2 Interpreters and the others mentioned in can. 983 §2, who violate the secret, are to be punished with a just penalty, not excluding excommunication.

Can. 1389 §1 A person who abuses ecclesiastical power or an office, is to be punished according to the gravity of the act or the omission, not excluding by deprivation of the office, unless a penalty for that abuse is already established by law or precept.

§2 A person who, through culpable negligence, unlawfully and with harm to another, performs or omits an act of ecclesiastical power or ministry or office, is to be punished with a just penalty.

TITLE IV: THE OFFENCE OF FALSEHOOD

Can. 1390 §1 A person who falsely denounces a confessor of the offence mentioned in can. 1387 to an ecclesiastical Superior, incurs a *latae sententiae* interdict and, if a cleric, he incurs also a suspension.

§2 A person who calumniously denounces an offence to an ecclesiastical Superior, or otherwise injures the good name of another, can be punished with a just penalty, not excluding a censure.

§3 The calumniator can also be compelled to make appropriate amends.

Can. 1391 The following can be punished with a just penalty, according to the gravity of the offence:

1° a person who composes a false public ecclesiastical document, or who changes or conceals a genuine one, or who uses a false or altered one;

2° a person who in an ecclesiastical matter uses some other false or altered document;

3° a person who, in a public ecclesiastical document, asserts something false.

TITLE V
OFFENCES AGAINST SPECIAL OBLIGATIONS

Can. 1392 Clerics or religious who engage in trading or business contrary to the provisions of the canons, are to be punished according to the gravity of the offence.

Can. 1393 A person who violates obligations imposed by a penalty, can be punished with a just penalty.

Can. 1394 §1 Without prejudice to the provisions of can. 194, §1, n. 3, a cleric who attempts marriage, even if only civilly, incurs a *latae sententiae* suspension. If, after warning, he has not reformed and continues to give scandal, he can be progressively punished by deprivations, or even by dismissal from the clerical state.

§2 Without prejudice to the provisions of can. 694, a religious in perpetual vows who is not a cleric but who attempts marriage, even if only civilly, incurs a *latae sententiae* interdict.

Can. 1395 §1 Apart from the case mentioned in can. 1394, a cleric living in concubinage, and a cleric who continues in some other external sin against the sixth commandment of the Decalogue which causes scandal, is to be punished with suspension. To this, other penalties can progressively be added if after a warning he persists in the offence, until eventually he can be dismissed from the clerical state.

§2 A cleric who has offended in other ways against the sixth commandment of the Decalogue, if the crime was committed by force, or by threats, or in public, or with a minor under the age of sixteen years, is to be punished with just penalties, not excluding dismissal from the clerical state if the case so warrants.

Can. 1396 A person who gravely violates the obligation of residence to which he is bound by reason of an ecclesiastical office, is to be punished with a just penalty, not excluding, after a warning, deprivation of the office.

TITLE VI
OFFENCES AGAINST HUMAN LIFE AND LIBERTY

Can. 1397 One who commits murder, or who by force or by fraud abducts, imprisons, mutilates or gravely wounds a person, is to be punished, according to the gravity of the offence, with the deprivations and prohibitions mentioned in can. 1336. In the case of the murder of one of those persons mentioned in can. 1370, the offender is punished with the penalties there prescribed.

Can. 1398 A person who actually procures an abortion incurs a *latae sententiae* excommunication.

TITLE VII: GENERAL NORM

Can. 1399 Besides the cases prescribed in this or in other laws, the external violation of divine or canon law can be punished, and with a just penalty, only when the special gravity of the violation requires it and necessity demands that scandals be prevented or repaired.

Book VII
PROCESSES

Part I
TRIALS IN GENERAL

Can. 1400 §1 The objects of a trial are:
1° to pursue or vindicate the rights of physical or juridical persons, or to declare juridical facts;
2° to impose or to declare penalties in regard to offences.
§2 Disputes arising from an act of administrative power, however, can be referred only to the Superior or to an administrative tribunal.

Can. 1401 The Church has its own and exclusive right to judge:
1° cases which refer to matters which are spiritual or linked with the spiritual;
2° the violation of ecclesiastical laws and whatever contains an element of sin, to determine guilt and impose ecclesiastical penalties.

Can. 1402 All tribunals of the Church are governed by the canons which follow, without prejudice to the norms of the tribunals of the Apostolic See.

Can. 1403 §1 Cases for the canonisation of the Servants of God are governed by special pontifical law.
§2 The provisions of this Code are also applied to these cases whenever the special pontifical law remits an issue to the universal law, or whenever norms are involved which of their very nature apply also to these cases.

TITLE I: THE COMPETENT FORUM

Can. 1404 The First See is judged by no one.

Can. 1405 §1 In the cases mentioned in can. 1401, the Roman Pontiff alone has the right to judge:
1° Heads of State;
2° Cardinals;
3° Legates of the Apostolic See and, in penal cases, Bishops;
4° other cases which he has reserved to himself.
§2 A judge cannot review an act or instrument which the Roman Pontiff has specifically confirmed, except by his prior mandate.

§3 It is reserved to the Roman Rota to judge:

1° Bishops in contentious cases, without prejudice to can. 1419 §2;

2° the Abbot primate or the Abbot superior of a monastic congregation, and the supreme Moderator of a religious institute of pontifical right;

3° dioceses and other ecclesiastical persons, physical or juridical, which have no Superior other than the Roman Pontiff.

Can. 1406 §1 If the provision of can. 1404 is violated, the acts and decisions are invalid.

§2 In the cases mentioned in can. 1405, the non-competence of other judges is absolute.

Can. 1407 §1 No one can be brought to trial in first instance except before a judge who is competent on the basis of one of the titles determined in cann. 1408–1414.

§2 The non-competence of a judge who has none of these titles is described as relative.

§3 The plaintiff follows the forum of the respondent. If the respondent has more than one forum, the plaintiff may opt for any one of them.

Can. 1408 Anyone can be brought to trial before the tribunal of domicile or quasi-domicile.

Can. 1409 §1 A person who has not even a quasi-domicile has a forum in the place of actual residence.

§2 A person whose domicile, quasi-domicile or place of actual residence is unknown, can be brought to trial in the forum of the plaintiff, provided no other lawful forum is available.

Can. 1410 Competence by reason of subject matter means that a party can be brought to trial before the tribunal of the place where the subject matter of the litigation is located, whenever the action concerns that subject matter directly, or when it is an action for the recovery of possession.

Can. 1411 §1 Competence by reason of contract means that a party can be brought to trial before the tribunal of the place in which the contract was made or must be fulfilled, unless the parties mutually agree to choose another tribunal.

§2 If the case concerns obligations which arise from some other title, the party can be brought to trial before the tribunal of the place in which the obligation arose or in which it is to be fulfilled.

Can. 1412 A person accused in a penal case can, even though absent, be brought to trial before the tribunal of the place in which the offence was committed.

Can. 1413 A party can be brought to trial:

1° in cases concerning administration, before the tribunal of the place in which the administration was exercised;

2° in cases concerning inheritances or pious legacies, before the tribunal of the last domicile or quasi-domicile or residence of the person whose inheritance or pious legacy is at issue, in accordance with the norms of cann. 1408–1409. If, however, only the execution of the legacy is involved, the ordinary norms of competence are to be followed.

Can. 1414 Competence by reason of connection means that cases which are inter-connected can be heard by one and the same tribunal and in the same process, unless this is prevented by a provision of the law.

Can. 1415 Competence by reason of prior summons means that, if two or more tribunals are equally competent, the tribunal which has first lawfully summoned the respondent has the right to hear the case.

Can. 1416 A conflict of competence between tribunals subject to the same appeal tribunal is to be resolved by the latter tribunal. If they are not subject to the same appeal tribunal, the conflict is to be settled by the Apostolic Signatura.

TITLE II
DIFFERENT GRADES AND KINDS OF TRIBUNALS

Can. 1417 §1 Because of the primacy of the Roman Pontiff, any of the faithful may either refer their case to, or introduce it before, the Holy See, whether the case be contentious or penal. They may do so at any grade of trial or at any stage of the suit.

§2 Apart from the case of an appeal, a referral to the Apostolic See does not suspend the exercise of jurisdiction of a judge who has already begun to hear a case. The judge can, therefore, continue with the trial up to the definitive judgement, unless the Apostolic See has indicated to him that it has reserved the case to itself.

Can. 1418 Every tribunal has the right to call on other tribunals for assistance in instructing a case or in communicating acts.

Chapter I
THE TRIBUNAL OF FIRST INSTANCE

Article 1: The Judge

Can. 1419 §1 In each diocese and for all cases which are not expressly excepted in law, the judge of first instance is the diocesan Bishop. He can exercise his judicial power either personally or through others, in accordance with the following canons.

§2 If the case concerns the rights or temporal goods of a juridical person represented by the Bishop, the appeal tribunal is to judge in first instance.

Can. 1420 §1 Each diocesan Bishop is obliged to appoint a judicial Vicar, or 'Officialis', with ordinary power to judge. The judicial Vicar is to be a person distinct from the Vicar general, unless the smallness of the diocese or the limited number of cases suggests otherwise.

§2 The judicial Vicar constitutes one tribunal with the Bishop, but cannot judge cases which the Bishop reserves to himself.

§3 The judicial Vicar can be given assistants, who are called associate judicial Vicars or 'Vice-officiales'.

§4 The judicial Vicar and the associate judicial Vicars must be priests of good repute, with a doctorate or at least a licentiate in canon law, and not less than thirty years of age.

§5 When the see is vacant, they do not cease from office, nor can they be removed by the diocesan Administrator. On the coming of the new Bishop, however, they need to be confirmed in office.

Can. 1421 §1 In each diocese the Bishop is to appoint diocesan judges, who are to be clerics.

§2 The Episcopal Conference can permit that lay persons also be appointed judges. Where necessity suggests, one of these can be chosen in forming a college of judges.

§3 Judges are to be of good repute, and possess a doctorate, or at least a licentiate, in canon law.

Can. 1422 The judicial Vicar, the associate judicial Vicars and the other judges are appointed for a specified period of time, without prejudice to the provision of can. 1420 §5. They cannot be removed from office except for a lawful and grave reason.

Can. 1423 §1 With the approval of the Apostolic See, several diocesan Bishops can agree to establish one tribunal of first instance in their dioceses, in place of the diocesan tribunals mentioned in cann. 1419–1421. In this case the group of Bishops, or a Bishop designated by them, has all the powers which the diocesan Bishop has for his tribunal.

§2 The tribunals mentioned in §1 can be established for all cases, or for some types of cases only.

Can. 1424 In any trial a sole judge can associate with himself two assessors as advisers; they may be clerics or lay persons of good repute.

Can. 1425 §1 The following matters are reserved to a collegiate tribunal of three judges, any contrary custom being reprobated:

1° contentious cases: a) concerning the bond of sacred ordination; b) concerning the bond of marriage, without prejudice to the provisions of cann. 1686 and 1688;

2° penal cases: a) for offences which can carry the penalty of dismissal from the clerical state; b) concerning the imposition or declaration of an excommunication.

§2 The Bishop can entrust the more difficult cases or those of greater importance to the judgement of three or of five judges.

§3 The judicial Vicar is to assign judges in order by rotation to hear the individual cases, unless in particular cases the Bishop has decided otherwise.

§4 In a trial at first instance, if it should happen that it is impossible to constitute a college of judges, the Episcopal Conference can for as long as the impossibility persists, permit the Bishop to entrust cases to a sole clerical judge. Where possible, the sole judge is to associate with himself an assessor and an auditor.

§5 Once judges have been designated, the judicial Vicar is not to replace them, except for a very grave reason, which must be expressed in a decree.

Can. 1426 §1 A collegiate tribunal must proceed in a collegiate fashion and give its judgement by majority vote.

§2 As far as possible, the judicial Vicar or an associate judicial Vicar must preside over the collegiate tribunal.

Can. 1427 §1 If there is a controversy between religious, or houses of the same clerical religious institute of pontifical right, the judge at first instance, unless the constitutions provide otherwise, is the provincial Superior or, if an autonomous monastery is concerned, the local Abbot.

§2 Without prejudice to a different provision in the constitutions, when a contentious matter arises between two provinces, the supreme Moderator, either personally or through a delegate, will be the judge at first instance. If the controversy is between two monasteries, the Abbot superior of the monastic congregation will be the judge.

§3 Finally, if a controversy arises between physical or juridical persons of different religious institutes or even of the same clerical institute of diocesan right or of the same lay institute, or between a religious person and a secular cleric or a lay person or a non-religious juridical person, it is the diocesan tribunal which judges at first instance.

Article 2: Auditors and Relators

Can. 1428 §1 The judge or, in the case of a collegiate tribunal, the presiding judge, can designate an auditor to instruct the case. The auditor may be chosen from the tribunal judges, or from persons approved by the Bishop for this office.

§2 The Bishop can approve clerics or lay persons for the role of auditor. They are to be persons conspicuous for their good conduct, prudence and learning.

§3 The task of the auditor is solely to gather the evidence in accordance with the judge's commission and, when gathered, to submit it to the judge. Unless the judge determines otherwise, however, an auditor can in the meantime decide what evidence is to be collected and the manner of its collection, should any question arise about these matters while the auditor is carrying out his role.

Can. 1429 The presiding judge of a collegiate tribunal is to designate one of the judges of the college as 'ponens' or 'relator'. This person is to present the case at the meeting of the judges and set out the judgement in writing. For a just reason the presiding judge can substitute another person in the place of the 'ponens'.

Article 3: The Promotor of Justice, the Defender of the Bond and the Notary

Can. 1430 A promotor of justice is to be appointed in the diocese for penal cases, and for contentious cases in which the public good may be at stake. The promotor is bound by office to safeguard the public good.

Can. 1431 §1 In contentious cases it is for the diocesan Bishop to decide whether the public good is at stake or not, unless the law prescribes the intervention of the promotor of justice, or this is clearly necessary from the nature of things.

§2 If the promotor of justice has intervened at an earlier instance of a trial, this intervention is presumed to be necessary at a subsequent instance.

Can. 1432 A defender of the bond is to be appointed in the diocese for cases which deal with the nullity of ordination or the nullity or dissolution of marriage. The defender of the bond is bound by office to present and expound all that can reasonably be argued against the nullity or dissolution.

Can. 1433 In cases in which the presence of the promotor of justice or of the defender of the bond is required, the acts are invalid if they were not summoned. This does not apply if, although not summoned, they were in fact present or, having studied the acts, able to fulfil their role at least before the judgement.

Can. 1434 Unless otherwise expressly provided:
    1° whenever the law directs that the judge is to hear the parties or either of them, the promotor of justice and the defender of the bond are also to be heard if they are present;
    2° whenever, at the submission of a party, the judge is required to decide some matter, the submission of the promotor of justice or of the defender of the bond engaged in the trial has equal weight.

Can. 1435 It is the Bishop's responsibility to appoint the promotor of justice and defender of the bond. They are to be clerics or lay persons of good repute, with a doctorate or a licentiate in canon law, and of proven prudence and zeal for justice.

Can. 1436 §1 The same person can hold the office of promotor of justice and defender of the bond, although not in the same case.

§2 The promotor of justice and the defender of the bond can be appointed for all cases, or for individual cases. They can be removed by the Bishop for a just reason.

Can. 1437   §1 A notary is to be present at every hearing, so much so that the acts are null unless signed by the notary.

§2 Acts drawn up by notaries constitute public proof.

Chapter II
THE TRIBUNAL OF SECOND INSTANCE

Can. 1438   Without prejudice to the provision of can. 1444 §1, n. 1:

1° an appeal from the tribunal of a suffragan Bishop is to the metropolitan tribunal, without prejudice to the provisions of can. 1439.

2° in cases heard at first instance in the tribunal of the Metropolitan, the appeal is to a tribunal which the Metropolitan, with the approval of the Apostolic See, has designated in a stable fashion;

3° for cases dealt with before a provincial Superior, the tribunal of second instance is that of the supreme Moderator; for cases heard before the local Abbot, the second instance court is that of the Abbot superior of the monastic congregation.

Can. 1439   §1 If a single tribunal of first instance has been constituted for several dioceses, in accordance with the norm of can. 1423, the Episcopal Conference must, with the approval of the Holy See, constitute a tribunal of second instance, unless the dioceses are all suffragans of the same archdiocese.

§2 Even apart from the cases mentioned in §1, the Episcopal Conference can, with the approval of the Apostolic See, constitute one or more tribunals of second instance.

§3 In respect of the second instance tribunals mentioned in §§1–2, the Episcopal Conference, or the Bishop designated by it, has all the powers that belong to a diocesan Bishop in respect of his own tribunal.

Can. 1440   If competence by reason of the grade of trial, in accordance with the provisions of cann. 1438 and 1439, is not observed, then the non-competence of the judge is absolute.

Can. 1441   The tribunal of second instance is to be constituted in the same way as the tribunal of first instance. However, if a sole judge has given a judgement in first instance in accordance with can. 1425 §4, the second instance tribunal is to act collegially.

Chapter III

THE TRIBUNALS OF THE APOSTOLIC SEE

Can. 1442   The Roman Pontiff is the supreme judge for the whole catholic world. He gives judgement either personally, or through the ordinary tribunals of the Apostolic See, or through judges whom he delegates.

Can. 1443   The ordinary tribunal constituted by the Roman Pontiff to receive appeals is the Roman Rota.

Can. 1444   The Roman Rota judges:
    1° in second instance, cases which have been judged by ordinary tribunals of first instance and have been referred to the Holy See by a lawful appeal;
    2° in third or further instance, cases which have been processed by the Roman Rota itself or by any other tribunal, unless there is question of an adjudged matter.

§2   This tribunal also judges in first instance the cases mentioned in can. 1405 §3, and any others which the Roman Pontiff, either on his own initiative or at the request of the parties, has reserved to his tribunal and has entrusted to the Roman Rota. These cases are judged by the Rota also in second or further instances, unless the rescript entrusting the task provides otherwise.

Can. 1445   §1   The supreme Tribunal of the Apostolic Signatura hears:
    1° plaints of nullity, petitions for total reinstatement and other recourses against rotal judgements;
    2° recourses in cases affecting the status of persons, which the Roman Rota has refused to admit to a new examination;
    3° exceptions of suspicion and other cases against Auditors of the Roman Rota by reason of things done in the exercise of their office;
    4° the conflicts of competence mentioned in can. 1416.

§2   This same Tribunal deals with controversies which arise from an act of ecclesiastical administrative power, and which are lawfully referred to it. It also deals with other administrative controversies referred to it by the Roman Pontiff or by departments of the Roman Curia, and with conflicts of competence among these departments.

§3   This Supreme Tribunal is also competent:
    1° to oversee the proper administration of justice and, should the need arise, to take notice of advocates and procurators;
    2° to extend the competence of tribunals;
    3° to promote and approve the establishment of the tribunals mentioned in cann. 1423 and 1439.

TITLE III
THE DISCIPLINE TO BE OBSERVED IN TRIBUNALS

Chapter I

THE DUTIES OF THE JUDGES AND OF THE OFFICERS
OF THE TRIBUNAL

Can. 1446 §1 All Christ's faithful, and especially Bishops, are to strive earnestly, with due regard for justice, to ensure that disputes among the people of God are as far as possible avoided, and are settled promptly and without rancour.

§2 In the early stages of litigation, and indeed at any other time as often as he discerns any hope of a successful outcome, the judge is not to fail to exhort and assist the parties to seek an equitable solution to their controversy in discussions with one another. He is to indicate to them suitable means to this end and avail himself of serious-minded persons to mediate.

§3 If the issue is about the private good of the parties, the judge is to discern whether an agreement or a judgement by an arbitrator, in accordance with the norms of cann. 1717–1720*, might usefully serve to resolve the controversy.

Can. 1447 Any person involved in a case as judge, promotor of justice, defender of the bond, procurator, advocate, witness or expert cannot subsequently, in another instance, validly determine the same case as a judge or exercise the role of assessor in it.

Can. 1448 §1 The judge is not to undertake the hearing of a case in which any personal interest may be involved by reason of consanguinity or affinity in any degree of the direct line and up to the fourth degree of the collateral line, or by reason of guardianship or tutelage, or of close acquaintanceship or marked hostility or possible financial profit or loss.

§2 The promotor of justice, the defender of the bond, the assessor and the auditor must likewise refrain from exercising their offices in these circumstances.

Can. 1449 §1 In the cases mentioned in can. 1448, if the judge himself does not refrain from exercising his office, a party may object to him.

§2 The judicial Vicar is to deal with this objection. If the objection is directed against the judicial Vicar himself, the Bishop in charge of the tribunal is to deal with the matter.

§3 If the Bishop is the judge and the objection is directed against him, he is to refrain from judging.

§4 If the objection is directed against the promotor of justice, the defender of the bond or any other officer of the tribunal, it is to be dealt

---

*Translators' note: It would appear that this reference should read 'cann. 1713–1716'.

with by the presiding judge of a collegial tribunal, or by the sole judge if there is only one.

Can. 1450 If the objection is upheld, the persons in question are to be changed, but not the grade of trial.

Can. 1451 §1 The objection is to be decided with maximum expedition, after hearing the parties, the promotor of justice or the defender of the bond, if they are engaged in the trial and the objection is not directed against them.

§2 Acts performed by a judge before being objected to are valid. Acts performed after the objection has been lodged must be rescinded if a party requests this within ten days of the admission of the objection.

Can. 1452 §1 In a matter which concerns private persons exclusively, a judge can proceed only at the request of a party. In penal cases, however, and in other cases which affect the public good of the Church or the salvation of souls, once the case has been lawfully introduced, the judge can and must proceed ex officio.

§2 The judge can also supply for the negligence of the parties in bringing forward evidence or in opposing exceptions, whenever this is considered necessary in order to avoid a gravely unjust judgement, without prejudice to the provisions of can. 1600.

Can. 1453 Judges and tribunals are to ensure that, within the bounds of justice, all cases are brought to a conclusion as quickly as possible. They are to see to it that in the tribunal of first instance cases are not protracted beyond a year, and in the tribunal of second instance not beyond six months.

Can. 1454 All who constitute a tribunal or assist in it must take an oath to exercise their office properly and faithfully

Can. 1455 §1 In a penal trial, the judges and tribunal assistants are bound to observe always the secret of the office; in a contentious trial, they are bound to observe it if the revelation of any part of the acts of the process could be prejudicial to the parties.

§2 They are also obliged to maintain permanent secrecy concerning the discussion held by the judges before giving their judgement, and concerning the various votes and opinions expressed there, without prejudice to the provisions of can. 1609 §4.

§3 Indeed, the judge can oblige witnesses, experts, and the parties and their advocates or procurators, to swear an oath to observe secrecy. This may be done if the nature of the case or of the evidence is such that revelation of the acts or evidence would put at risk the reputation of others, or give rise to quarrels, or cause scandal or have any similar untoward consequence.

Can. 1456 The judge and all who work in the tribunal are forbidden to accept any gifts on the occasion of a trial.

Can. 1457   §1 Judges can be punished by the competent authority with appropriate penalties, not excluding the loss of office, if, though certainly and manifestly competent, they refuse to give judgement; if, with no legal support, they declare themselves competent and hear and determine cases; if they breach the law of secrecy; or if, through deceit or serious negligence, they cause harm to the litigants.

§2 Tribunal officers and assistants are subject to the same penalties if they fail in their duty as above. The judge also has the power to punish them.

Chapter II
THE ORDERING OF THE HEARING

Can. 1458   Cases are to be heard in the order in which they were received and entered in the register, unless some case from among them needs to be dealt with more quickly than others. This is to be stated in a special decree which gives supporting reasons.

Can. 1459   §1 Defects which can render the judgement invalid can be proposed as exceptions at any stage or grade of trial; likewise, the judge can declare such exceptions ex officio.

§2 Apart from the cases mentioned in §1, exceptions seeking a delay, especially those which concern persons and the manner of trial, are to be proposed before the joinder of the issue, unless they emerge only after it. They are to be decided as soon as possible.

Can. 1460   §1 If an exception is proposed against the competence of the judge, the judge himself must deal with the matter.

§2 Where the exception concerns relative non-competence and the judge pronounces himself competent, his decision does not admit of appeal. However, a plaint of nullity and a total reinstatement are not prohibited.

§3 If the judge declares himself non-competent, a party who complains of being adversely affected can refer the matter within fifteen canonical days to the appeal tribunal.

Can. 1461   A judge who becomes aware at any stage of the case that he is absolutely non-competent, is bound to declare his non-competence.

Can. 1462   §1 Exceptions to the effect that an issue has become an adjudged matter or has been agreed between the parties, and those other peremptory exceptions which are said to put an end to the suit, are to be proposed and examined before the joinder of the issue. Whoever raises them subsequently is not to be rejected, but will be ordered to pay the costs unless it can be shown that the objection was not maliciously delayed.

§2 Other peremptory exceptions are to be proposed in the joinder of the issue and treated at the appropriate time under the rules governing incidental questions.

Can. 1463 §1 Counter actions can validly be proposed only within thirty days of the joinder of the issue.

§2 Such counter actions are to be dealt with at the same grade of trial and simultaneously with the principal action, unless it is necessary to deal with them separately or the judge considers this procedure more opportune.

Can. 1464 Questions concerning the guarantee of judicial expenses or the grant of free legal aid which has been requested from the very beginning of the process, and other similar matters, are normally to be settled before the joinder of the issue.

Chapter III

TIME LIMITS AND POSTPONEMENTS

Can. 1465 §1 The so-called canonical time limits are fixed times beyond which rights cease in law. They cannot be extended, nor can they validly be shortened except at the request of the parties.

§2 After hearing the parties, or at their request, the judge can, for a just reason, extend before they expire times fixed by himself or agreed by the parties. These times can never validly be shortened without the consent of the parties.

§3 The judge is to ensure that litigation is not unduly prolonged by reason of postponement.

Can. 1466 Where the law does not establish fixed times for concluding procedural actions, the judge is to define them, taking into consideration the nature of each act.

Can. 1467 If the day appointed for a judicial action is a holiday, the fixed term is considered to be postponed to the first subsequent day which is not a holiday.

Chapter IV

THE PLACE OF TRIAL

Can. 1468 As far as possible, the place where each tribunal sits is to be an established office which is open at stated times.

Can. 1469 §1 A judge who is forcibly expelled from his territory or prevented from exercising jurisdiction there, can exercise his jurisdiction and deliver judgement outside the territory. The diocesan Bishop is, however, to be informed of the matter.

§2 Apart from the circumstances mentioned in §1, the judge, for a just reason and after hearing the parties, can go outside his own territory to gather evidence. This is to be done with the permission of, and in a place designated by, the diocesan Bishop of the place to which he goes.

Chapter V

THOSE WHO MAY BE ADMITTED TO THE COURT AND THE MANNER OF COMPILING AND PRESERVING THE ACTS

Can. 1470 §1 Unless particular law prescribes otherwise, when cases are being heard before the tribunal, only those persons are to be present whom the law or the judge decides are necessary for the hearing of the case.

§2 The judge can with appropriate penalties take to task all who, while present at a trial, are gravely lacking in the reverence and obedience due to the tribunal. He can, moreover, suspend advocates and procurators from exercising their office in ecclesiastical tribunals.

Can. 1471 If a person to be interrogated uses a language unknown to the judge or the parties, an interpreter, appointed by the judge and duly sworn, can be employed in the case. Declarations are to be committed to writing in the original language, and a translation is to be added. An interpreter is also to be used if a deaf and dumb person must be interrogated, unless the judge prefers that replies to the questions he has asked be given in writing.

Can. 1472 §1 Judicial acts must be in writing, both those which refer to the merits of the case, that is, the acts of the case, and those which refer to the procedure, that is, the procedural acts.

§2 Each page of the acts is to be numbered and bear a seal of authenticity.

Can. 1473 Whenever the signature of parties or witnesses is required in judicial acts, and the party or witness is unable or unwilling to sign, this is to be noted in the acts. At the same time the judge and the notary are to certify that the act was read verbatim to the party or witness, and that the party or witness was either unable or unwilling to sign.

Can. 1474 §1 In the case of an appeal, a copy of the acts is to be sent to the higher tribunal, with a certification by the notary of its authenticity.

§2 If the acts are in a language unknown to the higher tribunal, they are to be translated into another language known to it. Suitable precautions are to be taken to ensure that the translation is accurate.

Can. 1475 §1 When the trial has been completed, documents which belong to private individuals must be returned to them, though a copy of them is to be retained.

§2 Without an order from the judge, notaries and the chancellor are forbidden to hand over to anyone a copy of the judicial acts and documents obtained in the process.

TITLE IV: THE PARTIES IN THE CASE

Chapter I
THE PLAINTIFF AND THE RESPONDENT

Can. 1476   Any person, baptised or unbaptised, can plead before a court. A person lawfully brought to trial must respond.

Can. 1477   Even though the plaintiff or the respondent has appointed a procurator or advocate, each is always bound to be present in person at the trial when the law or the judge so prescribes.

Can. 1478   §1 Minors and those who lack the use of reason can stand before the court only through their parents, guardians or curators, subject to the provisons of §3.

§2 If the judge considers that the rights of minors are in conflict with the rights of the parents, guardians or curators, or that these cannot sufficiently protect the rights of the minors, the minors are to stand before the court through a guardian or curator assigned by the judge.

§3 However, in cases concerning spiritual matters and matters linked with the spiritual, if the minors have the use of reason, they can plead and respond without the consent of parents or guardians; indeed, if they have completed their fourteenth year, they can stand before the court on their own behalf; otherwise, they do so through a curator appointed by the judge.

§4 Those barred from the administration of their goods and those of infirm mind can themselves stand before the court only to respond concerning their own offences, or by order of the judge. In other matters they must plead and respond through their curators.

Can. 1479   A guardian or curator appointed by a civil authority can be admitted by an ecclesiastical judge, after he has consulted, if possible, the diocesan Bishop of the person to whom the guardian or curator has been given. If there is no such guardian or curator, or it is not seen fit to admit the one appointed, the judge is to appoint a guardian or curator for the case.

Can. 1480   §1 Judicial persons stand before the court through their lawful representatives.

§2 In a case of absence or negligence of the representative, the Ordinary himself, either personally or through another, can stand before the court in the name of juridicial persons subject to his authority.

Chapter II

PROCURATORS AND ADVOCATES

Can. 1481   §1 A party can freely appoint an advocate and procurator for him or herself. Apart from the cases stated in §§2 and 3, however, a party can plead and respond personally, unless the judge considers the services of a procurator or advocate to be necessary.

§2 In a penal trial the accused must always have an advocate, either appointed personally or allocated by the judge.

§3 In a contentious trial which concerns minors or the public good, the judge is ex officio to appoint a legal representative for a party who lacks one; matrimonial cases are excepted.

Can. 1482   §1 A person can appoint only one procurator; the latter cannot appoint a substitute, unless this faculty has been expressly conceded.

§2 If, however, several procurators have for a just reason been appointed by the same person, these are to be so designated that there is the right of prior claim among them.

§3 Several advocates can, however, be appointed together.

Can. 1483   The procurator and advocate must have attained their majority and be of good repute. The advocate is also to be a catholic unless the diocesan Bishop permits otherwise, a doctor in canon law or otherwise well qualified, and approved by the same Bishop.

Can. 1484   §1 Prior to undertaking their office, the procurator and the advocate must deposit an authentic mandate with the tribunal.

§2 To prevent the extinction of a right, however, the judge can admit a procurator even though a mandate has not been presented; in an appropriate case, a suitable guarantee is to be given. However, the act lacks all force if the procurator does not present a mandate within the peremptory time-limit to be prescribed by the judge.

Can. 1485   Without a special mandate, a procurator cannot validly renounce a case, an instance or any judicial act; nor can a procurator settle an action, bargain, promise to abide by an arbitrator's award, or in general do anything for which the law requires a special mandate.

Can. 1486   §1 For the dismissal of a procurator or advocate to have effect, it must be notified to them and, if the joinder of the issue has taken place, the judge and the other party must be notified of the dismissal.

§2 When a definitive judgement has been given, the right and duty to appeal lie with the procurator, unless the mandating party refuses.

Can. 1487   For a grave reason, the procurator and the advocate can be removed from office by a decree of the judge given either ex officio or at the request of the party.

Can. 1488 §1 Both the procurator and the advocate are forbidden to influence a suit by bribery, seek immoderate payment, or bargain with the successful party for a share of the matter in dispute. If they do so, any such agreement is invalid and they can be fined by the judge. Moreover, the advocate can be suspended from office and, if this is not a first offence, can be removed from the register of advocates by the Bishop in charge of the tribunal.

§2 The same sanctions can be imposed on advocates and procurators who fraudulently exploit the law by withdrawing cases from tribunals which are competent, so that they may be judged more favourably by other tribunals.

Can. 1489 Advocates and procurators who betray their office because of gifts or promises, or any other consideration, are to be suspended from the exercise of their profession, and be fined or punished with other suitable penalties.

Can. 1490 As far as possible, permanent advocates and procurators are to be appointed in each tribunal and to receive a salary from the tribunal. They are to exercise their office, especially in matrimonial cases, for parties who may wish to choose them.

TITLE V: ACTIONS AND EXCEPTIONS

Chapter I

ACTIONS AND EXCEPTIONS IN GENERAL

Can. 1491 Every right is reinforced not only by an action, unless otherwise expressly provided, but also by an exception.

Can. 1492 §1 Every action is extinguished by prescription in accordance with the law, or in any other lawful way, with the exception of actions bearing on personal status, which are never extinguished.

§2 Without prejudice to the provision of can. 1462, an exception is always possible, and is of its nature perpetual.

Can. 1493 A plaintiff can bring several exceptions simultaneously against another person, concerning either the same matter or different matters, provided they are not in conflict with one another, and do not go beyond the competence of the tribunal that has been approached.

Can. 1494 §1 A respondent can institute a counter action against a plaintiff before the same judge and in the same trial, either by reason of the case's connection with the principal action, or with a view to removing or mitigating the plaintiff's plea.

§2 A counter action to a counter action is not admitted.

Can. 1495   The counter action is to be proposed to the judge before whom the original action was initiated, even though he has been delegated for one case only, or is otherwise relatively non-competent.

Chapter II
ACTIONS AND EXCEPTIONS IN PARTICULAR

Can. 1496   §1 A person who advances arguments, which are at least probable, to support a right to something held by another, and to indicate an imminent danger of loss of the object unless it is handed over for safekeeping, has a right to obtain from the judge the sequestration of the object in question.

§2 In similar circumstances, a person can obtain a restraint on another person's exercise of a right.

Can. 1497   §1 The sequestration of an object is also allowed for the security of a loan, provided there is sufficient evidence of the creditor's right.

§2 Sequestration can also extend to the assets of a debtor which, on whatever title, are in the keeping of others, as well as to the loans of the debtor.

Can. 1498   The sequestration of an object, and restraint on the exercise of a right, can in no way be decreed if the loss which is feared can be otherwise repaired, and a suitable guarantee is given that it will be repaired.

Can. 1499   The judge who grants the sequestration of an object, or the restraint on the exercise of a right, can first impose on the person to whom the grant is made an undertaking to repay any loss if the right is not proven.

Can. 1500   In matters concerning the nature and effect of an action for possession, the provisions of the civil law of the place where the thing to be possessed is situated, are to be observed.

Part II
THE CONTENTIOUS TRIAL

Section I: The Ordinary Contentious Trial

TITLE I: THE INTRODUCTION OF THE CASE

Chapter I
THE PETITION INTRODUCING THE SUIT

Can. 1501 A judge cannot investigate any case unless a plea, drawn up in accordance with canon law, is submitted either by a person whose interest is involved, or by the promotor of justice.

Can. 1502 A person who wishes to sue another must present a petition to a judge who is lawfully competent. In this petition the matter in dispute is to be set out and the intervention of the judge requested.

Can. 1503 §1 A judge can admit an oral plea whenever the plaintiff is impeded from presenting a petition or when the case can be easily investigated and is of minor significance.

§2 In both cases, however, the judge is to direct a notary to record the matter in writing. This written record is to be read to, and approved by, the plaintiff, and it takes the place of a petition written by the plaintiff as far as all effects of law are concerned.

Can. 1504 The petition by which a suit is introduced must:
    1° state the judge before whom the case is being introduced, what is being sought and from whom it is being sought;
    2° indicate on what right the plaintiff bases the case and, at least in general terms, the facts and evidence to be submitted in support of the allegations made;
    3° be signed by the plaintiff or the plaintiff's procurator, and bear the day, the month and the year, as well as the address at which the plaintiff or the procurator resides, or at which they say they reside for the purpose of receiving the acts;
    4° indicate the domicile or quasi-domicile of the respondent.

Can. 1505 §1 Once he has satisfied himself that the matter is within his competence and the plaintiff has the right to stand before the court, the

267

sole judge, or the presiding judge of a collegiate tribunal, must as soon as possible by his decree either admit or reject the petition.

§2 A petition can be rejected only if:

1° the judge or the tribunal is not legally competent;

2° it is established beyond doubt that the plaintiff lacks the right to stand before the court;

3° the provisions of can. 1504 nn. 1–3 have not been observed;

4° it is certainly clear from the petition that the plea lacks any foundation, and that there is no possibility that a foundation will emerge from a process.

§3 If a petition has been rejected by reason of defects which can be corrected, the plaintiff can draw up a new petition correctly and present it again to the same judge.

§4 A party is always entitled, within ten canonical days, to have recourse, based upon stated reasons, against the rejection of a petition. This recourse is to be made either to the tribunal of appeal or, if the petition was rejected by the presiding judge, to the collegiate tribunal. A question of rejection is to be determined with maximum expedition.

Can. 1506 If within a month of the presentation of a petition, the judge has not issued a decree admitting or rejecting it in accordance with can. 1505, the interested party can insist that the judge perform his duty. If, notwithstanding this, the judge does not respond within ten days of the party's request, the petition is to be taken as having been admitted.

Chapter II

THE SUMMONS AND THE INTIMATION OF JUDICIAL ACTS

Can. 1507 §1 In the decree by which a plaintiff's petition is admitted, the judge or the presiding judge must call or summon the other parties to court to effect the joinder of the issue; he must prescribe whether, in order to agree the point at issue, they are to reply in writing or to appear before him. If, from their written replies, he perceives the need to convene the parties, he can determine this by a new decree.

§2 If a petition is deemed admitted in accordance with the provisions of can. 1506, the decree of summons to the trial must be issued within twenty days of the request of which that canon speaks.

§3 If the litigants in fact present themselves before the judge to pursue the case, there is no need for a summons; the notary, however, is to record in the acts that the parties were present at the trial.

Can. 1508 §1 The decree of summons to the trial must be notified at once to the respondent, and at the same time to any others who are obliged to appear.

§2 The petition introducing the suit is to be attached to the summons, unless for grave reasons the judge considers that the petition is not to be communicated to the other party before he or she gives evidence.

§3 If a suit is brought against a person who does not have the free exercise of personal rights, or the free administration of the matters in dispute, the summons is to be notified to, as the case may be, the guardian, the curator, the special procurator, or the one who according to law is obliged to undertake legal proceedings in the name of such a person.

Can. 1509   §1 With due regard to the norms laid down by particular law, the notification of summonses, decrees, judgements and other judicial acts is to be done by means of the public postal service, or by some other particularly secure means.

§2 The fact and the manner of notification must be shown in the acts.

Can. 1510   A respondent who refuses to accept a document of summons, or who circumvents the delivery of a summons, is to be regarded as lawfully summoned.

Can. 1511   Without prejudice to the provision of can. 1507 §3, if a summons has not been lawfully communicated, the acts of the process are null.

Can. 1512   Once a summons has been lawfully communicated, or the parties have presented themselves before a judge to pursue the case:

1° the matter ceases to be a neutral one;
2° the case becomes that of the judge or of the tribunal, in other respects lawfully competent, before whom the action was brought;
3° the jurisdiction of a delegated judge is established in such a way that it does not lapse on the expiry of the authority of the person who delegated;
4° prescription is interrupted, unless otherwise provided;
5° the suit begins to be a pending one, and therefore the principle immediately applies 'while a suit is pending, no new element is to be introduced'.

TITLE II: THE JOINDER OF THE ISSUE

Can. 1513   §1 The joinder of the issue occurs when the terms of the controversy, as derived from the pleas and the replies of the parties, are determined by a decree of the judge.

§2 The pleas and the replies of the parties may be expressed not only in the petition introducing the suit, but also either in the response to the summons, or in statements made orally before the judge. In more difficult cases, however, the parties are to be convened by the judge, so as to agree the question or questions to which the judgement must respond.

§3 The decree of the judge is to be notified to the parties. Unless they have already agreed on the terms, they may within ten days have recourse to the same judge to request that the decree be altered. This question, however, is to be decided with maximum expedition by a decree of the judge.

Can. 1514 Once determined, the terms of the controversy cannot validly be altered except by a new decree, issued for a grave reason, at the request of the party, and after the other parties have been consulted and their observations considered.

Can. 1515 Once the joinder of the issue has occurred, the possessor of another's property ceases to be in good faith. If, therefore, the judgement is that he or she return the property, the possessor must return also any profits accruing from the date of the joinder, and must compensate for damages.

Can. 1516 Once the joinder of the issue has occurred, the judge is to prescribe an appropriate time within which the parties are to present and to complete the evidence.

TITLE III: THE TRIAL OF THE ISSUE

Can. 1517 The trial of the issue is initiated by the summons. It is concluded not only by the pronouncement of the definitive judgement, but also by other means determined by law.

Can. 1518 If a litigant dies, or undergoes a change in status, or ceases from the office in virtue of which he or she was acting:

1° if the case has not yet been concluded, the trial is suspended until the heir of the deceased, or the successor, or a person whose interest is involved, resumes the suit;

2° if the case has been concluded, the judge must proceed to the remaining steps of the case, having first summoned the procurator, if there is one, or else the heir or the successor of the deceased.

Can. 1519 §1 If the guardian or the curator or the procurator required in accordance with can. 1481 §§1 and 3, ceases from office, the trial is suspended for the time being.

§2 However, the judge is to appoint another guardian or curator as soon as possible. He can appoint a procurator ad litem if the party has neglected to do so within the brief time prescribed by the judge himself.

Can. 1520 If over a period of six months, no procedural act is performed by the parties, and they have not been impeded from doing so, the trial is abated. Particular law may prescribe other time limits for abatement.

Can. 1521   Abatement takes effect by virtue of the law itself, and it is effective against everyone, even minors and those equivalent to minors; moreover, it must be declared even ex officio. This, however, is without prejudice to the right to claim compensation against those guardians, curators, administrators and procurators who have not proved that they were without fault.

Can. 1522   Abatement extinguishes the acts of the process, but not the acts of the case. The acts of the case may indeed be employed in another instance, provided the case is between the same persons and about the same matter. As far as those outside the case are concerned, however, these acts have no standing other than as documents.

Can. 1523   When a trial has been abated, the litigants are to bear the expenses which each has incurred.

Can. 1524   §1 The plaintiff may renounce a trial at any stage or at any grade. Likewise, both the plaintiff and the respondent may renounce the acts of the process either in whole or only in part.

§2 To renounce the trial of an issue, guardians and administrators of juridical persons must have the advice or the consent of those whose agreement is required to conduct negotiations which exceed the limits of ordinary administration.

§3 To be valid, a renunciation must be in writing, and must be signed either by the party, or by a procurator who has been given a special mandate for this purpose; it must be communicated to the other party, who must accept or at least not oppose it; and it must be admitted by the judge.

Can. 1525   Once a renunciation has been admitted by the judge, it has the same effects for the acts which have been renounced as has an abatement of the trial. Likewise, it obliges the person renouncing to pay the expenses of those acts which have been renounced.

TITLE IV: PROOFS

Can. 1526   §1 The onus of proof rests upon the person who makes an allegation.

§2 The following matters do not require proof:

1° matters which are presumed by the law itself;

2° facts alleged by one of the litigants and admitted by the other, unless their proof is nevertheless required either by law or by the judge.

Can. 1527   §1 Any type of proof which seems useful for the investigation of the case and is lawful, may be admitted.

§2 If a party submits that proof, which has been rejected by the judge, should be admitted, the judge is to determine the matter with maximum expedition.

Can. 1528   If a party or a witness refuses to testify before the judge, that person may lawfully be heard by another, even a lay person, appointed by the judge, or asked to make a declaration either before a public notary or in any other lawful manner.

Can. 1529   Unless there is a grave reason, the judge is not to proceed to collect the proofs before the joinder of the issue.

Chapter I

THE DECLARATIONS OF THE PARTIES

Can. 1530   The judge may always question the parties the more closely to elicit the truth. He must do so if requested by one of the parties, or in order to prove a fact which the public interest requires to be placed beyond doubt.

Can. 1531   §1 A party who is lawfully questioned is obliged to respond and to tell the whole truth.

§2 If a party has refused to reply, it is for the judge to evaluate what, as far as the proof of the facts is concerned, can be deduced therefrom.

Can. 1532   Unless a grave reason suggests otherwise, in cases in which the public good is at stake the judge is to administer to the parties an oath that they will tell the truth, or at least that what they have said is the truth. In other cases, it is left to the prudent discretion of the judge to determine whether an oath is to be administered.

Can. 1533   The parties, the promotor of justice and the defender of the bond may submit to the judge propositions upon which a party is to be questioned.

Can. 1534   The provisions of cann. 1548 §2, n. 1, 1552 and 1558–1565 concerning witnesses are to be observed, with the appropriate qualifications, in the questioning of the parties.

Can. 1535   A judicial confession is an assertion of fact against oneself, concerning a matter relevant to the trial, which is made by a party before a judge who is legally competent; this is so whether the assertion is made in writing or orally, whether spontaneously or in response to the judge's questioning.

Can. 1536   §1 In a private matter and where the public good is not at stake, a judicial confession of one party relieves the other parties of the onus of proof.

§2 In cases which concern the public good, however, a judicial confession, and declarations by the parties which are not confessions, can have a probative value that is to be weighed by the judge in association with the other circumstances of the case, but the force of full proof cannot be attributed to them unless there are other elements which wholly corroborate them.

Can. 1537   It is for the judge, having considered all the circumstances, to evaluate the weight to be given to an extra-judicial confession which is introduced into the trial.

Can. 1538   A confession, or any other declaration of a party, is devoid of all force if clearly shown to be based on an error of fact or to have been extracted by force or grave fear.

Chapter II

DOCUMENTARY PROOF

Can. 1539   In every type of trial documentary proof is admitted, whether the documents be public or private.

Article 1: The Nature and Reliability of Documents

Can. 1540   §1 Public ecclesiastical documents are those which an official person draws up in the exercise of his or her function in the Church and in which the formalities required by law have been observed.

§2 Public civil documents are those which are legally regarded as such in accordance with the laws of each place.

§3 All other documents are private.

Can. 1541   Unless it is otherwise established by contrary and clear arguments, public documents constitute acceptable evidence of those matters which are directly and principally affirmed in them.

Can. 1542   A private document, whether acknowledged by a party or admitted by a judge, has the same probative force as an extra-judicial confession, against its author or the person who has signed it and against persons whose case rests on that of the author or signatory. Against others it has the same force as have declarations by the parties which are not confessions, in accordance with can. 1536 §2.

Can. 1543   If documents are shown to have been erased, amended, falsified or otherwise tampered with, it is for the judge to evaluate to what extent, if any, they are to be given credence.

Article 2: The Production of Documents

Can. 1544 Documents do not have probative force at a trial unless they are submitted in original form or in authentic copy and are lodged in the office of the tribunal, so that they may be inspected by the judge and by the opposing party.

Can. 1545 The judge can direct that a document common to each of the parties is to be submitted in the process.

Can. 1546 §1 No one is obliged to exhibit documents, even if they are common, which cannot be communicated without danger of the harm mentioned in can. 1548 §2, n. 2, or without the danger of violating a secret which is to be observed.

§2 If, however, at least an extract from a document can be transcribed and submitted in copy without the disadvantages mentioned, the judge can direct that it be produced in that form.

Chapter III
WITNESSES AND TESTIMONY

Can. 1547 Proof by means of witnesses is admitted in all cases, under the direction of the judge.

Can. 1548 §1 Witnesses must tell the truth to a judge who lawfully questions them.

§2 Without prejudice to the provisions of can. 1550 §2, n. 2 the following are exempted from the obligation of replying to questions:

1° clerics, in those matters revealed to them by reason of their sacred ministry; civil officials, doctors, midwives, advocates, notaries and others who are bound by the secret of their office, even on the ground of having offered advice, in respect of matters subject to this secret;

2° those who fear that, as a result of giving evidence, a loss of reputation, dangerous harassment or some other grave evil will arise for themselves, their spouses, or those related to them by consanguinity or affinity.

Article 1: Those who can be Witnesses

Can. 1549 Everyone can be a witness, unless expressly excluded, whether wholly or in part, by the law.

Can. 1550 §1 Minors under the age of fourteen years and those who are of feeble mind are not admitted to give evidence. They can, however, be heard if the judge declares by a decree that it would be appropriate to do so.

§2 The following are deemed incapable of being witnesses:

1° the parties in the case or those who appear at the trial in the name of the parties; the judge and his assistant; the advocate and those others who in the same case assist or have assisted the parties;

2° priests, in respect of everything which has become known to them in sacramental confession, even if the penitent has asked that these things be made known. Moreover, anything that may in any way have been heard by anyone on the occasion of confession, cannot be accepted even as an indication of the truth.

Article 2: The Introduction and the Exclusion of Witnesses

Can. 1551   A party who has introduced a witness may forego the examination of that witness, but the opposing party may ask that the witness nevertheless be examined.

Can. 1552   §1 When proof by means of witnesses is sought, the names and addresses of the witnesses are to be communicated to the tribunal.

§2 The propositions on which the interrogation of the witnesses is requested, are to be submitted within the time-limit determined by the judge; otherwise, the request is to be deemed abandoned.

Can. 1553   It is for the judge to curb an excessive number of witnesses.

Can. 1554   Before witnesses are examined, their names are to be communicated to the parties. If, in the prudent opinion of the judge, this cannot be done without great difficulty, it is to be done at least before the publication of the evidence.

Can. 1555   Without prejudice to the provisions of can. 1550, a party may request that a witness be excluded, provided a just reason for exclusion is established before the witness is examined.

Can. 1556   The summons of a witness is effected by a decree of the judge lawfully notified to the witness.

Can. 1557   A properly summoned witness is to appear, or to make known to the judge the reason for being absent.

Article 3: The Examination of Witnesses

Can. 1558   §1 Witnesses are to be examined at the office of the tribunal unless the judge deems otherwise.

§2 Cardinals, Patriarchs, Bishops, and those who in their own civil law enjoy a similar favour, are to be heard at the place selected by themselves.

§3 Without prejudice to the provisions of can. 1418 and 1469 §2, the judge is to decide where witnesses are to be heard for whom, by reason of distance, illness or other impediment, it is impossible or difficult to come to the office of the tribunal.

Can. 1559   The parties cannot be present at the examination of the witnesses unless, especially when there is question of a private interest, the judge has determined that they are to be admitted. Their advocates or procurators, however, may attend, unless by reason of the circumstances of matter and persons, the judge has determined that the proceedings are to be in secret.

Can. 1560   §1 The witnesses are to be examined individually and separately.

§2 If in a grave matter the witnesses disagree either among themselves or with one of the parties, the judge may arrange for those who differ to meet or to confront one another, but must, in so far as possible, eliminate discord and scandal.

Can. 1561   The examination of a witness is conducted by the judge, or by his delegate or an auditor, who is to be attended by a notary. Accordingly, unless particular law provides otherwise, if the parties or the promotor of justice or the defender of the bond or the advocates who are present at the hearing have additional questions to put to the witness, they are to propose these not to the witness, but to the judge, or to the one who is taking the judge's place, so that he or she may put them.

Can. 1562   §1 The judge is to remind the witness of the grave obligation to tell the whole truth and nothing but the truth.

§2 The judge is to administer an oath to the witness in accordance with can. 1532. If, however, a witness refuses to take an oath, he or she is to be heard unsworn.

Can. 1563   The judge is first of all to establish the identity of the witness. The relationship which the witness has with the parties is to be probed, and when specific questions concerning the case are asked of the witness, enquiry is to be made into the sources of his or her knowledge and the precise time the witness came to know the matters which are asserted.

Can. 1564   The questions are to be brief, and appropriate to the understanding of the person being examined. They are not to encompass a number of matters at the same time, nor be captious or deceptive. They are not to be leading questions, nor give any form of offence. They are to be relevant to the case in question.

Can. 1565   §1 The questions are not to be made known in advance to the witnesses.

§2 If, however, the matters about which evidence is to be given are so remote in memory that they cannot be affirmed with certainty unless they are recalled beforehand, the judge may, if he thinks this can safely be done, advise the witness in advance about certain aspects of the matter.

Can. 1566   The witnesses are to give evidence orally. They are not to read from a script, except where there is a question of calculations or accounts; in this case, they may consult notes which they have brought with them.

Can. 1567   §1 The replies are to be written down at once by the notary. The record must show the very words of the evidence given, at least in what concerns those things which bear directly on the matter of the trial.

§2 The use of a tape-recorder is allowed, provided the replies are subsequently committed to writing and, if possible, signed by the deponents.

Can. 1568   The notary is to mention in the acts whether the oath was taken or excused or refused; who were present, parties and others; the questions added ex officio; and in general, everything worthy of record which may have occurred while the witnesses were being examined.

Can. 1569   §1 At the conclusion of the examination, the record of the evidence, either as written down by the notary or as played back from the tape-recording, must be communicated to the witness, who is to be given the opportunity of adding to, omitting from, correcting or varying it.

§2 Finally, the witness, the judge and the notary must sign the record.

Can. 1570   Before the acts or the testimony are published, witnesses, even though already examined, may be called for re-examination, either at the request of a party or ex officio. This may be done if the judge considers it either necessary or useful, provided there is no danger whatever of collusion or of inducement.

Can. 1571   Witnesses must be refunded both the expenses they incurred and the losses they sustained by reason of their giving evidence, in accordance with the equitable assessment of the judge.

Article 4: The Credibility of Evidence

Can. 1572   In weighing evidence the judge may, if it is necessary, seek testimonial letters, and is to take into account:
    1° the condition and uprightness of the witness;
    2° whether the knowledge was acquired at first hand, particularly if it was something seen or heard personally, or whether it was opinion, rumour or hearsay;
    3° whether the witness is constant and consistent, or varies, is uncertain or vacillating;
    4° whether there is corroboration of the testimony, and whether it is confirmed or not by other items of evidence.

Can. 1573   The deposition of one witness cannot amount to full proof, unless the witness is a qualified one who gives evidence on matters carried out in an official capacity, or unless the circumstances of persons and things persuade otherwise.

Chapter IV
EXPERTS

Can. 1574   The services of experts are to be used whenever, by a provision of the law or of the judge, their study and opinion, based upon their art or science, are required to establish some fact or to ascertain the true nature of some matter.

Can. 1575   It is for the judge, after hearing the opinions or suggestions of the parties, to appoint the experts or, if such is the case, to accept reports already made by other experts.

Can. 1576   Experts can be excluded or objected to for the same reasons as witnesses.

Can. 1577   §1   The judge in his decree must define the specific terms of reference to be considered in the expert's task, taking into account whatever may have been gathered from the litigants.

§2   The expert is to be given the acts of the case, and any documents and other material needed for the proper and faithful discharge of his or her duty.

§3   The judge, after discussion with the expert, is to determine a time for the completion of the examination and the submission of the report.

Can. 1578   §1   Each expert is to complete a report distinct from that of the others, unless the judge orders that one report be drawn up and signed by all of them. In this case, differences of opinion, if there are such, are to be faithfully noted.

§2   Experts must clearly indicate the documents or other appropriate means by which they have verified the identity of persons, places or things. They are also to state the manner and method followed in fulfilling the task assigned to them, and the principal arguments upon which their conclusions are based.

§3   If necessary, the expert may be summoned by the judge to supply further explanations.

Can. 1579   §1   The judge is to weigh carefully not only the expert's conclusions, even when they agree, but also all the other circumstances of the case.

§2   When he is giving the reasons for his decision, the judge must state on what grounds he accepts or rejects the conclusions of the experts.

Can. 1580   Experts are to be paid their expenses and honorariums. These are to be determined by the judge in a proper and equitable manner, with due observance of particular law.

Can. 1581   §1   Parties can designate their own experts, to be approved by the judge.

§2 If the judge admits them, these experts can inspect the acts of the case, in so far as required for the discharge of their duty, and can be present when the appointed experts fulfil their role. They can always submit their reports.

Chapter V
JUDICIAL ACCESS AND INSPECTION

Can. 1582   If, in order to decide the case, the judge considers it opportune to visit some place, or inspect some thing, he is to set this out in a decree. After he has heard the parties, the decree is to give a brief description of what is to be made available for this access.

Can. 1583   After the inspection has been carried out, a document concerning it is to be drawn up.

Chapter VI
PRESUMPTIONS

Can. 1584   A presumption is a probable conjecture about something which is uncertain. Presumptions of law are those stated in the law; human presumptions are those made by a judge.

Can. 1585   A person with a presumption of law in his or her favour is freed from the onus of proof, which then falls on the other party.

Can. 1586   The judge is not to make presumptions which are not stated in the law, other than on the basis of a certain and determinate fact directly connected to the matter in dispute.

TITLE V: INCIDENTAL MATTERS

Can. 1587   An incidental matter arises when, after the case has begun by the summons, a question is proposed which, even though not expressly raised in the petition which introduced the case, is yet so relevant to the case that it needs to be settled before the principal question.

Can. 1588   An incidental matter is proposed before the judge who is competent to decide the principal case. It is raised in writing or orally, indicating the connection between it and the principal case.

Can. 1589   §1 When the judge has received the petition and heard the parties, he is to decide with maximum expedition whether the proposed incidental matter has a foundation in, and a connection with, the principal matter, or whether it is to be rejected from the outset. If he admits it, he must decide whether it is of such gravity that it needs to be determined by an interlocutory judgement or by a decree.

§2 If, however, he concludes that the incidental matter is not to be decided before the definitive judgement, he is to determine that account be taken of it when the principal matter is decided.

Can. 1590 §1 If the incidental matter is to be decided by judgement, the norms for a contentious oral process are to be observed unless, because of the gravity of the issue, the judge deems otherwise.

§2 If it is to be decided by decree, the tribunal can entrust the matter to an auditor or to the presiding judge.

Can. 1591 Before the principal matter is concluded, the judge or the tribunal may for a just reason revoke or alter an interlocutory judgement or decree. This can be done either at the request of a party or ex officio by the judge after he has heard the parties.

Chapter I

THE NON-APPEARANCE OF PARTIES

Can. 1592 §1 If a respondent is summoned but does not appear, and either does not offer an adequate excuse for absence or has not replied in accordance with can. 1507 §1, the judge is to declare the person absent from the process, and decree that the case is to proceed to the definitive judgement and to its execution, with due observance of the proper norms.

§2 Before issuing the decree mentioned in §1, the judge must make sure, if necessary by means of another summons, that a lawful summons did reach the respondent within the canonical time.

Can. 1593 §1 If the respondent thereafter appears before the judge, or replies before the trial is concluded, he or she can bring forward conclusions and proofs, without prejudice to the provisions of can. 1600; the judge is to take care, however, that the process is not deliberately prolonged by lengthy and unnecessary delays.

§2 Even if the respondent has neither appeared nor given a reply before the case is decided, he or she can challenge the judgement; if the person can show that there was a just reason for being absent, and that there was no fault involved in not intimating this earlier, a plaint of nullity can be lodged.

Can. 1594 If the plaintiff does not appear on the day and at the hour arranged for the joinder of the issue, and does not offer a suitable excuse:
    1° the judge is to summon the plaintiff again;
    2° if the plaintiff does not obey the new summons, it is presumed that the case has been abandoned in accordance with cann. 1524–1525;

3° if the plaintiff should want to intervene at a subsequent stage in the process, the provisions of can. 1593 are to be observed.

Can. 1595 §1 A party, whether plaintiff or respondent, who is absent from the trial, and who does not establish the existence of a just impediment, is bound to pay the expenses which have been incurred in the case because of this absence, and also, if need be, to indemnify the other party.

§2 If both the plaintiff and the respondent were absent from the trial, they are jointly bound to pay the expenses of the case.

Chapter II

THE INTERVENTION OF A THIRD PARTY IN A CASE

Can. 1596 §1 Any person with a legitimate interest can be allowed to intervene in a case in any instance of the suit, either as a party defending his or her own right or, in an accessory role, to help one of the litigants.

§2 To be admitted, however, the person must, before the conclusion of the case, produce to the judge a petition which briefly establishes the right to intervene.

§3 A person who intervenes in a case is to be admitted at that stage which the case has reached. If the case has reached the evidence stage, a brief and peremptory time-limit is to be assigned within which to bring forward evidence.

Can. 1597 A third party whose intervention is seen to be necessary must be called into the case by the judge, after he has consulted the parties.

TITLE VI: THE PUBLICATION OF THE ACTS, THE CONCLUSION OF THE CASE AND THE PLEADINGS

Can. 1598 §1 When the evidence has been assembled, the judge must, under pain of nullity, by a decree permit the parties and their advocates to inspect at the tribunal office those acts which are not yet known to them. Indeed, if the advocates so request, a copy of the acts can be given to them. In cases which concern the public good, however, the judge can decide that, in order to avoid very serious dangers, some part or parts of the acts are not to be shown to anyone; he must take care, however, that the right of defence always remains intact.

§2 To complete the evidence, the parties can propose other items of proof to the judge. When these have been assembled the judge can, if he deems it appropriate, again issue a decree as in §1.

Can. 1599 §1 When everything concerned with the production of evidence has been completed, the conclusion of the case is reached.

§2 This conclusion occurs when the parties declare that they have nothing further to add, or when the canonical time allotted by the judge for the production of evidence has elapsed, or when the judge declares that he considers the case to be sufficiently instructed.

§3 By whichever way the case has come to its conclusion, the judge is to issue a decree declaring that it is concluded.

Can. 1600 Only in the following situations can the judge, after the conclusion of the case, still recall earlier witnesses or call new ones, or make provision for other evidence not previously requested:

1° in cases in which only the private good of the parties is involved, if all the parties agree;

2° in other cases, provided that the parties have been consulted, that a grave reason exists, and that all danger of fraud or subornation is removed;

3° in all cases, whenever it is probable that, unless new evidence is admitted, the judgement will be unjust for any of the reasons mentioned in can. 1645 §2, nn. 1–3.

§2 The judge can, however, command or permit the presentation of a document which, even without fault of the interested party, could not be presented earlier.

§3 New evidence is to be published according to can. 1598 §1.

Can. 1601 When the case has been concluded, the judge is to determine a suitable period of time for the presentation of pleadings and observations.

Can. 1602 §1 Pleadings and observations are to be in writing unless the judge, with the consent of the parties, considers it sufficient to have a discussion before the tribunal in session.

§2 If the pleadings and the principal documents are to be printed, the prior permission of the judge is required, and the obligation of secrecy, where it exists, is still to be observed.

§3 The directions of the tribunal are to be observed in questions concerning the length of the pleadings, the number of copies and other similar matters.

Can. 1603 §1 When the pleadings and observations have been exchanged, each party can make reply within a brief period of time determined by the judge.

§2 This right is given to the parties once only, unless for a grave reason the judge considers that the right to a second reply is to be given; if this right is given to one party, it is to be considered as given to the other as well.

§3 The promotor of justice and the defender of the bond have the right to respond to every reply of the parties.

Can. 1604   §1 It is absolutely forbidden that any information given to the judge by the parties or the advocates, or by any other persons, be excluded from the acts of the case.

§2 If the pleadings in the case are made in writing, the judge may, in order to clarify any outstanding issues, order that a moderate oral discussion be held before the tribunal in session.

Can. 1605   The notary is to be present at the oral discussion mentioned in cann. 1602 §1 and 1604 §2, so that, if the judge so orders, or the parties so request and the judge consents, the notary can immediately make a written report of what has been discussed and concluded.

Can. 1606   If the parties neglect to prepare their pleadings within the time allotted to them, or if they entrust themselves to the knowledge and conscience of the judge, and if at the same time the judge perceives the matter quite clearly from the acts and the proofs, he can pronounce judgement at once. He must, however, seek the observations of the promotor of justice and the defender of the bond if they were engaged in the trial.

TITLE VII
THE PRONOUNCEMENTS OF THE JUDGE

Can. 1607   A principal case which has been dealt with in judicial fashion is decided by the judge by a definitive judgement. An incidental matter is decided by an interlocutory judgement, without prejudice to can. 1589 §1.

Can. 1608   §1 To give any judgement, the judge must have in his mind moral certainty about the matter to be decided in the judgement.

§2 The judge must derive this certainty from the acts of the case and from the proofs.

§3 The judge must conscientiously weigh the evidence, with due regard for the provisions of law about the efficacy of certain evidence.

§4 A judge who cannot arrive at such certainty is to pronounce that the right of the plaintiff is not established and is to find for the respondent, except in a case which enjoys the favour of law, when he is to pronounce in its favour.

Can. 1609   §1 The presiding judge of a collegiate tribunal decides the day and time when it is to meet for discussion. Unless a special reason requires otherwise, the meeting is to be at the tribunal office.

§2 On the day appointed for the meeting, the individual judges are to bring their written conclusions on the merits of the case, with the reasons in law and in fact for reaching their conclusions. These conclusions are to be added to the acts of the case and to be kept in secrecy.

§3 Having invoked the divine Name, they are to offer their conclusions in order, beginning always with the 'ponens' or 'relator' in the case, and then in order of precedence. Under the chairmanship of the presiding judge, they are to hold their discussion principally with a view to establishing what is to be stated in the dispositive part of the judgement.

§4 In the discussion, each one is permitted to depart from an original conclusion. A judge who does not wish to accede to the decision of the others can demand that, if there is an appeal, his or her conclusions be forwarded to the higher tribunal.

§5 If the judges do not wish, or are unable, to reach a decision in the first discussion, they can defer their decision to another meeting, but not beyond one week, unless the instruction of the case has to be completed in accordance with can. 1600.

Can. 1610 §1 If there is a sole judge, he will draw up the judgement.

§2 In a collegiate tribunal, the 'ponens' or 'relator' is to draw up the judgement, using as reasons those tendered by the individual judges in their discussion, unless the reasons to be preferred have been defined by a majority of the judges. The judgement must then be submitted to the individual judges for their approval.

§3 The judgement is to be issued not later than one month from the day on which the case was decided, unless in a collegiate tribunal the judges have for grave reasons stipulated a longer time.

Can. 1611 The judgement must:
1° define the controversy raised before the tribunal, giving appropriate answers to the individual questions;
2° determine the obligations of the parties arising from the trial and the manner in which these are to be fulfilled;
3° set out the reasons or motives, both in law and in fact, upon which the dispositive part of the judgement is based;
4° apportion the expenses of the suit.

Can. 1612 §1 The judgement, after the invocation of the divine Name, must state in order the judge or tribunal, and the plaintiff, respondent and procurator, with names and domiciles duly indicated. It is also to name the promotor of justice and the defender of the bond if they were engaged in the trial.

§2 It must then briefly set out the alleged facts, with the conclusions of the parties and the formulation of the doubt.

§3 Then follows the dispositive part of the judgement, prefaced by the reasons which support it.

§4 It ends with the date and the place in which it was given, and with the signature of the judge or, in the case of a collegiate tribunal, of all the judges, and of the notary.

Can. 1613 The rules set out above for a definitive judgement are to be adapted also to interlocutory judgements.

Can. 1614 A judgement is to be published as soon as possible, with an indication of the ways in which it can be challenged. Before publication it has no effect, even if the dispositive part may, with the permission of the judge, have been notified to the parties.

Can. 1615 The publication or notification of the judgement can be effected by giving a copy of the judgement to the parties or to their procurators, or by sending them a copy of it in accordance with can. 1509.

Can. 1616 §1 A judgement must be corrected or completed by the tribunal which gave it if, in the text of a judgement, there is an error in calculations, or a material error in the transcription of either the dispositive part or the presentation of the facts or the pleadings of the parties, or if any of the items required by can. 1612, §4 are omitted. This is to be done either at the request of the parties or ex officio, but always after having consulted the parties and by a decree appended to the foot of the judgement.

§2 If one party is opposed, an incidental question is to be decided by a decree.

Can. 1617 Other pronouncements of a judge apart from the judgement, are decrees. If they are more than mere directions about procedure, they have no effect unless they give at least a summary of their reasons or refer to motives expressed in another act.

Can. 1618 An interlocutory judgement or a decree has the force of a definitive judgement if, in respect of at least one of the parties, it prevents the trial, or brings to an end the trial itself or any instance of it.

TITLE VIII: CHALLENGING THE JUDGEMENT

Chapter I

THE PLAINT OF NULLITY OF THE JUDGEMENT

Can. 1619 Without prejudice to cann. 1622 and 1623, whenever a case concerns the good of private individuals, acts which are null with a nullity established by positive law are validated by the judgement itself, if the nullity was known to the party making the plaint and was not raised with the judge before the judgement.

Can. 1620 A judgement is null with a nullity which cannot be remedied, if:

  1° it was given by a judge who was absolutely non-competent;
  2° it was given by a person who has no power to judge in the tribunal in which the case was decided;

3° the judge was compelled by force or grave fear to deliver judgement;

4° the trial took place without the judicial plea mentioned in can. 1501, or was not brought against some party as respondent;

5° it was given between parties of whom at least one has no right to stand before the court;

6° someone acted in another's name without a lawful mandate;

7° the right of defence was denied to one or other party;

8° the controversy has not been even partially decided.

Can. 1621   In respect of the nullity mentioned in can. 1620, a plaint of nullity can be made in perpetuity by means of an exception, or within ten years of the date of publication of the judgement by means of an action before the judge who delivered the judgement.

Can. 1622   A judgement is null with a nullity which is simply remediable, if:

1° contrary to the requirements of can. 1425, §1, it was not given by the lawful number of judges;

2° it does not contain the motives or reasons for the decision;

3° it lacks the signatures prescribed by the law;

4° it does not contain an indication of the year, month, day and place it was given;

5° it is founded on a judicial act which is null and whose nullity has not been remedied in accordance with can. 1619;

6° it was given against a party who, in accordance with can. 1593, §2, was lawfully absent.

Can. 1623   In the cases mentioned in can. 1622, a plaint of nullity can be proposed within three months of notification of the publication of the judgement.

Can. 1624   The judge who gave the judgement is to consider the plaint of its nullity. If the party fears that the judge who gave the judgement is biased, and consequently considers him suspect, he or she can demand that another judge take his place in accordance with can. 1450.

Can. 1625   Within the time limit established for appeal, a plaint of nullity can be proposed together with the appeal.

Can. 1626   §1 A plaint of nullity can be made not only by parties who regard themselves as injured, but also by the promotor of justice and the defender of the bond, whenever they have a right to intervene.

§2 Within the time-limit established in can. 1623, the judge himself can retract or correct an invalid judgement he has given, unless in the meantime an appeal joined to a plaint of nullity has been lodged, or the nullity has been remedied by the expiry of the time-limit mentioned in can. 1623.

Can. 1627   Cases concerning a plaint of nullity can be dealt with in accordance with the norms for an oral contentious process.

Chapter II
THE APPEAL

Can. 1628   Without prejudice to the provisions of can. 1629, a party who considers him or herself to be injured by a judgement has a right to appeal from the judgement to a higher judge; in cases in which their presence is required, the promotor of justice and the defender of the bond have likewise the right to appeal.

Can. 1629   No appeal is possible against:
1° a judgement of the Supreme Pontiff himself, or a judgement of the Apostolic Signatura;
2° a judgement which is null, unless the appeal is lodged together with a plaint of nullity, in accordance with can. 1625;
3° a judgement which has become an adjudged matter;
4° a decree of the judge or an interlocutory judgement, which does not have the force of a definitive judgement, unless the appeal is lodged together with an appeal against the definitive judgement;
5° a judgement or a decree in a case in which the law requires that the matter be settled with maximum expedition.

Can. 1630   §1 The appeal must be lodged with the judge who delivered the judgement, within a peremptory time-limit of fifteen canonical days from notification of the publication of the judgement.
§2 If it is made orally, the notary is to draw up the appeal in writing in the presence of the appellant.

Can. 1631   If a question arises about the right of appeal, the appeal tribunal is to determine it with maximum expedition, in accordance with the norms for an oral contentious process.

Can. 1632   §1 If there is no indication of the tribunal to which the appeal is directed, it is presumed to be made of the tribunal mentioned in cann. 1438 and 1439.
§2 If the other party has resorted to some other appeal tribunal, the tribunal which is of the higher grade is to determine the case, without prejudice to can. 1415.

Can. 1633   The appeal is to be pursued before the appeal judge within one month of its being forwarded, unless the originating judge allows the party a longer time to pursue it.

Can. 1634   §1 To pursue the appeal, it is required and is sufficient that the party request the assistance of the higher judge to amend the judge ment which is challenged, enclosing a copy of the judgement and indicating the reasons for the appeal.

§2 If the party is unable to obtain a copy of the appealed judgement from the originating tribunal within the canonical time-limit, this time-limit is in the meantime suspended. The problem is to be made known to the appeal judge, who is to oblige the originating judge by precept to fulfil his duty as soon as possible.

§3 In the meantime, the originating judge must forward the acts to the appeal court in accordance with can. 1474.

Can. 1635 The appeal is considered to be abandoned if the time-limits for an appeal before either the originating judge or the appeal judge have expired without action being taken.

Can. 1636 §1 The appellant can renounce the appeal, with the effects mentioned in can. 1525.

§2 Unless the law provides otherwise, an appeal made by the defender of the bond or the promotor of justice, can be renounced by the defender of the bond or the promotor of justice of the appeal tribunal.

Can. 1637 §1 An appeal made by the plaintiff benefits the respondent, and vice versa.

§2 If there are several respondents or plaintiffs, and the judgement is challenged by only one of them, or is made against only one of them, the challenge is considered to be made by all and against all whenever the thing requested is an individual one or the obligation is a joint one.

§3 If one party challenges a judgement in regard to one ground, the other party can appeal incidentally on the other grounds, even if the canonical time-limit for the appeal has expired. This incidental case is to be appealed within a peremptory time-limit of fifteen days from the day of notification of the principal appeal.

§4 Unless the contrary is clear, an appeal is presumed to be against all the grounds of the judgement.

Can. 1638 An appeal suspends the execution of the judgement.

Can. 1639 §1 Without prejudice to the provision of can. 1683, a new ground cannot be introduced at the appeal grade, not even by way of the useful accumulation of grounds. So the joinder of the issue can concern itself only with the confirmation or the reform of the first judgement, either in part or in whole.

§2 New evidence is admitted only in accordance with can. 1600.

Can. 1640 With the appropriate adjustments, the procedure at the appeal grade is to be the same as in first instance. Unless the evidence is to be supplemented, however, once the issue has been joined in accordance with can. 1513 §1 and can. 1639 §1, the judges are to proceed immediately to the discussion of the case and the judgement.

TITLE IX: ADJUDGED MATTER AND TOTAL REINSTATEMENT

Chapter I
ADJUDGED MATTER

Can. 1641 Without prejudice to can. 1643, an adjudged matter occurs when:

1° there are two conforming judgements between the same parties about the same matter and on the same grounds;

2° no appeal was made against the judgement within the canonical time-limit;

3° the trial has been abated or renounced in the appeal grade;

4° a definitive judgement has been given from which, in accordance with can. 1629, there is no appeal.

Can. 1642 §1 An adjudged matter has the force of law and cannot be challenged directly, except in accordance with can. 1645 §1.

§2 It has the effect of law between the parties; it gives the right to an action arising from the judgement and to an exception of an adjudged matter; to prevent a new introduction of the same case, the judge can even declare such an exception ex officio.

Can. 1643 Cases concerning the status of persons never become an adjudged matter, not excepting cases which concern the separation of spouses.

Can. 1644 §1 If two conforming sentences have been given in cases concerning the status of persons, recourse to a tribunal of appeal can be made at any time, to be supported by new and serious evidence or arguments which are to be submitted within a peremptory time limit of thirty days from the time the challenge was made. Within one month of receiving the new evidence and arguments, the appeal tribunal must declare by a decree whether or not a new presentation of the case is to be admitted.

§2 Recourse to a higher tribunal to obtain a new presentation of the case does not suspend the execution of the judgement, unless the law provides otherwise or the appeal tribunal orders a suspension in accordance with can. 1650 §3.

Chapter II
TOTAL REINSTATEMENT

Can. 1645 §1 Against a judgement which has become an adjudged matter there can be a total reinstatement, provided it is clearly established that the judgement was unjust.

§2 Injustice is not, however, considered clearly established unless:

1° the judgement is so based on evidence which is subsequently shown to be false, that without this evidence the dispositive part of the judgement could not be sustained;

2° documents are subsequently discovered by which new facts demanding a contrary decision are undoubtedly proven;

3° the judgement was given through the deceit of one party to the harm of the other;

4° a provision of a law which was not merely procedural was evidently neglected;

5° the judgement runs counter to a preceding decision which has become an adjudged matter.

Can. 1646 §1 Total reinstatement based on the reasons mentioned in can. 1645 §2, nn. 1–3, is to be requested from the judge who delivered the judgement within three months from the day on which these reasons became known.

§2 Total reinstatement based on the reasons mentioned in can. 1645 §2, nn. 4 and 5, is to be requested from the appeal tribunal within three months of notification of the publication of the judgement. In the case mentioned in can. 1645 §2, n. 5, if the preceding decision is not known until later, the time-limit begins at the time the knowledge was obtained.

§3 The time-limits mentioned above do not apply for as long as the aggrieved party is a minor.

Can. 1647 §1 A plea for total reinstatement suspends the execution of a judgements which has not yet begun.

§2 If there are probable indications leading the judge to suspect that the plea was made to cause delays in execution, he may decide that the judgement be executed. The person seeking total reinstatement is, however, to be given suitable guarantees that, if it is granted, he or she will be indemnified.

Can. 1648 Where total reinstatement is granted, the judge must pronounce judgement of the merits of the case.

TITLE X
JUDICIAL EXPENSES AND FREE LEGAL AID

Can. 1649 §1 The Bishop who is responsible for governing the tribunal is to establish norms concerning:

1° declarations that parties are liable for the payment or reimbursement of judicial expenses;

2° the honorariums for advocates, experts and interpreters, and the expenses of witnesses;

3° the granting of free legal aid and the reduction of expenses;

    4° the payment of damages owed by a person who not merely lost
        the case, but was rash in having recourse to litigation;
    5° the money to be deposited, or the guarantee to be given, for the
        payment of expenses and the compensation of damages.

§2 No distinct appeal exists from a pronouncement concerning
expenses, honorariums and damages. The parties can, however, have
recourse within ten days to the same judge, who can change the sum
involved.

TITLE XI: THE EXECUTION OF THE JUDGEMENT

Can. 1650   §1 A judgement which becomes adjudged matter can be
executed, without prejudice to the provision of can. 1647.

§2 The judge who delivered the judgement and, if there has been an
appeal, the appeal judge, can either ex officio or at the request of a party
order the provisional execution of a judgement which has not yet become
an adjudged matter, adding if need be appropriate guarantees when it is a
matter of provisions or payments concerning necessary support. They can
also do so for some other just and urgent reason.

§3 If the judgement mentioned in §2 is challenged, the judge who must
deal with the challenge can suspend the execution or subject it to a
guarantee, if he sees that the challenge is probably well founded and that
irreparable harm could result from execution.

Can. 1651   Execution cannot take place before there is issued the judge's
executing decree directing that the judgement be executed. Depending on
the nature of the case, this decree is to be either included in the judgement
itself or issued separately.

Can. 1652   If the execution of the judgement requires a prior statement
of reasons, this is to be treated as an incidental question, to be decided by
the judge who gave the judgement which is to be executed.

Can. 1653   §1 Unless particular law provides otherwise, the Bishop of
the diocese in which the first instance judgement was given must, either
personally or through another, execute the judgement.

§2 If he refuses or neglects to do so, the execution of the judgement, at
the request of an interested party or ex officio, belongs to the authority to
which the appeal tribunal is subject in accordance with can. 1439 §3.

§3 Between religious, the execution of the judgement is the responsibility of the Superior who gave the judgement which is to be executed, or
who delegated the judge.

Can. 1654   §1 The executor must execute the judgement according to
the obvious sense of the words, unless in the judgement itself something is
left to his discretion.

§2 He can deal with exceptions concerning the manner and the force of the execution, but not with the merits of the case. If he has ascertained from some other source that the judgement is null or manifestly unjust according to cann. 1620, 1622 and 1645, he is to refrain from executing the judgement, and is instead to refer the matter to the tribunal which delivered the judgement and to notify the parties.

Can. 1655 §1 In real actions, whenever it is decided that a thing belongs to the plaintiff, it is to be handed over to the plaintiff as soon as the matter has become an adjudged matter.

§2 In personal actions, when a guilty person is condemned to hand over a movable possession or to pay money, or to give or do something, the judge in the judgement itself, or the executor according to his discretion and prudence, is to assign a time limit for the fulfilment of the obligation. This time-limit is to be not less than fifteen days nor more than six months.

Section II: The Oral Contentious Process

Can. 1656 §1 The oral contentious process dealt with in this section can be used in all cases which are not excluded by law, unless a party requests an ordinary contentious process.

§2 If the oral process is used in cases other than those permitted by the law, the judicial acts are null.

Can. 1657 An oral contentious process in first instance is made before a sole judge, in accordance with can. 1424.

Can. 1658 §1 In addition to the matters enumerated in can. 1504, the petition which introduces the suit must:

1° set forth briefly, fully and clearly the facts on which the plaintiff's pleas are based;
2° indicate the evidence by which the plaintiff intends to demonstrate the facts and which cannot be brought forward with the petition; this is to be done in such a way that the evidence can immediately be gathered by the judge.

§2 Documents which support the plea must be added to the petition, at least in authentic copy.

Can. 1659 §1 If an attempt at mediation in accordance with can. 1446 §2 has proven fruitless, the judge, if he deems that the petition has some foundation, is within three days to add a decree at the foot of the petition. In this decree he is to order that a copy of the plea be notified to the respondent, with the right to send a written reply to the tribunal office within fifteen days.

§2   This notification has the effects of a judicial summons that are as mentioned in can. 1512.

Can. 1660   If the exceptions raised by the respondent so require, the judge is to assign the plaintiff a time-limit for a reply, so that from the material advanced by each he can clearly discern the object of the controversy.

Can. 1661   §1   When the time-limits mentioned in cann. 1659 and 1660 have expired, the judge, after examining the acts, is to determine the point at issue. He is then to summon all who must be present to a hearing, which is to be held within thirty days; for the parties, he is to add the formulation of the point at issue.
§2   In the summons the parties are to be informed that, to support their assertions, they can submit a short written statement to the tribunal at least three days before the hearing.

Can. 1662   In the hearing, the questions mentioned in cann. 1459–1464 are considered first.

Can. 1663   §1   The evidence is assembled during the hearing, without prejudice to the provision of can. 1418.
§2   A party and his or her advocate can assist at the examination of the other parties, of the witnesses and of the experts.

Can. 1664   The replies of the parties, witnesses and experts, and the pleas and exceptions of the advocates, are to be written down by the notary in summary fashion, restricting the record to those things which bear on the substance of the controversy. This record is to be signed by the persons testifying.

Can. 1665   The judge can admit evidence which is not alleged or sought in the plea or the reply, but only in accordance with can. 1452. After the hearing of even one witness, however, the judge can admit new evidence only in accordance with can. 1600.

Can. 1666   If all the evidence cannot be collected during the hearing, a further hearing is to be set.

Can. 1667   When the evidence has been collected, an oral discussion is to take place at the same hearing.

Can. 1668   §1   At the conclusion of the hearing, the judge can decide the case forthwith, unless it emerges from the discussion that something needs to be added to the instruction of the case, or that there is something which prevents a judgement being correctly delivered. The dispositive part of the judgement is to be read immediately in the presence of the parties.
§2   Because of the difficulty of the matter, or for some other just reason, the decision of the tribunal can be deferred for up to five canonical days.

§3   The full text of the judgement, including the reasons for it, is to be notified to the parties as soon as possible, normally within fifteen days.

Can. 1669   If the appeal tribunal discerns that a lower tribunal has used the oral contentious procedure in cases which are excluded by law, it is to declare the judgement invalid and refer the case back to the tribunal which delivered the judgement.

Can. 1670   In all other matters concerning procedure, the provisions of the canons on ordinary contentious trials are to be followed. In order to expedite matters, however, while safeguarding justice, the tribunal can, by a decree and for stated reasons, derogate from procedural norms which are not prescribed for validity.

Part III
CERTAIN SPECIAL PROCESSES

TITLE I: MATRIMONIAL PROCESSES

Chapter I
CASES CONCERNING THE DECLARATION OF NULLITY OF MARRIAGE

Article 1: The Competent Forum

Can. 1671 Matrimonial cases of the baptised belong by their own right to the ecclesiastical judge.

Can. 1672 Cases concerning the merely civil effects of marriage pertain to the civil courts, unless particular law lays down that, if such cases are raised as incidental and accessory matters, they may be heard and decided by an ecclesiastical judge.

Can. 1673 The following tribunals are competent in cases concerning the nullity of marriage which are not reserved to the Apostolic See:
1° the tribunal of the place where the marriage was celebrated;
2° the tribunal of the place where the respondent has a domicile or quasi-domicile;
3° the tribunal of the place where the plaintiff has a domicile, provided that both parties live within the territory of the same Episcopal Conference, and that the judicial Vicar of the domicile of the respondent, after consultation with the respondent, gives consent;
4° the tribunal of the place in which in fact most of the evidence is to be collected, provided that consent is given by the judicial Vicar of the domicile of the respondent, who must first ask the respondent whether he or she has any objection to raise.

Article 2: The Right to Challenge the Validity of Marriage

Can. 1674   The following are able to challenge the validity of a marriage:

1° the spouses themselves;

2° the promotor of justice, when the nullity of the marriage has already been made public, and the marriage cannot be validated or it is not expedient to do so.

Can. 1675   §1 A marriage which was not challenged while both parties were alive, cannot be challenged after the death of either or both, unless the question of validity is a necessary preliminary to the resolution of another controversy in either the canonical or the civil forum.

§2 If a spouse should die during the course of a case, can. 1518 is to be observed.

Article 3: The Duties of the Judges

Can. 1676   Before he accepts a case and whenever there appears to be hope of success, the judge is to use pastoral means to persuade the spouses that, if it is possible, they should perhaps validate their marriage and resume their conjugal life.

Can. 1677   §1 When the petition has been accepted, the presiding judge or the 'ponens' is to proceed to the notification of the decree of summons, in accordance with can. 1508.

§2 If, within fifteen days of the notification, neither party has requested a session to contest the suit, then within the following ten days the presiding judge or 'ponens' is, by a decree, to decide ex officio the formulation of the doubt or doubts and to notify the parties accordingly.

§3 The formulation of the doubt is not only to ask whether the nullity of the particular marriage is proven, but also to determine the ground or grounds upon which the validity of the marriage is being challenged.

§4 If the parties have not objected to this decree within ten days of being notified, the presiding judge or 'ponens' is, by a new decree, to arrange for the hearing of the case.

Article 4: Proofs

Can. 1678   §1 The defender of the bond, the advocates of the parties and, if engaged in the process, the promotor of justice, have the right:

1° to be present at the examination of the parties, the witnesses and the experts, without prejudice to can. 1559;

2° to see the judicial acts, even if they are not yet published, and to inspect documents produced by the parties.

§2 The parties themselves cannot be present at the sessions mentioned in §1, n. 1.

Can. 1679   Unless the evidence brought forward is otherwise complete, in order to weigh the depositions of the parties in accordance with can. 1536, the judge is, if possible, to hear witnesses to the credibility of the parties, as well as to gather other indications and supportive elements.

Can. 1680   In cases concerning impotence or defect of consent by reason of mental illness, the judge is to use the services of one or more experts, unless from the circumstances this would obviously serve no purpose. In other cases, the provision of can. 1574 is to be observed.

Article 5: The Judgement and the Appeal

Can. 1681   Whenever in the course of the hearing of a case a doubt of a high degree of probability arises that the marriage has not been consummated, the tribunal can, with the consent of the parties, suspend the nullity case and complete the instruction of a case for a dispensation from a non-consummated marriage; eventually it can forward the acts to the Apostolic See, together with a petition, from either or both of the parties, for a dispensation, and with the Opinions of the tribunal and of the Bishop.

Can. 1682   §1   The judgement which has first declared the nullity of a marriage, together with the appeals, if there are any, and the judicial acts, are to be sent ex officio to the appeal tribunal within twenty days of the publication of the judgement.

§2   If the judgement given in first instance was in favour of the nullity of the marriage, the appeal tribunal, after weighing the observations of the defender of the bond and, if there are any, of the parties, is by its decree either to ratify the decision at once, or to admit the case to ordinary examination in the new instance.

Can. 1683   If a new ground of nullity of marriage is advanced in the appeal grade, the tribunal can admit it and give judgement on it as at first instance.

Can. 1684   §1   After the judgement which first declared the nullity of the marriage has been confirmed on appeal either by decree or by another judgement, those whose marriage has been declared invalid may contract a new marriage as soon as the decree or the second judgement has been notified to them, unless there is a prohibition appended to the judgement or decree itself, or imposed by the local Ordinary.

§2   The provisions of can. 1644 are to be observed even if the judgement which declared the nullity of the marriage is confirmed not by a second judgement, but by a decree.

Can. 1685   As soon as the sentence is executed, the judicial Vicar must notify the Ordinary of the place where the marriage was celebrated. This Ordinary must ensure that a record of the decree of nullity of the marriage, and of any prohibition imposed, is as soon as possible entered in the registers of marriage and baptism.

Article 6: The Documentary Process

Can. 1686   A marriage can be declared invalid on the basis of a document which proves with certainty the existence of a diriment impediment, a defect of lawful form or the lack of a valid proxy mandate; the document must not be open to any contradiction or exception. It must be equally certain that no dispensation has been given. When a petition in accordance with can. 1677 has been received alleging such invalidity, the judicial Vicar, or a judge designated by him, can omit the formalities of the ordinary procedure and, having summoned the parties, and with the intervention of the defender of the bond, declare the nullity of the marriage by a judgement.

Can. 1687   §1   If the defender of the bond prudently judges that the defects mentioned in can. 1686, or the lack of dispensation, are not certain, he must appeal to the judge of second instance. The acts must be sent to the appeal judge and he is to be informed in writing that it is a documentary process.

§2   A party who considers him or herself injured retains the right of appeal.

Can. 1688   The judge of second instance, with the intervention of the defender of the bond and after consulting the parties, is to decide in the same way as in can. 1686 whether the judgement is to be ratified, or whether the case should rather proceed according to the ordinary course of law, in which event he is to send the case back to the tribunal of first instance.

Article 7: General Norms

Can. 1689   In the judgement the parties are to be reminded of the moral, and also the civil, obligations by which they may be bound, both towards one another and in regard to the support and upbringing of their children.

Can. 1690   Cases for the declaration of nullity of marriage cannot be dealt with by the oral contentious process.

Can. 1691   In other matters concerning the conduct of the process, the canons concerning judicial powers in general and concerning the ordinary contentious process are to be applied, unless the nature of the case demands otherwise; the special norms concerning cases dealing with the status of persons and cases pertaining to the public good are also to be observed.

Chapter II

CASES CONCERNING THE SEPARATION OF SPOUSES

Can. 1692   §1   Unless lawfully provided otherwise in particular places, the personal separation of baptised spouses can be decided by a decree of the diocesan Bishop, or by the judgement of a judge in accordance with the following canons.

§2 Where the ecclesiastical decision does not produce civil effects, or if it is foreseen that there will be a civil judgement not contrary to the divine law, the Bishop of the diocese in which the spouses are living can, in the light of their particular circumstances, give them permission to approach the civil courts.

§3 If the case is also concerned with the merely civil effects of marriage, the judge is to endeavour, without prejudice to the provision of §2, to have the case brought before the civil court from the very beginning.

Can. 1693 §1 The oral contentious process is to be used, unless either party or the promotor of justice requests the ordinary contentious process.

§2 If the ordinary contentious process is used and there is an appeal, the tribunal of second instance is to proceed in accordance with can. 1682 §2, observing what has to be observed.

Can. 1694 In matters concerning the competence of the tribunal, the provisions of can. 1673 are to be observed.

Can. 1695 Before he accepts the case, and whenever there appears to be hope of success, the judge is to use pastoral means to induce the parties to be reconciled and to resume their conjugal life.

Can. 1696 Cases of separation of spouses also concern the public good; the promotor of justice must, therefore, always intervene, in accordance with can. 1433.

Chapter III

THE PROCESS FOR THE DISPENSATION FROM A RATIFIED AND
NON-CONSUMMATED MARRIAGE

Can. 1697 The parties alone, or indeed one of them even if the other is unwilling, have the right to seek the favour of a dispensation from a ratified and non-consummated marriage.

Can. 1698 §1 Only the Apostolic See gives judgement on the fact of the non-consummation of a marriage and on the existence of a just reason for granting the dispensation.

§2 The dispensation, however, is given by the Roman Pontiff alone.

Can. 1699 §1 The diocesan Bishop of the place of domicile or quasi-domicile of the petitioner is competent to accept the petition seeking the dispensation. If the request is well founded, he must arrange for the instruction of the process.

§2 If, however, the proposed case has special difficulties of a juridical or moral order, the diocesan Bishop is to consult the Apostolic See.

§3 Recourse to the Apostolic See is available against the decree of a Bishop who rejects the petition.

Can. 1700 §1 Without prejudice to the provisions of can. 1681, the Bishop is to assign the instruction of these processes, in a stable manner or case by case, to his own tribunal or to that of another diocese, or to a suitable priest.

§2 If, however, a judicial plea has been introduced to declare the nullity of the same marriage, the instruction of the process is to be assigned to the same tribunal.

Can. 1701 §1 In these processes the defender of the bond must always intervene.

§2 An advocate is not admitted, but the Bishop can, because of the difficulty of a case, allow the petitioner or respondent to have the assistance of an expert in the law.

Can. 1702 In the instruction of the process both parties are to be heard. As far as possible, and provided they can be reconciled with the nature of these processes, the canons concerning the collection of evidence in the ordinary contentious process and in cases of nullity of marriage are to be followed.

Can. 1703 §1 There is no publication of the acts, but if the judge sees that, because of the evidence tendered, a serious obstacle stands in the way of the plea of the petitioner or the exception of the respondent, he can prudently make it known to the party concerned.

§2 To the party requesting it the judge can show a document which has been presented or evidence which has been received, and he can set a time for the production of arguments.

Can. 1704 §1 When the instruction is completed, the judge instructor is to give all the acts, together with a suitable report, to the Bishop. The Bishop is to express his Opinion on the merits of the case in relation to the alleged fact of non-consummation, the adequacy of the reason for dispensation, and the opportuneness of the favour.

§2 If the instruction of the process has been entrusted to another tribunal in accordance with can. 1700, the observations in favour of the bond of marriage are to be prepared in that same tribunal. The Opinion spoken of in §1 is, however, the province of the Bishop who gave the commission and the judge instructor is to give him, together with the acts, a suitable report on the case.

Can. 1705 §1 The Bishop is to transmit all the acts to the Apostolic See, together with his Opinion and the observations of the defender of the bond.

§2 If, in the judgement of the Apostolic See, a supplementary instruction is required, this will be notified to the Bishop, with a statement of the items on which the acts are to be supplemented.

§3 If, however, the answer of the Apostolic See is that the non-consummation is not proven from the evidence produced, then the expert in law mentioned in can. 1701 §2 can inspect the acts of the case, though not the Opinion of the Bishop, in the tribunal office, in order to decide whether anything further of importance can be brought forward to justify another submission of the petition.

Can. 1706   The rescript of dispensation is sent by the Apostolic See to the Bishop. He is to notify the parties of the rescript, and also as soon as possible direct the parish priests of the place where the marriage was contracted and of the place where baptism was received, to make a note of the granting of the dispensation in the registers of marriage and baptism.

Chapter IV

THE PROCESS IN THE CASE OF THE PRESUMED DEATH OF A SPOUSE

Can. 1707   §1 Whenever the death of a spouse cannot be proven by an authentic ecclesiastical or civil document, the other spouse is not regarded as free from the bond of marriage until the diocesan Bishop has issued a declaration that death is presumed.

§2 The diocesan Bishop can give the declaration mentioned in §1 only if, after making suitable investigations, he has reached moral certainty concerning the death of the spouse from the depositions of witnesses, from hearsay and from other indications. The mere absence of the spouse, no matter for how long a period, is not sufficient.

§3 In uncertain and involved cases, the Bishop is to consult the Apostolic See.

TITLE II: CASES FOR THE DECLARATION OF NULLITY OF SACRED ORDINATION

Can. 1708   The right to impugn the validity of sacred ordination is held by the cleric himself, or by the Ordinary to whom the cleric is subject, or by the Ordinary in whose diocese he was ordained.

Can. 1709   §1 The petition must be sent to the competent Congregation, which will decide whether the case is to be determined by the Congregation of the Roman Curia, or by a tribunal designated by it.

§2 Once the petition has been sent, the cleric is by the law itself forbidden to exercise orders.

Can. 1710   If the Congregation remits the case to a tribunal, the canons concerning trials in general and the ordinary contentious trial are to be observed, unless the nature of the matter requires otherwise and without prejudice to the provisions of this title.

Can. 1711   In these cases the defender of the bond has the same rights and is bound by the same duties as the defender of the bond of marriage.

Can. 1712   After a second judgement confirming the nullity of the sacred ordination, the cleric loses all rights proper to the clerical state and is freed from all its obligations.

TITLE III: WAYS OF AVOIDING TRIALS

Can. 1713   In order to avoid judicial disputes, agreement or reconciliation can profitably be adopted, or the controversy can be submitted to the judgement of one or more arbiters.

Can. 1714   The norms for agreements, for mutual promises to abide by an arbiter's award, and for arbitral judgements are to be selected by the parties. If the parties have not chosen any, they are to use the law established by the Episcopal Conference, if such exists, or the civil law in force in the place where the pact is made.

Can. 1715   §1 Agreements and mutual promises to abide by an arbiter's award cannot validly be employed in matters which pertain to the public good, and in other matters in which the parties are not free to make such arrangements.
   §2 Whenever the matter concerned demands it, in questions concerning temporal ecclesiastical goods the formalities established by the law for the alienation of ecclesiastical goods are to be observed.

Can. 1716   §1 If the civil law does not recognise the force of an arbitral judgement unless it is confirmed by a judge, an arbitral judgement in an ecclesiastical controversy has no force in the canonical forum unless it is confirmed by an ecclesiastical judge of the place in which it was given.
   §2 If, however, the civil law admits of a challenge to an arbitral judgement before a civil judge, the same challenge may be brought in the canonical forum before an ecclesiastical judge who is competent to judge the controversy at first instance.

Part IV
THE PENAL PROCESS

Chapter I
THE PRELIMINARY INVESTIGATION

Can. 1717 §1 Whenever the Ordinary receives information, which has at least the semblance of truth, about an offence, he is to enquire carefully, either personally or through some suitable person, about the facts and circumstances, and about the imputability of the offence, unless this enquiry would appear to be entirely superfluous.

§2 Care is to be taken that this investigation does not call into question anyone's good name.

§3 The one who performs this investigation has the same powers and obligations as an auditor in a process. If, later, a judicial process is initiated, this person may not take part in it as a judge.

Can. 1718 §1 When the facts have been assembled, the Ordinary is to decide:

1° whether a process to impose or declare a penalty can be initiated;

2° whether this would be expedient, bearing in mind can. 1341;

3° whether a judicial process is to be used or, unless the law forbids it, whether the matter is to proceed by means of an extra judicial decree.

§2 The Ordinary is to revoke or change the decree mentioned in §1 whenever new facts indicate to him that a different decision should be made.

§3 In making the decrees referred to in §§1 and 2, the Ordinary, if he considers it prudent, is to consult two judges or other legal experts.

§4 Before making a decision in accordance with §1, the Ordinary is to consider whether, to avoid useless trials, it would be expedient, with the parties' consent, for himself or the investigator to make a decision, according to what is good and equitable, about the question of harm.

Can. 1719 The acts of the investigation, the decrees of the Ordinary by which the investigation was opened and closed, and all those matters which preceded the investigation, are to be kept in the secret curial archive, unless they are necessary for the penal process.

Chapter II
THE COURSE OF THE PROCESS

Can. 1720 If the Ordinary believes that the matter should proceed by way of an extra-judicial decree:

1° he is to notify the accused of the allegation and the evidence, and give an opportunity for defence, unless the accused, having been lawfully summoned, has failed to appear;

2° together with two assessors, he is accurately to weigh all the evidence and arguments;

3° if the offence is certainly proven and the time for criminal action has not elapsed, he is to issue a decree in accordance with cann. 1342–1350, outlining at least in summary form the reasons in law and in fact.

Can. 1721 §1 If the Ordinary decrees that a judicial penal process is to be initiated, he is to pass the acts of the investigation to the promotor of justice, who is to present to the judge a petition of accusation in accordance with cann. 1502 and 1504.

§2 Before a higher tribunal, the promotor of justice constituted for that tribunal adopts the role of plaintiff.

Can. 1722 At any stage of the process, in order to prevent scandal, protect the freedom of the witnesses and safeguard the course of justice, the Ordinary can, after consulting the promotor of justice and summoning the accused person to appear, prohibit the accused from the exercise of the sacred ministry or of some ecclesiastical office and position, or impose or forbid residence in a certain place or territory, or even prohibit public participation in the blessed Eucharist. If, however, the reason ceases, all these restrictions are to be revoked; they cease by virtue of the law itself as soon as the penal process ceases.

Can. 1723 §1 When the judge summons the accused, he must invite the latter to engage an advocate, in accordance with can. 1481 §1, but within the time laid down by the judge.

§2 If the accused does not do this, the judge himself is to appoint an advocate before the joinder of the issue, and this advocate will remain in office for as long as the accused has not engaged an advocate.

Can. 1724 §1 At the direction or with the consent of the Ordinary who decided that the process should be initiated, the promotor of justice in any grade of the trial can resign from the case.

§2 For validity, this resignation must be accepted by the accused person, unless he or she has been declared absent from the trial.

Can. 1725 In the argumentation of the case, whether done in writing or orally, the accused person or the advocate or procurator of the accused, always has the right to write or speak last.

Can. 1726 If in any grade or at any stage of a penal trial, it becomes quite evident that the offence has not been committed by the accused, the judge must declare this in a judgement and acquit the accused, even if it is at the same time clear that the period for criminal proceedings has elapsed.

Can. 1727   §1   The offender can appeal, even if discharged in the judgement only because the penalty was facultative, or because the judge used the power mentioned in cann. 1344 and 1345.

§2   The promotor of justice can appeal whenever he considers that the reparation of scandal or the restitution of justice has not been sufficiently provided for.

Can. 1728   §1   Without prejudice to the canons of this title, and unless the nature of the case requires otherwise, in a penal trial the judge is to observe the canons concerning judicial procedures in general, those concerning the ordinary contentious process, and the special norms about cases which concern the public good.

§2   The accused person is not bound to admit to an offence, nor may the oath be administered to the accused.

Chapter III

THE ACTION TO COMPENSATE FOR HARM

Can. 1729   §1   In accordance with can. 1596, a party who has suffered harm from an offence can bring a contentious action for making good the harm in the actual penal case itself.

§2   The intervention of the harmed party mentioned in §1 is no longer admitted if the intervention was not made in the first instance of the penal trial.

§3   An appeal in a case concerning harm is made in accordance with cann. 1628–1640, even if an appeal cannot be made in the penal case itself. If, however, there is an appeal on both headings, there is to be only one trial, even though the appeals are made by different persons, without prejudice to the provision of can. 1734*.

Can. 1730   §1   To avoid excessive delays in a penal trial, the judge can postpone the trial concerning harm until he has given a definitive judgement in the penal trial.

§2   When the judge does this he must, after giving judgement in the penal trial, hear the case concerning harm, even though the penal trial is still pending because of a proposed challenge to it, or even though the accused has been acquitted, when the reason for the acquittal does not take away the obligation to make good the harm.

Can. 1731   A judgement given in a penal trial, even though it has become an adjudged matter, in no way creates a right for a party who has suffered harm, unless this party has intervened in accordance with can. 1733**.

*Translators' note: It would appear that this reference should read 'can. 1730'.
**Translators' note: It would appear that this reference should read 'can. 1729'.

Part V
THE MANNER OF PROCEDURE IN ADMINISTRATIVE RECOURSE AND IN THE REMOVAL OR TRANSFER OF PARISH PRIESTS

Section I
Recourse Against Administrative Decrees

Can. 1732 Whatever is laid down in the canons of this section concerning decrees, is also to be applied to all singular administrative acts given in the external forum outside a judicial trial, except for those given by the Roman Pontiff himself or by an Ecumenical Council.

Can. 1733 §1 When a person believes that he or she has been injured by a decree, it is greatly to be desired that contention between that person and the author of the decree be avoided, and that care be taken to reach an equitable solution by mutual consultation, possibly using the assistance of serious-minded persons to mediate and study the matter. In this way, the controversy may by some suitable method be avoided or brought to an end.

§2 The Episcopal Conference can prescribe that in each diocese there be established a permanent office or council which would have the duty, in accordance with the norms laid down by the Conference, of seeking and suggesting equitable solutions. Even if the Conference has not demanded this, the Bishop may establish such an office or council.

§3 The office or council mentioned in §2 is to be diligent in its work principally when the revocation of a decree is sought in accordance with can. 1734 and the time-limit for recourse has not elapsed. If recourse is proposed against a decree, the Superior who would have to decide the recourse is to encourage both the person having recourse and the author of the decree to seek this type of solution, whenever the prospect of a satisfactory outcome is discerned.

Can. 1734 §1 Before having recourse, the person must seek in writing from its author the revocation or amendment of the decree. Once this petition has been lodged, it is by that very fact understood that the suspension of the execution of the decree is also being sought.

§2 The petition must be made within the peremptory time-limit of ten canonical days from the time the decree was lawfully notified.

§3 The norms in §§1 and 2 do not apply:

1° in having recourse to the Bishop against decrees given by authorities who are subject to him;

2° in having recourse against the decree by which a hierarchical recourse is decided, unless the decision was given by the Bishop himself;

3° in having recourse in accordance with cann. 57 and 1735.

Can. 1735 If, within thirty days from the time the petition mentioned in can. 1734 reaches the author of the decree, the latter communicates a new decree by which either the earlier decree is amended or it is determined that the petition is to be rejected, the period within which to have recourse begins from the notification of the new decree. If, however, the author of the decree makes no decision within thirty days, the time-limit begins to run from the thirtieth day.

Can. 1736 §1 In those matters in which hierarchical recourse suspends the execution of a decree, even the petition mentioned in can. 1734 has the same effect.

§2 In other cases, unless within ten days of receiving the petition mentioned in can. 1734 the author of the decree has decreed its suspension, an interim suspension can be sought from the author's hierarchical Superior. This Superior can decree the suspension only for serious reasons and must always take care that the salvation of souls suffers no harm.

§3 If the execution of the decree is suspended in accordance with §2 and recourse is subsequently proposed, the person who must decide the recourse is to determine, in accordance with can. 1737 §3, whether the suspension is to be confirmed or revoked.

§4 If no recourse is proposed against the decree within the time-limit established, an interim suspension of execution in accordance with §§1 and 2 automatically lapses.

Can. 1737 §1 A person who contends that he or she has been injured by a decree, can for any just motive have recourse to the hierarchical Superior of the one who issued the decree. The recourse can be proposed before the author of the decree, who must immediately forward it to the competent hierarchical Superior.

§2 The recourse is to be proposed within the peremptory time-limit of fifteen canonical days. In the cases mentioned in can. 1734 §3, the time-limit begins to run from the day the decree was notified; in other cases, it runs in accordance with can. 1735.

§3 Even in those cases in which recourse does not by law suspend the execution of the decree, or in which the suspension is decreed in accordance with can. 1736 §2, the Superior can for a serious reason order that the execution be suspended, but is to take care that the salvation of souls suffers no harm.

Can. 1738   The person having recourse always has the right to the services of an advocate or procurator, but is to avoid futile delays. Indeed, an advocate is to be appointed ex officio if the person does not have one and the Superior considers it necessary. The Superior, however, can always order that the one having recourse appear in person to answer questions.

Can. 1739   In so far as the case demands, it is lawful for the Superior who must decide the recourse, not only to confirm the decree or declare that it is invalid, but also to rescind or revoke it or, if it seems to the Superior to be more expedient, to amend it, to substitute for it, or to obrogate it.

Section II: The Procedure for the Removal or Transfer of Parish Priests

Chapter I
THE PROCEDURE FOR THE REMOVAL OF PARISH PRIESTS

Can. 1740   When the ministry of any parish priest has for some reason become harmful or at least ineffective, even though this occurs without any serious fault on his part, he can be removed from the parish by the diocesan Bishop.

Can. 1741   The reasons for which a parish priest can lawfully be removed from his parish are principally:
    1° a manner of acting which causes grave harm or disturbance to ecclesiastical communion;
    2° ineptitude or permanent illness of mind or body, which makes the parish priest unequal to the task of fulfilling his duties satisfactorily;
    3° the loss of the parish priest's good name among upright and serious-minded parishioners, or aversion to him, when it can be foreseen that these factors will not quickly come to an end;
    4° grave neglect or violation of parochial duties, which persists after a warning;
    5° bad administration of temporal goods with grave harm to the Church, when no other remedy can be found to eliminate this harm.

Can. 1742   §1 If an investigation shows that there exists a reason mentioned in can. 1740, the Bishop is to discuss the matter with two parish priests from a group stably chosen for this purpose by the council of priests, at the proposal of the Bishop.   If he then believes that he should proceed with the removal, the Bishop must, for validity, indicate to the parish priest the reason and the arguments, and persuade him in a fatherly manner to resign his parish within fifteen days.

§2 For parish priests who are members of a religious institute or a society of apostolic life, the provision of can. 682 §2 is to be observed.

Can. 1743   The resignation of the parish priest can be given not only purely and simply, but even upon a condition, provided the condition is one which the Bishop can lawfully accept and does in fact accept.

Can. 1744   §1 If the parish priest has not replied within the days prescribed, the Bishop is to renew his invitation and extend the canonical time within which a reply is to be made.

§2 If it is clear to the Bishop that the parish priest has received this second invitation but has not replied, even though not prevented from doing so by any impediment, or if the parish priest refuses to resign and gives no reasons for this, the Bishop is to issue a decree of removal.

Can. 1745   If, however, the parish priest opposes the case put forward and the reasons given in it, but advances arguments which seem to the Bishop to be insufficient, to act validly the Bishop must:

    1° invite him to inspect the acts of the case and put together his objections in a written answer, indeed to produce contrary evidence if he has any;

    2° after this, complete the instruction of the case, if this is necessary, and weigh the matter with the same parish priests mentioned in can. 1742 §1, unless, because of some impossibility on their part, others are to be designated;

    3° finally, decide whether or not the parish priest is to be removed, and without delay issue the appropriate decree.

Can. 1746   When the parish priest has been removed, the Bishop is to ensure that he is either assigned to another office, if he is suitable for one, or is given a pension in so far as the case requires this and the circumstances permit.

Can. 1747   §1 A parish priest who has been removed must abstain from exercising the function of a parish priest, leave the parochial house free as soon as possible, and hand over everything pertaining to the parish to the person to whom the Bishop has entrusted it.

§2 If, however, it is a question of a sick man who cannot be transferred elsewhere from the parochial house without inconvenience, the Bishop is to leave to him the use, even the exclusive use, of the parochial house for as long as this necessity lasts.

§3 While recourse against a decree of removal is pending, the Bishop cannot appoint a new parish priest, but is to make provision in the meantime by way of a parochial administrator.

Chapter II

THE PROCEDURE FOR THE TRANSFER OF PARISH PRIESTS

Can. 1748 The good of souls or the necessity or advantage of the Church may demand that a parish priest be transferred from his own parish, which he governs satisfactorily, to another parish or another office. In these circumstances, the Bishop is to propose the transfer to him in writing and persuade him to consent, for the love of God and of souls.

Can. 1749 If the parish priest proposes not to acquiesce in the Bishop's advice and persuasion, he is to give his reasons in writing.

Can. 1750 Despite the reasons put forward, the Bishop may judge that he should not withdraw from his proposal. In this case, together with two parish priests chosen in accordance with can. 1742 §1, he is to weigh the reasons which favour and those which oppose the transfer. If the Bishop still considers that the transfer should proceed, he is again to renew his fatherly exhortation to the parish priest.

Can. 1751 §1 If, when these things have been done, the parish priest still refuses and the Bishop still believes that a transfer ought to take place, the Bishop is to issue a decree of transfer stating that, when a prescribed time has elapsed, the parish shall be vacant.

§2 When this time has elapsed without result, he is to declare the parish vacant.

Can. 1752 In cases of transfer, the provisions of can. 1747 are to be applied, always observing canonical equity and keeping in mind the salvation of souls, which in the Church must always be the supreme law.

TABLE OF CANONS

Table of Canons

Table of Canons

GLOSSARY

advena	the term to describe a person when he or she is actually present in the place where he or she has a quasi-domicile.
ferendae sententiae	the term to describe one of the two forms of penalty, namely, that which is imposed by the judgement of a court or by the decree of a Superior, when a person has been found guilty of an offence. (cf *latae sententiae* below.)
incola	the term to describe a person when he or she is actually present in the place where he or she has a domicile.
inter vivos	the term to describe a legal arrangement whereby, during lifetime, a person at once transfers property to another person or corporate body. (cf *mortis causa* below).
latae sententiae	the term to describe one of the two forms of penalty, namely, that which is automatically incurred on committing an offence, without the intervention of a judge or Superior. (cf *ferendae sententiae* above.)
magisterium	the term to describe the teaching authority of the Church.
mortis causa	the term to describe a legal arrangement made by a person during lifetime, whereby only after his or her death property is transferred to another person or corporate body. (cf *inter vivos* above.)
motu proprio	the term to describe a rescript (cf can. 59 §1) which grants a favour not on the request of a petitioner, but on the sole initiative of the granting authority.
peregrinus	the term to describe a person when he or she is outside the place where he or she has a domicile or quasi-domicile, while still retaining that domicile or quasi-domicile. The plural is *peregrini*.
presbyterium	the term to describe the body of priests who are dedicated to the service of a particular Church, under the authority of the Bishop or other Superior equivalent to a Bishop.
vagus	the term to describe a person who has neither a domicile nor a quasi-domicile anywhere. The plural is *vagi*.